**MEDIA TECHNOLOGY
AND THE VOTE**

**A SOURCE BOOK**

# MEDIA TECHNOLOGY AND THE VOTE

## A SOURCE BOOK

JOEL L. SWERDLOW, EDITOR

**THE ANNENBERG**
**WASHINGTON PROGRAM**
COMMUNICATIONS POLICY STUDIES
NORTHWESTERN UNIVERSITY

WESTVIEW PRESS ✶ BOULDER, COLORADO

Drawings by Arthur Asa Berger

ISBN 0-933441-02-9

Distributed by WESTVIEW PRESS
to libraries and bookstores

The Annenberg Washington Program
The Willard Office Building
1455 Pennsylvania Avenue, N.W., Suite 200
Washington, DC 20004
Telephone: (202) 393-7100
Telex: 4949457
Fax: (202) 638-2745

ISBN 0-8133-0869-0 (Westview)

# DEDICATION

*New communications technologies make many wondrous
things possible. But technology will never change the basic
obligations of citizenship. We must, as Walt Whitman
noted in an earlier era, "work for democracy."*

*This book is dedicated to those who keep the faith and
continue the struggle.*

# ACKNOWLEDGMENTS

The talents and hard work of dozens of people made this book possible. These include:

All participants in the February 2, 1988 Annenberg Washington Program colloquium and all who contributed their writing.

*David Beiler,* an extremely versatile political editor, writer and analyst, who organized the colloquium. He is well known and respected among campaign professionals.

*Jeff Porro,* who gave his editorial skills and helped transform a huge amount of material into manageable portions.

*Jill Edy* and *Rebecca Reeves,* who did copy-editing and proofreading and research—all with great ability and enthusiasm.

*Yvonne Zecca* and *Beth Laverty* of The Annenberg Washington Program. They have the unique and invaluable ability to help creative projects blend with real-world needs. Without their skill and good nature this book would never have happened.

*Arthur Asa Berger,* who teaches at San Francisco State and writes provocative books. His cartoons bring ideas and public-policy issues to life.

*Elizabeth Dixon,* certainly one of America's top designers. That a book such as this one is possible is due in large part to her skills.

*Steve Behrens,* editor for The Annenberg Washington Program. His insights and editorial eye improved every part of this book.

*Suzan Wynne* and *Barbara Bruce,* who did excellent jobs indexing and proof-reading (respectively) this complex book.

*Maurice Mitchell,* founding Director of The Annenberg Washington Program, who helped make possible all that is achieved here. He remains an active Program adviser, and his counsel has been of great value.

*Newton N. Minow,* current Annenberg Washington Program Director, possesses a unique combination of wisdom based on experience and enthusiasm based on idealism without illusions. He believes in getting done what at first does not seem possible.

In addition, each of the following deserves a special thank you for their talent and generosity:

*Julie A. Aquian* of Nielsen Media Research; *Tiffany Barnard; Frank A. Bennack,*

*Jr.* of the Hearst Corporation; *Paul Cahberg; Sheryl E. Cohen; John Convy* of Grass Roots Software Systems; *Roger Craver; Peggy DeBell* of Craver, Mathews, Smith & Company; *Kim Downes; James Dwinell,* Publisher of *Campaigns & Elections* magazine; *Joan L. Fiddle* of Professional Video Transmission Services; *Kathleen Fraovich; David Fruitman; Mark Ganguzza* of Calhoun Satellite Communications; *Cristina M. Gilmour; Joe Glick; Samuel Greenhouse; Toni Grueninger* of the Center for Media and Public Affairs; *Jeffrey J. Hallett* of the Presidential Campaign Hotline; *Todd Hanks* of Conus Communications; *Helen Hanson; Gary Jacobson; Montague Kern; Julie King* of Below, Tobe & Associates; *Roma Klimczak; Everett Carl Ladd; Larry Lichty; Frank Lloyd; Linda Miller* and *Paul Hoff* of the Center for Responsible Politics; *Joe Palaia; Mike Platt; Reynolds Cafferata; Michael Robinson; William L. Rosenberg* of Drexel University; *William L. Rosenthal; Marjorie L. Share; Mike Skiidan; Harry Sommer; Susan Swain* of C-SPAN; *Aaron B. Swerdlow; David Webster; Tracy Westen; Martin Zwick*

# FOREWORD

When the idea of democracy developed thousands of years ago in ancient Greece, philosophers thought a democratic system would not endure with more than 30,000 people. Why 30,000? That was the number of people who could climb on a hill in Athens to see and hear one speaker at one time.

Now we have a huge nation spanning thousands of miles and a population of 250 million people. We continue to try to govern ourselves through the democratic process. Central to this effort in today's environment are new communications technologies whose impact prompts some philosophers to wonder whether they are doing more harm than good. Experts agree, however, that communications technologies have fundamentally changed American politics and that this change is accelerating.

To examine current communications public policy and the public interest, and to provide a neutral meeting place in the nation's capital for scholars, public policymakers and others, The Annenberg Washington Program was established in 1983.

Thus, in 1983, under founding director Maurice B. Mitchell, the Program hosted a colloquium on issues raised by the use of computers in political campaigns. This highly successful event led to publication of a book, *New Communication Technologies in Politics*, which has prompted discussion and debate among scholars, students, journalists and political professionals.

On February 2, 1988, The Program hosted a second colloquium on these issues. The 1988 discussion went beyond computers to examine the effects on political campaigns of communication technologies ranging from cable television and videocassette recorders to instantaneous public opinion analyzers. This second colloquium was entitled "New Technologies in Political Communications" and led to this publication, which we hope is only the second in a continuing series.

At the colloquium, Professor Larry Sabato, a leading academic expert on political campaigns, presented a paper analyzing new technologies. Leading industry representatives then discussed these unique technologies and gave hands-on demonstrations. Following came a discussion by a distinguished panel of Michael Barone, editorial writer for the *Washington Post*, Curtis B. Gans, director of the Committee for the Study of the American Electorate, and Edward J. Rollins, a successful and effective campaign consultant who served as President Reagan's political director in 1984. The colloquium was organized by David Beiler, a former editor of *Campaigns & Elections* magazine.

The participants all gave generously of their time. There was no endorsement of any particular company or technique, and the speakers' list was balanced between firms with Republican and Democratic clients.

This book was edited by Joel L. Swerdlow, a Senior Fellow at The Annenberg Washington Program. Dr. Swerdlow is well known throughout the academic and journalistic communities as a respected scholar and as a writer on contemporary politics and communications technologies.

*Media Technology and the Vote: A Source Book* raises complex issues, highlights the need for more research, and offers a wide range of views. Like its predecessor, it is intended to help and stimulate scholars, students, journalists, public officials, political professionals and interested members of the public. It may be read in its entirety, or topics of particular interest may be selected. Thus, this book can serve well as a resource and reference guide.

One special feature is the especially thorough index. *Media Technology and the Vote: A Source Book* makes available an unusually broad spectrum of material whose sources range from previously unpublished scholarly studies to articles in the popular press.

As a young man, I was with Adlai Stevenson when he ran for president in 1956. He finished a speech in San Francisco where a woman came up to him and said, "Governor Stevenson, after hearing that speech, every thoughtful American is going to vote for you." He replied, "Madam, that is not enough. I need a majority."

In this book, we hope you will consider the following questions: Are new communications technologies producing more thoughtful voters? Are they advancing or endangering the democratic process? What can be done to take full advantage of these technologies consistent with the democratic process?

*Newton N. Minow*
*Director*
*The Annenberg Washington Program*

# INTRODUCTION

*by Joel L. Swerdlow*

*In the spring of 1988, a business executive running for a Democratic gubernatorial nomination seemed poised for victory. A few days before the election, however, one of his opponents began televising spots saying the executive had been an owner and director of a company that had filed for bankruptcy, endangering millions of dollars in the workers' pension fund.*

*Most voters in the state were strongly pro-labor, and overnight tracking polls soon revealed that the commercials were hurting badly—perhaps mortally. The executive's support was hemorrhaging.*

*With the election only days away, there seemed no way to get a response on the air. But new technology saved the candidate. He produced an effective 30-second commercial responding to the charges, and, for less than $1,000, leased time on a communications satellite to relay the commercial to television stations throughout the state. The commercial ran, the decline in his support stopped, and he won.[1]*

*Such stories are becoming common as new communications technologies—and the various techniques through which they are applied—change the rhythms and content of American politics.*

*Many experts regard these changes as positive. New technologies, they say, improve communications between candidate and citizen. Information flows more quickly. Others are less optimistic. They lament the "technocratic flavor" that they say has robbed American politics of passion. Many long for the days when Robert F. Kennedy campaigned in black neighborhoods because his "gut" and not "number-crunching" told him it was right; others find it especially refreshing when a candidate like Pierre DuPont stakes out positions he feels are more correct than popular.*

*But almost all experts who have looked closely at campaigns agree that a quiet revolution—based on communications technologies—is transforming American politics. Public policymakers, scholars, journalists and political professionals must recognize this revolution if they are to understand—and shape—it.*

*This understanding will be helped if it includes three major steps. The first is to clarify language. As recently as the early 1980s, "new politics" meant grassroots* organizations and going directly to the people. "New" technology meant broadcast television.

But broadcast television _per se_ is no longer fresh and dramatic. When Theodore H. White noted in the mid-1970s that "the action has moved to the studios," he was full of wonderment. For today's voters, however, politics by television is the norm. More than two-thirds of Americans alive today were born after television became the nation's dominant means of communication.

Politicians who understand _only_ broadcast television are as outdated as the oldtime ward heeler. "New" technology means cable, computers and satellites. New politics no longer means going directly to the grassroots.

It now means speed in data collection and manipulation, overnight tracking polls, highly reactive campaigns in which debate focuses on 15-second television commercials, targeting based on complex demographic information, and a volatile electorate prone to last-minute decisions and non-voting. To be informed, a political professional must know what "digital" means and how rain affects Ku-band satellite transmissions.

The second step is to recognize the size of the campaign marketplace. Candidates now spend over half a billion dollars each election cycle. Referenda and other ballot measures generate another $100 million. "Democracy," one consultant recently noted, "is a growth business."

This huge market stimulates innovation and competition in the political uses of communications technologies. Computers, for example, first enjoyed widespread usage in California campaigns because television costs were prohibitive, and targeted mailings were the most economical way to reach voters.

At the same time, political campaigns—whether at the presidential, state or local level—rarely involve new uses of communications technologies. What becomes "new" in politics has long since been proven in the nonpolitical marketplace. As journalist James Perry noted in _The New Politics_ as early as 1968, "It's not show biz that's taking over in politics; it's industrial and business technology."

Thus, the next cycle of new technologies in campaigns will probably be those we are accustomed to in offices and supermarkets. Bar-codes and portable scanning devices that can easily computerize telephone or door-to-door canvassing are already available. After that will come three-dimensional commercials, huge portable video screens at shopping malls and subway stops, and highly personalized electronic mail.

The final step is to recognize that the revolution in American politics has worldwide implications. American campaigns are frequently a prelude to what happens in other democracies—and nondemocracies. The governments of the USSR and mainland China, for example, are moving towards using sophisticated public opinion polls—which involve many of the technologies discussed in this book—to mold public opinion and to affect the results of elections of delegates to Communist Party Congresses.[2]

Of course, the revolution in communications technologies should not be exaggerated. Technology brings change, but those who believe the change is significant bear the burden of proof. Focusing on the communication mechanisms of politics, furthermore, may unduly emphasize political process over substance. As George F. Will notes in _The New Season_, "America has a surplus of people who know everything about the nuts and bolts of politics [but] do not have a clue as to why Americans pull one voting lever rather than another." Any understanding of communications technologies must include such clues.

*Media Technology and the Vote: A Source Book* identifies significant changes, areas in need of scholarly research and important public policy issues.

The book has three sections. First is a scholarly analysis of new technologies as presented at the February 2, 1988 Annenberg Washington Program colloquium. Next are industry representatives' descriptions of their technologies as presented at this colloquium.

The third and largest section builds upon the panel discussion that followed the industry presentations. Articles, excerpts, scholarly studies and essays address 11 crucial campaign variables examined in the February discussion. Much of this material was commissioned for this volume and has never been published before. This is the first time, furthermore, that such a wide range of material has been gathered in one book.

To help make all three sections most accessible to readers, this book offers a detailed index at the end. An annotated bibliography also offers guidance for further research.

*Media Technology and the Vote: A Source Book* is nonpartisan. It addresses campaigns at all levels—from local to presidential—and will be timely well into the 1990s. It lays out an agenda for Members of Congress, Federal Communications Commission officials, state legislators and other policymakers; for students and scholars; for political reporters and editors; for candidates, consultants and other political professionals; and for interested members of the public. All will find useful information and ideas, and all will see the need to define and defend the "public interest" in campaigns.

It offers a window into the future of political campaigns.

## NOTES

1. Lloyd Grove, "Where TV Saturation Spelled Success," *Washington Post*, 12 May 1988, p. A7. "Republicans Back Governor More Again," *New York Times* 12 May 1988, p. A32. "Campaign Trail," *New York Times* 12 May 1988, p. A32.
2. Michael Dobbs, "Soviets Offer Curbs on Party's Power," *Washington Post* 27 May 1988, p. A1. Biller Keller, "Muscovites, in Poll, Are Split on What Their Future Holds," *New York Times* 27 May 1988, p. A1.

# CONTENTS

## IV  RESOURCE MATERIAL

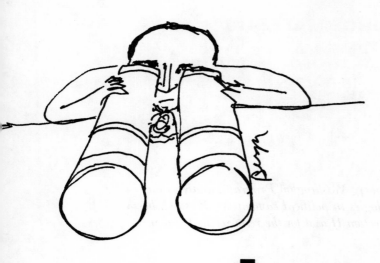

# I

# MAGIC ... OR BLUE SMOKE AND MIRRORS?

*This paper, commissioned by The Annenberg Washington Program, analyzes the state-of-the-art in the use of new technologies in political campaigns. It establishes the framework for the presentations in Section II and for the resource material in Section III.*

# MAGIC ... OR BLUE SMOKE AND MIRRORS?

## REFLECTIONS ON NEW TECHNOLOGIES AND TRENDS IN THE POLITICAL CONSULTANT TRADE

*Larry Sabato and David Beiler*

It was 1936, and Republican presidential nominee Alfred M. Landon had a revealing brush with the new campaign technology of public opinion polls, then in its infancy. The *Literary Digest* had taken a poll by mailing a sample presidential ballot to ten million Americans, and the returns suggested a stunning upset was in the making: Landon would handily defeat President Franklin D. Roosevelt.[1] As Landon later recalled it, the poll was the "one time in that 1936 campaign when I thought I might beat Roosevelt. For an hour or so that night, I could see myself in the White House."[2] The technology plainly failed Landon—primarily by an extreme oversampling of wealthy Republican-leaning citizens—as FDR won one of the greatest landslides in presidential history.

Polling has become far more sophisticated in the decades since, and other technologies, from media advertising to direct mail, have been invented and refined. Yet the technologies still often fail candidates and campaigns; the political consultants who develop and master the technologies frequently make mistakes in judgment that startle amateurs; and despite popular lore and journalistic legend, few candidates can truly be said to be creations of their clever consultants and dazzling campaign techniques.

Partly this is because politics always has been (and always will be) far more art than science, not subject to precise manipulation or formulaic computation. *In the end—in most cases—the candidate wins or loses the race according to his or her abilities, qualifications, communications skills and weaknesses.* Although this simple truth is warmly reassuring to most of us, it has been remarkably overlooked by election analysts and reporters seemingly mesmerized by the exorbitant claims of consultants and the flashy computer lights of their technologies.

The voter deserves much of the credit for whatever encouragement we can draw from this candidate-centered view of politics. Most voters want to take the real measure of candidates, and retain a healthy skepticism about the techniques of running for office. Political cartoonist Tom Toles suggested as much when he depicted the seven preparatory steps the modern candidate takes: (1) Set out to discover what voters want; (2) Extensive polling; (3) Study of demographic trends; (4) Sophisticated interpretation of in-depth voter interviews; (5) Analyze results; (6) Discover that what the voters want is a candidate who doesn't need to do steps one through five; (7) Pretend you didn't. The chastened politician tells his assembled throng, "I follow my conscience."[3]

### Technology's Worth

Having opened this essay by debasing its subject, we hasten to add that consultants and new campaign technologies *can* contribute a great deal to campaigns. The best political professionals add extensive political experience spanning scores of separate campaigns, a background which can confer the instinctive judgment and analytical ability often vital to a campaign's success. The technologies confer efficiency and knowledge, above all. They make it possible for campaigns to make the best use of limited resources, to transfer information to voters in appealing and potentially effective ways, and provide vital data about the preferences of individual voters and the collective electorate. All of this comes at a high price, of course; campaign techniques can be enormously expensive (though in the politician's view, the most costly campaign is the one that is lost).

Therefore, consultants and their technologies not only have worth—their value may indeed be growing. In general, the new techniques we will cover here are more effective than the methods they are replacing. Moreover, consultants and the new techniques can and do influence virtually every significant part of a campaign, and the campaign certainly makes some difference in the outcome of an election. While it is still true that most voters make their general election choices in good part on the basis of party loyalty, in most of these contests as much as a third or even more of the electorate is honestly uncommitted or switchable; that proportion will probably increase even further as the strength of party identification declines. Primaries present a particularly fluid opportunity for campaign influence because of their relatively low turnouts, and the lack of party ties might well provide the new technologies with their broadest potential use.

Another decisive election variable susceptible to campaign manipulation is voter turnout. Even if conversions prove elusive, a campaign's success depends heavily on its ability to stimulate those favorable to it to vote and, alas, to encourage those unfavorable to it to stay at home, mainly through negative advertising directed at the opponent's weaknesses.

While the influence of professionals and their technologies over election results is probably substantial and growing, anyone who attempts to assess the effectiveness of modern campaign techniques is humbled by the scarcity of empirical evidence to support hard and fast conclusions. Compared to the extensive privately supported research in product advertising, there has been little thorough testing of the impact of various political communications during campaigns. As a result, the impact of any consultant or any technology can usually only be guessed at. No one has even a vague idea of what percentage of a candidate's vote is added, under any given circumstances, by a consultant's work or by the use of new campaign technology. Campaign observers rarely even have a precise idea of what event or series of events produced the election result. Campaigning remains complex, unpredictable and very unscientific, and one may expect and be grateful that it always will be.[4]

### The Technology and Profession Develop

There have always been political consultants in one form or another in American politics, but campaign professionals of earlier eras were strategists without benefit of the complex technologies so standard today. Usually, they were tied to one or a few candidates, or perhaps to a state or local party organization.

On a separate track, the profession of public relations was developing with the support of the business community. As Stanley Kelley, Jr. has stated, "Business was, and is still, the public relations man's most important patron."[5] Business executives saw image-making as a way to counter a rising tide of criticism. The federal government followed in close pursuit of public relations professionals, expanding their role considerably during the New Deal. State and local governments, charities, religions and colleges in succession all saw the "P.R. promise."

Dan Nimmo has called political consultants the "direct descendants" of the public relations professionals[6], and the growth of both groups is clearly related to some similar phenomena, especially the revolution in mass media communications. Yet political consulting has causes all its own. The decline of the political parties has created opportunities for consultants and the tools of their trade. As party power waned, new means of financing campaigns, telling the candidate's story and getting the candidate's voters to the polls became necessary.

The fact that the new campaign techniques quickly became too complex for lay people to grasp—consultants themselves were forced to specialize to keep up with changes—and Americans' acknowledged need for, and trust in, experts, made professionals that much more attractive. The belief that consultants' tricks could somehow bring order out of campaign chaos, even if it was mistaken, was enormously reassuring to a candidate. And rising campaign costs (and limitations on expenditures and contributions) placed a premium on the wise use of every campaign dollar. All of these alterations of the political map seemed powerful arguments for hiring political consultants, who became an unquestioned essential for serious campaigns. Every campaign now needs them, if only because the opposition always seems to have them.[7]

Partly as a result of this inherent tendency toward political arms races, and partly because recently developed technologies have made complex information and communication systems simpler and more affordable, campaign professionalism has gradually reached farther down the ballot. Today, races for local and lesser state office often employ paid consultants and utilize technologies that even the wealthiest campaigns only dreamt of a decade ago. Will these new, accessible technologies bring candidate and voter closer together, place barriers between them, or create a firmer grasp over our democratic system by an undemocratically chosen elite of campaign technocrats? This is one of the central questions faced by our inquiry.

### A Sampler of the New Campaign Technology

Some of the technological wonders now breaking on the political campaign horizon include: (1) computerized network communications—specifically, the *Presidential Campaign Hotline*; (2) audio/visual voter targeting through the use of cable television transmissions and videocassette distribution; (3) campaign-sponsored satellite feeds; (4) instantaneous pulse-reading of focus groups; (5) video image generators; and (6) micro-mapping. There is some overlap among the categories. Satellite feeds, for example, could be used to facilitate A/V targeting. But, by and large, each category supports its own new cadre of specialists in the political arena, each with a distinct portfolio of techniques.

While a comprehensive review of all these campaign technologies is well beyond the modest scope of this paper, selective commentary can suggest the breadth of the recent changes technology has wrought in our politics—and the depth of the problems that have accompanied their advent.

### Computerized Network Communications

A new branch of political media went on-line September 15, 1987 in the form of *The Presidential Campaign Hotline*. The brainchild of Democratic direct mailer Roger Craver and Republican media consultant Doug Bailey, *Hotline* is a computer network that transmits campaign information each morning to nearly 200 subscribers (half of them media outlets) for a basic fee of $250 per month.[8]

The intended purpose of this service is to keep subscribers fully apprised of timely developments in the race for the White House. Various devices are used: reporting late-breaking news of events in the field; forwarding news stories, editorials and columns from influential periodicals and local newspapers in battleground states (often as they hit the streets); and providing up-to-the-minute analysis from assorted campaign experts.[9] *Hotline* performs this mission with precision, and has quickly become a valuable executive news summary for busy journalists and other professional observers of the political scene. It should also prove to be an important academic resource, providing useful assistance for scholars in their teaching and research by recording—for the present and posterity—the actual messages each campaign tried to communicate each day, without the filtering, altering or discounting of the media.

It has quickly become apparent, however, that the greatest potential impact of this enterprise lies not in its function as a high-tech, specialized wire service, but rather as an elaborate means of rapid mass communication among political campaigns, the media and interest-group power-brokers. *Hotline*'s practice of carrying daily reports from each presidential campaign press secretary has created a unique opportunity for "spin control" of events *before* they have had the chance to make an impact on their own.

The ease and speed with which this service disseminates information might also be a source of concern. In an age when belt-tightening measures are reducing news staffs across the country, the temptation to cut corners in coverage is substantial. *Hotline* appeals to that inclination by providing a front-row seat to the campaign action to anyone with a modem-equipped personal computer and the subscription fee, an expense considerably lower than the cost of sending someone into the field or developing original sources. This encourages "pack journalism" through an inevitable centralization of the reporting process, with the few experts and journalists cited in the *Hotline's* 15-page daily digest wielding ever more influence over America's perception of its presidential selection process.

### Audio/Visual Targeting

The process of "targeting" involves cross-referencing polling and census data to enable a campaign to send key voters the precise message they want to hear. Until recently that has meant defining demographic "clusters" that react with supposedly predictable political behavior, identifying their geographic presence, and then exposing them to highly specific and often dramatic direct mail.[10]

This technique created quite a stir when it was devised in the late 1970s primarily because of its "Big Brother" implications, and it was used with some reported effect early in this decade. But in recent years the luster of targeting has appeared to fade, largely because cutbacks in the Census Bureau program have left its demographic data too dated to be useful late in the decade. A fresh census is looming, however, and a revolutionary process, which targets audio/visual messages, is now developing. It may soon prove to be one of the most effective and cost-efficient means of communicating with the electorate.

The most important new technology facilitating this development is cable television. Seven years ago, fewer than one in five American homes with a television set had access to cable, and cable's selection of channels was quite limited. Today half of these homes have hookups, most with a wide variety of programming choices. Cable services are becoming more segmented, but the expanding scope of system "interconnects"—computer networks organized by groups of local cable systems that can facilitate placement of messages in numerous demographically homogeneous communities simultaneously—will further "fine-tune" the audience. The cost per thousand viewers is as much as one third lower than the shotgun approach of network television.[11]

Another new technology contributing to the impact of audio/visual targeting is the rapid proliferation of household videocassette recorders (VCRs). The practice of distributing campaign videos as a centerpiece for living room fundraisers began with George Bush's 1980 presidential campaign; applications of this technology have recently expanded to include A/V press kits and mass-mailings to highly targeted political activists. Eight current presidential candidates have already distributed such tapes or have them in production.[12]

Although the penetration of VCR technology is about equal to that of cable—both are found in about half the homes with TV sets[13]—the costs involved in producing and distributing a cassette have limited its application. But those costs are rapidly falling, and mass-produced videos can now be produced and delivered for about $5 per unit. Thus, we may soon see them used in targeted voter contact by extremely well-heeled campaigns. By combining television's persuasive power with the pinpoint impact of a forceful, carefully tailored message, A/V targeting may prove to be one of the most influential communications tools introduced to political campaigning since television itself.

The press has in the past served as a muting influence on such "flexible" strategies, with the media pointing out any conflicting information emanating from a single campaign. But reporters, with so many media cable outlets to cover and A/V tapes to review, might be forced to limit such scrutiny to only the highest-profile campaigns.

Targeting with cable does have its limitations, of course. It is less flexible than direct mail, since it does not conform as readily to geodemographic boundaries. Yet cable systems are smaller, more numerous and more homogeneous than many political media strategists have supposed. Pennsylvania consultant Bill Cromer's analysis of his home state reveals the existence of 112 cable systems *outside* the state's seven Areas of Dominant Influence (major media markets), averaging about 10,000 subscribers each. Half of these systems (including 75 percent of the larger ones) accept advertising locally.[14] Such geographic dispersal, coupled with selective placement on the various special-interest channels, *could* result in audiences of remarkable psychographic (if not demographic) homogeneity.

We emphasize "could" because demographic information about particular audiences within a cable system is often sketchy at best. Political time-buyers are usually reduced to cross-referencing neighborhood demographics with the national audience makeup of cable networks and drawing on their artistic judgment when matching spots with slots. But that information is becoming more precise all the time. In one recent development, Nielsen Media Research and the National Cable Television Association merged their databases to produce an on-line service that identifies cable advertising possibilities by congressional district, complete with demographic indexing and a listing of current "avails" (open ad slots).[15]

Still, largely because cable audience data has a reputation for less precision than broadcasters' data, political media specialists (except for a noted few on the local level) have yet to use its targeting potential. Nineteen eighty-eight might be the breakthrough year for political cable advertising, however: at least two presidential campaigns are planning regional cable buys in preparation for the South's March 8th super-primary.

The impact of campaign videos on the political landscape may be less spectacular than cable's, but it almost certainly will be felt sooner. Commercial video press releases now comprise a $3 billion business that is expected to triple over the next two years.[16] Political applications of this technology remain a cottage industry, but they are already moving beyond the initial stage of living room fundraisers.

The peculiar power of video press releases in the political arena was graphically demonstrated last September when two officials of the presidential campaign of Massachusetts Governor Michael Dukakis surreptitiously released a tape which interspersed segments of a debate performance by rival Senator Joseph Biden (D-Del.) with an earlier campaign commercial for British Labour Party chief Neil Kinnock. By powerfully demonstrating Biden's rhetorical plagiarism, this "attack video" set in motion a chain of events that helped drive its victim from the race in 11 days.

The far more common use of campaign videos remains the persuasion of targeted groups, particularly contributors and activists. These productions are typically six to twelve minutes long, cost about $10,000 to produce, and are designed to acquaint viewers with the candidate in a favorable way. While these tapes invariably feature rugged terrain, broad sunsets and happy families, they often include substantive material on the candidate's public record and policy positions as well. Such hard facts are usually considered prerequisites in motivating political activists and contributors.

The campaign practice of selectively distributing videocassettes as a means of attracting allies is now even being utilized in reverse: Interest groups have started to use VCRs to help them decide who to support. Last summer, for example, the AFL-CIO taped four-minute stand-up segments with each of the 13 major presidential contenders then in the race. These performances were linked in a video production, 15,000 copies were dispatched to union halls across the country and the tapes were screened by rank-and-file audiences. The union officials' expressed purpose was not to build a consensus behind a single candidate but to encourage members to become involved in the campaign of their choice and run for delegate to the national conventions.[17]

### *Focus Groups and Instantaneous Pulse-Reading*

It is sometimes difficult to imagine that as recently as the 1930s, no one had yet utilized the scientific public opinion survey as a means of communication between political candidates and voters. In the late 1980s, campaigns often take such readings daily and use "guinea pig" focus groups of voters to guide political strategy.

A focus group is usually comprised of 10 to 15 individuals marshaled by a trained discussion leader. The individuals are drawn from predetermined population subgroups, are often recruited in random selections at shopping centers, and are paid a nominal amount for their participation. Once gathered, the group discusses possible campaign themes or looks at advertisements and answers open-ended questions. Political consultants often watch the dialogue from behind a two-way mirror and tape-record the discussion for later analysis. Despite the nonscientific structure of the focus group, it can probe in more detail and elicit more unstructured responses than is possible with most surveys.[18]

The extent to which this technology has progressed was dramatically revealed in July 1987 when a battalion of 80 carefully selected Iowa caucus-goers registered their reactions to a debate among presidential aspirants while the event was in progress. As candidates pleaded their cases in a Houston arena, the chosen Iowans used individual dial boxes to indicate thumbs up, down, or various intermediate degrees of approval. Their collective judgment was instantaneously computed, converted into pulsating bar graphs and superimposed over the debate action.[19]

Never has opinion research so graphically portrayed or so quickly registered voters' political reflexes. But for all their virtues, there are considerable dangers involved in relying on focus groups. Even in a more conventionally probed group, a couple of strong personalities can stifle discussion or heavily influence the conclusions of other participants. Most importantly, even though focus groups are not random samples, they often are treated as such. The more concrete and structured conclusions of a focus group should be tested in a poll with a representative sample, but campaigns rarely use this fail-safe device. Instead, presidential or statewide campaigns sometimes make fundamental advertising and thematic decisions based on the expressed opinions of at most a few dozen individuals in focus group sessions.[20]

The Iowa "applause meter" approach to focus group research is additionally troubling because it also represents the latest version of "instant polling," an insidious practice that has been lately proliferating in various forms. A number of local television stations have established "yes" or "no" voting on current issues by calling one of two telephone numbers as part of their nightly newscasts. The samples are nonrandom and the results subject to easy manipulation by organized interest groups. But the stations rarely note as much on-air, and unsophisticated viewers undoubtedly fail to distinguish scientific polls from this bogus variety.

NBC News created a stir in the summer of 1979 when it employed an instant polling device called the Qube system, a viewer-response set-up fitted to the television sets of some cable subscribers. Used on an experimental basis following President Carter's crucial "crisis of confidence" speech, the immediate reactions of 29,000 viewers in Columbus, Ohio were given national attention.[21] While the network gave warnings that the nonrandom sample was the equivalent of a "man on the street" interview, the definition was probably lost on most viewers, especially when the commentator also referred to Qube as an "electronic poll." NBC was severely chastised by Albert H. Cantril, president of the National Council on Public Polls, who correctly noted that the "poll" results cited on the air were not an accurate measure of opinion even in Columbus, much less the nation.[22]

The ABC network tried a different sort of instant participation poll after the Carter-Reagan presidential debate in October 1980. Viewers called special telephone lines to "vote" for the candidate they believed had "won" the debate. ABC's results (about two-to-one for Reagan) were skewed by a number of methodological problems, including: (1) timing—the East Coast was retiring, while Reagan's western strongholds were in prime time, (2) the 50-cent charge to participate, (3) the self-selection involved (as opposed to random sampling), and (4) the discrimination introduced by the telephone setup, which apparently recorded "votes" from rural regions more readily than those from congested urban areas. While ABC commentators occasionally mentioned on air that their poll was "unscientific," an untrained public could hardly be expected to make the distinction, particularly when the results were presented on an official-looking tally board of the kind used on election night. Judging by the banner headlines accorded the ABC "poll" results on the day after the debate, many journalists also apparently failed to recognize the phony nature of the ABC gimmick.

The new generation of "instant polling" techniques—as represented by the wired "pulse-reading" exercise in Des Moines—is a technological marvel, but of questionable value. The participants are nonrandomly selected, and even if they had been randomly chosen, the group would be far too small to be a useful sample (and even less valid when broken down into demographic subsamples). The meter reading is a shallow, unidimensional gauging of a complex set of reactions. Moreover, instantaneous response can be purely impulsive, unrepresentative of the more important opinion arrived at after leisurely consideration and reflection (not to mention after the intervening mediation of the press and other informed commentary). This kind of instant poll is a clumsy attempt to quantify the unquantifiable—which some campaign consultants, to their credit, already discount. As Roger Ailes, Vice President Bush's media consultant, commented while watching one debate "instant poll" in November 1987:

> I still don't know how the graph works and I don't care. I believe that technology is useful up to a point. But when I make a commercial, I don't paint by numbers. I once asked a great jazz saxophonist if he read music. And he said, 'Sure, but only as much as it doesn't hurt my playing.'[23]

### Micro Mapping

The capabilities of computer graphics have made enormous strides in the past four years, and nowhere are the political implications more intriguing than in the field of micro-mapping. Mapping Information Systems, a New York software firm catering to that state's legislature, has recently developed a program series which will enable a redistricter to draw boundaries on a computer screen map with a "mouse," then sit back and receive a complete analysis of the area's demographic composition and voting behavior. Canvassers will be able to trace a proposed route, then receive a list of all registered voters along the way, including address and party registration.[24] The visual displays of such programs are splendidly detailed when used in conjunction with the latest generation of high-resolution monitors.

The real artwork here, however, at least with the redistricting programs, is age-old gerrymandering—the drawing of legislative districts with an eye toward political advantage. If old-school redistricters could achieve their results using only precinct maps, city directories, scouting interns and electronic slide rules,[25] one can only imagine what might be achieved once new-tech pols start to use the new micro-mapping programs to carve up the electorate.

Of course, the Supreme Court *did* indicate in *Bandemer v. Davis* (1986) that redistrictings that consistently favor one party over another may be held unconstitutional.[26] But the full impact of that decision awaits further adjudication, and in the meantime the gerrymander appears to be anything but an endangered species.

### Video Image Generators

When Pat Caddell signed on as a strategist with Gary Hart on New Year's Day, 1984, the campaign began to crystallize the theme of "a new generation of leadership." Television time was reserved for the closing days of the Iowa caucus campaign and new spots aimed at the "Baby Boomer" generation were ordered to fill it. The campaign was short of funds and time, however, so documentary footage of Hart was culled to carry the message. To smooth out the jarring jump cuts made necessary by this approach, Ray Strother employed a "peeling page" graphics technique made possible by "Mirage," a viewed image generator which had made its American debut only days before at his editing house, Reeves of New York City. Media pundits gave some credit for Hart's surprising second-place showing in Iowa to the "high-tech" spirit engendered by these computer-generated graphics.[27]

The communicative power of video image generation stems from its ability to turn a television screen into a precise reflection of the producer's mind. An immediate concern rises when one thinks of political messages being crafted with surrealistic wizardry. Aren't electronic gizmos such as ADO, Cyron, Paint

Box and Dubner really just so much added camouflage between a candidate and the voters?

Some of this anxiety is unwarranted, if only because it gives the professionals too much credit and the voters too little. Ads perceived as too slick have traditionally aroused voters' suspicions about the sponsor. But video image generation *can* enhance certain types of political messages if used with the proper mix of imagination and restraint.

An apparently successful series of ads produced by Ian and Betsy Weinschel for Republican Senate candidate Ed Zschau in the 1986 California primary provides a textbook example. Largely unknown when the campaign began, Zschau faced a formidable obstacle in his early quest for name recognition: connecting the name's spelling and pronunciation (the first syllable in "shower") was difficult for most voters. The Weinschels decided to draw out the sibilance of the name to create a whispering effect that would enhance subliminal recall. To make sure the viewer's attention was attracted at the critical time, an ADO was employed to move the logo dramatically into the picture with the effect of a swooping spaceship, action that might be associated with the "whooshing" pronunciation of the candidate's name.[28] Zschau won the nomination in a field crowded with well-known monikers; his distinctive commercials may have helped (though, as always, one can never be certain).

### Satellite Feeds

We have often heard the complaint that the news media, particularly television, have trivialized the presidential selection process by covering only candidates who are leading—or precipitously climbing—in the polls. Having allegedly reduced the whole affair to "horserace" entertainment, the campaign press stands accused of stifling any substantive consideration of issues and records.

This damning theory has some merit, but fortunately advances made in satellite communications over the past four years are bringing with them the prospect of campaign coverage that is at once potentially more extensive and less superficial. At the same time, these developments may have pronounced positive impacts on races for lesser office as they permit candidates more direct access to local media markets at reasonable cost. And the changes are coming quickly. Of the 13 major candidates now seeking the presidency, only Gary Hart and Alexander Haig have yet to avail themselves of the new satellite technology, which can create an ad-hoc independent television network for as little as $5,000 (less, if expenses are shared with another candidate). Several statewide campaigns are now gearing up with the same capabilities.

In a sense, this satellite-sparked revolution began with Walter Mondale's presidential effort of 1984, which used a satellite to simulcast a fundraising event convened at numerous locations across the country.[29] But the Mondale production belonged more to an earlier generation of "closed-circuit" television events;

based on "C-band" technology, it was more costly, less flexible and more logistically difficult than the "Ku-band" systems being used by campaigns today. The difference is that C-band transmissions are susceptible to interference from microwave transmissions such as those used to transmit long-range telephone calls and Ku-band is unaffected—enabling it to avoid location coordination fees, FCC red tape, bulky antennas and restrictive placement.[30]

Several days in advance of an event, a networking campaign will send letters to local stations with satellite reception capability (there are now about 1,000 in the U.S.). In addition to informing these outlets of the time of the feed and the nature of the transmission (interview opportunity, policy speech, prepared video release, debate with another sponsoring candidate, etc.), the letter will direct the station engineer to the proper coordinates for "tuning in" the transmission.

Whether or not the station chooses to receive and air the feed is a crucial concern of campaign press aides, of course, and they often turn lobbyist with phoned follow-ups after the notification letters have arrived. "Live" interviews (which may be taped or fed directly by the station) have by far the greatest success in attracting coverage, but these one-on-one sessions are the least efficient for the candidate in terms of unit resource cost and are sometimes reserved for the larger, more strategic markets. The big markets often require this added attention: contrary to their smaller-budgeted provincial brethren, they are unlikely to consider such transmissions an exotic mark of prestige.

While candidate-sponsored satellite coverage has provided an important big step toward reducing the high cost of covering campaigns for television outlets, it is also proving to be a boon to campaign budgets. As part of a notable campaign appearance in Iowa last November, presidential candidate Paul Simon succeeded in parlaying his own satellite transmission into interviews that were carried "live" on six stations in three states. Several other outlets taped Simon for broadcast later, leaving the campaign to calculate that it had corralled more than $10,000 worth of commercial air time at a cost of only $2,300.[31] One should add to this calculation the media consultant's axiom that time in a newscast, because of its enhanced credibility, is worth at least three times as much as the same amount of paid advertising time.

As might be expected, the political use of the new satellite technology is rapidly proliferating. Several competing satellite companies now provide a mobile satellite transmission unit with crew for about $3,000 per day (down to $1,000 per day over an extended engagement), and can supply a fully equipped production staff for an additional $2,000. Satellite time rents for an average of roughly $600 per hour.

Though its arrival has been sudden, satellite campaigning will not be a passing gimmick. It is destined to greatly expand television campaign coverage (particularly outside the major metropolitan areas) and it will do so in a substantive way—by allowing stations to cover lesser-known candidacies at no charge. It will also provide campaigns with some control over that coverage. (As has recently been demonstrated by George Bush in his celebrated showdown with anchorman Dan Rather on the *CBS Evening News*, candidates can often turn "live" coverage to their advantage.)

Of course, such a development ought to be of some concern to the the rest of us, particularly if satellite feeds encourage laziness in media outlets. Less aggressive reporting and fewer station-generated segments might result. Voters will be the losers if stations choose to substitute canned campaign video feeds for hard-hitting political coverage.

### Conclusions

The effectiveness of democracy depends in part upon how well representative government reflects the will of the people. There has been much concern in recent years that the trend toward technocracy has clouded that reflection. Our survey of the latest advances in political campaign technology suggests, however, that this concern is not justified, on balance. (The more established techniques of basic public opinion polling and television advertising are more troubling.)

Some developments discussed in this paper *do* tend to garble or distort transmissions between politicians and the people—most particularly through such pseudo-scientific methods of opinion research as focus groups, "instant polling" and "instantaneous pulse-reading." But for the most part, campaigns' use of such distortion-prone techniques will contribute to the natural selection process of politics: Candidates who rely too heavily on them will ultimately damage their own cause. The principal danger posed by pseudo-scientific technologies occurs when the media sponsor their usage or take their results too seriously. Magnified and sanctified by the media, distortions may then become self-fulfilling realities.

Most of the new technologies, however, will probably enhance democratic communications as much as they obscure them. For instance, while the proliferation of television outlets and candidate-sponsored satellite feeds may lead to increased influence of an un-elected consultant elite, it also suggests that a more complete and substantive picture of campaigns can potentially be provided to the electorate, though the potential may remain unrealized. Computerized network communications may encourage "pack journalism," but by increasing the information available to smaller media outlets at a modest cost, they might increase the quality of campaign coverage. And although excessive use of video image generators can introduce a measure of distracting glitz to campaign communications, the technology can also effectively communicate certain helpful information—such as the correct pronunciation of a candidate's name.

In conclusion, these latest campaign technologies, much as those of the preceding technological generation, are double-edged swords, ever capable of wounding representative democracy as much as defending it. Wisely used, they offer considerable opportunity for enhanced (albeit indirect) two-way communication between campaigns and voters. To the extent they contribute to citizen and candidate education, and to voter participation, the new technologies should be praised. But they retain a capacity for danger if abused, and should be carefully monitored by thoughtful citizens who must remain critical, vocal and vigilant.

## NOTES

1. Larry Sabato, *The Rise of Political Consultants: New Ways of Winning Elections* (New York: Basic Books, 1981), p. 69.
2. As quoted in *Washington Post*, October 13, 1987, p. A6.
3. From a 1987 cartoon by Tom Toles, copyrighted by *The Buffalo News*.
4. See Sabato, *The Rise of Political Consultants*, pp. 14-17.
5. Stanley Kelley, Jr., *Professional Public Relations and Political Power* (Baltimore: Johns Hopkins, 1956), p. 16; see also pp. 9-25, 26-38.
6. Dan Nimmo, *The Political Persuaders: The Techniques of Modern Election Campaigns* (Englewood Cliffs, N.J.: Prentice-Hall, 1970), p. 35.
7. See Sabato, *The Rise of Political Consultants*, pp. 10-11.
8. Telephone interview with Ron Rosenblith, president of the Presidential Campaign Hotline, conducted October 28, 1987.
9. Mickey Kaus, with Eleanor Clift, "Fresh-Baked Political Wisdom," *Newsweek* (November 2, 1987): p. 83.
10. See Jonathan Robbin, "Geodemographics: The New Magic," *Campaigns & Elections* (Spring, 1980): pp. 25-34.
11. John Power, "Plug Into Cable TV," *Campaigns & Elections* (September/October, 1987): pp. 12-14.
12. Lloyd Grove, "Campaigns Courting Voters via Their VCRs," *The Washington Post*, October 28, 1987, p. A7.
13. Roger Brown, "Sophisticated Market Research Tools Targeting Diverse Demographic Groups," *Cablevision* (August 17, 1987): pp. 58-60.
14. Taken from remarks made by William Cromer before the conference "Cable Political Advertising," convened by the Cable Advertising Bureau in Washington, D.C., January 15, 1988.
15. Interview with Julie A. Aquan of Nielsen Media Research, conducted January 15, 1988.
16. Sandra Sugawara, "Putting Out the News on Videos," *Washington Post*, August 10, 1987, page 9 of the special section, "Washington Business."
17. Andrew Rosenthal, "Videotape Is Labor's Way to Shun '84 Mistake," *New York Times*, September 8, 1987, p. A5.
18. See Sabato, *The Rise of Political Consultants*, pp. 138-139. For examples of how focus groups have been used (or misused) in recent campaigns, see "Campaign Ads with a Woman's Voice," *National Journal* 19 (December 19, 1987): p. 3214; and "Finding Out if the Message Is Clear," *National Journal* 19 (October 31, 1987): 2722.
19. Howard Fineman, "The Vox Pop Hit Parade," *Newsweek* (August 10, 1987): p. 17.
20. See Sabato, pp. 138-139; *National Journal* 19 (December 19, 1987): p. 3214 and *National Journal* 19 (October 31, 1987): p. 2722 for examples of the process. Since each separate focus group session can cost $3,000 or more, most campaigns organize just a few of them, adding to the problem of conclusions based on too limited a database.
21. The Qube system was installed in 29,000 homes in Columbus, Ohio, by Warner Amex Cable. Each subscriber paid an additional $3.45 monthly for the use of ten extra free channels and access to ten more special pay-per-view ones. The polling component operated through a miniature computer terminal in each home connected to the television set, which had buttons respondents could push to answer questions superimposed on the screen.

22. See *Washington Post*, July 7, 1979, and August 24, 1979.
23. See, for example, Lloyd Grove, "Candidates Experiment With Instant Feedback," *Washington Post*, November 13, 1987, p. A8.
24. Telephone Interview with Michael Marvin, president of Mapping Information Systems, Inc., conducted January 6, 1988.
25. See, for example, *The Wall Street Journal*, August 24, 1987, p. 22.
26. David Beiler, "Court Sends Gerrymander to Open Air Zoo," *Campaigns & Elections* (July/August, 1986): p. 43.
27. David Beiler, *The Classics of Political Television Advertising* (Washington: Campaigns & Elections, Inc.), p. 7.
28. *Campaigns & Elections* (November/December, 1986): p. 53.
29. Andrew Rosenthal, "Via Satellite, Candidates Make Their Own News," *New York Times*, July 21, 1987, p. 16.
30. David Fruitman, "Understanding Ku-band and C-band Satellite Applications," promotional pamphlet provided by Calhoun Satellite Communications, Inc. of Miami.
31. Lloyd Grove, "Campaigning 'Live' by Satellite Feed," *Washington Post*, November 18, 1987, p. A18.

*David Beiler* is Senior Partner in Democracy, Inc., a political communications consulting firm in Washington, D.C. which restricts its clientele to nonpartisan and bipartisan institutions. After serving as a political consultant with Cumberland Campaigns of Nashville, Beiler began a career in journalism with *The* (Nashville) *Tennessean* in 1981 and continued it with *Campaigns & Elections* magazine in 1984, where he served as editor until July, 1986. He is the writer and producer of the video documentary *The Classics of Political Television Advertising* and author of an attendant viewer handbook. He also remains a contributing editor of *Campaigns & Elections*.

*Larry Sabato* is an election analyst and Associate Professor of Government and Foreign Affairs at the University of Virginia. He is a former Rhodes Scholar and Danforth Fellow. After he received his B.A. in government from the University of Virginia as a Phi Beta Kappa in 1974, he did a year's graduate study in public policy at Princeton University's Woodrow Wilson School of Public and International Affairs. Upon receipt of the Rhodes scholarship in 1975, he left Princeton to begin study at Queen's College, Oxford University. In less than two years he received his doctorate in politics from Oxford, and was invited to become a tutor (instructor) for students in the Politics, Philosophy, and Economics (PPE) program. In January, 1978, he was elected Lecturer in Politics at New College, Oxford. He assumed his present post at the University of Virginia in September 1978.

# II

# PRESENTATIONS

*In these reports delivered at the February 1988 colloquium, industry representatives explain why they think their technological specialties will increasingly help shape America's political campaigns. Since communications technology is far from monolithic, the industries promoting and selling these services and products employ a variety of approaches and arguments. Differing priorities can often be seen. To read these presentations is to get a feel for what a candidate or campaign official hears throughout the run for office.*

# THE PRESIDENTIAL CAMPAIGN HOTLINE

*Larry Checco in consultation with Jeffrey Hallett,*
*co-founder of the Presidential Campaign Hotline.*

" 'It's Super Bluesday,' according to Dole staffers; Lacy says Bush may win 16 or 17 states. . . . 'The lights are going out for Bob Dole' (Boston Globe). 'Trying to avoid being written off' (USA Today)."

*Excerpt from the Presidential Campaign Hotline,*
*American Political Network, Inc. March 8, 1988*

This litany on the demise of Senator Robert Dole's presidential aspirations was already available electronically to hundreds of media outlets and campaign staffs by 10 a.m. Eastern Standard Time, March 8, 1988. The date is better known as Super Tuesday. The newspapers cited by the Hotline barely had time to circulate, and the voting polls in most states weren't even opened.

The Presidential Campaign Hotline, which went into operation September 15, 1987, added a new twist to the 1988 presidential campaigns. In effect, the Hotline's ability to technologically flash "insider" political information nationwide—even before such information had time to become "news" in the broader sense of the word—changed the way candidates conducted their campaigns. More importantly, it had an impact on the "news" prospective voters received.

The Hotline's uniqueness lies in its creative use of "low-end" computer and telecommunications technology. Personal computers and modems enabled many Hotline subscribers— including hundreds of media outlets, all 13 campaign organizations, and a bevy of high-powered political consultants and analysts— to contribute to the content of each day's 20-page edition of the Hotline, creating an exclusive dialogue among key players.

Described as an "insidious electronic tip sheet" by some, "a great tool for [campaign] damage control" by others, the Hotline may revolutionize, or perhaps already has revolutionized, the way future political campaigns of all kinds will be conducted, and could permanently influence the type and scope of information prospective voters will receive.

Is the Presidential Campaign Hotline a boon or bust for the American political process? Will it increase political campaign coverage? Or will it reduce the incentive for journalists to "cover" campaign stories on their own, thereby homogenizing information disseminated to the public? Will there ever be such a thing as "a local event" in politics again? Will the Hotline ultimately hinder or help campaign strategists? And will candidates' political messages truly be communicated via this political and technological medium?

The Hotline is accessible to anyone with a computer and modem willing to pay the $150 to $350 upfront monthly subscriber's fee (spring 1988 prices). Its founder foresees a long and bright future for this marriage of technology and politics.

Beginning Labor Day 1988, the American Political Network plans to launch the "First-Ever Daily Presidential Tracking Poll." Each night, from September 5 onward, 333 randomly selected voters will be asked which candidate they support, demographic information about themselves, and their opinions of advertising, debates, issues and gaffes as they arise in the campaign. The American Political Network is banking that television stations and newspapers will be willing to pay from $10,000 to $35,000—depending on their size—for exclusive use of this service in select media markets. In addition, starting November 15, 1988, the Campaign Hotline will become the Transition Hotline, covering the personnel and systems of the new administration.

In short, with the help of today's computer and telecommunications technology, the American Political Network's long-term goal is to become the single most reliable source of data and information that reflect political developments in the United States. In the words of one of its co-founders, "our goal is to be to American politics what Dow Jones is to the American economy."

The entire inventory of technology employed to put out the 20-page Hotline each weekday at 10:00 a.m. consists of: eight PC-XT clones, four modems, three facsimile (fax) machines, one television set, three videocassette recorders, three audio recorders for taping telephone interviews, 10 telephones, a copier and 10 computer printers.

Initial capital investment for the above was approximately $35,000. In addition, 16 people—some part-time—work to collect, edit, redraft and format incoming data before it is disseminated to subscribers. A covey of renowned political analysts lend their professional insight to some of the major news items contained in any given day's edition of the Hotline.

### The Process—From Start to Finish

Each evening, between 7 p.m. and 2 a.m., Hotline headquarters in McLean, Virginia receives the bulk of data that staff will sift through for its next edition. This raw data is received electronically in five different ways:

—Direct electronic feeds—used by 40 to 60 regional and local newspapers nationwide, which send to the Hotline relevant campaign stories that will appear in their next-day editions.

—Electronic mail—used mostly by campaigns and other contributors to the Hotline.

—Facsimile (fax) machines—used by political analysts, campaigns, newspapers, and others to send material to the Hotline.

—News wire services and other electronic information services—These services are scanned by Hotline staff for relevant news.

—Television—All major news broadcasts are taped, reviewed, and abstracted appropriately.

Crunch time for the Hotline staff is between 4 a.m. and 9:30 a.m. The primary selection process from all the accumulated data is handled by two senior editors. Supporting them at any given moment are four to eight analysts and associated editors. Once the first selection process is completed, one or more of the publishers reviews and assists in the final selection and analysis for that day's edition. All information contained in the Hotline is fully attributed to the appropriate source. (Part of the impact of the Hotline comes from a subscriber knowing that a particular story ran in a certain number of different media outlets.)

By 9:30 a.m., the selected information is entered into a word processing program. When the document reaches its final draft stage, a special program is run that automatically prepares the document for printed publication and properly formats the text for automatic uploading to one private and three public-access electronic information services, including Dialcom, Newsnet and Compuserve. The document is formatted to the tight specifications of each of the services.

In many respects, the Hotline is very technologically similar to any news wire-service operation. In fact, most subscribers have set up their equipment to automatically connect with their electronic information services to retrieve the Hotline. At 10 a.m. on any week-day morning, several hundred subscribers can simultaneously have access to the Hotline.

The day does not end at 10 in the morning, however, for the Hotline staff. No sooner is the day's edition out than the review process begins. The managing editors and publishers meet to decide which of the important political developments contained in the the current day's edition will warrant follow-up for the next day's edition. Decisions are also made regarding which political event or development most justifies an "insider" commentary by one of the Hotline's 24 contributing political analysts.

### What Hotline Contains and Who Receives It

Each day, the Hotline includes:

—Hotline Highlights—a four-page summary of the top items and a quick reference index to the remaining 20 pages.

—Poll Update—a daily report from all sources.

—Campaign Reports—a daily report from each campaign with the candidate's schedule, press release and other news.

—Insider Commentary—daily analysis by the Hotline's contributing analysts, well-known pollsters and consultants in both parties.

—National Briefing—a summary of that day's coverage of each candidate—in major newspapers, on network TV, and in target states such as Iowa and New Hampshire, for example.

—Senate Race Briefing—a daily report on 1988 Senate races and the coverage in leading newspapers in the states with the hottest contests.

The Hotline's subscriber list breaks down as follows: media outlets (60 percent); campaigns, and campaign-related individuals such as pollsters, analysts, and consultants (20 percent); and a mix of political action committees, embassies, universities, corporations and political junkies of all sorts (20 percent). As mentioned earlier, many of these subscribers contribute to the content of the Hotline, as well. "Participating subscribers"—*i.e.*, media outlets, campaigns and others who contribute stories and information to the Hotline—receive the Hotline at a discounted rate.

It doesn't take much technological know-how or equipment to become a subscriber. Virtually any computer and modem can receive the Hotline. Each subscriber receives a guide that describes the procedures for accessing the Hotline via modem. Those without an existing communications program receive a pre-set disk to make the connection automatic (for IBM PC-compatible and Macintosh computers only). The Hotline staff provides a subscriber with any assistance needed to retrieve the information, and a Hotline HELP telephone number is shown on the computer screen at all times.

It should be noted that not everyone receives the Hotline electronically. Approximately 100 subscribers on Capitol Hill and downtown D.C. receive a printed version by noon on weekdays.

### Archiving Hotline Information

Today's availability of low-cost computer storage plus new database software has made it possible to maintain an archive which contains every Hotline edition put out, starting from September 15. This database grows at the rate of 100 pages a week and it is to politics what Lexis is to the legal profession. It allows campaign staffers, reporters or any other Hotline subscriber to retrieve a universe of information pertaining to a particular candidate, issue, state, etc., as it appeared in Hotline. The fee for this additional service is based on use. In the end, this electronic archival database will represent the most concise and insightful history of the 1988 presidential campaign available.

In short, the Presidential Campaign Hotline is one of the most impressive demonstrations of the political impact of interactive news transmitted at the speed of light. The Hotline is unique in that the creative use of technology allows for the gathering of important information and its distribution to a variety of interested parties in a manner whereby the subscriber, in many cases, is also part of the information source.

As the 1988 presidential campaign narrows to two candidates, the Hotline will extend its coverage of the key House and Senate races for 1988.

*The Presidential Campaign Hotline*
*1489 Chain Bridge Rd., Suite 300*
*McLean, Va. 22101*

# AUDIO/VISUAL TARGETING THROUGH CABLE TELEVISION

*Lloyd Trufelman,*
*Cabletelevision Advertising Bureau*

A few quick facts: right now, approximately 45 million homes subscribe to cable television. In 1987, cable passed the 50 percent penetration mark and is continuing to grow. By penetration, we mean homes connected and subscribing, not homes passed. This means that for the first time now more homes in America are getting their TV programming through a wire than over the air. Another way of putting it is that cable TV subscribers are no longer the minority.

Actual viewing of cable has grown as well. On a 24-hour basis in the viewing year 1986-87, viewing of basic cable networks was up 14 percent and viewing of pay channels was up 24 percent. Cable programming now accounts for 33 percent of total viewing in all cable households, while programming fed by the three broadcast networks accounts for 35 percent. In cable households with pay service, the cable programming share is 40 percent versus 31 percent for the broadcast networks. While these cable audiences are growing, the three broadcast networks' share of prime-time viewing continues to erode, from a 91 percent share in 1977-78, to an 80 share in 1981-82 and a 71 share in 1986-87. This is because in homes where cable is available, people naturally tend to watch more cable programming and less broadcast programming. In more basic terms, if you have a TV bringing you 35 channels of television, you are going to watch a little bit of all of those 35 channels, rather than dividing your viewing time among three or four. Thus, no matter how much broadcast programming is coming into a household with cable, a certain segment of that cable audience is not going to be reached by the over-the-air signal.

If you want to reach these cable viewers, the best way to do so is to advertise on cable channels. We are not saying to advertisers, "Use cable instead of broadcast." Instead, it's a matter of re-allocating. By shifting some advertising onto the cable channels, candidates could reach voters who are wandering up and down the cable box. Why is it important to reach cable viewers?

Cable viewers watch TV differently. Since they have more channels they move around on the dial a lot more.

Cable subscribers are 24 percent more likely to vote than non-cable viewers. This is because, in general, the cable household is better paid and better educated than the general voting-age population—demographics that spell a higher-than-average turnout at the polls. The cable household is paying $10, $15, $20 or $30 a month for their television programming. It has more disposable income, and wider-ranging interests. According to studies, cable subscribers are 26 percent more likely to support a political party or a candidate than non-cable viewers. By a 30 percent margin, cable subscribers are more likely to engage in political fundraising; they are 36 percent more likely to be involved in local issues, 56 percent more likely to have personally visited an elected official in the past year, and 34 percent more likely to have expressed an interest in writing to public officials.

C-SPAN recently released a study showing that their audience is competitive with *MacNeil/Lehrer, Face the Nation, Meet the Press* and *This Week with David Brinkley*. All the political activists who watch C-SPAN are cable viewers. Indeed, C-SPAN has become synonymous with politics and therefore, in a way, so has cable.

This brings us to the ways cable can reach this more desirable cable audience. Specific groups of voters can be targeted. The selectivity of cable programming allows candidates to choose the most favorable audience for their messages: all-news, all-sports, cultural, educational and so on. Cable can target geographically, nationally, statewide, regionally or simply by congressional district.

Cable advertising is cost-efficient both on an overall-cost basis and a cost-per-thousand basis. And cable is more flexible. The spots are not limited to 15 or 30 seconds in length.

The principal cable system in Des Moines has so far received political advertising revenues of more than $50,000, compared to under $4,000 in 1984. Candidates using cable in Iowa and New Hampshire included Dole, Jackson, Babbitt, Dukakis, DuPont, Kemp, Gephardt and Simon. Before "Super-Tuesday," Al Gore bought national time on four cable networks, the first time such advertising appeared prior to a national convention. Interconnects allowed candidates to buy on a statewide basis, rather than negotiating with each individual system. National buys might come in handy for candidates looking to maximize strength before arriving on the convention floor, perhaps looking for a vice presidential slot.

Cable opens many new opportunities. For example: on January 21, 1988, the Dukakis campaign produced an hour-long program featuring the candidate and distributed it via satellite to cable systems throughout the Midwest. This was a leased-access network established by purchasing time on midwestern cable systems. In this case, the Dukakis people did not downlink to the local broadcast station, which requires sending out field people to ask news directors to clear a few minutes of the feed on the local news. Instead, they bought a half-hour of cable time, bypassed the gatekeepers and used the field operation to promote the telecast and get people to tune in to that particular cable channel. The entire cost came to about $15,000. So rather than going from satellite-to-station-to-viewer, they went from satellite-to-viewer via cable.

Presidential elections receive the most attention, but cable is really having its strongest effect at the local level. Cable is opening up television advertising for the first time to congressional, city council, state assembly and virtually all other races. Cable is targeted and inexpensive, with little or no waste. Until now, candidates in these races could not afford television advertising. More importantly, the waste on over-the-air broadcast was just too great because the broadcast reached too many viewers who could not vote in a particular race. With cable, a candidate's message is isolated down to a congressional or smaller district. Statewide candidates can even break down different congressional districts via cable systems that zero in on the kind of people they are trying to reach. And more than advertising is involved. Local cable systems are increasing the amount of time devoted to any local news. Cablevision, for example, has a 24-hour, county-wide local news channel, News 12, that has been an extraordinary success.

Pay-per-view also has come to cable, offering programs purchased by subscribers on a per-program basis rather than a per-month basis. This is made possible through addressable cable converters that allow cable operators at the subscriber's request to activate, disconnect and descramble the signal received by each individual subscriber. More than 13.5 million homes have addressable converters. Six pay-per-view networks now reach over 7.3 million homes, mostly with movies and sporting events. If you want to watch a movie, you press the code, you watch that night's or that afternoon's movie, and you get billed.

None of this pay-per-view technology has reached a critical mass yet, but how might it be used in politics? In 1988, the rage was tape parties. Campaigns produced them and circulated them. They could do the same sort of thing with pay-per-view. The field operation could tell supporters, "Please activate your converter from 9:00 to 10:00 tonight for a special message on pay-per-view Channel 2." Or you could use addressable technology to send different messages to different households in a given district. Again, cable is expanding television choices and fragmenting the television audience to the point where campaigns can reach smaller and smaller groups of people simultaneously with different messages.

*Cabletelevision Advertising Bureau*
*757 3rd Avenue*
*New York, NY 10017*

# CANDIDATE-CONTROLLED SATELLITE FEEDS

*Cheryl Cohen,*
*Calhoun Satellite Communications*

Now and into the future, the growing pressure to stay competitive will force many politicians to make decisions about new technology that's as far removed from their usual duties as satellites are from the earth.

In the past few years, a number of innovative developments have occurred that collectively resulted in nothing less than a communications revolution. Communication satellites have had a tremendous role to play in this revolution and in changing the exchange of information.

Mobile satellite earth stations, *i.e.*, vehicles with transmission capabilities, make it possible for individuals to stay at their headquarters/home base, yet still transmit their message all over the country with impact and immediacy.

Case in point: When Vice President George Bush decided to throw his hat into the 1988 presidential race, he wanted to declare his intentions from Houston. His campaign personnel contacted Calhoun Satellite Communications, which is a private mobile satellite facilities company, to coordinate the arrangements. The Bush people wanted a lot more than just a live declaration announcement for television stations to pick up as a news event. They wanted to enable questions and answers to be transmitted as part of the live event from strategic areas throughout the county. Therefore, Calhoun set up a video teleconference of sorts, which a growing number of private companies now utilize as part of their corporate communications strategies.

Satellite conferencing is a cost-effective means of increasing an individual's productivity, a fast and efficient way of disseminating information and a way of allowing increased participation.

You don't have to have an engineering degree to understand the satellite communications industry. Television networks have been involved with satellite communications for over five years. They first used the C-band type of satellites. To transmit in the C-band required a 45-foot tractor-trailer rig, a five-meter transmission dish and a frequency clearance to avoid microwave interference.

With the launch of the first Ku-band satellite in the mid-1980s, a new era of satellite technology was born. Ku-band satellites are more powerful and require smaller transmitting and receiving dishes and smaller transmitters. Thus, a more compact vehicle can be used. TV news operations were enabled, at a more cost-effective rate, to reach those fast-breaking news stories.

More and more, the broadcast television industry is cutting its high-cost terrestrial communications links in favor of satellites as a means of increasing its programming flexibility, news-gathering capabilities, and reach. Many new stations now own their own Ku-band vehicles, and there are about 20 independent Ku transportable companies throughout the country that serve networks, television stations, corporations, organizations and, now, the political arenas.

NBC selected Ku-band as their choice to distribute network programming to affiliates and as the most efficient method of backhauling remotely organized programming into the network. From an operation viewpoint, NBC's actions to date have indicated that rain attenuation, one of the feared drawbacks of Ku-band, is not a major concern. This is due to a combination of high satellite power and the antenna sizes selected by NBC to transmit and receive signals. Other broadcasters also are rapidly realizing the benefits of Ku-band transmission.

Furthermore, private networking by business via satellite has increased substantially with the introduction of Ku-band satellite systems. Unlike C-band satellites, Ku-band has made practical the use of small transmit/receive antennas for business.

With all of the interest in Ku-band satellites, their applications, affordability and other advantages over C-band, Ku-band satellites have taken the leading technological edge in the satellite industry.

One of the key assets of exclusive access to direct uplinking technology for campaigns in 1988 will be the the ability to create the illusion of being in many more places at one time. In addition, the candidate could more effectively address issues pertaining to key markets. Without ever getting on a plane, today's candidate can be in Iowa, New Hampshire, Florida and California all during a single day—live.

Through satellites, live video can be received at multiple locations. Through telephone hook-ups, questions can be asked of the candidates, with responses given immediately, as in a face-to-face meeting. News stations can pick up the live event without having to rely exclusively on footage from the networks.

The possibilities are endless. The future is now. The satellite industry presents a golden opportunity, and by incorporating these developments into campaign plans . . . the sky's the limit for the candidate of '88.

*Calhoun Satellite Communications*
*14871 NE 20th Avenue*
*North Miami, FL 33181*

# THE EVOLUTION OF ELECTRONIC DATA COLLECTION: THE PERCEPTION ANALYZER

*Michael Malone,*
*Columbia Information Systems*

It is important when you look at new technology to understand why it was developed. A comprehensive understanding of why the Perception Analyzer was developed requires consideration of:
—the assumptions implicit in the research approach;
—the major challenges research professionals encounter and have been trying to overcome for the last 30 years; and
—how the Perception Analyzer works, along with actual examples of research applications.

## *Traditional Research: Implicit Assumptions*

Traditional research relies on three common assumptions. The first is that sample size—given that the sample is randomly selected—is the primary determinant of validity. This assumption implies that the sampling error, a function of how many people you talk to, is more important than measurement error. To take it one step further, what we are really saying is that larger sample sizes are always better. This assumption has not received enough scrutiny. We fail to understand that when we say we want a big sample size we are, in effect, giving up several important things. Furthermore, we are also supporting the notion that the statistical rules of probability are more important and appropriate than the real foundation of science, the scientific method.

Though statistically derived estimates of error are a useful tool for evaluating alternative hypotheses, they are notoriously unreliable in explaining the true nature of any dynamic phenomenon. Statistics are a useful tool in the research process but they are used too often in lieu of a comprehensive, logical examination of alternative explanations. A larger sample size may improve the statistical reliability of a prediction, but this increased reliability is not that valuable if it limits the breadth of information considered during the research process or the ease with which alternative hypotheses may be examined.

A second statistically biased assumption common in the research industry is that there is a critical difference between "qualitative," which often implies focus groups or small-sample-size research, and "quantitative," which is generally considered to include survey or large-sample-size research. A corollary of this tenet is that numbers have no place in the qualitative domain lest they be misinterpreted as implying statistical validity. What this assumption really means is that qualitative research need not be concerned with measurement precision.

When you ask people to verbally indicate the magnitude of a reaction, they really have only three reliable increments of differentiation: "Not at all," "Somewhat," and "A whole lot." Semantics do not afford any reliable scale that exceeds three categories of differentiation.

Numbers, however, provide great precision because numeric references communicate differences in magnitude. But because the domain of qualitative research is often deemed inappropriate for numbers, the precision available with the Arabic numeral system is often not used, and is instead replaced by a limited, three-category semantic alternative.

A third statistically biased assumption is that technique is synonymous with technology. In other words, the strategy used for framing the test protocol involved in a research project is inseparable from the technology used to collect and communicate the information.

In reality, three established research technologies and an emerging fourth alternative—telephone interviewing, mail surveys and person-to-person interaction (one-on-one interviews, focus groups, mall intercepts)—are all capable of supporting a wide variety of research techniques. The newest kid on the block, electronic data collection, is often considered only appropriate for the moment-to-moment testing techniques for which it is best known. This limiting assumption can be tied directly to the failure of research professionals to maintain a crisp distinction between research technologies and the techniques they can support.

The Perception Analyzer, for example, is an interactive group testing system that allows us to collect information electronically without having to rely on verbal communication. It is a technology, a "stupid" data collection tool. Its value and potential benefit are tied not to any one research technique but to the quality of the technique with which it is used. To imply that this technology can be used with only one research technique reflects narrow thinking.

### The Challenge of the Information Gauntlet

What is responsible for these deeply flawed assumptions? I attribute their continued presence, in part, to a phenomenon we refer to as the information gauntlet. The information gauntlet begins when a question of significance arises among a group of decision-makers. Information pertaining to this question is requested from the organization's research manager, who in turn talks to the research vendor, who translates the question into an appropriate test protocol. He or she then talks to the research project manager, who in turn talks with the data collection staff, who will talk directly to the audience of interest. Once the information is collected, it must go back through these six steps to the person who asked the question in the first place.

An important objective of research is to shorten the distance between target population and decision-maker. But there are significant logistical problems involved. There is a high, positive correlation between the length of an information gauntlet and the distortion that will occur as information passes through the gauntlet.

The response to the challenge of the information gauntlet thus far has been to structure questions in great detail at the beginning of a project and to maintain this rigid structure throughout the entire effort. Though inflexible and narrow, this rigid structure allows questions to survive the gauntlet with some semblance of what was originally intended.

Prior to microprocessors, information in the gauntlet was unavailable to the decision-maker until the entire project was complete. Even though unanticipated findings of critical importance were often discovered during the research process, the rigidity of the research process often prevented them from reaching the decision-maker, making research a black-box phenomenon rather than a discovery process ("black box" in this case meaning the common situation of a data-collection process invisible to the individual who will use the information).

The black-box orientation creates an environment in which research becomes a fixed commodity bought by the pound. Because a solid deductive examination is not compatible with the black-box approach, quality becomes synonymous with sample size. And the decision-maker, being uninvolved in the research process, cannot make distinctions between numbers used for reporting statistical precision and numbers used for reporting measurement precision. Distinctions between technique and technology are also too subtle for the black-box research user, so they are also left out. The end result of the rigid black-box orientation are findings almost completely dictated by the phrasing of the original question.

The limitation of a black-box approach to research was one of the major reasons we developed the Perception Analyzer.

Another challenge faced by the research industry is communication distortion. In research, we often pull people off the street who may not necessarily be versed in public speaking and ask them to describe what are often contextually bound reactions in an anxiety-provoking group setting. The nature of this information collection process produces two very significant problems (which also occur with telephone surveys). First, the typical respondent is going to keep his answer simple because the more he talks, the greater the likelihood he won't appear as sharp as he'd like. Second, he will tend to gravitate toward the most socially acceptable answers. Suppose that I think that women should never ever be allowed to work, and I am being asked questions by a female interviewer.

There is a nasty tendency to start filtering my answers in order to make them more socially acceptable. Though the filtering is a very understandable social phenomenon, it certainly distorts research, undermining our ability to provide the most reliable assessment possible of what people think, and more importantly, what they are most likely to do. This problem was another factor influencing the development of the Perception Analyzer.

A third challenge concerns the negative correlation between speed and processing accuracy. Every time a research project's timeline is accelerated, error inevitably increases. This error, which is generally referred to as non-sampling error, is actually more likely to distort research findings than error associated with sampling limitations. Its potential for distorting data, however, is often overlooked in the effort to rush information to a decision-maker. The black-box approach to research, spawned in response to the challenge of the information gauntlet, rarely concerns itself with the details of the information collection process.

### The Perception Analyzer

The Perception Analyzer was designed to create an interactive feedback loop between the decision-maker and the audience of interest. It is an electronic data collection tool that allows respondents to instantly express an opinion with a minimum of effort. It can accommodate both close-ended and open-ended questions *and* is generally used in a two-step process.

The first portion of a group session is devoted to using the Perception Analyzer to record what respondents think. The results of the first step are then used to direct moderator-led discussions during the second step, which explore *why* participants reacted the way they did. The hand-held dials used with the Perception Analyzer are easy to use and do not intimidate the participants. The instructional phase of a session rarely lasts more than 10 minutes, with most participants mastering the concept immediately. From the participant perspective, there is only one control. The most difficult exercise requires no more than turning the dial from side to side in reaction to video or audio material. If there is a question, the moderator can quickly provide an answer and demonstrate the proper use of the dial. We have never encountered participants intimidated by the dials. Most find it much easier to respond using a dial rather than standing up in front of 60 people and trying to describe a reaction.

A typical Perception Analyzer session has about 60 participants. Each participant has a dial with values ranging from 0 to 100, connected directly to a microprocessor, which allows him/her to indicate reactions to questions or the presentation of test material. The computer then measures respondents' reactions and the magnitude of the variation that emerges. This allows us to instantaneously monitor respondents' thoughts; they do not need to verbalize their reactions. The data are immediately available to the client, providing instant access to respondents' opinions.

There is little contamination; individuals have not had to screen their opinions for the social setting because their responses are anonymous. If a participant does not want to have other participants know how he is answering a question, the dial can easily be covered with one hand. We usually ask participants at the end of a session whether they thought they had been able to answer questions with anonymity. After more than 200 sessions, we have yet to encounter a participant who said their answers were not anonymous. Furthermore, the speed with which we transfer the information does not increase the probability of distortion, so we are able to obtain a much more reliable channel of information.

When we conduct national studies, we have up to eight Perception Analyzer machines at different sites simultaneously using the same test protocol; results are transmitted by modem to a central site, where they are combined to provide an instantaneous profile of respondent reactions on a second-by-second basis. The Perception Analyzer provides one of the fastest data collection and reporting systems available in the United States.

One of the applications of the Perception Analyzer system is in determining attitudes toward political candidates. Contrary to the opinions expressed by some political consultants, our goal was not to become an agent in a manipulative process that distorts and harms the American political process. Our objective was to create a technology that would allow quality research to be conducted within a short time, *without* compromising quality or analytical flexibility.

A candidate's image often changes constantly throughout a campaign, and this dynamic phenomenon is extremely difficult to monitor. A wide variety of factors influences the volatility of a candidate's image, and the importance of any one factor is also likely to change over time.

With the Perception Analyzer, it is possible to measure a candidate's image relative to his opponents, identify the factors influencing his image, and evaluate alternative strategies for changing the candidate's image within a two-hour session. The speed of the Perception Analyzer allows the collection of more than 600 separate pieces of information during one session. The immediate reporting of information to the client viewing the session creates an interactive link that provides the opportunity to explore any issue of interest or pursue questions that were not anticipated prior to the session. This flexibility ensures that the client receives definitive results from the research process and need not be concerned about the possibility of having asked the wrong questions.

This technology also allows the candidate to actually incorporate the results of the research into the presentation being studied. During the intermission in a debate, the candidate can quickly be informed of his earlier performance and make adjustments in his strategy accordingly. If statistical rigor is desired, several sessions can be conducted simultaneously with the results sent via modem to a central site for immediate analysis.

The Perception Analyzer allows the user to simultaneously track different segments during the research process. Results can be broken down into four subsets, based upon classification questions asked of the group. Not only does the user see how the aggregate has reacted, but he/she can also monitor how any subset has reacted. By using our session simulation software, users can examine any number of segments after the session until they find significant points of differentiation. Because the software was designed to support simulation, the limit of analysis is determined only by the imagination of the users.

When something interesting is discovered, the Perception Analyzer software allows the user to fine-tune his analysis. For example, I can display the standard deviation of any reading if I have questions regarding how much variability is found within a segment; this feature is particularly valuable when dealing with small sample sizes. Statistics can help determine how robust results are. The most important feature is that the data are coming back in real time without any group contamination. Hypotheses can be generated *and* tested during the same session, ensuring that the research investment will produce actionable results.

You will notice that throughout this presentation I have described how the Perception Analyzer can be used to expedite information generated during the session. And though the speed and flexibility of the Perception Analyzer will influence the amount of information collected during a session, the majority of questions asked of participants will probably not be any different from those asked in telephone surveys, focus groups, from all intercept studies.

Ultimately, decisions regarding which questions will be asked and how the results will be interpreted have a much greater impact than the technology used to collect and report information. This decision process is the appropriate focus of concerns regarding the role of research in politics, not the speed with which information can be processed. The Perception Analyzer is basically a stupid machine whose value is tied to the research technique it is used to support.

*Columbia Information Systems*
*333 SW 5th Street*
*Portland, Oregon 97204*

# VIDEO IMAGE GENERATORS

*Tom Angell,*
*Interface Video Systems*

Modern post-production facilities use many new and different electronic devices to acquire, generate and/or manipulate video. Five deserve special attention. They are: (1) the digital video effects unit, (2) the robotically controlled camera, (3) electronic art stations, (4) digital video recorders and (5) three-dimensional computer animation devices. These machines are at the heart of a producer's ability to efficiently create many of the stunning visual effects we see every day on television. They are of special importance in political spot production for five major reasons.

First, it is almost impossible to buy commercial spot time longer than 30 seconds. To be effective, visual images must have a high impact in such short periods. One way to create higher impact is to create complex, visually-arresting, textured images.

Second, political issues can be complex and are thus often more easily explained in graphic or animated form instead of what we pejoratively refer to in the industry as the "BTF," Big Talking Face. A good example of this: the amount of televised coverage about Supreme Court decisions or economic issues has increased dramatically now that the networks have imaging devices with which to animate and thus better illustrate these relatively abstract, non-visual stories. Before this technology existed, such stories were carried in highly abbreviated form, if at all.

Third, a candidate's messages must stand out in the video stream. During an election year, there is a tremendous amount of noise on television—the commercials for the other candidates. You must rise above that noise in order to be heard. Obviously, to have visually interesting images is essential. Our technological boxes, judiciously used, help accomplish this task.

Fourth, these devices not only speed up production and increase quality but also shorten the time needed to change course and alter your TV message. In today's highly reactive political campaigns, time really is of the essence.

Fifth, voters expect political commercials that measure up to the material they normally see on television. You cannot have a pedestrian spot, lacking production value, and expect it to capture the imagination of your viewing audience. Usually image generators can create enough production value to attract and hold an audience whose prime concern that evening is not waiting for and watching a political message.

Let's take a look at each of these devices, see how they work and how they are applied to political commercials, and talk about their strengths and weaknesses.

### Digital Video Effects Units (DVEs)

DVEs are often called flat-plane manipulators because they are designed to take the normal image on your TV ("the flat plane") and, through mathematical algorithms, distort it into other useful shapes. They are common now and are the backbone of most effects in any modern post-production facility. There are probably more than 15 brands on the market. They are also referred to as "freeze and squeeze boxes," because some of their most common uses are to compress, twist, turn, flip or warp the existing video image. This ability to compress one picture and place it on top of another is key to getting multiple images on the screen. Since people can easily "read" images at high speed (much faster than an announcer can say the words), heavily layered or collaged images can communicate a more complex message in a much shorter period of time. The only disadvantage of this technology is that its ease of use tends to result in overuse. Virtually no political commercial today is made without this machine.

### Interactive Motion Control Devices

Sometimes referred to as motion control cameras, these devices are a wedding of a camera (film or video) with a robotic arm similar to those used for welding in large factories. They allow complex moves to be completed with ease and precision on flat art, photos and even three-dimensional objects. The final recorded images exhibit in their movement the grace of a ballet dancer combined with the repetitive accuracy of a computer. Integrated with other equipment, these devices permit many other interesting special effects that were until recently unknown; *e.g.*, time-lapse videography and other types of in-camera effects.

This device is still relatively rare but will soon be a common sight in most high-end post-production houses. Its advantages are speed, precision and cost-effectiveness. Its disadvantage is that its size and weight tie it to the studio. Also, the images it records are almost always best if they are of inanimate objects. The robotic arm (like its factory cousin) expects the objects of its attention to move only as instructed by the computer.

### Electronic Art Stations

These "paintbox" workstations are the electronic equivalent of a complete artist's studio. By combining electronic tablet, computer and specialized software, they allow artists to draw, design, lay out and compose two-dimensional, static art-work. They can set type and use chalk, paint, airbrush or watercolors as their medium. Most important, they accomplish all of this work entirely within the electronic medium. Even exotic effects such as rotoscoping—animation created by overdrawing live action material—are easily accomplished.

Work proceeds so rapidly that often the producer sits through the session adding ideas and changing concepts as the product evolves! In addition to making production highly interactive, the advantages of electronic paint systems are the speed at which the artist can work (no need to wait weeks for artist material to come off story boards), the quality of the finished image, and, there-fore, the cost-effectiveness of the machinery. There are no real disadvantages as long as only a video image—*i.e.*, no print or film—is needed.

### Digital Disc Recorders or Digital Video Recorders

The secret of these phenomenal new video recorders is that they capture video as digital data, not as an analog signal. In many ways they are quite similar to the new digital audio tape recorders (DATs) that are about to revolutionize the music industry. The advantage of a digital recording is that it can be copied and added to hundreds of times without any loss in quality. This allows techniques such as multi-layering video to be accomplished quite easily.

The possibilities of this instrument are just beginning to be explored. Cam-paign commercials using it are visually arresting and often possess a deep-textured look that can convey significant amounts of information in a very short time. Many other technologies surrounding this development are now being explored; for example, multi-matting images (*i.e.*, non-detectable compositing masking such as your familiar weatherman superimposed over his satellite maps) can now be repeatedly employed with full confidence that the final master will look identical to the source material, even though it might be 50 to 100 genera-tions removed from the original. Such techniques are possible only via digital video recording.

### Three-Dimensional Computer Animation Devices

These computer graphic imagined devices (often called CGIs) perform a unique style of animation often used in the production of moving logos. Emphasis here should be placed on the words "three-dimensional," since these computers depict all possible sides of an object. The effect is distinctly different from that of their distant cousin, the DVE, which can only manipulate a two-dimensional or flat-plane image.

This is high-end animation, created with a large computer and specialized software. It is basically a three-step process that, unlike the previously described devices, does not function in "real time." That is, the result of your work does not instantly appear on the screen but first must be "processed" much the same way a word processor is used in revising a speech.

The first step, modeling, is used to build a mathematical model of a three-dimensional object. These objects at this stage resemble a skeleton or wire frame of the final object you will need for your commercial. The wire-frame objects can then be set into motion using other software. This second step, often referred to as "motion scripting," defines how the object will move through space—swooping, tumbling and turning to reveal all its sides. In the third step, the wire frame is wrapped with a skin that can simulate almost any texture such as glass, stone or metal.

Then, the images are electronically "rendered." This means that the computer computes what each individual frame would look like with the predescribed texture, light, and positioning along its predetermined motion-scripted path. These rendered frames are stored and eventually called back, one by one, and put on videotape.

It often takes 10 minutes for the computer to render, or think out, each individual frame. With 30 frames of video per second, 10 seconds of an animated logo—300 frames rendered at the rate of 10 minutes each—would require about 50 hours of computing time to be rendered.

Producing this type of material is difficult, expensive and slow. The payoff is that the images are unique and visually stunning. Due to cost and time considerations, this technique has mostly been used for opens and closes of spots instead of longer pieces.

It is important to note that no commercial is made using a single device. A combination of many different pieces of equipment and of many different talents is required. Moreover, these machines do not guarantee a quality product. Great commercials are created by a delicate balance of talent and technology, creative ideas and excellent execution.

Prospective purchasers of such services must not only evaluate the available hardware, but also the talents of the staff and the desire of the management of a facility to do political work. Many of the greatest political spots have been produced without any special effects whatsoever. They key element has always been and will continue to be a political consultant/producer with a thorough understanding of the candidate, the issues and the voters—combined with a certain undefinable genius for linking these elements through television.

The direction is clear. Fast-paced, responsive political campaigns will become increasingly dependent on the latest video technology to keep the broadcast component of their campaigns effective and on target.

*Interface Video Systems*
*1333 New Hampshire Avenue, N.W.*
*Washington, DC 20036*

# MAKING DATA-RICH MAPS WITH A PC

*Laszlo Bardof,*
*MapInfo Corp.*

We have a package that can take a map of any scale and overlay data onto it—take an existing database and throw it into the map. The geographic analysis that we can do will help with (1) finding out where particular points are in a political campaign's database, (2) overlaying this database onto actual maps and seeing what it means; and (3) comparing the geographic relationships among different sets of data. Thus, we can facilitate redistricting because the computer can now draw experimental boundaries and tell us what those boundaries mean. We can then shift the boundaries as desired.

Users can quickly modify a boundary on the screen and ask, "How does this affect the density of a certain age group, party affiliation or ethnic group?" Then they can shift the boundaries again and repeat the calculations. The significance of tables of figures also can be easily grasped when they are displayed geographically.

MapInfo can work with multiple layers of data. On a street map of a city we can display points representing the location of voters, and in addition, show boundaries. We can display up to 50 layers of data and independently turn any of them on or off. We can also zoom in or out of any area, giving the user detail ranging from a neighborhood to the whole country. In this way one can see the "nitty-gritty" —where each voter lives, his or her party affiliation, race, sex or age—or zoom back and see the summary of the data for a county.

MapInfo Corp. can supply state, county, MCD, ADI, DMA, MSA and ZIP Code boundary files. In the urbanized parts of over 300 metropolitan areas, MapInfo's MetroMaps are detailed street maps, which include all the streets, rivers, railroad tracks and address ranges for each block. These maps are drawn to scale and correct to about 60 feet.

With the maps as a base, MapInfo can locate information from the user's database and even find addresses in a metropolitan area, correct to the block and side of the street. A database with addresses can appear as a "push-pin map" with symbols representing the location of the database records. Moving the cursor to any of the points on the screen will retrieve the detailed record behind the point.

By combining a database with a map, the user can perform analyses that were never before possible. What would you like to see on a map? Voter registration? Locations of contributors who donated more than $1,000? The user can sort information, write reports, make mail labels and search and retrieve records in the database program and run MapInfo to display the results on a map. Conversely, analysis done in MapInfo can be sent back to the database.

For example, in a redistricting application, the user can draw boundaries interactively on the screen and calculate the population of the areas. With database queries, he or she can also selectively analyze sex, income, race or party affiliation.

MapInfo can also be used for all sorts of campaign work. Let's say you are planning a fundraiser, you can use large dots to show big contributors and small dots for lesser ones. The databases are flexible. You can store any information you want and then call it up. You move your cursor to a little dot and pull up all the detail related to that dot. You can use our basic pin map to draw boundaries and to conduct searches such as depicting all the contributions the campaign has received within a given area. It will do a complex search in just seconds. You can even take that one step further. Instead of showing the detail, you can summarize it. You can take a broader view than is provided by simply looking at streets, and you can impose shading based on how many dollars the campaign has received from an area. Then you can add another layer on top of that and put in legends and text.

*MapInfo Corp.*
*200 Broadway*
*Troy, NY 12180*

# COMPUTER SOFTWARE

*John A. Phillips,*
*Aristotle Industries*

The political campaign software industry has its roots in the use of mainframe computers in the presidential campaigns of the 1960s and 1970s. In the early 1980s, the advent of inexpensive, easy to use personal computers and the growth of specialized campaign-management programs have changed the way the modern American political campaign is run.

Almost 75 percent of federal campaigns (House, Senate and presidential) and 25 percent of state legislative campaigns now utilize personal computers. At the local level, computers are used by about one of every 10 campaigns.

Challengers are more likely than incumbents to use computers. Younger candidates, perhaps more comfortable with the cathode ray tube than the bumper sticker as a tool of political persuasion, are more likely to utilize a computer and specialized software.

In the next five years, the campaign technology industry is likely to introduce new products geared toward expert systems of artificial intelligence. Such programs permit users to incorporate "rules" or specialized "if-then" statements, which will further enhance their decision-making ability.

The same thing happened in the political campaign industry as in other industries. As the cost went down, availability increased and cost-standardization increased. Even low-budget campaigns began to use computers for both voter persuasion and voter turnout.

There have been previous technological breakthroughs, such as television advertising in the presidential race and Senate and House races. But not until technology reaches candidates for county sheriff or county commissioner do you see the full impact of technology. We are moving rapidly in that direction.

There are approximately 1,700 federally registered campaigns in a presidential election year. Candidates will spend approximately $550 to $750 million in the election cycle of 1987-88 on campaign technology. About half a million more candidates run for state and local office in a typical election cycle. These local campaigns are traditionally run grassroots efforts. In the past, technology has geared towards the high end of the market, but now companies are selling to the bottom of the market where a significant number of candidates are.

Among other uses, software now available will: help you raise money in compliance with state and federal guidelines, assist the campaign in conducting its own poll, run cross-tabulations, assist in opposition research, help plan the candidate's schedule, help send out news releases, and generate mailings to specific groups of swing voters or to voters already identified as committed.

We are going to see greater use of computers at the grassroots level. Thirty to 40 percent of campaigns at the state and local level already utilize a computer in some context. It might be a parent borrowing their child's computer to run for school board, or it may be a state legislator who uses a computer borrowed from the district office. But such *ad hoc* arrangements are giving way to more formalized planning, and we will see the wider and wider infiltration of personal computers into campaigns.

*Aristotle Industries*
*205 Pennsylvania Avenue, S.E.*
*Washington, DC 20003*

# III

# CRUCIAL CAMPAIGN VARIABLES

*The future of political campaigns is unknown and exciting. Section III considers political campaigns in terms of 11 crucial variables. Leading off the analysis of each variable are statements from participants in the February 2, 1988 Annenberg Washington Program colloquium. Among the participants quoted, besides David Beiler and Larry Sabato, are Michael Barone, Curtis B. Gans, Newton N. Minow and Edward J. Rollins.*

*__Michael Barone__ is a senior writer on the editorial staff of The Washington Post, for which he writes editorials and occasional columns. He is the editor of the Almanac of American Politics and was senior vice president of Peter D. Hart Research Associates, Inc., a public opinion research firm. He is a graduate of Harvard College and Yale Law School.*

*__Curtis B. Gans__ is the Director of the Committee for the Study of the American Electorate and, until last year, wrote a self-syndicated column, which appeared in more than 20 newspapers in major urban centers. As director of the Committee, Gans is the ranking expert on voter turnout and participation. On matters of voting, he has become the primary source of information for many newspapers, wire services, news magazines and columnists. His writings have appeared in a number of major publications, and he has appeared on numerous talk shows, including Today, Good Morning America, All Things Considered and The MacNeil/Lehrer Report, among others. He has spoken in various capacities on more than 200 college campuses and before political and trade associations.*

*__Newton N. Minow__ is the Director of The Annenberg Washington Program in Communications Policy Studies of Northwestern University. Mr. Minow was Chairman of the Federal Communications Commission during the Kennedy Administration, and has served as Chairman of the Public Broadcasting Service (PBS) and the Rand Corporation. He is a partner in the law firm of Sidley & Austin. A graduate of Northwestern, he is a Life Trustee of the University and a Professor of Communications Law and Policy. He is the recipient of two of broadcasting's most valued honors, the George Foster Peabody Award and the Ralph Lowell Medal. He was a Visiting Fellow at the Kennedy School of Government at Harvard in 1986.*

*__Edward J. Rollins__ is managing partner of Russo Watts and Rollins, a political and governmental affairs consulting firm with offices in Washington, D.C. and Sacramento, California. Mr. Rollins has served in the administrations of Presidents Nixon and Ford, and on the White House staff of President Reagan from January 20, 1981 until he resigned as Assistant to the President for Political and Intergovernmental Affairs on October 1, 1985. In 1983, he took a leave of absence from the White House to serve as the National Director of the President's re-election campaign.*

# BROADCAST REGULATION

"When television began, people in broadcasting took a map of the United States and drew circles to correspond with television signals. It was quickly apparent that television signals bore no relationship to political boundaries. A television signal goes out in a circle of about 70 miles in radius no matter where city, county, town or state borders may be. The people in the business of television drew circles around all the television signals, and discovered they had over 150 markets. They called them ADIs, or 'areas of dominant influence,' and created a commercial map that made sense. They didn't know that by so doing, they had also amended the U.S. Constitution, because politics would never be the same again."

*Newton N. Minow*

*New technologies, particularly cable and satellites, are changing the way television is transmitted. Thus, the basic public policy agenda related to campaigns—how to ensure each candidate equitable opportunity to reach voters—has become far more complicated.*

*Much of the public policy terrain—such as access, equal time and right of reply— will sound familiar. But many of the questions are new. For example, are rights created at the local cable system level when a national candidate buys commercial time on a superstation? This essay and its rejoinder outline the new public policy, and present the opposing views about the proper role of government.*

# CANDIDATES, NEW TECHNOLOGIES AND REGULATION

*Daniel J. Swillinger and*
*Andrew S.A. Levine*

New communications technologies are slowly changing American political campaigns. Television news programs and paid commercials constitute the overwhelming source of the information about candidates received by the electorate.

New technologies are giving campaigns quicker, better access to the nation's television screens, especially through the use of satellite communication between the candidate and local TV stations thousands of miles away.

The 1988 presidential campaign has seen the first significant use of satellites by candidates. It allowed Sen. Albert Gore, for example, to hold a "press conference" in Iowa that was made available to local stations in the southern "Super Tuesday" states. The local stations pick up the feed, edit the tape and present excerpts from the "press conference," just as if the station had a reporter and camera crew present in Des Moines.

Many of the dozen major Republican and Democratic candidates used this type of satellite "availability," especially when the tight early primary schedule made it physically impossible to be every place a candidate would have liked to be.

Perhaps by the time of the next presidential election, candidates will have the capacity to send their messages from a satellite to individual voters' television sets. While the advent of direct broadcast satellite (DBS) systems has been slower than earlier projected, it will likely come, especially if a small rooftop receiving dish is successfully marketed.

There was also a measurable increase in the placement of commercials on cable systems, as a way of targeting both certain geographic areas and certain demographic groups. As cable reaches a larger part of the electorate, candidates presumably will make correspondingly greater use of it.

This would seem to be particularly true in metropolitan areas, where broadcast television time is prohibitively expensive for most congressional and state legislative candidates. Cable, as well as multipoint distribution service (MDS) systems, gives candidates running in geographically small districts the opportunity to reach voters through television at much lower costs.

Overlaying these technological advances—indeed, casting a shadow upon them—is the question of the regulation of broadcast, cable and satellite media by the Federal Communications Commission through the Communications Act of 1934 and its many amendments.

Federal law includes a number of specific provisions regulating candidates' and broadcasters' rights to access to the airwaves. These provisions, such as the so-called "equal time" requirement, are viewed by most candidates as implementing their right to the public airwaves, and by most broadcasters as impinging on their First Amendment rights.

The FCC during the Reagan Administration has been a hotbed of deregulatory fervor. In usefully cleaning out much of the regulatory undergrowth that had developed during the nearly 70 years of government regulation of the airwaves, the Commission took on some of the "trees" as well.

In particular, the FCC decided in August 1987 that the "fairness doctrine," which requires stations to provide reasonably balanced coverage of controversial issues of public importance, was no longer justified because people now have access to news through so many additional channels of communications; the Commission said it would no longer enforce the doctrine unless Congress forced it to. Congress did pass such legislation, but the President vetoed it.

A lawsuit challenging the FCC's decision is working its way through the courts.[1] It seems clear that legislative or judicial resolution of this issue is some ways off.

While the fairness doctrine itself does not apply to candidates, it underlies other rules, such as those giving a right to reply to someone who is personally attacked in a broadcast, or the political candidate's right to respond to editorials endorsing an opponent.

These are politically sensitive issues, made more so by new technologies that are stretching many decades-old regulatory systems. Concern for the First Amendment rights of broadcasters and related providers of information is legitimate. But in the sensitive area of political campaigns—where, as the Supreme Court has noted, meaningful "alternative channels of communication" do not exist—the countervailing right of citizens to learn about candidates and issues must be given great weight.

Failure to require roughly equal treatment of candidates by broadcasters may well undermine democratic processes. Thus, just as the state may impose reasonable restrictions to facilitate the electoral process—*e.g.*, barring the sale of alcoholic beverages on election day, or preventing campaigning within 50 feet of polling places—it may reasonably regulate to ensure the free flow of vital political information.

Our purpose here is to review the current political information regulatory scheme of several of the new communications technologies, and to suggest how the traditional regulatory scheme should be applied.

### Cable Television

Cable television is the most regulated, and most confusing medium in the application of equal opportunity and fairness doctrine requirements. The FCC first applied these rules to cable systems under the standard, "reasonably ancillary to broadcasting." Subsequently, Section 315 (c) of the Federal Communications Act was amended to include cable operators under political broadcasting rules. As a result, the FCC adjusted its regulatory scheme to reflect court decisions and decided not to apply the equal opportunity and fairness doctrine requirements to public-access programming on cable, while maintaining the requirements on "local origination" channels controlled directly by the operators.

While the equal opportunity requirement has been specifically applied to cable operators by statute, the fairness doctrine's application is a creature of regulation. It is essential to continue to apply the fairness doctrine to cable to preserve the integrity of the political arena. The Supreme Court held in *Red Lion Broadcasting Co. v. FCC*,[2] a seminal case in this area, that "[i]t is the right of the viewers and listeners, not the right of the broadcasters, which is paramount." The Court has recognized that "it is of particular importance that candidates have the . . . opportunity to make their views known so that the electorate may intelligently evaluate the candidates' personal qualities and their positions on vital public issues before choosing among them on election day." Scarcity of frequencies available in the electromagnetic spectrum required the regulatory protection of this right.

Scarcity also exists in the franchising of cable systems. Just as constitutionally permissible government regulation prohibits an individual from operating a radio or TV station without a license, local government franchising creates a monopoly for the local cable operator. There is almost never more than one cable operator in a particular community. This circumstance will continue well into the future, since most cable operators have long-term exclusive franchises. The cable operator, an unelected private individual or corporation selected by local government, has exclusive control over what channels subscribers receive. Because the number of cable systems generally is fixed at one, the scarcity in cable systems is at least as great as the scarcity of frequencies.

Cable television, unlike newspapers, involves a form of government regulated scarcity, which prevents virtually all members of the public from owning and operating cable systems. As a result, the government may regulate cable television to ensure that there is an opportunity for the presentation of views expressed by those excluded from cable ownership. As the Supreme Court stated in *Red Lion:*

> [T]he First Amendment confers no right . . . to an unconditional monopoly of a scarce resource which the Government has denied others the right to use. . . . It does not violate the First Amendment to treat licensees given the privilege of using scarce radio frequencies as proxies for the entire community, obligated to give suitable time and attention to matters of great public concern.

Cable operators also are proxies for the community, and they should provide response time for a candidate whose opponent has been endorsed on the cable system.

One way to discuss application of the equal opportunity and fairness doctrine principles under current regulation, the potential effects of ending regulation, and some proposals to meet existing and potential problems, is to look at the four general sources of programming carried on cable systems.

**RETRANSMISSION OF IMPORTED SIGNALS**

Transmission of "superstations" and the importation of distant signals is a staple of cable systems across the country. The FCC maintains that the superstations, as local broadcasters, are subject to the equal opportunity and fairness doctrine requirements, but concludes that cable systems retransmitting the signals are not similarly obligated. This is clearly contrary to the statute, which places cable operators in the same posture as local television stations. They are responsible for all programs they transmit, not just those they originate.

Assume that a congressional candidate from northern Virginia is interviewed on a *Geraldo*-type program on WGN in Chicago. It would constitute an "equal opportunity use" on WGN only if he were a Chicago-area candidate. But if a cable system in northern Virginia carries WGN, this broadcast also would not give his opponent the right to an equal opportunity, since the local cable system does not "control" the retransmission. The opponent has no right to an equal opportunity on WGN since he is not a candidate in the station's local service area.

What about a presidential candidate? In the event that a "use" occurred, the right to an equal opportunity on WGN would be available to the opponent. The effect, however, is not clear if a local cable system preempted the opponent's time. The ability to preempt might constitute "control" and subject the local system to an equal opportunity claim.

If national candidates in 1988 purchase advertising on the "superstations," this will create an equal opportunity right for opponents to purchase time because the advertising is being broadcast locally. The unresolved issue, however, is what equal opportunity rights are created at the local cable system level. Should the local operator at least be obliged to carry that candidate's advertising?

### ORIGINAL SATELLITE PROGRAMMING

Local cable systems carry a number of channels of original programming provided by satellite. ESPN, C-SPAN, and the Movie Channel are prominent examples. Unlike superstations, these programmers are not regulated by the FCC or anyone else. Under current FCC policy, neither equal time nor fairness doctrine requirements apply to this original satellite programming. ESPN, for example, could sell advertising to a candidate and would be under no obligation to provide equal time. Similarly, it could endorse a candidate, carry programming constituting a personal attack on a person or institution, or treat a controversial issue of public importance without being obligated to carry opposing views.

The equal opportunity and fairness doctrine rules should be applied to satellite programming. The programmer has a choice of whether to carry advertising or endorsements. If they are carried, then the programmer should be required to provide equal time or response time.

The current communications statutory and regulatory scheme does not provide an obvious basis for the imposition of regulation on the satellite programmer. The FCC regulates satellites used by the programmers only as common carriers; there is no content regulation. The issue, however, is as much about election regulation as communications regulation. A combination of sound public policy, a legitimate governmental interest in regulating elections, and the intrusiveness of television provide a basis for regulating satellite programmers in the narrow context of political candidate broadcasting.

In the 1974 case of *Miami Herald Publishing Co. v. Tornillo*,[3] the Supreme Court held unconstitutional a Florida statute requiring newspapers to afford a right of reply to candidates. It has been argued that according to this decision, the First Amendment rights of cable operators would be abridged by obligating them to comply with equal opportunity and fairness doctrine rules. The Court has noted that the varying characteristics of the news media justify differences in the First Amendment standards applied to them. The almost absolute ability of newspapers to operate free of governmental restriction has never been available to broadcasters. At least in their current mode of operation, cable systems are not so different from broadcasters that they should be treated like newspapers. The impact of the television screen, whether the program is broadcast or cablecast, is immense. When the impact is felt in political campaigns and elections, the public interest requires that full and vigorous debate be available to the electorate.

Alternatively, the cable operator who makes the editorial decision to carry ESPN or C-SPAN and who is already regulated by the FCC and local government, could be obligated to adhere to equal opportunity and fairness doctrine requirements. The FCC position of imposing equal opportunity and fairness doctrine obligations only on cable origination is the result of rulemaking, and the FCC has the authority to amend its rules to impose requirements on the local operator in this context.

This approach creates practical difficulties: the cable operator would have to know in advance that political advertising was to be carried by the programmer, he would have to have the contractual right to delete it, and he would need something to replace it. It would seem easier to place the burden on the originator, who is benefiting economically by selling the advertising time and can most easily, as a mechanical matter, make equal time available.

### "MUST-CARRY" REQUIREMENTS

In the past, FCC "must-carry" rules required local cable operators to carry "significantly viewed local area television stations." A recent case struck down the commission's second attempt at a constitutionally acceptable must-carry regulation.[4] Nonetheless, at the present time, a major portion of a local system's cable channels is devoted to these "significantly viewed local area television stations."

All such programming carried on a cable system is subject to equal opportunity and fairness doctrine requirements because the originator is a broadcaster. The requirements would not apply only when there is a discontinuity between the service area of a broadcast station and the significantly viewed area (as defined for must-carry purposes). For instance, a candidate for office outside of the station's service area could appear, create a "use," and have the broadcast "must-carried" on cable within the electoral district, where the candidate's opponent would have no equal-time right.

### LOCAL ORIGINATION

FCC rules apply equal opportunity and fairness doctrine requirements to local cable-originated programming. The regulations are essentially identical to those governing broadcasters, with the same news program exemptions for equal time. The rules apply to locally originated programs and advertising—a very small portion of cable programs. This presumably includes local ads inserted in non-local programs. It does not include access channels. It is these rules that the FCC has opened for repeal or modification.

Since the Commission recognizes that it cannot repeal the equal opportunity requirement, it is seeking to minimize regulation. A proposal submitted in 1983 suggests that equal time obligations be met through use of access channels. This proposal would effectively repeal equal opportunity requirements, since it would mean that candidate ads aired during a popular prime time program merely trigger the opponent's right to appear on the access channel. An appearance on the access channel would not be an equal opportunity in terms of audience and would not be on the same channel.

Equal opportunity rules as currently applied to cable origination should remain unchanged. This will be important in the future as cable reaches more homes, and candidates in districts where broadcast advertising is prohibitively expensive begin to use cable as a significant part of their advertising campaigns.

Similarly, the fairness doctrine should remain intact and applicable to cable as a matter of policy. Candidates ought to be entitled to reply to editorials endorsing opponents. Individuals and institutions ought to be able to respond to personal attacks. Both sides of controversial issues of public importance should be carried. Commission-created political rights, such as the "Zapple doctrine" (a statement by a candidate's spokesperson invokes equal time for opponent), which is as much quasi-fairness as it is quasi-equal-opportunity, should remain available.

The proposal to substitute access channels for a real right to respond is inadequate. Equally deficient are such ideas as grouping all channels on a cable system to determine whether fairness doctrine requirements are being met. The political process is too important for candidates and the partisans of public issues to be without certain extraordinary rights to reach the public.

### Direct Broadcast Satellites

The direct broadcast satellite service (DBS) is a radio-communication service in which signals from earth stations are retransmitted by satellite for direct reception by home terminals. Direct broadcast satellites can transmit signals much more powerful than those of current communications satellites, allowing reception of television broadcasts by small home dishes. DBS is currently a mode of program distribution in Japan and is operative in Europe.

Application of equal opportunity and fairness doctrine rules to DBS is determined by whether the FCC classifies a particular DBS applicant's proposal as broadcasting or as common carriage. If the proposed usage closely resembles broadcasting, then the requirements generally imposed on broadcasting, including those relating to political content, apply. The FCC has decided that DBS is not "broadcasting," a position that has been affirmed by a recent court decision.[5]

The commission has provided a general account of the standards that guide its classification decision-making. If an applicant proposes to provide direct service and retains control over the content of transmissions, the service is probably a broadcast. If the applicant offers its satellite transmission services indiscriminately to the public pursuant to tariff under the [common carrier] provisions of . . . the Act, it will be treated as a common carrier. The applicant may have some stations in each category.

Programmer-customers of common carrier DBS operators will not be subject to content regulation. The commission has argued that any control of this sort would: (1) merely duplicate the more pervasive access obligations already imposed upon the carrier itself; (2) go against the wishes of Congress, which probably did not intend for the customers of common carriers to be licensed and regulated as broadcasters; and (3) be unnecessary because similar systems are in operation without regulation and without harm to the public. Thus, common carrier DBS will be completely insulated from the political broadcasting rules.

The advent of DBS, of course, provides yet another way for political advertisers to target potential voters. Although we believe that there is little doubt that DBS programming is broadcasting, and therefore subject to equal opportunity and fairness doctrine rules, the commission and the courts have decided otherwise. The program originator, be it the satellite owner or a company leasing a transponder, is, therefore, not obligated to carry out the requirements of Section 315.

### Teletext

Teletext systems transmit textual and graphic material to home viewing screens. The information transmitted between the fields of the regular television picture is known as the "vertical blanking interval," which can be used for transmission of textual and graphic matter that appears on the television screen of a subscriber with a decoder.

Application of the political broadcasting rules to teletext was approved in a 1986 federal court decision,[6] in which the court found that teletext is broadcasting. The FCC's position was that teletext should not be subject to the political broadcasting rules, because teletext is similar to a print medium and *Tornillo* prohibited any content regulation. The court held that teletext, because it uses broadcast frequencies, is a form of broadcasting and is therefore covered by political broadcasting rules, as permitted in *Red Lion*.

From this seemingly simple conclusion, the court proceeded to follow a labyrinthian course of reasoning to determine that while equal opportunity rules did apply to teletext, reasonable access rules and the fairness doctrine did not apply.

The commission argued that teletext services were utterly incapable of a "use" under Section 315 and therefore equal opportunity rules did not apply. The court disagreed and concluded that teletext is capable of high-resolution graphics and can transmit a recognizable image of a candidate.

The court's reasoning that led to this conclusion seemed to be based on a realistic comprehension of the principles underlying the political broadcasting rules and how they should be equitably applied to new technologies. The court, however, then turned its back on these principles in concluding that the commission was not unreasonable in determining that the reasonable access rules did not apply to teletext transmissions. The court's rationale was deference to the expertise of the commission. It is perplexing that the same court had just found that this "expert" commission had completely misunderstood the basic nature of teletext, *i.e.*, whether it is broadcasting.

In deciding that the fairness doctrine need not be applied to teletext, the court said that the fairness doctrine had not been codified by the 1959 amendments to the Communications Act of 1934. Therefore, it reasoned, the commission was entirely justified in not "extending" one of its own regulations to the new technology of teletext.

The origin of the fairness doctrine is in the commission's power to regulate in the "public interest." Other mechanisms, such as reasonable access, could also be adopted under the public interest standard, perhaps in modified versions. The commission's failure to address these provisions effectively excluded discussion as to whether they should be adopted as a matter of discretion. The FCC failed even to seek comment on alternatives which might be better suited to the special circumstances of teletext, but which would accommodate the needs of the viewing public.

This court decision underlies the FCC's current policy decision not to enforce the fairness doctrine in any medium.

### Other New Media

Other new technologies present similar problems. Videotex is a two-way medium, permitting subscribers to respond to information provided textually and graphically. Subscribers may bank, pay bills, purchase goods and services, as well as respond to requests for opinions. Videotex is usually considered a common carrier service, since information is transmitted over telephone wires or cable. Videotex services are widespread in France which has more than 10 million subscribers. In the United States, the future scope of videotex is dependent upon market developments and the outcome of current litigation.[7]

If videotex, which is essentially a television set hooked up to a central computer, is limited to home banking and shopping, it is unlikely that political content will become an issue. The potential exists for local programming, however, at least over those videotex operators using cable rather than telephone wires. Unlike teletext, which is clearly broadcasting, regulation of political information on videotex raises the same issues as with cable. Equal opportunity and fairness doctrine requirements as now applied to local cable origination ought to be applicable to videotex.

Multipoint distribution service (MDS) is a microwave transmission service capable of line-of-sight transmission of a signal, typically no more than 25 miles. It is the non-cable conduit for such services as Home Box Office and Showtime. Additionally, there is a service known as multichannel multipoint distribution service (MMDS). MMDS and MDS should be treated in the same ways for purposes of political regulation.

The FCC's view is that MDS is a common carrier and therefore not subject to those regulatory aspects applicable specifically to broadcasters. Review of the commission's classification of MDS services is currently pending.

Subscription television (STV) is "pay TV"—the broadcasting of a scrambled television signal, which paying subscribers can unscramble with a decoder. The commission has decided that STV is a nonbroadcast service, a view upheld by a federal court.[8]

The commission bases its conclusion on the concept that subscription television is not "intended for the use of the general public," but only for subscribers. This disregards the reality that subscription providers "intend" to reach as many members of the general public as possible. Nonetheless, it has been finally decided that STV is not broadcasting and is not subject to the same regulations regarding political broadcasting as other broadcasters.

Before the current dispute over the broad applicability of broadcast regulation to STV, the commission had afforded STV special treatment for the application of the "reasonable access" requirement, based on its special characteristics.

The purpose of giving federal candidates the access right to purchase ads on prime time programming is because prime time (8-11 p.m.) is usually the period of maximum audience potential. However, subscription television programming—sporting events, for instance—is "generally" geared to selective audiences. It would appear that those stations engaged in STV would have their periods of maximum audience potential outside of normal prime time viewing periods. The commission believes, however, that reasonable access does not require STV stations to make available to federal candidates those periods of time in which they are engaged in STV programming, even though they are the times for maximum audiences.

Low power television (LPTV) uses very weak signals to broadcast over a small area, perhaps 10 to 15 miles, without interfering with other signals. The stations are limited to 1,000 watts of power, compared to 5 million watts for some standard broadcast stations. There are about 350 LPTV stations on the air and 1,700 construction permits outstanding. The potential exists for LPTV stations to target particular ethnic or racial communities, or, perhaps, suburban areas now served only by metropolitan-wide stations.

The FCC has decided that equal opportunity and fairness doctrine requirements will apply to programs originated by the LPTV station.

Since LPTV is broadcasting, these requirements should certainly continue to apply. To the extent that LPTV stations are engaged principally in the retransmission of other broadcast stations, or of satellite programming, the issues raised regarding cable television also arise here. While it may be premature to attempt to define the scope of regulation of political broadcasting, the potential of LPTV for candidate use is enormous, and the originator must be held responsible for assuring that both sides of issues and campaigns are presented.

In satellite master antenna television (SMATV) systems, earth stations pull down signals from satellites, including pay channel signals, and programming is provided to tenants of apartment buildings and complexes, to hotels and to other densely populated buildings which are internally wired to distribute the signals. In 1983, the FCC ruled that federal regulations preempt state and local regulation of SMATV; the commission has not decided whether political broadcasting rules apply to SMATV.

Electronic mail is a type of videotex, in which the sender types a letter on a personal computer, which transmits it as digital data over telephone lines or cable. A central computer sorts and delivers the message to the "electronic address" of the recipient's personal computer, where the signal is reconstructed into words on a screen or printed on paper. Electronic mail as currently conceived is a common carrier service, and therefore not subject to political content rules.

### Conclusion

This review of the current regulation of political broadcasting demonstrates a confusing pattern of FCC, judicial and congressional efforts to define candidates' and stations' rights and responsibilities. The net result is a lack of an underlying policy for regulation, or deregulation. Needed are policies that promote access to the airwaves for candidates and issues.

This can be done only with access rights that candidates may exercise, such as "equal time," the right to purchased or free time when an opponent buys or is given the time; "reasonable access," the right that a candidate cannot be denied the right to purchase time; and "lowest unit rate," a rule ensuring that candidates are not gouged by stations when buying advertising. Existing protections against stations' censorship of candidates' ads ought to remain as well.

Broadcasters raise legitimate concerns about their First Amendment rights, which they see as government intrusion into their programming. While sensitive to those concerns, we are convinced that nothing is more important than the greatest possible flow of information during elections—a flow that requires candidates to have certain minimum rights to air their views.

New technologies provide alternatives for candidates to communicate, but the need for access remains constant. The broadcast airwaves remain a limited commodity. Anyone with sufficient capital may start a newspaper, but to open a radio or TV station, or to launch a satellite, requires surmounting enormous government licensing procedures.

As long as those limitations exist, and candidates have a finite number of broadcast outlets from which to choose, those outlets must

be required to provide access to candidates. Maintenance of democratic processes requires no less.

NOTES

1. *Syracuse Peace Council et al. v. FCC* (D.C. Cir., No. 87-1516)
2. 395 U.S. 367 (1969)
3. 418 U.S. 241 (1974)
4. *Century Communications Corp. v. FCC* 835 F.2d 242 (D.C. Cir. 1987)
5. *National Association for Better Broadcasting v. FCC* (D.C. Cir., No 87-1198, June 17, 1988)
6. *Telecommunications Research & Action Center v. FCC*, 801 F.2d 501 (D.C. Cir. 1986)
7. *U.S. v. Western Electric Co.* (CA82-0192, D.C.D.C.)
8. *National Association for Better Broadcasting v. FCC, supra.*

*Daniel J. Swillinger* is a partner in the Washington, D.C. law firm of Barnett & Alagia. He is a former congressional staff member, former Assistant General Counsel of the Federal Election Commission and Deputy Special Counsel to the U.S. Senate Ethics Committee. Mr. Swillinger has been involved in dozens of political campaigns as a staff member and consultant and as legal counsel on both election and communication law matters. This piece is based on an article he wrote for the Winter 1984 *University of Missouri Law Review*, "Candidates and New Technologies: Should Political Broadcasting Rules Apply?"

*Andrew Steven Appel Levin* is admitted to practice by the Supreme Judicial Court of Massachusetts. He received his J.D. from Boston University School of Law in 1977.

## COMMENT
### Daniel L. Brenner

The problems of campaigning in the electronic age are real and disturbing. The trends? The generally baleful aspects of political action committees; the use of computers to vary direct mail campaign literature based on a recipient's profile; the presence of media consultants who script how a candidate will face the voters.

But the solution to these real problems will not come by pounding away at 40-year-old nails that have long lost their heads. That is my problem with the message of Swillinger and Levine. Talk to us about public financing of campaigns leading to limitations on overall expenditures. Address the structural rights of access to electronic media, and we'll be getting someplace. Dragging broadcast election law into the new technologies is not the way to go.

The authors initially state that it is "essential" to apply the fairness doctrine to cable "to preserve the integrity of the political arena." Leave aside whether said arena is now, or has recently been, a hot seat of integrity. The fact is, the fairness doctrine in cable possesses the same infirmities as fairness in broadcasting.

Covering newsworthy events and attempting to insure that all sides are heard—the twin prongs of the doctrine—are sound journalistic practices. But it is one thing for editors at CNN to make these judgments. It is another, less desirable, scheme when the government decides whether a cablecaster has provided sufficient opportunity for contrasting viewpoints.

Government-ordered balancing makes even less sense in cable. For there is less likelihood that the audience, say for one segment of CNN, will be watching when an FCC-ordered balancing viewpoint is aired. Cable's audience is more chopped up than the limited-channel environment present when the fairness doctrine was advanced for radio in 1949.

Nor do the authors convince me that scarcity applies to cable, even if we were to accept its application to radio and TV for the moment. There is no physical limit to the number of cables that can be strung overhead or underground, although the economics of cable and the resulting blight of unlimited wiring pose obstacles. Cities can, and some do, permit overbuilding of cable systems.

Moreover, the Cable Communications Policy Act of 1984 mandates leased access for most systems, and many franchises provide for free public access. Operators are therefore not entirely "proxies for the community," as the authors state. Congress's access scheme says, "Speak for yourself, citizen!"

The authors perform a service in pointing to the difficulties of an FCC regime that holds cable systems liable only for what is "originated" by the operator. The problem of a distant signal carrying Candidate "A" but not her opponent is a loophole that could require correction. But in the decades of distant signal importation, this problem has never been serious. Moreover, the likelihood of frequent appearances by a local candidate via imported signals is quite remote.

And contrary to the suggestion of the authors, presidential candidates generally would be carried without deletion by the local oper-

ator. As a practical matter, operators do not know when an originating distant station or superstation will air a particular candidate's spot.

The authors' approach to other new media—cable satellite services, teletext, MDS—is to impose the same scheme applied to broadcasting. But if their logic is correct, why stop there? Why not apply such rules to local theaters that exhibit films containing the "use" of a candidate? Why not require VCR rental shops to suppress tapes 45 days before a general election?

And why, really, don't the authors require newspapers to provide equal opportunity and reasonable access and obey the fairness doctrine, with the same range of sanctions that noncompliance triggers for broadcasting?

"Anyone with sufficient capital may start a newspaper," comes the reply. True? Just ask Time Inc., purchasers of the now defunct *Washington Star*, whether tens of millions of dollars was "sufficient capital". Their rueful answer is "No."

I live in Los Angeles, and even the mighty Hearst Corporation, with its feisty *Herald Examiner*, cannot compete with the influence of the *Los Angeles Times* in setting the political agenda. In an age when two-paper towns are disappearing, it approaches casuistry to suggest that we may all yet be newspaper publishers.

The reason neither the authors nor I would impose equal opportunity or fairness doctrine duties on newpapers is the basis identified in *Miami Herald Publishing Co. v. Tornillo:* the First Amendment. The authors acknowledge that broadcasters (and, I presume, cablecasters) have First Amendment rights. But they would subordinate those interests and transfer the matrix developed for broadcasting to whatever media develop. I wonder whether the authors seriously believe that insisting we impose these duties on stillborn technologies like teletext and DBS will affect media's influence on our political process.

A better way? Let's first acknowledge that radio and especially television (broadcast and cable) are important in our political process. At the same time, let's recognize that broadcast expenditures do not constitute anywhere near the majority of a campaign's expenditures when print ads, mailing, travel and the like are factored in.

Further, sometimes the best financed campaigns, with the biggest media expenditures, do not succeed. Many factors influence election results. Opinion leaders within small groups—often the locus of power in molding the opinions of others—can be crucial to outcomes and yet they are obviously beyond regulation.

Despite these caveats, broadcasting and cablecasting might be subject to some regulations relating to a right of access for candidates and the cost of such access. And the same rules could apply to both sides of ballot initiatives.

Accepting this as an agenda for regulating political speech does not call for a wholesale adoption of the current FCC regime. For instance, current law only assures reasonable access for federal candidates. Why not candidates for state offices?

Current law provides only for opportunities for a candidate on the same terms that her opponent receives. But that does nothing for a poor candidate who is outspent by her rich opponent.

Current law requires stations to provide their lowest unit charges to buyers of certain campaign time. But why should broadcasters be asked to subsidize the political process when it is in all of our interests that candidates have reasonable opportunities to address the electorate?

I do not know the full contours of a revised political broadcasting/cablecasting law. The outline of such a law will not come by trying to uphold the falling rafters of the old scheme, however. The considerable deregulation of radio and television already accomplished is unlikely to be undone, given the increasing importance of nonbroadcast video. What is needed is a national commission of prominent citizens from politics, the media and academia to recommend a new scheme. What might new rules look like? Consider for discussion these openers:

—candidates for local or federal office would be given a set number of television minutes, (with more for presidential candidates) to divide as they wish. Rich candidates could buy no more, poor candidates would obtain no less.

—the cost of media time might be paid for by public financing, but acceptance of such financing would place restrictions on the other sources of funds a candidate could use.

—an index would be developed to weigh the time value of spots on local cable TV against their greater exposure value on local broadcast TV.

—all candidates and all sides of a ballot proposition would be entitled to some access to radio and television.

—spots of 10 seconds, or perhaps 30 seconds, would be limited or banned, requiring candidates and initiative sponsors to discusss the merits of issues and not market candidates or issues like brands of soda pop.

Some of these ideas may be wrong-headed. And I would be reluctant to endorse government regulation of broadcasters or cable political speech if satisfactory access policies prevailed through market forces.

There's reason to believe they would. Because a TV network must appeal to audiences and advertisers year-round, it is most unlikely that it will routinely deny access or show favoritism.

Government solutions also can be overbroad, and we will be back to the problems that plague the fairness doctrine. And, less direct means of regulation, such as public financing and spending limits, could make big media power less significant to campaigns altogether. Furthermore, creating a tight set of rules for radio and TV ignores the other media of communication now so instrumental in elections: direct mail, billboards, absentee ballot drives, get-out-the-vote squads and the essentially unregulated news and interview shows on TV themselves.

Spot television's role in electing officials, however, may be sufficiently important to consider regulations. In any case, we need to focus initially on reasonable access and limitations of expenditures, not whether the fairness doctrine applies to the little ad message flashed by my bank teller machine.

As the authors state, "The political process is too important for candidates and issues not to have certain extraordinary rights to reach the public." Agreed. Now, let's set about the business, as a nation, of determining what those rights should be.

*Daniel L. Brenner* is Director of the Communications Law Program at the U.C.L.A. School of Law. From 1979 to 1984, he served as Legal Advisor to the Chairman of the Federal Communications Commission, Mark Fowler. From 1984 to 1986, he was Senior Advisor to the Chairman.

# BASIC POLITICS IN THE AGE OF NEW TECHNOLOGY

"There has been a tendency to forget the basic rules of politics, whether you are a consultant or a pollster, a candidate or a media specialist.

Three basic rules are essential in any campaign: First, find a district that you can win in. Second, find your potential voters, communicate with those voters and reinforce them. Third, get your voters to the polls.

The last rule is something we often forget in this wonderful age of communication. When I was White House political director in 1982, there was a special congressional election in Mississippi. We had a candidate who was winning all the way. He was ahead in the polls. We were doing nightly tracking that showed him to be a runaway winner. He was getting 58 percent of the vote.

Unfortunately, on election day he lost by seven points. So we decided to see what happened. We went back in the field and did an expensive post-election poll and found that he was still getting 54 percent of the vote. Fifty percent of those polled had actually voted for him. Unfortunately, what we missed somewhere along the line was that our voters did not bother to vote on election day.

In this age of the super technology, anything that relates back to these three basic rules helps you, and is worth the time and effort devoted to it. This technology is fantastic. But it always works a lot better if you have the votes."

*Ed Rollins*

"In the eight years that Ronald Reagan has been President, the Republican Party has raised and spent three-quarters of a *billion* dollars. But when Ronald Reagan leaves office there will not be one more Republican in this country. There may not be one additional Republican House member or senator, and there will be only a few more governors. The Republican Senate committee spent a hundred million dollars above and beyond what the Senate campaigns did in 1986 and we did not win one close election.

Meanwhile, the Democrats who have had nearly one-tenth of that money, have gone back to the grassroots and have rebuilt by using coalitions. They did not have all the money and all the technology, and they are winning races everywhere."

*Ed Rollins*

---

"Over the last 20 years, we have made it easier to vote and yet a smaller proportion of Americans are voting, election by election. We have an electorate that is not terribly interested in politics."

*Michael Barone*

---

"Is the demography going to be used ever increasingly to target likely voters and therefore make the non-voter someone who never gets contacted by anybody? Is the message honing going to be used in ever-more-sophisticated demagogic commercials that will turn more and more voters off—some of it by intent?"

*Curtis Gans*

---

*"All politics," former House speaker Thomas P. O'Neill, Jr. used to say, "is local politics." This insight leads to another: All politics involves the same basics—finding your supporters and motivating them, locating undecided voters and trying to win them over, minimizing the motivation of your opponent's supporters, and getting your people to the polls on election day.*

*Contact between candidate and voter may be via handshake or a television commercial, but it is the single most important element of basic politics. The ultimate form of basic politics—grassroots campaigning—is every campaign's most prized commodity. Even candidacies with no real grassroots effort try to create a grassroots image through photo opportunities and television commercials that show the candidate with real voters. Scholars and journalists reinforce the value of grassroots support by asserting that money spent on "direct voter contact" is more virtuous than money spent for other purposes.*

*How much have communications technologies really changed basic politics? Paid workers and volunteers, for example, have always compiled information on voters. Until recently such information was on three-by-five cards. Now it is in computers. Does this change mean anything? Does technology ever replace the need for sweat and shoe leather?*

*The following excerpts help provide answers. M. Ostrogorski describes basic politics in turn-of-the-century America. Next are descriptions of basic politics in the context of 1960s activism and a 1986 congressional campaign. Also included are portions of a manual designed to accompany campaign computer software.*

*In reading these excerpts, it is useful to keep in mind the question of what <u>motivates</u> campaign workers. A variety of motivations are evident, and it becomes obvious that one key variable distinguishing grassroots from purely high-tech campaigns is that the latter need people motivated only by money.*

*Finally, the essay on presidential debates shows how one key aspect of basic politics—two candidates standing in front of voters and discussing issues—has been shaped by communications technologies.*

## DEMOCRACY AND THE PARTY SYSTEM IN THE UNITED STATES
A Study in Extra-Constitutional Government, 1910

*M. Ostrogorski*

### Preliminary Polls

. . . The real campaign begins by reconnoitering the electoral ground and making an estimate of the forces available on each side. All over the Union, in each locality, polling lists are drawn up showing which party each elector is going to vote for; if he has not made up his mind or has not given an indication of his choice, he is ranked among the doubtful.

Special agents, paid by the party committees, scour the country. . . . A sort of political and social survey is made for each locality. The data supplied by it are grouped and transmitted from one committee to another, along the whole line, up to the national committee. Each committee will derive from it useful information for determining its policy in its respective territorial area: the national committee will . . . concentrate all its efforts on the States in which the majority is inconsiderable or uncertain, where the parties are so well matched in point of numbers that a small group of electors may turn the scale in favour of either side. . . . The local committees may plunge into the fray with all their might in the several districts of that State in which the

party is able to return congressmen, members of the local legislature, and other office-holders . . .

### Meetings

Foremost among the electoral campaign weapons is the public meeting. Eloquence is lavished on the electors in a continuous series of meetings of every kind, from mass-meetings which attract thousands of people, to small gatherings in out-of-the-way country spots, attended by a handful of farmers. . . . It is only in the "presidential years" that this great flocking together of voters occurs. . . . The meetings are got up by the committees; this is one of the most important, if not the most important, of their duties.

### Speakers

The national committee supplies eminent orators, who have a national reputation, and who travel, by its direction, from one State to another, to make the great hits; the State committees procure the less important speakers. The best speakers are engaged, like tenors, at so much a night for a certain number of evenings, or by the week, and are more or less highly paid. True, they have met recently with the mighty competitor in the phonograph, which reproduces before audiences the great speeches of the presidential candidates themselves. The speakers who come next in order of merit only get their traveling expenses and perhaps a small allowance for their time.

Lastly, the great majority give their service gratuitously in the hope of obtaining a share of the booty, after the victory, in the form of some place or other. Yet the number of paid speakers is on the increase. The speakers are taken principally from among politicians and lawyers; they also include journalists and business men; one meets, too, with clergymen who are sometimes more successful on the stump than in the pulpit.

The candidates, of course, have their place marked on the list of orators, which, however, is not the most important one; they are lost in the crowd of speakers who have to fight for the ticket, especially at the general election of the presidential year, when all the notabilities of the party descend into the arena. . . . The presidential candidates are stumping the country all the time. They run from one State to another, from East to West, from North to South, in a "whirlwind tour," and speak before audiences flocking as to a show, until they become hoarse. . . . It not infrequently happens that the committee asks a speaker sent on an important campaign to submit to it beforehand his speech, which it will touch up, perhaps, pointing out what should be said and what left unsaid. Sometimes there have been at the headquarters regular training schools for the campaign speakers.

The committees take care to suit the speakers to the audiences. To meetings mainly composed of Irishmen speakers of the same race are told off. . . . The "hard-headed" districts must be dealt with by speakers who can appeal to reason, who can present good logical arguments; in other places it will be enough to excite passions and prejudices and to tickle the innate sense of humour of the Americans.

### Stump Oratory

It is eloquence of this last kind which is the predominant type in the party meetings, and which has given the terms of "stump" and "stump oratory" their peculiar meaning. The fact is that beneath a frigid exterior, under a reserved and taciturn appearance, the American is a highly sensitive, emotional, and excitable being . . .

### Political Literature

The type of "campaign literature" which is the most read, and which produces the most effect, is represented by leaflets, or even little bits of cardboard, with a few dogmatic asser-

tions unaccompanied by argument. . . . The greatest success is obtained by "pictorial literature," that is to say, by cartoons in newspapers and by illustrated leaflets and handbills with symbolic pictures, caricatures, etc. . . .

### The Election Campaign

The means of propaganda which have just been reviewed and which aim, or are supposed to aim, at the intelligence of the electors, are very largely supplemented by others which appeal to the senses, and are meant to "raise enthusiasm." . . . The noise is produced by a set of regular devices, to which the American organizers themselves give the collective title of the "Chinese business."

Foremost among the usual methods come the mass-meetings, whose principal attraction for the crowd that cares little for political eloquence consists of musical interludes executed by orchestras and choruses. Far more picturesque are the processions and the big demonstrations called parades, of which we have already had a foretaste at the National Convention. Every city and every rural district treats itself to these during the campaign, and people would think themselves almost disgraced if they were deprived of them. . . . Some of these demonstrations attain really gigantic proportions, such as the great parades in New York, for instance, when more than a hundred thousand men march past a few leading members of the party, sometimes with the presidential candidate himself at their head, accompanied by bands, flags, and banners, in the midst of a million spectators. All classes of the population are represented in the procession, from the princes of finance down to the common people; heads of business firms and members of the bar fall in, shouting themselves hoarse, in honour of the candidates of the party, just like ordinary labourers . . .

The electioneering propaganda also resort to picnics, dances, and dramatic entertainments, etc., with political speeches as interludes. In the old days, before the Civil War, political picnics were in vogue, especially in the South, and were known by the name of "barbecues." In the South and in the West the barbecues still take place; occasionally the programme includes, besides the political speeches and the meals, athletic contests, dances, sports, horse races. In the East the barbecue is less common and not so picturesque; it is more a sort of fair for which the railroad companies consider it a good opportunity to organize excursion trains.

### Campaign Buttons

Lastly, another external device, and a very popular one, is the display of political emblems. The most common party emblems are the badges, and especially the "buttons," small, round tin plates bearing the portraits of the candidates in enamel, with or without a motto. As soon as the election campaign opens all and sundry, old and young, men "worth millions of dollars" and ragamuffins who sell newspapers or black boots at street-crossings, adorn their buttonholes with a party "button" . . .

### Charges

Another set of practices may be included in the "Chinese business" which tries to impress the imagination through the intellect. These are the charges, the claims, the bets, and the straw votes. The "charges" are libelous accusations brought against the candidates of the opposite party. They occur so regularly in the course of each election campaign that nobody believes them: they are only "campaign lies." Yet they are brought all the same; they resemble a firework which leaves nothing behind, although for the moment it has made a noise.

### Claims

The "claims" are forecasts backed by figures which predict success for the party; so many votes are "claimed" for it in advance, so many counties, or such and such a State. . . . These estimates or claims are always exaggerated with the object of stimulating the ardour of the "workers" and the generosity of the subscribers to the party funds . . .

To confirm belief in the success of the candidates of the party and to decide the waverers, bets laid on the candidates as on racehorses are largely resorted to. It is an old national habit to back one's opinion, even on the most trivial subjects, by laying a bet . . .

### Straw Votes

The "straw votes" are a general rehearsal of the impending election, conducted in certain sections of the population or in certain localities. These polls are held on the stock exchange, in large factories, or other establishments where there are a great number of electors. The result of these anticipating votes furnish "evidence" of the strength of the candidate and of the "hopeless" weakness of his rival. Being often taken in a genuine way by a newspaper, for instance, for the purpose of gauging public opinion, these ballots are always apt to influence those electors who like to be on the winning side.

### Personal Canvass of the Voters

The extraordinary development of these electioneering methods, which operate collectively on large masses of electors, by no means excludes the direct action of man on man, first of all in the classic form of the canvass, of the personal solicitation of votes. . . . Wherever parties are evenly matched, in all the "doubtful" States, it is carried on energetically. The *modus operandi* varies a good deal. The lower strata of the electorate are canvassed by paid "workers." They strive not so much to argue with the electors as to make themselves pleasant; they shake hands with negroes, they invite the bystanders to have a drink. As the decisive moment approaches, redoubled efforts are made to win the "doubtful" electors, one by one; emissaries are sent to them who have a special influence over them, to whom they are under an obligation, or with whom they wish or are obliged to stand well. The canvassers of this sort are zealous auxiliaries who look for no reward but the success of the party and the satisfaction of having contributed to it. The Organization has the moral right to requisition, on the eve of the election, every faithful follower of the party for the work of conversion; and all respond to the pious appeal.

### Part of the Candidate

The candidate himself does not always take a personal part in the election, but he must, especially the candidate for the less exalted positions, exert himself in some way or other. . . . The personal letters, typewritten with the hand signature of the candidate, are the most effective. He sends out cards with his portrait, pamphlets and leaflets dwelling on his qualifications. He advertises in the newspapers and has there, perhaps, a testimonial published above the signatures of men of note. He contributes to charities, he allows himself to be bled by the little politicians for one dollar apiece and upwards, while his campaign managers spend money in the saloons—a thing which he pretends to ignore entirely. He may pay a visit to the most important electors, or even if he is an inferior man, go from one drinking-saloon to another to ingratiate himself with the frequenters of the bars.

### Undue Influence of Employers

The civilities of the candidate and the endless variety of arguments employed by the canvassers act, or are supposed to act, by free persuasion. But sometimes these arguments are supplemented or replaced by the pressure exerted, for instance, by employers of labour . . .

### Getting Out the Voters

. . . The success of the efforts made to "get out the vote," as the phrase goes, will, however, be incomplete if care is not taken, at the eleventh hour, to "get out" the voters. Apathy and want of public spirit are so great with many electors that they would abstain from voting if they were left to themselves on the polling-day, as is the case in England. Yet the American elector shows more eagerness to vote. The belief in the duty of voting is more common in the United States, perhaps not so much from the fact that the civic conscience is more enlightened there, as owing to the civic "cant" which, to a certain extent, prevails in the American democracy. . . . With grand words about his sacred rights and duties constantly dinned into his head and with a genuine appreciation of them, the American elector, while wholly wrapped up in his affairs, readily cherishes a platonic cult for his civic duties. . . . Again, nowhere is the elector so canvassed as he is by the party organization in the United States. This twofold pressure put on the elector reaches its height in the presidential years. The result is that the vote yields at that time very high proportions—as much as 95 percent of the total electorate. The maximum is reached in the "doubtful" States, where the parties fight tooth and nail over the slender majority which may issue from the contest. It should be noted, however, that the total of 100 percent represents only electors on the register, that is to say, under the American system, those only who have got on it of their own accord. A good many, in fact, abstain from registering. . . .

From M. Ostrogorski, *Democracy and the Party System in the United States: A Study in Extra-Constitutional Government*, New York, The Macmillan Company, 1910, pp. 179–222.

## THE SCHEER CAMPAIGN
Organization of the 1966 Robert Sheer Congressional Campaign
*Serge Lang*

. . . Six Scheer offices were to open throughout Berkeley and Oakland, while Cohelan had only one. Campaign literature came out in an overwhelming flow—I have never seen any group with the same urge to get rid of their frustration by using the mimeograph and photo-offset machines, eventually running up a printing bill which constituted a good part of the 69,000 dollars spent during the two months of active campaigning . . .

There were 1,000 volunteer workers for the campaign, and only about a dozen paid workers, at 125 dollars a month. There were 500 precinct workers.

*[Following are parts of interviews Serge Lang conducted with Carl Bloice, the campaign coordinator, and other campaign workers.]*

SL   So how did you go about organizing? What does it mean?

CB   First of all, trying out some semblance of a strategy, which way to go, getting committees set up. I'd say more than anything else, it means recruiting people, talking to people, convincing them to take on certain tasks.

SL   Specifically, what committees, what tasks?

CB   Well, there was a research committee, a literature committee, getting the information on the issues, and getting all the leaflets out. There was a speaker's bureau, which lined up engagements for Scheer to speak. And then all the precinct work had to be organized. There was also an office committee, taking care of opening the offices and keeping them running . . .

CB   We had sometimes two or three such meetings a night. It was really going strong. That was one of the ways that made him known to the community. Next to precinct work. But precinct work just gave the issues, it didn't give a sense of the personality. The things that we did, while at the same time designed to make people think, and challenge their accepted political notions, were also designed to win them over.

SL   So you liked the way the campaign ended up?

CB   Yes. Given the circumstances, we did the best we could with what we had. The things that we did were very exciting. The park rallies were very exciting.

SL   How many people showed up at the park rallies?

CB   Varied a great deal. At one we had 200 people, other times, nobody showed up. At the De Fremery Park, I think we had two, three hundred people. We had park rallies once a week, Saturday or Sunday, for two months. A lot of the things in the campaign had to do with Scheer's view of politics. That you have to relate to people, do things that aren't a drag, routine.

SL   What else beside park rallies, and precinct work?

CB   House meetings. They would vary between some that would draw 150 people to their house, and some that would draw only three. Almost every night. The idea of the campaign was to speak to as many people as possible as often as possible.

SL   Except that Scheer didn't do handshaking in supermarkets.

CB   That's right. In fact, he didn't do any handshaking anywhere. But we made Scheer speak at many little meetings. Even if only four people were there, they'd be the active type so they would convince others afterwards. . . .

CB   I am convinced that a good political activity like this, the Scheer campaign, results in spiritual and psychological salvation—no, that may not be the word—say, stability—for the people of my generation. The temptation to go mad while everybody else around is going mad, or opt out for some kind of escape—it's there, it's all very tempting. A lot of people who were ready to give up got heart from the Scheer campaign. . . .

### Precinct Workers

Scheer's name was unknown in the district three months before election time except to a small minority of people interested in politics. The situation was to be radically changed in the subsequent weeks. A mushrooming of window signs, bumper stickers, and precinct workers in the district was to carry Scheer's name and message to about two thirds of all registered democrats. The greatest exception was the white middle class of Oakland, living in central Oakland. In this section, Scheer had no contacts and little opportunity to reach the people. A systematic newspaper campaign of ads in *The Oakland Tribune*, for instance, designed to affect this group, was much too expensive to be considered.

Even with 500 precinct workers volunteering from Berkeley and Oakland, there was not enough to try to make a dent in the sprawling sections of urban Oakland. . . .

It was going to be proved over and over again that people, from any walk of life, are sensitive to the attention paid to their political opinions, and will give a positive response to efforts designed at contacting them.

Dick Clair, who organized precinct work in Berkeley, told me some things about precinct work during the Scheer campaign which were different from precinct work in other campaigns: "It was not just a matter of dropping literature, but we wanted the precinct workers to talk about issues. They warmed up to their jobs toward the end of the campaign, and become more and more conscientious. They also enjoyed it very much, especially as they found a much better response than they had expected. Each worker devised his own approach, we never told them what to say. Furthermore, each worker had the responsibility of his own precinct. . . ."

LANG   Do you think precinct work is effective?

[Precinct worker John] McELHENEY   I've always had the feeling that precinct work done by people like me . . . is very effective. Both I and the people whom I visit, who are on the fence, are impressed if one of their neighbors has the dedication to walk the streets—in a dignified way, of course! Precinct work, in my view, is the hardest political job. There are many theories whether it is valuable and how to go about it. The people I'm most effective with are those in my neighborhood. People resent outsiders. One's peers are the most effective precinct workers. Actually, there are a couple of people in the neighborhood who look forward to my yearly visits.

SL   Yearly?

McELHENEY   Yes, I do this kind of thing regularly, for school board election, things like that. We are established there for a long time. People are receptive when one of theirs does this kind of thing, Saturday, Sunday, evenings, openly and directly, I get good reception.

SL   So you rang doorbells?

[Marcia Gean]   So I rang doorbells, and tried to convince other people. One of the things that excited me—after working for several weeks, ringing doorbells extensively, I found out most people hadn't heard of him. I felt I was relatively successful in persuading them to vote for him.[Scheer]

SL   If someone hadn't heard of Scheer, what did you tell him?

MG   I first mentioned the war. I thought there wasn't too much interest, or maybe not too much disapproval for the war. So I began to emphasize his criticism of conditions obtaining in Oakland, and I found that by being very specific, and quoting Government dollars, Federal dollars going to the war, and the general corruption—that may be too strong a word—of the Oakland government, that somehow, I was able to convey to these people that Scheer had guts, and this impressed them. Somehow, I really don't know how. Many of these people are cynical and suspicious when you come to the door—they believed me. I even had the remarkable experience of going into a home—the family had never heard his name, and when I left, they put a sticker in their window, and I think the reason was, I was quoting Scheer's comments that directed themselves so much to the actual problems these people are living with.

SL   Did people ever slam doors in your face?

MG   No. I was staggered, I was amazed by the willingness to listen, the general politeness of these people. Considering that when they first opened the door and saw me, I could feel suspiciousness. I later joined up with my girl friend. When she went with me, we ended up being in everybody's living room! I personally felt pretty uncomfortable ringing at people's door, when I did it alone.

[George Gordon]   We didn't give up. We kept on pushing. We went into the houses, talked to the people, how it would be better for them, their children, their grandchildren. We covered most of the underprivileged people in the Flatlands.

SL   When you say we, whom do you mean?

GG   You see, we had a citizen's assembly set up, at least a dozen phones busy in the offices along San Pablo, all day, sometimes up to 10, 11 o'clock at night, reaching the people. Let them see what's better for their condition.

GG   You know, I've done a lot of talking to people. But this time is the most, the hardest pushing I've ever done in trying to put someone in office. I worked nights and days on this thing. I think the others who worked with me felt just the same way. A lot of these kids, I didn't actually know their names, we worked together, they did a lot of work in Berkeley, and they did some with me around here for a while. I think they did a good job.

SL   How did you do your precinct work?

GG   I'd go into the homes, with my briefcase, give them the literature, show them and explain to them. Show them what the men that were running were, what their programs were, so they'd know for themselves.

From Serge Lang, *The Scheer Campaign*, New York, W.A. Benjamin, Inc, 1967, pp. 45-73. Reprinted with permission.

---

# THE RACE FOR THE EIGHTH
The Making of a Congressional Campaign: Joe Kennedy's Successful Pursuit of a Political Legacy

*Gerald Sullivan and Michael Kenney*

. . . Every campaign field operation of any merit works according to a simple, two-part strategy: identify a sufficient number of voters pledged to, or strongly favoring, your candidate; then, get those voters to the polls on election day. Insiders and would-be opinion makers ask the question, "Does this candidate have the money and the troops to mount an effective field operation?"

George Bachrach knew that insider game well and understood the importance of the question to political insiders—and of obtaining the kind of support which their favorable opinion could give him. As this campaign progressed, Bachrach's public estimates of the number of workers committed to his field operation rose dramatically from 3,000 in midspring to an improbable 10,000 by September.

Rich Gatto set the goals for the Kennedy field operation: 60,000 voters to be identified and induced to vote. That figure seemed hopelessly high. In a crowded field, Gatto was hoping to draw for Joe Kennedy nearly 50 percent of that vote.

No other campaign could match the financial resources, the professional experience, or the sheer number of volunteers available to Joe Kennedy's field organization. It formed in the spring around the task of obtaining signatures to put Kennedy's name on the ballot. A goal was set and then met: 25,000 signatures, where only 2,000 were required. By the time summer rolled around, the campaign was ready to begin what it called its Issues Canvass.

The six-page handout of instructions given

to each volunteer began with a statement of purpose:

The Issues Canvass has many purposes, the single most important of which is to preference registered Democrats and Independent voters in the Eighth District. Using the walk sheets, voters can be identified as being decided supporters of Joe Kennedy (FOR), probable supporters (LF), undecided voters (UN), or voters who have decided to vote for another candidate (DA).

Subsidiary purposes included the solicitation of campaign donations, recruitment of new volunteers, and the request to put out yard signs. Kennedy himself seemed at times obsessed with yard signs: The only thing more depressing to him than a yard without the blue and white "Kennedy for Congress" sign was a sign promoting one of his many opponents.

The door-to-door Issues Canvass was under the direction of Jim Spencer.

Each afternoon throughout the summer, at 3:30 sharp, a dozen or so volunteers met with Spencer in a small, bare room of the Cambridge headquarters before setting out on the day's canvass. A meeting on July 22 was typical.

Spencer gave a pep talk: "Despite the high tech we have going for us, we're doing this the old fashioned way, face-to-face. By tomorrow night we'll have talked with 10,000 voters." He gave them some pointers on what he called "building a rap" and the buzzwords to use, principally "public-private cooperation." An example: "Suppose they say, 'I lean to George Bachrach.' Tell them he's a good guy, they'd vote alike—but Joe Kennedy can do more. How? The Citizens Energy idea. Joe has the proven ability to get people involved in problem solving—public and private cooperation."

Then, the veterans in the group staged a series of mock interviews. All the volunteers were in their twenties, a sub-Yuppie group, some almost preppy in appearance. None seemed to have money problems. Only one identified herself as a true local. Adam Landis, from Atlanta, was not atypical. He told how he had been finding work in a law firm boring, was thinking of moving into investment banking, when a friend spoke to him about Joe Kennedy. He came to Boston "for the kick-off speech" in January, quit his job, and signed on as a volunteer. By late summer, Landis was on the payroll. Another of the group, a serious-looking young man, declared, "Joe offered me hope for my generation."

The walk sheet assignments were distributed, and the meeting broke up.

On Tuesday evening, August 19, just four weeks before the primary, Rich Gatto called a district-wide field meeting, at the same VFW Mount Auburn Post 8188 where Joe Kennedy had announced his candidacy exactly seven months earlier. Three hundred workers turned out.

It was an upbeat event. Chuck McDermott reported that the TV ad campaign begun the previous night would continue as part of an overall media blitz through primary day. In a question period that followed, McDermott was quick to silence a worker who wondered if too much emphasis was being placed on Citizens Energy. "No," McDermott said, "it shows he can get things done. Joe's not going in as a back bencher." Rich Gatto cited the achievements to date: of 120,000 households in the district, 30,000 had been contacted by volunteers manning weekend phone banks; another 30,000 had been visited personally by the Spencer forces; local headquarters, soon to number seven or eight, were going into operation. "Give yourselves a round of applause," he told the workers and then introduced "the next Congressman from the Eighth Congressional District."

"Fantastic!" shouted an ebullient Kennedy. "You know how to make a candidate feel good!" The extemporaneous speech is not Kennedy's forte. However unsuited it was for this audience of the already converted, he took refuge in bits and pieces of his standard stump speech. The speech tailed off into anticlimax—the yard signs again: "It's about time we put up some Joe Kennedy signs around here. Where's Spencer?"

The meeting then got down to business under the direction of Alex Bledsoe, breaking into groups along town and ward lines. The handout set forth a detailed calendar for the next four weeks of rallies, visibilities, mailings, phone banks, a district-wide, one-day leaflet drop, two pages of election-day job descriptions—poll checkers, drivers, runners, telephoners, door knockers, sign carriers at the polling places—and, finally, an hour-by-hour election-day schedule. That schedule called for three attempts to contact "all identified supporters who have not voted"—one round of telephone calls by 2:30 p.m., a second round by 5:30 p.m., finally, door knocking, street by street, and continued phoning in certain predetermined precincts. With 222 polling places to service in the manner planned, an election-day turnout of 3,000 workers would be called for. "Everyone here tonight," Bledsoe said, "should personally recruit four others. Try to find people who can take a day off from work on September 16."

The Kennedy field organization pressed on toward election day. On Sunday, September 14, a meeting of the key players of what would be the central command post at headquarters convened to assess the state of readiness and receive election-day assignments. There seemed to be no loose ends. Steve Rothstein and Rich Gatto met beforehand to double check:
—2,000 precinct workers in the field
—100 cars and vans in the field, plus 60 more to be dispatched from headquarters
—70 phone lines at headquarters
—25 phone banks in the Boston area, plus 100-200 additional phones during the day
—60,000 phone calls to be made election day
—Three cars assigned to deliver people to phone banks, get students out, make food deliveries
—212 election day kits delivered to precinct captains; kits to include two phone lists, one for those over sixty years of age; voter turnout sheets; three copies of Kennedy voter lists; pencils and ruler to cross out names of those who have voted; letters of permission to be a poll checker; phone scripts for calls to elderly voters; instructions for door knockers.

After the staff assignments were distributed, Tom Kiley, who had conducted nine tracking polls since early July for Kennedy including four since Labor Day, spoke to the group. He told them that the last survey of 500 voters "showed Joe into the high 40s [in percentage] and Bachrach the low 30s. Somewhere around Wednesday [September 10], we gained the high road and George Bachrach lost control of his campaign." Kiley predicted that the voter turnout would exceed the 127,000 figure of 1982. "The next 48 hours are always the best of a campaign," he said. "Enjoy them."

### The Final Countdown

Joe Kennedy called it "the full-court press" as his campaign moved into its final days. The game plan placed a tremendous burden on his staff and field workers. It called upon them to mount a series of rallies calculated to build a frenzy of excitement and dedication among committed supporters that could be translated into hard work on Primary Day itself. . . .

The climax came on Saturday, September 13, a day reminiscent of the politics of an earlier age. There were few of the trappings of modern politics, for it relied little on polls or pollsters, media "spin" or computer banks. It was a day not shown on television, but nonetheless it happened.

It began for Kennedy at Mangini's Restaurant on Saratoga Street in the Orient Heights section of East Boston—a "walking tour of the community," Angelo Musto, a lifelong East Bostonian, called it.

. . . The walk, then, began as a piece of ordinary street campaigning, in and out of shops and stores for the traditional meet-and-greet, but it soon changed into something quite different. At Day Square another contingent of sign carriers and a small crowd were on hand. Kennedy spoke briefly and then led off again, taking a good portion of the crowd with him. Spencer had sent workers with signs ahead to the major intersections, and when the candidate swept past, they all fell in behind.

. . . They marched the length of the East Boston peninsula, then east up Webster Street to the yacht club at Jeffries Point, which claims to be the oldest on the eastern seaboard, then back to Maverick Square. Modica ushered Kennedy into other clubs along the way—the Sportsman's AC, the Progressive Club, the Chuckawalla Club, and ITAM, the Italian-American veterans club—and from each they emerged with new followers.

At Maverick Square, Boston's mayor, Ray Flynn, joined the traffic-snarling line to walk the final lap with Kennedy. . . . Two thousand people eventually made their way behind Kennedy and the mayor into Central Square for more speeches to a crowd exhilarated by what it had done.

The last event of the day, a rally at Kennedy's Somerville headquarters in Davis Square, was a throwback to the campaign nights of Honey Fitz. The crowd gathered outside the modest storefront office on Elm Street and was bent on enjoying itself.

That there was any crowd at all on a mild Saturday evening was due to local organizational skills, which had put a last-minute network of telephone callers and handbill distributors to work. By 8:30, the campaign office was packed full with a crowd of seventy or more supporters, while outside a throng—200 and growing—began to overflow the sidewalks. Among them was Ethel Kennedy, the candidate's mother, and two of her daughters, Courtney and Rory. An elderly gentleman had brought his grandson along. "I want him to have this to remember," he said, "the way I remember Jack Kennedy."

At last, a new cry sounded in the distance, and Joe Kennedy came in sight. He was on foot, preceded and surrounded by another throng of supporters, which included fifty persons waving placards. The noise became deafening as he moved closer.

Finally he found his footing in the doorway, turned toward the street and waited to speak as the cheering continued. "You know," Kennedy fairly shouted, "I was brought up by my mother and father to believe that this country really stands for something. . . ." It was the speech Joe Kennedy had given a hundred times over in the course of the previous eight months, but nobody seemed to mind.

On the last weekend before the primary, both candidates sought reassurance among their strongest supporters. . . .

. . . As the party for Kennedy workers continued, forty young people, too lightly clad for the chill night, were gathering in Mrs. Casamassima's tiny storefront on Bennington Street—it had once been her husband's cobbler shop—to start, long before midnight, the unseen work of Primary Day. Most had never set foot in East Boston before. They were volunteer workers, recruited over the previous spring and summer on the many college campuses in the Eighth district. Jim Spencer, the Kennedy field operative for whom they would work over the next twenty-four hours, called them foot soldiers.

Their task was to leave a Primary Day greeting and message from Joe Kennedy for each of East Boston's 15,100 registered voters—voters overwhelmingly Democratic. Musto and [Gus] Serra were certain that for every ten voters brought to the polls in East Boston, Joe Kennedy would gain eight or nine votes. The door-hanger message in blue lettering on a white background was simple: "VOTE TODAY." It continued: "Good Morning! Today is Election Day. We hope that you will join us in voting for Joe Kennedy for Congress." The polling hours were given plus a number to call for a ride to the polls and, in red letters, the address of the polling place for the individual precinct, sometimes with the added message: "ATTENTION: New Polling Place."

The operation was meticulously planned. The foot soldiers were dispatched in groups to each of the fourteen precincts of Ward 1 that make up East Boston. There, a precinct captain sent them out on predetermined routes. Still more volunteers arrived at Bennington Street and were sent out to the precincts—so many, in fact, that this part of the East Boston get-out-the-vote operation was done in forty-five minutes. By 10:30, Jim Spencer had returned to the main Kennedy headquarters near the Charles River in East Cambridge, where he stopped only long enough to make sure that wake-up calls had gone out to the second wave of foot soldiers due to report at midnight.

The city of Waltham, five miles up the Charles River, is the westernmost part of this compact district. It, too, is solid Kennedy territory, although it took some time to shape up as such. An intensive door-to-door campaign by Kennedy workers in Waltham throughout the summer and repeated visits to the city by the candidate—with the results tested each week by the campaign's tracking polls—had shown Joe Kennedy to be the overwhelming favorite. But the question was whether Waltham Democrats would go to the polls on Primary Day. Spencer and his foot soldiers, now augmented by a large contingent of Brandeis students and Waltham volunteers, went about their task of silent persuasion.

Waltham presented a bigger problem than did East Boston. There were more door hangers to be posted, and Waltham covers 13.5 square miles, about five times the size of East Boston. It was 4 a.m. before the foot soldiers' work was done.

### Primary Day

On primary morning, George Bachrach and Ken Goode met back at the second-floor campaign headquarters in Watertown Square about 6:30 and then were off on a round of visits to polling places. Part of the reason for Bachrach's being out early was to get him on local radio stations during "drive-time" news programs.

After a brief stop at a Somerville school, they were in Davis Square by 7:30 where, in the drenching rain, some twenty-five campaign volunteers were staging a "visibility"— the new word in political circles for what used to be called sign holding. Davis Square, an old urban commercial center in the process of economic revival, is a stop on the Red Line subway into Boston, and Bachrach stayed there until shortly before 9, greeting commuters. From there, the two went to the Haggerty School in Cambridge and, with the rain still coming down, got into the line of cars picking up elderly voters at the nearby housing project and transporting them to the polls.

. . . Two of Arlington's precincts vote at town hall.

Bachrach was on the town hall steps with fellow State Sen. Richard Kraus. Kraus thought that "Bachrach has had more people doing more things over the past few months—but Kennedy may have more people out today." A few steps away was evidence of the Kennedy effort. John Doyle, one of Kennedy's Arlington coordinators, was out on the sidewalk with a precinct captain. "We got started real fast," Doyle said. "We have a dozen drivers and vans circulating around town. This morning we had a bus for one of the senior citizen housing projects. The phone bank has been working since 9; we've already made the first check on who's voted, and we're about to make the second check. . . ."

. . . As Kennedy traveled around the district that day—to North Cambridge, to Concord, back home—he was receiving a constant stream of reports over the telephone in the front seat of his car—a $1,200 item for the last month of the campaign alone. The reports, guardedly optimistic, were of a high turnout in his strongholds, and they were being relayed from a windowless room at his headquarters in East Cambridge, where deputy campaign manager Steven Rothstein was masterminding a sophisticated vote-pulling operation.

It was the old boiler-room phone-bank operation considerably updated by the use of computers. Three walls of the room were papered with hand-lettered sheets identifying the phone banks, the number of phones available, the time they would be operating, and who would be manning them—all day at the Electrical Workers, the Bricklayers, and public employees' union AFSCME, and after work at several law offices. On the fourth wall were pasted up the computer printouts, which represented the information gathered by the phone banks and by workers at each polling place. For each precinct, there were the number of Democrats and independents, the average vote in past elections by number and percentage, the projected vote by number and percentage, the number of persons who had

actually voted at 11 a.m., 2:30 and 5:30 p.m., and—perhaps most important—a code signifying whether it was likely to vote heavily for Kennedy, and thus be one in which to pull out as many voters as possible.

After the 11 a.m. check, Rothstein had discovered that a predominantly Hispanic precinct in East Cambridge was voting very slowly. "We sent out some Spanish-speaking volunteers to do a house-by-house canvass, and we doubled the turnout by 2:30."

. . . By 4 p.m. the phone banks had made some 50,000 calls to voters who had been identified through personal contact or telephone canvassing as "ones" or "twos," persons highly likely, or probably likely, to vote for Kennedy, all of them coded by age, sex, and occupation on one of the campaign's computers. "We're now going deeper into our base," Rothstein said. From the weekly tracking polls, "We knew that the undecideds were breaking for Joe. So now that we've called our ones and twos, we're going back on the phones and calling the threes and fours." Also, he said, "People are just getting home from work so there's a whole new population to call."

Where the last Kennedy visibility of the campaign should occur had been the subject of intense discussion. Spencer's view prevailed. He believed that the voters of Waltham were most in need of last-minute prodding.

Main and Moody are the two heavily commercial streets of Waltham, an inescapable junction for the cars of shoppers and commuters in the evening rush hour.

Joe Kennedy was in high gear for this last push before the polls closed, the energy pent up throughout the day at last released. His mood carried over to others, first to his supporters—Spencer had brought more than fifty foot soldiers carrying huge signs—and then to motorists and pedestrians. The excitement that had stirred each time Kennedy entered a supporter-filled room during the campaign was now spilling over into the streets and sidewalks at the corner of Main and Moody. It mounted as the daylight began to fade and traffic grew more congested.

TV crews from the three local stations moved in to set up on the park grass to do live shots with Kennedy for the six o'clock news. The scene took on the aspects of a movie set, a mob scene filled with high spirits.

George Bachrach's roving visibility crew of some two dozen volunteers was set up at the kiosk above the Harvard Square station on the

Red Line subway to meet the late afternoon commuters, and Bachrach showed up there about 5:30 after a stop at headquarters. His Primary Night party was to be at the Charles Hotel, two short blocks away, and Bachrach walked down to check on the arrangements and give a final television interview. "I'm the ultimate realist," he told reporters. "We're the ultimate underdog." Then, Bachrach decided he wanted to be alone for a while and had Ken Goode drive him home to Watertown.

In the Charles Hotel ballroom, the press had been waiting around since early evening for their story which, once it began to unfold, was unlikely to last more than two hours. Bachrach campaign workers and supporters, as they began arriving shortly before 8, were quiet and subdued. The band—Sassy, a group of five Berklee College of Music graduates who play old standards in updated settings—was pretty much ignored.

The party, such as it was, was over just as it was starting. Channel 7's Delores Handy, moments after the polls closed at 8, announced that their exit polls showed Kennedy winning by 26 percentage points. . . .

## THE COMPUTERIZATION OF THE CAMPAIGN

*S. J. Guzzetta*

Throughout this manual I have stressed the advantages of having a computer to assist the campaign. I am convinced that it has become an indispensable tool for any campaign, regardless of its size. Just to re-cap, here are the basic lists that need to be maintained by virtually every campaign.

### Individual Support File

Records on every person who contributes, volunteers, or endorses the candidate. The file would contain the name, address, phone number, occupation, place of employment, source (how that person became a supporter), if a

volunteer, type of activity willing to do, if a contributor, the amount contributed and when, precinct, Area and Region designations, etc. This file could grow to thousands of records and needs to be maintained in alphabetical and zip code order.

### Individual Prospect File

Records on every prospective contributor, volunteer, or endorser. The file would contain the person's name, address, phone number, occupation, and source. This file could grow to thousands of records. Sources of names: professional membership directories, previous campaign contributors' lists, church membership lists, alumni membership lists, etc. File needs to be maintained in alphabetical and zip code order.

### Organization Support File

Records on every organizational source of support, usually contributions. This list includes the Party, PACs, and associations. Needs to be treated separately because most campaign reports require a separate accounting for organizations. File could grow to over 100 records.

### Organization Prospect File

Records on every prospective organizational source of support. Those PACs and associations from [which] the campaign hopes to obtain contributions, research support, or endorsements. Source: lists from State and National Party. File will probably be over 1,000 records and needs to be maintained in alphabetical and zip code order.

### Media File

Records on all media outlets impacting on the district, including the name of the contact person for each outlet. Depending on the district, could be over 100 records. Needs to be maintained separately to prevent accidental solicitation. File needs to be maintained in alphabetical order and by subcategory of specific type of outlet.

### Voter Registration File

Usually maintained by a computer service bureau for large districts, but can be maintained in-house for smaller districts. In either case, the campaign will probably want to transfer data of those voters who have been identified as positive supporters of the Candidate for possible solicitation and the GOTV [get-out-the-vote] program. This file could grow to thousands of records and would be maintained by precinct, in zip code, street number, and alphabetical order.

In addition to these files, the campaign needs to maintain records of all Requests for Appearances of the Candidate during the campaign, the schedule of events, i.e., the Campaign Calendar, the Time Line, the Political Game Plan, Budget and Cash Flow, plus innumerable letters and reports.

To attempt to do all of this manually, even for the smallest electoral districts, is a very inefficient use of time and resources. Today, it is possible to purchase an excellent starter computer system for a relatively small campaign that can be added to if a Candidate decides to seek higher office without having to re-enter all the accumulated data. . . .

The next consideration in the computerization of the campaign is the software necessary to make the computer do what the campaign wants it to do. There are a number of companies that have developed computer software for campaigns.

All of these companies distribute a fine product, but they have one drawback in common—they are too expensive and in some cases limited in their ability to do word-processing, which necessitates buying a word-processing program and then trying to integrate the two when the campaign wants to do letter-writing. In all fairness, I should point out that what makes them so expensive ($900-$1,900) is that they all contain two features that I consider unnecessary in most campaigns: the ability to do a PIPS analysis, and the ability to do internal polling. A number of them also require considerable capital for overhead, advertising, and distributors.

. . . [T]he PIPS [Precinct Indexing Prioritization, a system for arranging precinct priorities for field work] analysis requires so much keypunching that by the time this is done, there has been no effective savings for the campaign over doing the final calculations manually. The polling feature is nice, but I estimate less than five percent of all campaigns would ever have someone with the ability to do it properly, and a program like A-CROSS would still be necessary to prepare the cross-tabs.

Regardless of [what] software program, or configuration of hardware the campaign decides to use, the important thing is to computerize the campaign.

From S.J. Guzzetta, *The Campaign Manual: A Definitive Study of the Modern Political Campaign Process*, Revised 2nd Edition, pp. 192-197, Political Publishing Company, P.O. Box 4406, Alexandria, VA 22303. Reprinted with permission from S. J. Guzzetta, 1987.

---

# THE STRANGE—AND SOMETIMES SURPRISING—HISTORY OF PRESIDENTIAL DEBATES IN AMERICA

*Joel L. Swerdlow*

New eras in presidential politics are rare, and their arrival is frequently a time of opportunity.

Such an era is beginning now: the era of debates. There will be more presidential debates in 1988 than have occurred since the writing of the U.S. Constitution. And the 1990s promise to bring even more.

The story of presidential debates is characterized by contradictions and false starts. That such debates did not emerge much earlier is surprising, given the nature of our democracy, our politics, and our communications technology. At the same time, many of the factors contributing to the new era are only tangentially related to debates. The story of these surprises and of the strange causal factors is fascinating—and useful. Only through understanding the past can we have realistic expectations about, and take full advantage of, what the new era offers.

## Issue Debates

From our earliest days, Americans have loved to argue and to listen to arguments about public policy. Colonists debated during town meetings. Revolutionary leaders debated the shape of their new Constitution. Congress recorded discussions in its official Debates and Proceedings. Often these arguments were as much entertainment as they were politics, and they had so pervaded our culture by the 1830s that Alexis de Tocqueville wrote in *Democracy in America*,

To take a hand in the regulation of society and to discuss it is his [an American's] biggest concern and, so to speak, the only pleasure an American knows. This feeling pervades the most trifling habits of life; even the women frequently attend public meetings and listen to political harangues as a recreation from their household labors. Debating clubs are, to a certain extent, a substitute for theatrical entertainments.

Tocqueville visited America during what is now called the golden age of congressional oratory. Congress did not yet have an effective committee system, so issue argumentation occurred on the floor. Robert Y. Hayne, Daniel Webster, Henry Clay, John C. Calhoun, and other great speech makers used eloquent arguments to sway their immediate audience. They spoke largely to people within immediate earshot. At times, the most advanced technology of the day did bring key speeches to the nation; after the Hayne-Webster debate, one newspaper equipped a ship with "frames and cases and type and compositors" to work through the night as it carried Daniel Webster's words to New England printing presses.

These debates bear little resemblance to what a modern audience would tolerate. To speak for days was not unusual, and debate involved complex propositions aimed at an elite, well-informed audience. In a typical example, the 1830 Hayne-Webster encounter (called the "Great Debate" throughout the nineteenth century) centered on Hayne's assertion,

That this Assembly doth explicitly and pre-emptarily declare, that it views the powers of the federal government, as resulting from the compact to which the States are parties, as limited by the plain sense and intention of the instrument constituting that compact, as no farther valid than they are authorized by the grants enumerated in that compact; and that, in case of a deliberate, palpable, and dangerous exercise of other powers not granted by the said compact, the States who are parties thereto have the right, and are in duty bound, to interpose for arresting the progress of the evil, and for maintaining, within their respective limits, the authorities, rights, and liberties appertaining to them.

Great oratory died with the Civil War. Major contributors to its demise were the spread of the franchise, the growth of mass circulation newspapers, and the development of machine politics. Some historians assert that great constitutional issues also disappeared.

An idealized vision of past oratory took hold. "Oratory is the parent of liberty," de-

clared an early twentieth-century citizens' handbook. "It is in the interest of tyrants to cripple and debilitate every species of eloquence. They have no other safety. It is, then, the duty of free states to foster oratory." Schoolchildren read, memorized, and recited speeches. Families saved pennies and nickels to buy collections of great American orations.

Idealization of past oratorical excellence contributed to the unique American belief that "truth" will always somehow emerge from an open, aggressive exchange of views. And yet, this belief had little impact on America's political campaigns. From Locke and Hume to Jefferson and Madison there was no mention of the notion that democracy needed—or was even well served by—debates between candidates for public office. In subsequent generations, the thinkers and organizers who gave us political parties argued with great force and persuasiveness that party competition was necessary to inform the public, curtail apathy, minimize corruption, and promote healthy dialogue—and yet none ever claimed that democracy benefited when candidates debated. As generations passed, electoral reforms included the secret ballot, direct primary, recall, referendum, control over campaign contributions, and intra-party democracy—and still, no mention of campaign debates.

"Debate" remained largely an issue-oriented notion and not a device for either mass persuasion or election campaigning. Thus, a 1940s dictionary of American politics defined the word as something occurring in a "legislative assembly."

### Debates in Non-presidential Campaigns

Even though electoral competition was essential to the American political process from the beginning, American politicians did little campaigning. *Candidate* is derived from the Latin word *candidatus*, meaning "clothed in white," someone pure, above seeking votes.

In the late eighteenth century, when a few candidates dared to campaign, they usually did so at the risk of censure. Many newspapers condemned anyone who traveled around, in the words of a typical editorial, "for the purpose of inducing people to vote for him." Candidates, historian Samuel Eliot Morison notes in *The Oxford History of the American People*, "were supposed to play coy, obeying a call to service from their country, saving their energies for the task of government. Election-eering was done by newspapers, pamphlets and occasional public meetings." Surrogates would sometimes debate each other at such meetings, if debating means appearing before the same audience at the same time. These events were usually billed as discussions of the issues, not arguments about who should be elected.

"Vote-for-me" campaigns became accepted in local and statewide elections during and following the Jacksonian era, although as late as 1847 in Pennsylvania—one of the most politically sophisticated states—newspapers complained loudly when gubernatorial candidates first delivered stump speeches.

Active campaigning soon evolved into the speaking tour. Travel was by steamboat, canal, and railroad. In addition to partisan rallies, political club meetings, and parades, candidates appeared at non-political gatherings such as festivals, carnivals, barbecues, Fourth of July picnics, and church meetings. Political opponents would often meet at such events, speaking in turn. Rejoinders might be given if the crowd was interested.

Most candidates debated at one time or another; many also toured together, presenting a series of debates. This was particularly popular in the West and South where debates served more than just a political function. They often provided the year's most stimulating entertainment, as well as an opportunity for friends and relatives to socialize. In the South, the ultimate political debate—a duel using revolvers—was uncommon, yet real.

Debates, however, played neither a definitive nor an important role in the evolution of vote-for-me practices. They are most noteworthy, in fact, for their lack of impact and for the historical quirks they produced.

During the nation's first congressional elections, for example, two future presidents debated. James Madison and James Monroe were running against each other for a congressional seat from Virginia. Madison later described to a friend what happened:

We used to meet in days of considerable excitement and address the people on our respective sides; but there *never was an atom of ill-will* between us. On one occasion we met . . . at church. Service was performed, then they had music with two fiddles. They [the congregation members] are remarkably fond of music. When it was all over we addressed these people, and kept them standing in the snow listening to the discussion of Constitutional subjects. They stood it

out very patiently—seemed to consider it a sort of fight of which they were required to be spectators. I then had to ride in the night, twelve miles to quarters; and got my nose frost-bitten.

The frostbite made more of an impression on Madison than did the debate. Indeed, cold weather was the reason for the Madison-Monroe confrontations. Both men suffered terribly from the cold as they toured the district. As longstanding friends, they decided to travel together—not to better inform the public—but to keep one another warm in the coach.

Throughout U.S. history, from colonial times to the age of television, only one of these encounters is not forgotten: the series of senatorial debates between Abraham Lincoln and Stephen Douglas in 1858. Putting these debates in context shows just how limited the "debate" notion was.

Lincoln and Douglas had their first major conflict in 1854. Lincoln was a former one-term House member. Douglas, the incumbent senator, had recently introduced the Kansas-Nebraska bill, which repealed the 1820 Missouri Compromise, thus shaking the nation's sense that the slavery question might somehow be avoided. Douglas toured Illinois to sell his constituents on the virtues of this new measure, and Lincoln took to the stump in opposition. Because Douglas was by far the more popular and drew larger crowds, Lincoln, in what was an unusual move, began to follow him around the state. Douglas spoke in Springfield during state fair week, for example, and Lincoln appeared the next day. Two weeks later, they met by agreement in Peoria. Douglas spoke in the afternoon, Lincoln in the evening.

In 1858, when they were senatorial opponents, Lincoln once again followed Douglas. Beginning with the Chicago speech opening Douglas's campaign, Lincoln often stood in the crowd watching Douglas, sometimes shouting out that a rebuttal would be delivered later that same day or the next day.

Various newspapers, depending on their partisan preference, ridiculed or defended Lincoln. The papers also created their own mini-debates by printing excerpts from each of the candidates' speeches side by side. Live debates, however, did not seem to have been on anyone's mind.

Then Lincoln suggested to Douglas "an arrangement for you and myself to divide time, and address the same audiences." He did not say "to debate great issues," "to point out the differences in our opinions," or "to ask each other questions." He wanted to get out of the audience and onto the platform with Douglas.

Douglas had been irritated by Lincoln's tactics, and he knew from Republican party announcements that Lincoln intended to keep following him. This, as well as confidence in his own debating experience and skill, prompted Douglas to accept. Lincoln then wrote, "I shall be at no more of your exclusive meetings."

The Lincoln-Douglas debates are remembered for many reasons. They are, as debate specialist Lee Mitchell has pointed out, the first debates in an election with national significance. The debates addressed an issue—slavery—that was threatening to tear the nation apart. Newspapers, utilizing telegraph wires that made instantaneous communication possible, gave the debates a huge national audience. Lincoln went on to become a larger-than-life myth (no one refers to the Douglas-Lincoln debates). What is forgotten, however, is why the debates occurred in the first place: because they met the logistical and strategic needs of the candidates. Also forgotten is that the Lincoln-Douglas encounters were popular mostly because they were excellent theater, and not because what was said was particularly wise or revealing.

Even though historians report that an idealized "spectacle of debates captured the imaginations of the country," the Lincoln-Douglas debates sparked no debate era, no demand from the people or the press for more debates. Among politicians, the benefit to Lincoln—who nearly won the senatorial contest and went on to become president only twenty-four months later—of sharing a platform with a more popular incumbent was clear, as was the practical lesson: if you're ahead, why debate?

"After the Civil War," political scientist M. Ostrogorski noted in *Democracy and the Organization of Political Parties*, "the face-to-face debate, which enabled the citizen to grasp then and there the arguments pro and con presented by public men, disappeared almost entirely." Some debates did occur. Usually sponsorship was by local parties, and the format was roughly Lincoln-Douglas style. But these debates are memorable mostly for their social aspects.

The 1896 Tennessee gubernatorial race, for example, featured forty-one debates between the two major candidates. Tennessee history buffs remember this election not because of the debates, but because the opposing candidates were brothers. The brothers played fiddles and told stories and jokes. "The campaign was characterized by little that dealt with real issues," one local historian noted later. "The debates were pleasing, entertaining, and marked with dignity but were not profound. Everywhere the joint campaign took the form of social ritual." Like other debaters throughout the nineteenth century, the two candidates sometimes slept in the same bed while traveling in the back country.

One reason debates disappeared was that they were no longer needed. Debates had been largely a logistical convenience: travel was difficult for candidates and voters alike, and it simply made sense for opponents to appear together. As America became urbanized, and as railroads grew, logistics became less compelling. The slow emergence of an "objective" press, which promised to supply nonpartisan descriptions of what each candidate said, also made actually listening to the candidates seem less important. Indeed, politicians, newspaper editorialists, and civic reformers made no effort to institutionalize debates at any level or to convince the public that candidate debates were desirable—even though America experienced a growth in mass democracy during the last part of the nineteenth century.

Debates did experience a renaissance in the 1920s. Leading the way was the League of Women Voters, which was dismayed that after so much struggle to receive the franchise so few women actually voted. The League's national convention in 1921 discussed "a new kind of political meeting . . . which is more popular than the old fashioned political rally" that would help inform and energize female voters. By 1922, the League had sponsored candidate debates, including much-praised events in the Ohio and Indiana senatorial races. The League's national president called these debates "the dawn of a new kind of campaigning."

Challenging a frontrunner to debate became a popular technique. Indeed, the challenge often generated more attention than the debate itself. Robert Caro described in *Path to Power* what happened in the late 1930s, for example, when Lyndon B. Johnson was running for Congress:

Whenever, during the campaign, his path had crossed Johnson's, he [Emmett Shelton, Johnson's opponent] had attempted to shame Johnson into debating him. Arriving in a town to find Johnson's campaign car there, he would park his own right alongside, and would use his loudspeaker to challenge Johnson to debate. Johnson, aware of his weakness in debating, had refused to do so. In one particularly painful incident, Shelton had parked directly outside a store in which Johnson was shaking hands and had stayed there, blaring, over and over, a challenge to Johnson to come out and debate, for quite some time—and Johnson had not come out, refusing to leave the safety of the store until Shelton had driven away. Now, however, their paths crossed again—in Smithville on a Wednesday on which hundreds of farmers had come into town for a prize-drawing set up by the merchants—and, this time, when Shelton repeated the challenge, Johnson at last turned on his tormentor.

Johnson, according to witnesses, won the subsequent debate, during which each candidate spoke for about five minutes.

Such debates, as with most debates in American history, were quickly forgotten, except when a debater later became nationally prominent. A California member of Congress named Jerry Voorhis debated in 1936 and also participated in a series of 1946 encounters. The press, politicians, and public saw nothing noteworthy about these debates, which are remembered only because Voorhis's 1946 opponent was Richard Nixon. Nixon's successful debate tactics foreshadowed his later political techniques and helped to begin his climb to the White House.

### Presidential Elections in the Pre-broadcast Era

Until recently, debates played an even less important role in campaigns for the nation's highest office. Indeed, the pre-Jacksonian notion of the non-campaigning candidate endured into the twentieth century. Candidates, by custom, could work full time writing letters, conducting private meetings, and cajoling, but could do little publicly.

During the nation's first contested presidential election, in 1800, candidates openly consented to letting others, including hired speakers, campaign for them. No special value was seen, however, in having these surrogates debate. Thus, what was probably the first presidential campaign debate happened by chance.

New York's presidential electors were selected by the state assembly, and control of that assembly came down to perhaps a dozen contested seats in New York City. The leader of New York Republicans (the present-day Democrats) was Aaron Burr, the party's vice-presidential candidate. A close friend of Burr's later wrote:

It was understood that General [Alexander] Hamilton [leading spokesman for the Federalists] would personally attend the several polls during the three day election; that he would counsel and advise his political friends, and that he would address the people. Here again all seemed to feel that Colonel Burr was the man, and perhaps the only man, to meet General Hamilton on such an occasion.

The Federalist *Daily Advertiser*, reflecting popular beliefs of the time, lamented that a "would-be Vice President could stoop so low as to visit every corner in search of voters." When Hamilton and Burr met by chance at polling places, they debated. Little record of these encounters exists.

Burr's activities did nothing to shake the anti-campaigning tradition: would-be presidents had to remain decorously close-lipped. This is one reason why none of America's famous orators ever became president. Men such as Webster, Calhoun, and Clay, whose eloquence permeates America's history books, could not speak on their own behalf when running for president. The great congressional orators had another disadvantage—one that is relevant to understanding the behavior of today's presidential debate participants. Because these orators had made their views known on important, controversial issues, they were unable to hide behind the vagueness necessary for success in national elections. Their lack of electoral success, of course, was part of a larger phenomenon. The great orators of this era were congressional leaders, and no one in the nineteenth century—and so far in the twentieth—moved directly from a position of congressional leadership to the presidency.

Few people argued that presidential candidates should speak out. Indeed, their silence was often considered a strategic necessity. In 1836, for example, a prominent political leader wrote of Whig nominee William Henry Harrison, a retired general with little experience in the public arena:

[let him] say not one single word about his principles or his creed, let him say nothing—promise nothing. Let no Committee, no Convention, no town meeting ever extract from him a single word about what he thinks now and

will do hereafter. Let use of pen and ink be wholly forbidden as if he were a mad poet in Bedlam.

Harrison lost, but four years later did become the first presidential candidate to "take to the stump" and openly advocate his own election. His subsequent victory, however, was attributable not to these speeches but to a split among the Democrats.

Even though the nation was somewhat startled at the sight of Harrison asking for votes, the public began to expect that a presidential candidate would at least say something about his positions on key issues. In 1856, for example, Republican Thaddeus Stevens said about the soon-to-be-elected Democratic presidential nominee, "There is no such person running as James Buchanan. He is dead of Lockjaw."

The remainder of the century, however, saw only two major presidential vote-for-me efforts. In 1860 Stephen Douglas toured the country (the tours started under the guise of a trip to New England to visit his mother; Lincoln did not make one campaign speech in 1860). More than a quarter of a century later, in 1896, Democratic nominee William Jennings Bryan traveled 18,000 miles delivering speeches. Bryan's Republican opponent, William McKinley, rejected advice that he, too, go on a speaking tour. "I have to think when I speak," McKinley explained.

McKinley stayed home on his front porch, but what he did there was far more significant than a speaking tour would have been: he promoted the notion that even a stay-at-home candidate must actively engage in vote-for-me activities. McKinley delivered up to sixteen speeches a day to crowds estimated as large as 30,000. Margaret Leech's *In the Days of McKinley* described the scene:

. . . excursionists carried to all parts of the country enthusiastic reports of the Republican candidate. They had been right close to him, they had shaken his hand. They had seen him in his setting, and it was exactly right—the friendly town; the neat, unpretentious house and the porch hung with trumpet vines; and the First Methodist Church where McKinley worshiped with his mother every Sunday. Many of the visitors saw the dear old mother, sitting beside her son or rocking on her own front porch. Many saw and stared at the invalid wife.

Bryan ran again in 1900, prompting historian Charles Francis Adams, Jr., to describe him as "a talking machine, he can set his

mouth in action, and go away and leave it, sure that it will not stop until he returns." McKinley, now the incumbent, gave himself permission not to campaign; Vice President Theodore Roosevelt, feeling "as strong as a bull moose," traveled extensively.

McKinley's attitude—that the best strategy for an incumbent president is to remain presidential—has been followed by most of his successors even though many present-day commentators seem to believe that the presidential stay-at-home technique—often called the Rose Garden strategy—is something new. Television and Madison Avenue selling techniques have in many ways isolated incumbent presidents from the pressures and dangers of campaigning, but this is merely further development of stay-at-home tendencies that have always been present. Incumbent presidents have openly and aggressively campaigned mostly when in trouble (for example, Herbert Hoover in 1932, Harry S. Truman in 1948, and Gerald R. Ford in 1976), or when they wanted to roll up a huge majority (for example, Lyndon Johnson in 1964). Otherwise, they follow a strategy of minimal exposure to voter and press scrutiny. When asked to respond to his opponent's criticisms in the late summer of 1940, for example, Franklin D. Roosevelt responded, "I don't know nothin' about politics."

It is logical to believe, however, that the American public would have welcomed debates as presidential candidates started campaigning. Bryan-McKinley confrontations, for example, could have drawn hundreds of thousands of people and could have clearly delineated the basic issues—such as which economic classes should be the principal beneficiaries of federal policies—that still define American politics. But when presidential candidates met or came close to meeting during campaigns, the country's press and opinion makers—in sharp contrast to their present-day attitudes—encouraged nonconfrontational gentlemanly demeanor. In 1896, for example, Bryan visited Canton, Ohio, site of McKinley's front porch. Bryan stayed away, even though a large group of his supporters left his rally to pay McKinley a courtesy call. In 1912 Theodore Roosevelt and William Howard Taft, locked in a bitter and emotional battle for Republican convention delegates, passed through the same town yet avoided each other. That fall, incumbent Taft and Democratic challenger Woodrow Wilson stayed, by chance, in the same Boston hotel at the same time. They met for a friendly, non-political chat. During the 1936 presidential campaign Franklin D. Roosevelt and his Republican opponent, Kansas governor Alf Landon, participated in a governors' conference in Iowa. They earned praise from the press for treating each other with great courtesy and for not mentioning their differences.

### Presidential Elections: The Broadcast Era

Less than a decade after World War I, radio was broadcasting national political conventions, and paid and unpaid political speeches. Issue debates between civic leaders were also regularly scheduled, highly popular radio programs. Face-to-face encounters between presidential candidates would have been easy to stage, yet the history of radio yields only a few references to the possibility of such debates. During the 1936 presidential campaign, Republican senator Arthur Vandenberg of Michigan, who was not his party's presidential nominee, staged a fake radio debate with recordings of Franklin D. Roosevelt's speeches; and in 1940, Republican presidential nominee Wendell Wilkie challenged FDR to a series of debates on "fundamental issues." FDR simply ignored the challenge at no political cost because the press—and presumably the public— regarded the proposed debates as a ploy by a far-behind underdog. One radio debate did occur. In 1948 Republicans Harold Stassen and Thomas E. Dewey debated during the Oregon primary in a radio broadcast that attracted between 40 and 80 million listeners. Yet there was no demand for—or serious suggestion of—a radio debate in the subsequent Dewey-Truman general election.

The absence of radio debates is especially noticeable because a simple rule has guided the relationship between the broadcast media (radio and, later, television) and presidential campaigns: once something becomes technically feasible, it is quickly done. This has held true for coverage of national conventions, campaign events, and election returns, and for the use of paid time for partisan messages. Debates are the only major exception.

Of course, a change of the "equal time" law or in Federal Communications Commission (FCC) regulations would have been needed for radio debates to take place, but there is no evidence of public desire for such a change. Few people took seriously the notion that a president or would-be president should perform live over the air under adversarial circumstances. And, as in the past, politicians found it in their interest to avoid delineation of issue positions. Issue fuzziness was the best way to build electoral coalitions. "Every one takes part," Henry Adams wrote a friend during the 1884 presidential campaign, describing a phenomenon that has remained valid. "We are all doing our best, and swearing at each other like demons. But the amusing thing is that no one talks about real interests. By common consent they agree to let these pass. We are afraid to discuss them."

Underdogs, however, have always wanted to share the airwaves with incumbents, much as Lincoln had wanted to join Douglas on the platform. Thus, in 1944, the Republican party bought time for a radio address directly following time purchased for FDR. It was not a presidential campaign debate, but voters could sit back and listen to supporters of two principal candidates for president provide back-to-back explanations of why their choice deserved votes.

Television debates, however, did arrive right on schedule. In early May 1952 most major Democratic and Republican contenders made a joint appearance—broadcast live to a national radio and television audience—in front of the League of Women Voters' annual convention. In 1956 Estes Kefauver and Adlai Stevenson met in a nationally broadcast debate during the Democratic primaries. At the 1960 Democratic convention, John F. Kennedy and Lyndon B. Johnson debated in front of a joint session of the Massachusetts and Texas delegations, and a national television audience. And in the fall of 1960—the first general election in which television was the dominant national medium—the Kennedy-Nixon debates occurred.

That presidential debates took place in 1960, however, had little to do with debates per se and much to do with unique circumstances. In 1960 each of the major candidates had reasons to want to use television's enormous audience for his own purposes. Broadcasters wanted to carry debates as part of a larger effort to demonstrate that they were civic-minded and did not need federal regulation. Many debate advocates, frustrated and angered by commercial dominance of America's airways, saw debates as one way—and far from the most attractive way—to elicit free air time from the networks. And many people, dissatisfied with how America conducted its presidential campaigns, saw face-to-face debates as part of a larger reform. Thus Stevenson, who as the 1956 Democratic nominee had thought debates were a gimmick, wrote in early 1960:

I would like to propose that we transform our stumbling, fumbling, presidential campaign into a great debate, conducted in full view of all the people. Suppose that every Monday evening at peak viewing time, for an hour and a half, from Labor Day until election eve, the two candidates aired their views. They might on each evening take up a single issue. Each in turn might discuss it for a half hour, followed by rebuttal of one another for the third half hour. There are other possibilities, including face-to-face debate. But the central idea is that, in some manner, the principal figures, the candidates for president, appear together at the same prime time each week for a serious presentation of views on public questions. The time should cost them and their parties nothing.

The 1960 presidential debates generated high expectations. Debate planners, acutely aware of the Lincoln-Douglas glamour, wanted to initiate what they saw as "the TV debate era," when televised debates would be a fixture in presidential campaigns. To have presidential candidates meet face to face in front of the entire nation seemed—and was—nothing less than revolutionary. The optimism that accompanied this revolution was part of an idealism that surrounded television in general. In the early 1960s people still expected television to "ring with intelligence and leadership."

There was good reason to believe the debate era had indeed arrived. Throughout the 1960s television increasingly dominated all other aspects of the campaign. Partisan loyalties and political machines were dissolving, making the ever-nebulous "public opinion" an all-important determinant of electoral results. Democratization of the electorate—most notably, the addition of blacks and young people to voter rolls—greatly expanded the made-for-TV political audience. Intra-party democracy, in the form of more and increasingly contested primary elections, opened fertile ground for prenomination debates; indeed, Democratic would-be nominees met in 1968 and 1972.

Television itself, furthermore, encouraged a demand for debates by the very way it presented news and public affairs programs: every issue was depicted as always having two equal sides, covered one after the other, on roughly equal terms. One public official would say a tax increase was needed; another would

say it would be a disaster. One person would advocate changes in the nation's civil rights laws; another would say that action should be left to each state. The implicit message, copied by major newspapers, which began to feature "issue debates" on their op-ed pages, was powerful: the way to learn about public affairs is to see both sides. Public affairs discussion is adversarial, with winners and losers.

Yet the presidential debate era failed to appear: no more general-election presidential debates occurred until the middle of the next decade.

This hiatus in debates from 1960 to 1976 is most directly attributable to the equal-time provisions of the Communications Act of 1934. But Congress was free at any time during those years to eliminate or suspend these provisions, just as the FCC was free to do what it eventually did in 1976: issue administrative rulings permitting broadcast presidential debates by sidestepping equal-time rules.

Public opinion polls continued to show strong public support for presidential debates. Yet this support never translated into an organized or vocal demand for presidential debates.

No general-election presidential debates took place for sixteen years for one simple reason: in 1964, 1968, and 1972, the frontrunner did not want to share an audience with his opponent.

### The Age of Debate

The age of debates has evolved slowly over the past decade, but the evidence of its permanence is inescapable.

At the state and local level, more candidates have been debating much more often. Exact statistics have not been compiled, and much of the evidence is anecdotal, but it is impressive. A 1986 National Association of Broadcasters study found that "virtually all congressional candidates debated their opponents." In the 1986 Dallas mayoral election, candidates reportedly met more than sixty times. And on popular television entertainment programs, even judicial candidates debated.

Presidential debates have developed more slowly, just as presidential campaigning itself lagged behind. In 1976 a unique set of circumstances—an unelected incumbent; an unknown majority party challenger; a few key individuals such as Charles Benton, who funded early debate organizing efforts; and an organization, the League of Women Voters, which provided the necessary impartial organizational framework—helped produce presidential debates. Such debates recurred in 1980 and 1984. Debates, furthermore, now permeate the presidential nomination process. Joint candidate appearances begin more than six months before the first primary, and prospective nominees of the two major parties debate each other, as do would-be First Ladies.

Our idealized visions of a golden past—the great oratorical debates, the Lincoln-Douglas debates, and the aura of the 1960 Kennedy-Nixon encounters—obviously contributed to the current age of debates. But the causes of the age of debates have been complex.

—By the mid-1970s, the nation was entering a period of healing. Presidential debates had disappeared in the 1960s and early 1970s, precisely when America was fighting its most bitter, bloody, and divisive foreign war. By 1975 the Vietnam War was over, the Watergate scandals had been resolved by presidential resignation, and debates promised to be much less passionate—and less threatening to the established order—than they would have been in the 1960s.

—Technology has made possible—and encouraged—an increase in the debate-oriented approach to political campaigns. The *Congressional Quarterly Weekly Report* noted in late 1985, "The technology to produce commercials fast enough to stimulate a debate [has arrived]. One day's set of TV ads for one candidate was followed soon after by his opponent's set of counter-ads, and the process repeated several times in an intricate series of tactical moves." *Congressional Quarterly* called this "instant response politics."

—New technology is also making a variety of debates less expensive and easier to distribute. In mid-1987, for example, some presidential candidates organized a debate in Iowa and then bought satellite time to bounce their confrontation directly to interested local broadcast stations and to a roomful of political journalists gathered in Washington, D.C. Total cost was $11,000. Satellite transmission of television and radio programs, in the meantime, has prompted a number of programs in which members of Congress debate an issue for about sixty seconds each. Such programs can now be seen or heard in virtually every media market. This builds upon television's "two equal sides" approach to news, further solidifying the public's expectation that debates are the way to hear public policy discussed.

—A growing deregulatory mood in America—feelings only indirectly related to debates—has prompted the weakening and dissolution of federal equal-time restraints on the broadcast of debates. Until 1975, no broadcast station could carry a debate unless every candidate for that office was included or received equal time; until 1983, no broadcast station could host a debate. Now broadcast stations are free to do what they want within narrowly defined confines of fairness.

—Television coverage of the U.S. House of Representatives and Senate has inspired and sharpened debate. Unlike Hayne, Webster, and other great congressional orators of the past, today's legislators can—and must—speak directly to the public at large. Dramatic statements and subtly staged confrontations have become common. The result: still another reason for voters, journalists, and public officials themselves to believe that political dialogue should be in the "debate" mode.

—To sponsor a debate is to receive extraordinary media attention, so a wide variety of organizations—from newspapers to universities—now try to sponsor presidential confrontations. Likewise, candidates know that talking about debates, issuing challenges to debate, and best of all, actually organizing a debate, are sure ways to augment campaign coverage.

—Intra-party reforms since the early 1970s, by spawning primaries and caucuses, have created fertile ground for debating—especially since the public now expects all would-be presidents to campaign for their party's nomination. The last time a major party convention selected someone who had not actively sought the nomination was 1952; since then, there has been at least one prenomination debate in every election except 1964.

—As presidential candidates increasingly opt for a "selling-of-the-president" strategy that keeps the president hidden behind controlled media exposure, and as the campaign press conference atrophies, debates have become the prime vehicle through which journalists can ask questions. Thus, the news media have become—perhaps somewhat subconsciously—proponents of debates. New corporate concerns about news-gathering costs are also pro-debate. It is much cheaper to cover a debate than to travel around with a candidate.

Given the present ascendancy of campaign debates, there is every reason to believe that they will continue to flourish. Presidential candidates, always concerned with what historian Arthur M. Schlesinger, Jr., in *The Coming to*

*Power* calls "competition for visibility," will find it more and more difficult to reject the huge national audience that debates offer. Candidates will also increasingly use debates as an excuse to avoid something they invariably hate: frantic cross-country trips. Preparing for a debate and reaching voters via a debate are perfect excuses to stay home.

Television technology, in turn, will continue to encourage debates simply because it makes reaching so large an audience so easy. The ultimate proof of how technology drives debates is that other democracies with political and campaign traditions unlike our own are now turning to televised "American-style" presidential debates. In Great Britain, for example, the most recent parliamentary election began with a challenge that candidates for prime minister debate on television.

Debates will also flourish because the issue of whether broadcasters should be required to provide presidential candidates with free air time will remain very much alive. Considerable support for free air time currently exists in Congress and the nation as a whole. Reformers will press for dramatically enlarged debates, probably modeled after practices in other countries, where a candidate gets free time one evening and the opponent gets equal time to answer the next evening. The first candidate then gets additional time the third evening, and so on. Also attractive to reformers will be the notion that debates can be relied upon as an antidote to 30-second TV commercials.

At the same time, forces that will change presidential debates—and the debate process—are clearly at work. Debates are now the only major campaign device that invariably favors the underdog. This characteristic alone will prompt frontrunners to manipulate debates into minimal events that will satisfy the press and the public.

The increase in independent and cable channels, furthermore, will give viewers many choices other than debates. The potential impact of this on fall presidential debates is significant. One of the most extraordinary things about debates is that tens of millions of voters have watched them and then decided not to vote. No one knows how much of this consistently extraordinary debate audience has been the product of "roadblocking," or showing a debate on all three major broadcast networks.

Audience slippage—in 1980 millions of households switched to a movie on ABC rather than watch the Ronald Reagan-John Anderson debate—could force debates to become "better television." They could be made more compelling, more visually stimulating with computer graphics to highlight candidate arguments, and perhaps could even become more dangerous for the candidates.

On the other hand, debates may move in the opposite direction. Growing dissatisfaction with presidential campaigns, the feeling that reform has unnecessarily lengthened and complicated the nomination process, and the widespread belief that campaigns generate little useful information, may force debate planners to devise events that help convince citizens that rational choices do indeed exist. The solution here might be debate formats which permit more thoughtful, lengthy presentations of candidate positions.

No matter which way debates go, improvements are not hard to imagine. Adlai Stevenson's 1960 proposal—which had been developed in the mid-1950s by Newton Minow and other Stevenson aides—remains sound, insightful, and well worth a try in 1988. Why shouldn't major party nominees meet at least once a week on television to "discuss the great issues of the day"?

Change is certain. Television simply does not respect its own traditions. Every major area of the television-politics relationship—commercials, political convention coverage, press conferences, reportage of election-night returns—has been altered significantly since the advent of TV. Only presidential debates, at least so far, have remained the same.

As the next phase of presidential debates evolves, the crucial question is not whether we are for or against debates. They are inevitable. But it is essential to have realistic expectations. Looking for too much from debates can cause unnecessary confusion and disappointment.

Throughout American history, great and compelling issues have only rarely been addressed—let alone clearly delineated—during presidential campaigns. Debates cannot breathe life into an idealized past that never existed.

To avoid use of the word *debate*, furthermore, is not useful. Some people still want to call these events "joint discussions," because they are not "true debates."

Again, an idealized past serves as a poor guide. We have never had "true debates" for major office in this country. Lincoln and Douglas had no mutual interrogations, no sharp give-and-take. They took turns giving long speeches to the same audience. We call these encounters debates, as did the public at the time, because the name "the Lincoln-Douglas joint discussions" has no zing.

Debates, if not overused, do offer great practical opportunities. They give lesser known candidates a chance to be heard. They create new opportunities for discussion of the issues. They generate free air time for the candidates. But most importantly, they can make a profound contribution to the health of our democracy.

Writing in the late nineteenth century, scholar James Bryce noted in *The American Commonwealth* that "for three months [during U.S. presidential campaigns] processions, usually with brass bands, flags, badges, crowds of cheering spectators, are the order of the day and night from end to end of the country." These civic rituals somehow went to the heart of America, a nation that uniquely defined—and defines—itself by its political institutions.

The processions Bryce described no longer exist. Politics, particularly presidential politics, has gone indoors. "Three people in front of a television is a political rally," one campaign professional recently noted. But this shift has not changed the need for periodic civic rituals, part serious, part emotional, and part fakery, but in their totality an unabashed bow—however theatrical—to democracy and the sovereign will of the people. That is, in their own way, what debates have become.

Excerpted from *Presidential Debates: 1988 and Beyond*, Washington, D.C., Congressional Quarterly Books, 1987. Reprinted with permission from Congressional Quarterly, Inc.

# FUNDRAISING

"A few figures tell the story. In 1974, the cost of the five most expensive campaigns for the U.S. Senate was $1 million, of which $350,000 went to paid media. In 1984, the average cost of the five most expensive Senate campaigns was $10 million, of which $5 million went to paid media.

In 1974, the average overall cost per vote was 67 cents. In 1984, it was $7.74. In 1974, the average media cost per vote was 12 cents. In 1984, it was $3.54.

Overall campaign costs have increased since 1974 about fivefold. Media costs have increased tenfold; five, if you count constant dollars. The evidence is incontrovertible: It is television and the consultant industry that is fueling the engine of runaway cost."

*Curtis Gans*

"The Reagan campaign did more tracking in 1984 than any campaign in history. We absolutely did not have to do that much tracking; we just did not know what to do with all our money.

We started tracking nightly on June 1 and we tracked every single day through the election. We ran 49 separate television commercials based largely on this tracking, and spent over $30 million on television.

I wish I had been courageous enough to follow my instincts and not spend a penny on television. I felt I could utilize the money far more effectively as a campaign manager and just let the campaign be covered by national media."

*Ed Rollins*

*"Money," former California political leader Jesse Unruh once said, "is the mother's milk of politics."*

*The milk is overflowing. The California Commission on Campaign Financing reports, for example, that $57.1 million was spent on 100 California legislative races in 1986. Twelve races cost more than $1 million each. In 1984, 92 percent of money received by legislative candidates came from outside their districts. This prompted the Commission to conclude that in California—and presumably every other state—there now exist "two separate constituencies: the district residents who vote for them [state legislators] and the statewide contributors who pay for their campaigns."*

*Money—most of it spent on communications technologies—gets blamed for much that is wrong with our politics. For example, former Florida governor Reubin Askew in early 1988 was the runaway favorite for election to the U.S. Senate. Instead, he chose not to run. The reason, he said, was the inordinate amount of time fundraising would have required. The issues director of Askew's senatorial campaign later elaborated:*

*"Askew spent nearly all of his working time raising funds. The principal political event of the campaign was the fundraiser, where the price of admission often ranged from $500 to $1,000 a person. Askew would shake some hands, give a short speech and then head to the next city.*

*"When he was not attending fundraisers, he was often raising money by phone— 'dialing for dollars,' as professionals call it. While Askew talked on one phone, an assistant would dial another, get the potential contributor on the line and turn it over to the candidate. On a good day, this would go on for hours.*

*"Askew relished the rare occasion with the ordinary voter. At an old-style rally in a rural north Florida town last March, Askew and I sat at a picnic bench eating fried chicken. A hunched-over, withered dirt farmer approached the governor with a $100 check. " 'I want you to have this,' said the man, trembling with awe. 'I've supported you for years, and I'm behind you now.'*

*"With a 30-second television spot in Tampa costing around $6,000, the farmer's contribution paid for about half a second of television. I didn't have the heart to tell him. "While Askew spent little time milling around with the average Floridian, he spent an inordinate amount of time meeting with—and learning the concerns of—political action committees representing the narrowest of interests. . . ."[1]*

*Communications technologies are today's tin cup. Telephone solicitation and fundraising letters to computer target-lists, for example, are common. Imaginative new uses include videocassette recordings with financial appeals.*

*Since money-in-politics is a popular target, it is useful to remember at least one positive aspect: money-giving can be an important form of political participation. Fundraising expert Richard Viguerie points out: "In 1960, there were less than 50,000 contributors to Nixon and Kennedy combined. This year [1988] we can probably say 2 million people will donate to the campaigns."[2]*

*Senator Mitch McConnell (R-Ky.) argues that "most campaigns spend far too little money, not too much, given the positive effect of campaign spending on the democratic process [via modern technology.]"*[3]

Most government action vis-a-vis campaigns focuses on public financing, financial disclosure, political action committees and limitations on contributions and expenditures.

Reliable figures on how campaigns spend their money, however, are hard to find. Federal and state disclosure rules focus on sources. Even when data on allocation are required, the result is usually a list of consulting firms who cashed campaign checks— revealing little about how the money was spent. The broadcast industry and independent researchers, furthermore, sometimes disagree on how much is spent on television commercials and what percentage of overall campaign expenditure this represents. Broadcasters, anxious to minimize the liklihood of government action on proposals such as provision of free time for political candidates, tend to argue that television absorbs less campaign money than is sometimes claimed by those who favor free air time.

The basic patterns of allocation, however, have been established. Television receives the most money, followed by direct mail and then radio and newspapers. In large urban markets, mail absorbs the most money during congressional and local races.

The following tables provide some of the best available data on campaign expenditures. Following these tables are two excerpts that put expenditures into the overall context of a campaign. Finally, it is useful to listen to several U.S. senators as they tell their money stories.

1. Dexter Filkins, "For Senate Candidates, The Only Issue Is Money," *Washington Post*, May 25, 1988, p. A19.
2. Quoted in Andrew Rosenthal, "Politicians Yield to Computers," *New York Times*, May 9, 1988, p. D1.

3. Mitch McConnell, "Campaign Spending Is Good for Democracy," *Washington Post*, June 25, 1988, p. A23.

## POLITICAL ADVERTISING ON TELEVISION

Spending figures compiled by the National Association of Broadcasters

|      | *Network* | *Spot/Local* | *Total* |
|------|-----------|--------------|---------|
| 1970 | $ 260,900 | $ 11,789,000 | $ 12,049,900 |
| 1971 | 30,000 | 5,490,000 | 5,520,000 |
| 1972 | 6,519,100 | 18,061,000 | 24,580,100 |
| 1973 | 1,199,000 | 7,885,800 | 9,084,800 |
| 1974 | 1,486,200 | 21,781,600 | 23,267,800 |
| 1975 | 1,744,200 | 6,251,000 | 7,995,200 |
| 1976 | 7,906,500 | 42,935,700 | 50,842,200 |
| 1977 | —— | 14,992,600 | 14,992,600 |
| 1978 | 1,065,800 | 56,545,000 | 57,610,800 |
| 1979 | 255,000 | 16,891,700 | 17,146,700 |
| 1980 | 20,699,700 | 69,870,300 | 90,570,000 |
| 1981 | 713,100 | 20,114,300 | 20,827,400 |
| 1982 | 861,900 | 122,760,300 | 123,622,200 |

(POLITICAL ADVERTISING continued)

| | | | |
|---|---|---|---|
| 1983 | 2,739,700 | 24,609,700 | 27,349,400 |
| 1984 | 43,652,500 | 110,171,500 | 153,824,000 |
| 1985 | —— | 22,680,500 | 22,680,500 |
| 1986 | 459,300 | 161,184,000 | 161,643,300 |

*Source:* Broadcast Advertisers Reports. Reprinted with permission of the Television Bureau of Advertising.

## AGOURA HILLS: A PROGRESSIVE TOWN TRIES TO LASSO CAMPAIGN REFORM

From a report by the California Commission on Campaign Financing

The residents of Agoura Hills have always sought to maintain a small town simplicity in their community's civic life. Yet for a relatively young city, Agoura Hills has witnessed political shifts and changes that many municipalities take years to experience. Since its incorporation in December 1982, the city's campaign financing system has passed through stages of tranquility (1982-84), intense unrest (1985) and temporary quiescence (1987). Now, city leaders are considering whether campaign finance reforms are necessary to head-off the excessive campaign spending and undue contributor influence that they see looming on the horizon.

The City of Agoura Hills sits nestled in the Santa Monica Mountains, 40 miles west of downtown Los Angeles and 20 miles inland from the ocean. Its rural setting and gentle breezes easily wipe away residual thoughts of the sprawling metropolis just over the hill.

The Agoura area's rolling hills and remote setting boast a rustic past of cattle ranches, cowboys, stage-coach stops and saloons. Without knowing it, many Americans have seen Agoura Hills on the silver screen—for in the 1920s, Paramount Studios used an Agoura Hills ranch as a background for many movie westerns. For a time, the area was even named "Picture City."[1] Throughout the 1960s and much of the 1970s, the Agoura area was known mostly for its hosting of equestrian events and the annual Renaissance Pleasure Faire.

Though some of the rustic surroundings still exist, massive tract home developments and office building complexes have covered much of the area's bucolic past. The City of Agoura Hills is now a rapidly growing, upper-middle class bedroom community. Affluent refugees from the congested San Fernando Valley and other dense metropolitan Los Angeles areas have swarmed to the low-crime, clean-aired and spacious Agoura Hills, almost doubling the city's population—from 11,000 in 1980 to more than 20,000 in 1986.[2]

With a growing population has come increasing affluence. Between 1983 and 1986, the assessed value of property in the city climbed from $620 million to over $1 billion; average household income rose to $49,000 in 1986, almost double that of the county as a whole; and housing prices soared—homes selling for $100,000 in 1980 now sell for over $300,000.[3] "[Agoura Hills] has become a haven for yuppies seeking a new life where cowboys—real and movie versions—once roamed," the Los Angeles Herald Examiner observed in its 1986 exposé.[4]

### *"Quality of Life" Issues Drive Agoura Hills' Political System*

Agoura Hills' population explosion in the 1980s was substantially drawn by the area's beauty, open spaces and close proximity to the Santa Monica Mountains. Some residents commute several hours to their jobs in Los Angeles just to come back to Agoura Hills' serene, clean and simple atmosphere. Agoura Hills politics seek to maintain both the new and the old components of the city's lifestyle—the new higher standard of living and manicured community streets and lawns that have the affluent residents, and the old rustic and rural charm of the town.

#### CITY INCORPORATION

Agoura Hills in 1982 experienced a perceived threat to the area's "quality of life." According to some Agourans, Los Angeles County's land use decisions had stimulated "sloppy" and "haphazard" development along the area's main artery (the Ventura Freeway corridor). Commercial projects and large bill-board advertisements for housing developments "just up the road" or "at the next exit" were freely approved by the county supervisors.

"With the county seat 40 miles away [in downtown Los Angeles]," Mayor Fran Pavley recalled, "how could [the county supervisors] be sensitive to the needs of this community?" According to Pavley, residents of the then-unincorporated Agoura territory were denied control over planning decisions, inhibited in their attempts to influence these decisions, and therefore resented their tax dollars going to a county government that ignored their needs.[5] Agoura Hills resident and *Los Angeles Times* television critic Howard Rosenberg commented, "The county treated us like a toilet."[6]

Agoura Hills residents saw incorporation as a way to control development decisions and preserve their quality of life. One of Agoura Hills' land marks is a nine-foot tall statue of an Indian chief facing southwest with his arm outstretched and hand turned upward, seemingly motioning those coming towards him to "Stop." For Agoura Hills, this Indian statue symbolized the residents' actions to stop the metropolitan sprawl coming up over the hill.

**FRACTURING OF THE INCORPORATION COALITION**

The coalition of diverse city interests which was created in the drive for incorporation helped to produce an era of stability and calm following incorporation. A new city council had been elected and control over the city's planning decisions and its "quality of life" seemed finally to reside with the city.

Within the first three years of the city's existence, however, the incorporation coalition was torn apart by the first elected city council's aggressive growth policies. A pro-commercial development majority had apparently emerged on the council, voting approval after approval of many commercial and residential development projects. Four new housing tracts, three shopping centers and a half-million square feet of office space were approved and built by the mid-1980s. Proponents of this aggressive pro-growth maintained that the city's survival rested on broadening its tax base. More development meant more tax revenue, and more tax revenue promised better city services. But many Agoura Hills residents, who had previously been angered by Los Angeles County's planning policies, felt that their "quality of life" was in jeopardy once again. "[The first city council] gave everything away to the developers," one Agoura

Hills resident observed bitterly. "They never said 'no'!"[7]

One development, in particular, turned the residents' irritation over growth into anger. Katell Properties, a Torrance-based development firm, had obtained approval from the city council to erect a five-building office complex on the west end of town overlooking the Ventura Freeway. When construction workers broke ground on the project in late 1985, several of the city's 300-year-old oak trees were cut down. Only their stumps were left on the hillside development site. Residents were shocked. Some held "funeral services" for the trees that were "older than our country." Agoura Hills resident Eric Haupt later protested, "Don't rape our hills, don't spoil our beauty!"[8]

According to Council member Jack Koenig, the revelation of a $1,000 political contribution from Katell Properties to Mayor John Hood one week prior to council approval of the project further shocked Agoura Hills voters.[9] Katell had also contributed $400 to Council member Ernest Dynda one month before the deciding vote. These contributions prompted Katell's opponents to focus on the political process by which their community was being changed.

### Candidates' Campaign Finances Are Affected by Land Use Battles

Campaign financing in Agoura Hills followed a familiar pattern to other small and medium-sized cities. After its incorporation in late 1982, Agoura Hills witnessed a short-lived era of campaign financing and political stability. By 1985, however, a single issue—"land use planning"—exploded into local consciousness. As the city council made unpopular commercial land development decisions, political serenity quickly collapsed, voters took sides and campaign spending skyrocketed to startling levels. In the 1984 city council election, all candidates had raised and spent a total of approximately $15,000. By 1985, one candidate alone raised and spent around $20,000.[10] Then, as the land use issue receded from controversy, election costs diminished. The fluctuations between campaign spending in the 1984, 1985 and 1987 elections illustrate the power of the single development issue.

**RISING COSTS AND DEVELOPER CONTRIBUTIONS**

The 1984 election was relatively calm. High campaign spending was not a factor. The most controversial issue in this campaign involved the "non-residency" of candidates. According to Council member Koenig, two candidates had apparently stated falsely on their declaration of candidacy forms that they were Agoura Hills residents. "One address a candidate had listed as his home was in fact a chicken shack," Koenig said. "I don't know how you can live in a chicken shack."[11]

By 1985, however, Katell's project and its contributions to Mayor John Hood finally brought to a head the land use issue. The 1985 election became a referendum on the city's growth future.

Against this land use backdrop occurred a fundamental shift in the city's election structure. The city changed from district-by-district elections to at-large elections. After the 1984 election, city leaders and residents concluded that district elections were not practical. The highest vote-getter in 1984, for instance, received a total of 250 votes, and one city council member was elected by eight votes. In the 1985 election all candidates were elected citywide. In one year, the constituencies of each city council candidate grew from approximately 4,000 residents in individual districts to almost 22,000 residents in the entire city. Land use issues, together with this structural change, stimulated the explosive growth in 1985 campaign financing.

Development and real estate interests, feeling threatened by rapidly growing anti-development feelings sweeping the city, contributed unprecedented amounts to pro-development candidates. Over a five month period preceding the November 1985 election, Mayor John Hood's campaign accepted approximately $5,000 in campaign contributions from developer interests. Of that $5,000, over $4,000—including $1,500 from Katell Properties—came from out-of-town development and real estate interests.

Hayden Finley, another pro-development candidate, raised close to $21,000. Since a majority of his contributions were reported as "under-$100" donations, it was impossible to pin-point their sources. During the course of the election, however, Finley's opponents speculated openly that developers were simply trying to "hide" their contributions.

#### SUBSTANTIAL JUMP IN SPENDING ON VOTER CONTACTS

A comparison of Agoura Hills' 1984 and 1985 elections provides a striking comparison of the differences between spending and contribution patterns in an issue-charged at-large election and an issue-less districted race. One of the most startling differences lies in the percentage of expenditures devoted to voter contacts (expenditures for broadcast, outdoor and newspaper advertising and campaign literature).

Districted candidates in the low-spending election of 1984 devoted only 45 percent of their money to voter contacts expenditures. In 1985, candidates spent an average of 81 percent of their expenditures on voter contacts. The substantially larger city-wide constituency, coupled with controversial land use issues, caused a two-fold jump in the percentage amounts candidates spent on 1985 campaign literature alone.

The percentage of spending on campaign overhead significantly dropped between the two elections. Much less money was spent on fundraising and general expenses. The average candidate in the Commission's sample of jurisdictions spent almost 62 percent on campaign overhead, while Agoura candidates spent only 26 percent. Agoura Hills candidates lacked the "campaign organizations" used in big city campaigns. Political consultants were rarely used and virtually nothing was spent on personnel.

#### HIGH PERCENTAGE OF BUSINESS CONTRIBUTIONS

During the last two Agoura Hills elections, city council candidates accepted more than half of their contributions from business sources. This far out-paces the Commission's small city average and even exceeds the average for the Commission's entire sample.

However, the Agoura Hills business contribution figures are almost single-handedly skewed by Mayor John Hood's totals for 1985. Of almost $12,000 that Hood received in contributions of $100 or more, 84 percent came from business sources. Mayor Hood's business contributions alone—totaling more than $9,000—were more than the combined total of contributions raised by candidates Jack Koenig, Darlene McBane, Louise Rishoff and incumbent Fran Pavley.

### Residents Coalition Defeats Big-Spending Candidates

For the 1985 election, pro-development forces raised large war chests, solicited big contributions (the likes of which Agoura Hills residents had never seen before) and spent relatively huge amounts on campaign mail pieces. But angry residents, concerned over the explosion of new development, emulated the town's western history and formed a posse to "lasso" the city's pro-growth council members. The Katell project and the cutting of the oaks converted many residents into anti-development advocates.

PIZZA-PARLOR POLITICS

In early 1985, 14 Agoura Hills residents met at a local pizza parlor to discuss their frustrations with the city council decisions. If residents organized, they concluded, they could significantly impact the election of 1985. They called their new organization, "For Agoura '85."

Anti-development candidates pledged to disclose fully all campaign contributions and reject all donations from out-of-city sources. Pro-development candidates tried to undermine these full-disclosure tactics by charging that all anti-development monies were not being accurately reported. A paranoia towards development and developers swept the town. The formation of the citizens group, For Agoura '85, helped channel this paranoia into the political process.

In the months leading up to the election, For Agoura '85 registered voters, sent out "informational" mailers with news of the city council's pro-development actions, and held candidate debates. From the debates three candidates— incumbent Fran Pavley and candidates Jack Koenig and Darlene McBane— were endorsed in an attempt to retain one seat (Pavley's), defeat the incumbent mayor (Hood) and win an open seat.

Through numerous neighborhood meetings, mail parties and candidate forums, For Agoura '85 struck a responsive chord in the community. Membership in the group swelled to 426 two days before the election.[12] Raising $10 and $20 dollar contributions, For Agoura '85 was able to collect $8,000. The group even turned down a $3,000 contribution for fear it might be perceived as having an "obligation" attached to it.[13] On behalf of their endorsed candidates, For Agoura '85 sent out low-cost mailers listing their slate of candidates.

In November of 1985, For Agoura '85 candidates overwhelmingly defeated the pro-development candidates Hood and Finley by more than a three-to-one margin, even though Hood and Finley raised 87 percent more than the citizens' coalition and its candidates. In fact, Hood and Finley outraised all other candidates in the race combined by almost 50 percent.

In light of For Agoura '85's successes, opponents charged the organization with "political machine-like" tactics. Carol Dynda, wife of Council member Ernest Dynda, lodged claims that the organization had not reported all its $100 or more contributions. She felt it unlikely that For Agoura '85 could have raised $8,000 in "five and ten dollar contributions."[14] For Agoura '85 member Patricia MacGregor replied, "I'm really interested in how in just a few short weeks a bunch of housewives who care for this city has now become a 'political machine', as some of our critics have called us."[15] Eric Haupt, one of the original members of the group explained, "I see a machine as a fine-tuned instrument. If that is what we are, what is wrong with that?"[16]

To the victors of the 1985 race and other community activists, the true history of Agoura Hills begins, not with its 1982 incorporation, but with its 1985 election. At the city's administrative offices, a picture of the current city council hangs on the wall, with a sign in proud letters reading, "The City Council Re-Organization of 1985." This lack of any homage to the *first* pro-growth city council is quite deliberate.

DOMINANCE OF AGOURA HILLS POLITICS

The organization, For Agoura '85, due to its 1985 election activities, has become the dominant power in the city. The group's main target in the 1987 election, Council member Ernest Dynda, decided not to run for reelection. If he had decided to stay in the race, For Agoura '85 would have gone into action again as "For Agoura '87."

As a result, the 1987 election was relatively calm, compared to the 1985 contest. Candidates whose views matched those of For Agoura '85 won easily without significant effort. For Agoura '85 has positioned itself in a "threatening" role. If it believes that development-backed candidates reflect views that "endanger" the city's perceived "quality of life," For Agoura '85's members stand ready to organize. This "threat" may keep pro-development candidates out of Agoura Hills campaigns. As Council member Jack Koenig simply puts it, "If you're aligned with development, you're dead in this town."[17]

### Targeted Reforms May Be Needed

"To pour tens of thousands of dollars into a local election is ridiculous."[18]

*Council member Koenig*

In the wake of the 1985 election, the newly elected city council discussed various ideas for campaign reform. They spoke about the high spending and the dominance of developer and out-of-city contributions. Reflecting self-confessed paranoia over "developer money," council members Pavley, McBane and Koenig expressed interest in an ordinance that would require the "full disclosure" of all contributions as low as "a few dollars." "I feel the public and the citizens have a right to know where our money's coming from," Pavley said.[19] The current city council believes in the vigilance of city residents to "keep watch" on sources of candidate contributions.

The city council also considered their campaign finance remedies, such as a disqualification ordinance similar to those adopted by Orange County and the City of Modesto. Proposals including contribution limits and expenditure limits with partial public financing are also being examined. A majority of the city council members believe all or some of these provisions may be included in a campaign finance reform measure that will be approved in the coming year.

City Manager David Carmony is also currently pursuing a proposal to change the city from a "general law" to a charter municipality. This change would have the effect of, in his words, "locking reform in." If Agoura Hills became a charter city, a campaign reform measure could be passed by "charter amendment," and thus would require a vote of the people to change or repeal. Under the current general law structure, there is not a "charter amendment process." Laws are passed by the city council and could be potentially changed by future city councils.

Agoura Hills city officials and residents look at campaign reform as a way of preserving the small town simplicity of their elections; the fact that city officials are looking for a way to "lock reform in" is a measure of how important it is to them to "lock in" the simplicity and small town nature of their campaigns. For this reason, Agoura Hills might consider a broad range of innovative reforms that would go a long way to preserve the positive sides of their present situation.

### EXPENDITURE LIMITATIONS

Keeping the cost of campaigns checked at a reasonable limit would be, perhaps, the most important component of a comprehensive reform. Expenditure limits would immediately extinguish the possibility of a big spending campaign coming in and destroying the small town atmosphere of Agoura Hills elections, as was attempted by two candidates in the 1985

election. It would also ensure that, in the event of a truly competitive race, candidates would be on equal footing, playing by equal rules. In Agoura Hills elections, the highest amount ever spent was $18,152; in the low-charged elections of 1984 and 1987, campaign spending never reached above $3,000. Therefore, an expenditure cap of approximately $10,000 may be the most prudent limit to allow for reasonable competition by potential challengers and to take away the possibility of excessively high-spending campaigns using expensive campaign techniques (e.g., sophisticated campaign literature or campaign consultants).

Limited public matching funds are essential to the constitutional presence of expenditure limits under the 1976 U.S. Supreme Court decision *Buckley V. Valeo*. Agoura Hills could introduce a very low level of public matching funds, perhaps matching dollar-for-dollar up to the first $25 of each contribution. Under an expenditure limit of $10,000, the most a candidate could hope to receive per election would be $2,500. Eight candidates ran in the 1985 election; if all eight candidates raised and spent $10,000 (which is highly unlikely), the most in public matching funds that would have been provided under this proposal would have been $20,000—the cost of less than $1 per resident (or less than the price of a dozen eggs).

### CONTRIBUTION LIMITATIONS

As only a part of a comprehensive package of reforms, contribution limits would be essential for two reasons: to eliminate the possibility of large campaign contributions; and to attack potential fears of large contributor influence. A low contribution limit of $150 would fit the realities of Agoura Hills' fundraising patterns and help preserve the importance of the small contributor.

### A LIMITED BAN ON CONTRIBUTIONS FROM CITY CONTRACTORS

This provision, similar to one currently used in the City of Gardena, would prohibit anyone contracting with or bidding on contracts with the City of Agoura Hills from contributing to city council candidates or office holders. Due to the city's relatively young age, decisions on future city development and other city services may have yet to be made. This innovative provision would ensure that decisions regarding new city services would be above reproach and unaffected by campaign contributions. This proposal should only apply to businesses and individuals who must seek contract approval directly from the city council. A threshold level (e.g., contracts over $5,000) could be instituted to simplify enforcement. The city clerk could keep a current file of all city contractors that might be affected. During a campaign, this list would be distributed to all candidates for city office.

FULL DISCLOSURE OF DONORS

Under state law, candidates must only disclose the identities of contributors if their contributions total $100 or more. In Agoura Hills, however, approximately 37 percent of contributors give less than $100. Those concerned about developer influence have suspected that some candidates "hide" their contributors by receiving contributions in under-$100 amounts. Disclosure of donors giving $25 or more would inhibit such practices and ease public suspicion.

Some have suggested that disclosure should include all contributions down to a penny. Record keeping would be tedious and time consuming for the city clerk, however, who would be forced to check the correctness of all $1, $5 and $10 contributor information. It would also impose cumbersome reporting requirements on candidates accepting small cash contributions at local fundraising events (e.g., through the selling of campaign buttons and t-shirts).

Agoura Hills has a very unique situation. The city is less than a decade old, and yet it has experienced extremes in its campaign financing system that have prompted city officials to evaluate, already, the effectiveness of their election system. Agoura Hills city officials seem bent on correcting this system's problems while at the same time preserving its positive qualities.

Using this unique spirit for positive change, Agoura Hills city officials should move swiftly to adopt a comprehensive set of reforms. These reforms must be specifically tailored to these clear goals of preservation and positive change. Keeping election costs to a reasonable limit, limiting contributions and fully disclosing contributors may go a long way to help Agoura Hills achieve these ends.

NOTES

1. Richard Nordwind, *Escape to Agoura Hills*, Los Angeles Herald Examiner, Aug. 31, 1986.
2. *Id.*
3. *Id.*
4. *Id.*
5. Telephone interview with Fran Pavley, Mayor of Agoura Hills, June 11, 1987.
6. David Silver, *From Horse Ranch Haven to Rich Suburb*, Daily Commerce, June 1, 1987.
7. Interview with Eric Haupt, Member of For Agoura '85, July 1, 1987.
8. *Id.*
9. Telephone interview with Jack Koenig, Council member, City of Agoura Hills, July 1, 1987.
10. Hayden Finley, in the 1985 election, raised $20,556 and spent $18,152.
11. *Supra* note 9.
12. Cynthia Lee, *Councilman's Spouse Assails For Agoura '85*, Daily News, Nov. 2, 1986.
13. *Supra* note 7.
14. *Supra* note 12.
15. *Id.*
16. *Supra* note 7.
17. *Supra* note 9.
18. Cynthia Lee, *Agoura Hills Considers Enacting Municipal Election Laws*, Daily News, Feb. 14, 1986.
19. *Supra* note 5.

From "Money and Politics in the Golden State: Financing California's Local Elections," issued by the California Commission on Campaign Financing. Reprinted with permission.

## OVERVIEW: HOW CAMPAIGN MONEY IS SPENT IN CALIFORNIA

Cumulative campaign spending during 1980-86 in 17 representative California cities and counties, compiled by the California Commission on Campaign Financing:

Summary: Spending in All Surveyed Jurisdictions

| | | | | | |
|---|---|---|---|---|---|
| Broadcast Advertising | $ 2,698,806 | (7%) | Fundraising | 5,173,903 | 13%) |
| Newspaper | 795,833 | (2%) | General Overhead | 8,680,426 | (23%) |
| Literature | 10,174,832 | (26%) | Personnel | 2,042,640 | (5%) |
| Outdoor Advertising | 1,094,622 | (3%) | Travel | 379,060 | 1%) |
| Surveys | 1,230,881 | 3%) | Consulting | 3,740,898 | (10%) |
| Candidate Transfers | 2,399,215 | (6%) | Total | $38,411,116 | |

Spending (Percentage) by Size of Jurisdiction

| | *Small* | *Medium* | *Large* | *All* |
|---|---|---|---|---|
| Expenditures | | | | |
| Broadcast | 0% | 8% | 7% | 7% |
| Cand. Loan/Transfer | 2 | 2 | 8 | 6 |
| Fundraising | 7 | 11 | 15 | 13 |
| General | 17 | 16 | 26 | 23 |
| Consulting | 9 | 8 | 11 | 10 |
| Literature | 48 | 31 | 23 | 26 |
| Newspaper | 6 | 2 | 2 | 2 |
| Outdoor | 2 | 8 | 1 | 3 |
| Personnel | 4 | 10 | 4 | 5 |
| Survey | 5 | 3 | 3 | 3 |
| Travel | 0 | 1 | 1 | 1 |
| Total Expenditures | 100 | 100 | 100 | 100 |
| | | | | |
| Outreach Expenditures | | | | |
| Broadcast | 0 | 16 | 22 | 18 |
| Literature | 85 | 64 | 69 | 69 |
| Newspaper | 11 | 4 | 5 | 5 |
| Outdoor | 4 | 16 | 3 | 7 |
| Total Outreach | 100 | 100 | 100 | 100 |
| | | | | |
| Expenditures by Period[1] | | | | |
| Off-Year | 4.5 | 16.5 | 34.5 | 28.3 |
| On-Year, Period One | 15.4 | 21.4 | 14.1 | 15.9 |
| On-Year, Period Two | 31.6 | 27.3 | 27.8 | 27.9 |
| On-Year, Period Three | 48.5 | 34.9 | 23.6 | 28.0 |
| Total On-Year | 95.4 | 83.5 | 65.5 | 71.7 |
| Total Expenditures | 100.0 | 100.0 | 100.0 | 100.0 |

*Continued on next page*

(SPENDING *continued*)

| | Small | Medium | Large | All |
|---|---|---|---|---|
| **Expenditures by Status** | | | | |
| Incumbents | 45 | 66 | 66 | 65 |
| Challengers | 24 | 15 | 13 | 14 |
| Open Races | 6 | 18 | 21 | 19 |
| T-Type Races[2] | 25 | 0 | 0 | 1 |
| All Races | 100 | 100 | 100 | 100 |
| **Expenditures by Result** | | | | |
| Winners | 51 | 77 | 71 | 72 |
| Losers | 49 | 23 | 29 | 28 |
| All Candidates | 100 | 100 | 100 | 100 |

Spending (Actual Dollars) by Size of Jurisdiction

| | Small | Medium | Large | All |
|---|---|---|---|---|
| **Expenditures** | | | | |
| Broadcast | $ 4,601 | $ 749,246 | $ 1,944,959 | $ 2,698,806 |
| Cand. Loan/Transfer | 39,136 | 188,918 | 2,171,161 | 2,399,215 |
| Fundraising | 167,575 | 1,090,348 | 3,915,980 | 5,173,903 |
| General | 415,010 | 1,524,326 | 6,741,090 | 8,680,426 |
| Consulting | 211,146 | 753,697 | 2,776,055 | 3,740,898 |
| Literature | 1,177,742 | 2,973,763 | 6,023,327 | 10,174,832 |
| Newspaper | 146,353 | 205,000 | 444,480 | 795,833 |
| Outdoor | 60,755 | 738,264 | 295,603 | 1,094,622 |
| Personnel | 99,228 | 1,006,085 | 937,327 | 2,042,640 |
| Survey | 120,841 | 280,798 | 829,242 | 1,230,881 |
| Travel | 2,484 | 97,848 | 278,728 | 379,060 |
| Total Expenditures | 2,444,871 | 9,608,293 | 26,357,952 | 38,411,116 |
| **Outreach Expenditures** | | | | |
| Broadcast | 4,601 | 749,246 | 1,944,959 | 2,698,806 |
| Literature | 1,177,742 | 2,973,763 | 6,023,327 | 10,174,832 |
| Newspaper | 146,353 | 205,000 | 444,480 | 795,833 |
| Outdoor | 60,755 | 738,264 | 295,603 | 1,094,622 |
| Total Outreach | 1,389,451 | 4,666,273 | 8,708,369 | 14,764,093 |
| **Expenditures by Period[1]** | | | | |
| Off-Year | 124,710 | 1,857,785 | 9,272,682 | 11,255,177 |
| On-Year, Period One | 412,052 | 3,888,223 | 3,788,511 | 8,088,786 |
| On-Year, Period Two | 846,835 | 2,615,721 | 7,471,711 | 10,934,267 |
| On-Year, Period Three | 1,299,803 | 3,418,474 | 6,356,879 | 11,075,156 |
| Total On-Year | 2,558,690 | 9,922,418 | 17,617,101 | 30,098,209 |
| Total Expenditures | 2,683,400 | 11,780,203 | 26,889,783 | 41,353,386 |
| **Expenditures by Status** | | | | |
| Incumbents | 741,472 | 6,289,688 | 16,616,183 | 23,647,343 |
| Challengers | 393,445 | 1,452,113 | 3,369,695 | 5,215,253 |
| Open Races | 90,398 | 1,724,404 | 5,208,207 | 7,023,009 |
| T-Type Races[3] | 406,779 | 0 | 0 | 406,779 |
| All Races | 1,632,094 | 9,466,205 | 25,194,085 | 36,292,384 |

*Continued on next page*

(SPENDING *continued*)

|  | *Small* | *Medium* | *Large* | *All* |
|---|---|---|---|---|
| Expenditures by Result |  |  |  |  |
| Winners | 815,489 | 6,046,663 | 12,797,198 | 19,659,350 |
| Losers | 781,584 | 1,826,651 | 5,144,700 | 7,752,935 |
| All Candidates | 1,597,073 | 7,873,314 | 17,941,898 | 27,412,285 |
| Cost Per Vote |  |  |  |  |
| Total Expenditures | 1,648,363 | 9,142,112 | 22,168,273 | 32,950,748 |
| Total Voters | 521,824 | 3,042,687 | 5,091,447 | 8,655,958 |
| Average | 3.16 | 3.00 | 4.35 | 3.81 |

Spending (Percentage) by Candidate Status

|  | *Incumbents* | *Challengers* | *Winners* | *Losers* |
|---|---|---|---|---|
| Expenditures |  |  |  |  |
| Broadcast | 5% | 6% | 4% | 9% |
| Cand. Loan/Transfer | 10 | 1 | 9 | 1 |
| Fundraising | 18 | 5 | 18 | 5 |
| General | 27 | 18 | 27 | 17 |
| Consulting | 9 | 13 | 7 | 12 |
| Literature | 19 | 40 | 21 | 43 |
| Newspaper | 2 | 3 | 2 | 2 |
| Outdoor | 3 | 4 | 3 | 3 |
| Personnel | 4 | 4 | 4 | 4 |
| Survey | 2 | 5 | 3 | 4 |
| Travel | 1 | 0 | 2 | 0 |
| Total Expenditures | 100 | 100 | 100 | 100 |
| Outreach Expenditures |  |  |  |  |
| Broadcast | 17 | 12 | 12 | 16 |
| Literature | 67 | 76 | 70 | 75 |
| Newspaper | 7 | 5 | 8 | 4 |
| Outreach | 10 | 7 | 10 | 5 |
| Total Outreach | 100 | 100 | 100 | 100 |
| Expenditures by Period[1] |  |  |  |  |
| Off-Year | NA | NA | NA | NA |
| On-Year, Period One | NA | NA | NA | NA |
| On-Year, Period Two | NA | NA | NA | NA |
| On-Year, Period Three | NA | NA | NA | NA |
| Total On-Year | NA | NA | NA | NA |
| Total Expenditures | NA | NA | NA | NA |
| Expenditures by Status |  |  |  |  |
| Incumbents | 100 | — | 87 | 15 |
| Challengers | — | 100 | 4 | 44 |
| Open Races | — | — | 8 | 37 |
| T-Type Races[2] | — | — | 1 | 3 |
| All Races | — | — | 100 | 100 |

*Continued on next page*

(SPENDING *continued*)

| Expenditures by Result | Incumbents | Challengers | Winners | Losers |
|---|---|---|---|---|
| Winners | 93 | 19 | — | — |
| Losers | 7 | 81 | — | — |
| All Candidates | 100 | 100 | | |

## Spending (Percentage) by Type of Election

| | At-large Jurisdictions | Districted Jurisdictions | Off-Year | On-Year |
|---|---|---|---|---|
| Expenditures | | | | |
| Broadcast | 3% | 5% | 0% | 10% |
| Cand. Loan/Transfer | 1 | 9 | 14 | 3 |
| Fundraising | 11 | 16 | 26 | 8 |
| General | 17 | 27 | 34 | 18 |
| Consulting | 9 | 9 | 7 | 11 |
| Literature | 36 | 23 | 9 | 33 |
| Newspaper | 4 | 2 | 1 | 2 |
| Outdoor | 8 | 1 | 1 | 4 |
| Personnel | 7 | 5 | 3 | 6 |
| Survey | 3 | 3 | 2 | 4 |
| Travel | 1 | 1 | 3 | 0 |
| Total Expenditures | 100 | 100 | 100 | 100 |
| Outreach Expenditures | | | | |
| Broadcast | 6 | 17 | 3 | 20 |
| Literature | 71 | 74 | 81 | 68 |
| Newspaper | 7 | 5 | 9 | 5 |
| Outdoor | 16 | 4 | 7 | 8 |
| Total Outreach | 100 | 100 | 100 | 100 |
| Expenditures by Period[1] | | | | |
| Off-Year | 17 | 37 | 100 | — |
| On-Year, Period One | 32 | 15 | — | 27 |
| On-Year, Period Two | 21 | 26 | — | 36 |
| On-Year, Period Three | 29 | 23 | — | 37 |
| On-Year | 83 | 63 | — | 100 |
| Total Expenditures | 100 | 100 | — | — |
| Expenditures by Status | | | | |
| Incumbents | 74 | 73 | NA | NA |
| Challengers | 18 | 13 | NA | NA |
| Open Races | 2 | 15 | NA | NA |
| T-Type Races[2] | 5 | 0 | NA | NA |
| All Races | 100 | 100 | NA | NA |
| Expenditures by Result | | | | |
| Winners | 76 | 77 | NA | NA |
| Losers | 24 | 23 | NA | NA |
| All Candidates | 100 | 100 | NA | NA |

## NOTES

1. Based on incomplete figures. "Off-year" refers to years when no elections are held. On-year expenditures are divided into three periods: One, the first 40 days of the election year; Two, the next 60 days, and Three, the following 120 days. Period Three in many cases covers the month after the election.
2. "T-type" races are at-large elections in multi-seat districts with incumbents and open seats.

---

# CAMPAIGN TECHNOLOGY AND AMERICAN DEMOCRACY

*Frank Luntz*

"Under the current system, few candidates relish the task of getting elected. There is increasing awareness that modern campaign technologies have fostered a remoteness from the voters. . . . The expertise of campaign professionals—political consultants, media advisors, pollsters, direct mail specialists, lies in the techniques of mass marketing, not in fostering personal contact between candidates and the voters."[1]

*Former U.S. Senator Charles Mathias*

"Politics is and will always remain an art more than a science. Yet it would be foolish not to recognize that a scientific understanding of the hopes, fears and aspirations of the people provides crucial insight for the elected official. Modern campaign technology is information-intensive, and thus makes our candidates more responsive to the needs of the people."

*Richard Wirthlin, White House Pollster*

To focus on the candidates, the professional advisors, and the methods used to win elections is, in one sense, little more than a description of how a product (the candidate) is sold to the buyer (the electorate) by the ancient skill of marketing. Marketing in politics is not new. Image makers have packaged every successful presidential candidate from Dwight Eisenhower to Ronald Reagan. Modern campaign technology has developed and is increasingly utilized because it appears, at present, to be the best means for influencing mass behavior so as to obtain the desired political reward—victory at the polls. Political marketing is often reviled, though it is not inherently evil. It is disliked and distrusted, probably because some exponents have dared to discuss openly the marketing strategies and tactics

which less candid politicians and professional advisors prefer to discuss in private. Although the voter is subjected on all sides to marketing in one form or another, there seems to be particular resentment, justified or not, toward the marketing of those aspiring to public office.

Critics of the current system have, from time to time, complained about the negative impact of certain election legislation and the resultant new techniques in electioneering. There seems little doubt that the conventional wisdom, as reflected in newspapers, magazines, and television editorials, considers the style and strategy employed by candidates seeking elective office today to be at best uninspiring, and at worst a threat to democracy itself. On the surface, many of the criticisms contain some validity, but this author believes that the majority of electoral innovations since the mid-1970s have, in fact, had a positive impact on the American democratic process.

### Money in Politics

No issue in electoral politics has attracted as much attention and debate as the role of money in electing candidates. The average expenditure of a successful House candidate in 1976 was $87,000. A decade later, the average expenditure topped $350,000.[2] Since 1976, the cost of running a successful Senate race has risen from $610,000 to over three million dollars.[3] Candidate fundraising has gone from a campaign ingredient to an all-pervasive campaign obsession, and there is no question that money has become a key requirement on which paid advertising, polling, and all other techniques depend. The political agenda is set by those candidates and causes that can raise and spend vast sums of cash. "Money talks," claims *Campaigns & Elections* publisher James Dwinell, "and if you do not have it, few people hear you."[4]

Ironically, the debate over money in political campaigns is actually an outgrowth of the federal election laws designed to contain it. Political action committees were insignificant, and independent expenditures non-existent, until Congress decided to regulate the way candidates run for office. The unpredictability of human behavior led to the failure of well-intentioned election laws to work as planned. The Supreme Court undermined Congressional reformers when it struck down certain campaign laws while upholding others. In all fairness, candidates today are merely trying to use the current legal restrictions to their own best interests. It is not the rise of modern campaign technology but the campaign legislation of the 1970s that has forced candidates to spend endless hours in search of campaign contributions.

Many in the political world consider the extreme dependence on money for electoral success to be the single greatest threat to fair and open elections. Senator Charles Mathias (R-Md.), former Chairman of the Senate Rules and Administration Committee, said during a hearing regarding changes in campaign finance laws: "Many talented men and women choose not to enter the political arena because they simply cannot face, will not face, the need to raise hundreds of thousands, or even millions, of dollars to run a campaign."[5] While such an assertion is difficult to prove overall, it is known that, in 1986, four incumbent senators (Barry Goldwater (R-Ariz.), Thomas Eagleton (D-Mo.), Charles Mathias (R-Md.), and Russell Long (D-La.) chose retirement rather than having to raise millions of dollars for reelection. Distaste for long and costly campaigning was also a factor in the retirement of Senator Daniel Evans (R-Wash.) before the 1988 elections.

There is no question that too much of the valuable time of members of Congress is devoted to fundraising, and that this demand on their time comes, as it must, at the expense of legislative duties and personal contact with constituents. Nonincumbents, too, must spend a disproportionate amount of time dealing with the financial aspects of campaigning if they are to mount a serious challenge. The age of shoe-string campaign budgets and shoe-leather campaigning is dead. According to political columnist Tom Wicker: "Raising these necessary sums can be so time—and energy—consuming that a candidate has little of either for anything else. . . . Fundraising leaves little opportunity for live contact with the voting public."[6]

Of late, there is a growing feeling among some candidates and their advisors that a high percentage of expenditures is actually unnecessary and wasteful. Studies conducted by several consultants suggest that money spent beyond a certain threshold level, in both primaries and general elections, does not correlate to a higher percentage of the vote. The law of diminishing returns is applicable to politics, yet few candidates willingly respect it, particularly in tight races. The general attitude of most candidates is to get as much money as possible—and then spend it—since more ways to spend money can always be found. Yet an overflowing campaign treasury does not guarantee victory, and there are limitations on what it can do. Six of the top twelve Senate fundraisers in 1986 lost.[7] As a national party official noted, "There are only so many 30-second spots you can buy, only so many balloons you can inflate." Candidates need not match their opponent's financial resources as long as they have enough money to get a message across to the voters—provided, of course, it is a message the voters want to support.

In simpler times, wealthy candidates could use money to overwhelm opponents merely with extra political buttons, bumper stickers, billboards, lawn signs, leaflets, and similar modes of communication. The financially-deprived candidates, if they desired to maintain viability, had but one choice: to fight back with a grassroots campaign. These volunteer-intensive grassroots campaigns often succeeded because they were issue-oriented and stressed direct contact with voters. Even today, wealthy candidates are occasionally defeated (mostly in primaries) by aggressive challengers who have convinced voters that campaign funds are not a substitute for campaign ideas. Today, however, a massive paid media campaign—particularly in congressional races where there is less free media coverage—can usually blot out the opponent's message, even when that opponent has a strong grassroots organization. Television and radio have relegated buttons, bumper stickers, billboards and other traditional campaign paraphernalia to a quaint but meaningless role. A single television advertisement can have a greater impact on an election outcome than an army of volunteers. The rich have always had an advantage in American elections; and now, with the strict legal limits on how much individuals other than the candidate can contribute, the advantage of having personal money to buy air time is greater than ever.

### Modern Campaign Technology

Political observers as diverse as Arthur Schlesinger, Jr. and Barry Goldwater have suggested that the expertise of campaign professionals lies in the techniques of mass marketing, not in fostering personal contact between candidates and voters. The apparent increase in media emphasis and expenditures, and the corresponding decrease in personal campaigning, adds some credence to this observation. Moreover, few candidates have the time or inclination to master the increasingly sophisticated tools of electioneering. They have decided, quite correctly, that it is neither time nor cost effective to become experts in the latest campaign software package, to learn to operate complex film and video equipment, or to conduct their own public opinion polling. Candidates are thus forced to depend on the knowledge and advice of professionals in the art of electioneering. It can be argued, however, that the rise of political consultants and modern campaign technology, even with expensive price tags, have actually enhanced the dialogue between candidate and voter and encouraged greater participation in the electoral process. The communication techniques, for example, have clearly reestablished issues as an integral part of American politics.

### DIRECT MAIL

Direct mail, the technology most frequently employed to raise money and broaden campaign support, is a significant improvement on the old system of appealing to a few individuals for large contributions. Direct mail is more democratic. It reaches a greater number of people than did old fundraising techniques, and with a larger number of people financing a campaign, the less influence any single self-interest is likely to have. In addition, direct mail, being information intensive, brings issues to the forefront and thereby lessens the influence of personality and image. Through direct mail candidates explain their philosophy or contrast their vision of government with that of their opponents. Issues, therefore, are of crucial importance in direct mail fundraising.

A further example of direct communication between voter and candidate is the voter persuasion mailing. With modern campaign technology, direct mail specialists enable candidates to reach the desired audience with an appropriate message. Long gone are the days when candidates could limit the issue content of their appeal to reminders of party affiliation. Currently, the most effective candidate advocacy mail contrasts the opposing candidates' approach to the major issues and legislation of the day, and is demographically targeted to provide specific information sought by specific voters. Using the technological skills of the direct mail specialist, the campaign informs families with children about the candidate's position on education, the el-

derly about congressional votes on Social Security, and the unemployed about the jobs program advocated by the candidate. Thus, direct mail is technically neutral. Whether or not a candidate succeeds depends far less on the talent and inside manipulation of the direct mail experts than it does on voter acceptance of particular ideas and issue positions.

### SATELLITE TECHNOLOGY

One of the great changes in presidential electioneering has centered around satellite technology. First developed and implemented by former Vice President Walter Mondale in his successful 1984 Democratic presidential nomination effort, satellite technology exploded in the next four years. Mobile satellite trucks and advances in broadcasting capabilities have made the technology available to almost every national and statewide candidate.

This new technology has also made candidates more accessible and accountable to voters. At a cost of $9,000, Governor Mike Dukakis (D-Mass.) created his own instant television network when he addressed and responded to the questions of 2,500 college students live by satellite on 56 campuses around the country. In a matter of minutes, Senator Paul Simon (D-Ill.) was able to complete six "live" interviews with out-of-state broadcasters, at an expenditure of less than $3,000. Dukakis and Simon reached thousands of voters at about one-tenth the cost of a comparable political advertising media buy. At the same time, voters had the opportunity to view the candidate being questioned and challenged in a format that was more informative than the unresponsive 30-second TV spot.

### POLLING

Although today's voters may have less personal communication with the candidate than in the past, they do have considerable contact with at least one of the candidate's hired representatives, the pollster. Before the age of polling, candidates desiring a measure of the public's pulse had to rely on the advice of party bosses and business and religious figures, hardly a representative sample.

Today, nearly all elected officials can ascertain public opinion on issues, making them better informed and more responsive. Pollsters elicit information from voters, which is then given to media consultants to assist the candidate in responding to voter concerns. If, for instance, a candidate's constituency is primarily interested in one or two issues, then it is crucial that the candidate know and address those particular issues. Pollsters and media consultants, working together, have become a positive force in campaigns because they enable their clients to hear and be heard and understood by the voters they seek to reach. Advances in instant audience measurement systems, perfected just prior to the 1988 presidential contest, have even enabled pollsters to measure immediate pubic response to a candidate's speech or debate performance, indicating those areas where the candidate has failed to communicate effectively with voters. This two-way feedback between candidates and their constituents, even if conducted through a third party, contributes to maintaining an informed, representative, democratic system.

### Consultants and Campaign Imagery

"We have reached the point in political campaigning," claims Senator William Proxmire (D-Wis.), "where a candidate's most important campaign decision is not necessarily his stand on the issues but his choice of media advisor."[8] Media gurus have been accused of packaging clients so that the voter cannot distinguish between them. Former Senator Herman Talmadge (D-Ga.) voiced a common criticism of contemporary political advertising agencies when he said, "They take some fellow, dress him up in their fashion, teach him to read from some idiot board for 20 seconds. You can't separate the men from the boys."[9] Media consultant Doug Bailey candidly suggested in an article written early in the 1988 election season that "The personal attributes television best communicates attract to politics candidates better suited to public service by their smiles than by their substance."[10] But if these were true, every successful candidate would look, speak, and act similarly. Such is not the case.

One does not need to be handsome or even articulate to win. "Why is this man smiling?" asked a grinning Ed Zschau at a fundraising luncheon during his 1986 California Republican Senate campaign. "Because we know how we're going to win."[11] Zschau then went on to detail how millions of dollars were going to be spent on media advertising in his ultra-high technology campaign. Yet his opponent, Alan Cranston, a gaunt seventy-three year old veteran campaigner who could easily pass for eighty, was elected, even though he was pitted against the much younger and more charismatic Zschau. South Dakota's Senator George McGovern, despite his national stature, was defeated in 1980 by a candidate with a squeaky voice and a speech impediment, because Abdnor's ideology more closely represented the voters of South Dakota than did McGovern's. When questioned about his difficulty in addressing large crowds, successful 1986 congressional hopeful Clyde Holloway (R-Cal.) explained, "I'm a farmer. I speak to plants. But I'm learning to talk."[12] Democrat Bruce Babbitt was one of the most popular governors in Arizona history, yet he was never able to shake the television image of a stiff, awkward politician. When asked if this image would doom his presidential campaign, his response became one of the classic lines of the 1988 campaign: "If they can teach Mr. Ed [the TV horse] to talk, they can teach me."[13] It is arguable that Babbitt's presidential aspirations received considerably more exposure than his public support would have merited. Yet his message did not play well with voters, despite the spate of favorable publicity.

In today's elections, despite all the new techniques and gimmicks, it still takes more than good consultants and an attractive image to win. The crucial ingredient in good political communication is to go with lines of arguments, beliefs and themes in which the public is already inclined to believe—or ready to accept. Former presidential hopeful Senator Robert Dole (R-Kan.) may have been able to convince voters in neighboring Iowa that the was "One of Us," but the electorate in more distant regions remained unmoved. The most attractive, articulate candidates will still inevitably fail if they try to convince the electorate of something they know to be untrue; e.g., that times are prosperous when it is 1932. Image makers aside, the message remains as important as the messenger.

### Negative Advertising

There are also numerous complaints that candidates, with the assistance of professional advisors, have trivialized elections by using clever, negative advertising, making light of an opponent for such things as the opponent missing a vote or reversing an opinion. None of this, however is new. In America's first contested presidential election, Federalists branded Thomas Jefferson an anarchist, an atheist, and a coward; anti-Federalists lampooned Vice President John Adams as a monarchist and an egoist. From the campaigns of Andrew Jackson through Franklin Roosevelt, election contests were personal and vicious.

Character attacks were the rule, not the exception, and distortions of a candidate's record were commonplace. Smear tactics in American politics not only predate the development of the political consulting profession and negative advertising, but were considerably more slanderous in the days before television.

In comparison, modern negative-on-negative advertising may attack one or two sentences in an opponent's commercial, but it also adds information to the general debate. Moreover, since the ultimate effect of negative advertising is to focus attention on an elected officeholder's voting record, that in itself is important to the democratic process, a point that critics of current electioneering methods often miss or ignore. To accuse an opponent of having raised taxes may be a disconcerting charge, but if it can be substantiated then it is a fair, if uncommendable, campaign tactic. To their credit, candidates themselves are delivering more of the negative material, facing the camera head-on and telling voters where they disagree with their opponents.

In an ideal world, campaigns would be structured so that they defined the candidate's platform for voters. As long as the information is truthful, then comparative advertising—a more enlightening form of negative advertising—fulfills this goal and should remain a major element in campaigning. Once elected, senators and representatives will find they cannot vote irresponsibly and with disregard for the voters who put them in office. In this era of negative commercials, elected officeholders will have to give more thought to how they vote—or face the consequences back home. Comparative advertising exposes important differences among competing candidates. It is issue-oriented, and is specifically designed to stimulate an otherwise passive and uninformed electorate. As *Washington Post* columnist Michael Barone observed about the latest wave of comparative ads, "They tell you more about candidates' positions on substantive issues than those ads you saw a few campaigns back showing a candidate in shirtsleeves strolling down the beach with his suitcoat slung over his shoulder."[14]

Another anti-technology argument suggests that candidates can produce advertising with complete immunity. Columnist Tom Wicker maintains that consultants advise their candidate "to accuse the opponent of anything reprehensible that's remotely plausible; that failing, he should move on to charges that

aren't even plausible."[15] Democratic media consultant David Garth was equally critical of the media used in the 1988 nomination process, claiming that the candidates "can say *anything*, and by the time the truth catches up, they're gone to the next state."[16] If Wicker and Garth are correct, Congress would indeed have justification for passing legislation pertaining to reviewing, limiting, and where applicable, barring paid political advertising. Fortunately, certain checks against false advertising are already in place. If a candidate's commercials are patently untrue, the news media can be expected to expose this. Another check is the opponent, who can challenge factual distortions or inaccuracies. Finally, there are voters, the final arbiters, with the ultimate power to judge, and punish, a candidate.

All three media checks derailed the 1988 presidential campaign of Congressman Richard Gephardt (D-Mo.). Following his impressive victory in the Iowa Democratic Caucuses, Gephardt attempted to distance himself from the paid political advertising rhetoric that won him support in a farm-belt state but would be less popular in subsequent primaries. The news media, however, were entirely uncooperative. Michael Kramer, chief political correspondent for the *U.S. News & World Report*, observed that "every politically pejorative synonym in the book has been leveled at Gephardt: Expediency, opportunism, pandering, repackaging, flip-flopping, chameleon."[17] Following the media attack, Gephardt's opponents jumped on the flip-flop bandwagon. "Dick has taken cynicism [to] a depth it never had before," claimed Senator Al Gore (D-Tenn.).[18] Many Democratic primary voters agreed. Just days after his Iowa victory, Gephardt's national support began an unprecedented decline (for an Iowa winner) that led to his early withdrawal from the presidential contest. The press, the opposition, and the voters can—and do—hold candidates accountable for their actions on the campaign trail.

There has been the suggestion that paid media is used too often in politics today. There is significant evidence, however, to refute this argument. In the 1986 South Dakota Senate race both candidates were running as many as twenty radio ads a day, and had purchased all available television time weeks before the commercials were to air. Yet South Dakota had the highest voter turnout of any state holding a senatorial election. According to Senator Mitch McConnell (R-Ky.), voters in South Dakota were "turned on, not turned off, by a hot contest with a lot of money raised and a lot of money spent."[19] Vermont, Idaho and North Dakota were second, third and fourth in money spent per voter among Senate contests in 1986, but they were all among the top five states in voter turnout.[20] As McConnell concluded, "Show me a race in which not much money is spent and I will show you a race in which there is not much interest. . . ."[21]

The 1988 campaigns of Michael Dukakis, Rev. Jesse Jackson and Albert Gore bought hours of expensive airtime prior to the New York presidential primary, running commercials with more substance than their typical public and debate appearances. This paid advertising was the only redeemable feature in a contest that columnists as diverse as Jack Germond and Robert Novak criticized for otherwise becoming a "laughable, if not embarrassing joke."[22] If the way to inform an often apathetic electorate is to run costly political advertisements during and around popular TV shows, it seems worth the price. The 1988 presidential primaries and caucuses have witnessed an explosion in political advertising, as well as record-setting turnouts. Thus, the various modern campaign techniques are playing their part in reawakening the American people to the important world of electoral politics.

Some observers have even called for the total elimination of television advertising. "Truth, in politics, is a commodity packaged, twisted, stretched or ignored for convenience," wrote the *Washington Post* in an editorial following the 1986 elections.[23] Former Senator and presidential candidate Eugene McCarthy concluded: "The most direct way of avoiding the socially corrupting effects of political advertising is by banning it altogether. . . . Striking these ads from the airwaves would go a long way toward . . . developing a better-informed electorate."[24] Such an alternative, however, would be far more damaging to the American electoral process than the continued presence of the occasional misleading or uninformative ad. Public office holders seek to justify their reelection on the basis of performance and experience, whereas the opponents attack for the lack thereof. The longer voters dwell on this point, and the more evidence that is presented to them, the more likely they are to find something they do not like. Incum-

bents are usually better known than challengers and would stand to benefit if political advertising were regulated, limited, or even abolished. The ability to attack the incumbent, even if the attacks are somewhat slanted, is often the only way for the challenger to enter the campaign dialogue. Without having to answer viable challengers, incumbents could ignore opponents and run campaigns devoid of substance. Thus, barring political broadcast advertising would further enhance the incumbent's already powerful position while decreasing accountability in the political marketplace. Attacking an opponent is not unethical, and negative or comparative advertising can be a healthy addition to political discourse as long as it truthfully portrays what the opposition represents.

### Campaigns and the Free Press

Recent candidates have complained, with justification, that the only way to get free media coverage for their campaign was to introduce a new television ad. Before the 1988 primaries, political columnist David Broder wrote that "too few papers monitored what was being said—or evaded—in the face-to-face campaigning. Too few pushed aggressively for news conferences and interviews in which the candidate would have to speak for himself—not hide behind his media managers."[25] It would be difficult to argue otherwise.

Of the vast number of articles in nine leading national newspapers, on the individual 1986 Senatorial contests, a substantial proportion—perhaps half—focused on paid political advertising and other aspects of modern campaign technology, one-third dealt with money in politics, and only about 15 percent focused specifically on issues. The detailing of current and past candidate indiscretions—and the impact of their revelation on the candidate's standing in the polls—dominated early coverage of the 1988 presidential contest. Candidate issue positions were largely ignored. The television networks, in the words of Republican political consultant Eddie Mahe, "cover the elections as though they were covering a horse race, disregarding what the horses are saying." While the news media deplore the supposed mud-slinging and dearth of in-depth issues in campaigns, they actually bear much of the responsibility for creating the very situation they have spent so much print and air time criticizing. As Senator Jim Broyhill (R-N.C.) said during a campaign press conference, "It's you news people who try to make a negative campaign. You just asked me a question to try to get me to hit on my opponent."[26]

### Conclusion

One of the great myths of the American political system is that the democratic ideal means candidates talking directly to the voters and appealing, face-to-face, for support. Envisioned as old-fashioned politics, it is a fantasy, and has never really existed in twentieth-century America. There once was a time, about a century ago, when candidates could literally walk their district and personally greet many of their constituents. Today, no candidate has enough time and energy to meet even one-tenth of the roughly 600,000 people in a congressional district, or the millions of voters in a statewide race. If the two Senate candidates in Florida could shake the hands of 120 people an hour for 24 hours a day, it would take three years to meet every individual who voted in the 1986 election. If they made 10 speeches a day to audiences of 100 persons, it would take eight years to reach every voter.[27]

Integration of television into the political environment in the 1960s and 1970s enabled candidates, for the first time, to appear, in bodily form, in the homes of constituents. In the next decade, the typical statewide campaign will spend at least half of its dollars on political advertising, and will reach more voters, more often with more information. Although still far away in Washington, D.C., elected officials have become less obscure and more accountable figures to the average voter than in the days before television. Television advertising has given many American voters the ability to recognize the candidates' names and faces—and learn something about the background of the people they are electing. Thus, voters today have far more knowledge about the candidates than voters had as recently as the late 1950s or 1960s. Granted, the quantity and quality of information may be less than some would prefer, but today's voters still have the opportunity to acquire a sense of the personality and character of the candidates, and at least a superficial knowledge of their position on the issues.

At the same time, candidates also know more about the voters than they ever did before. Voter opinion research, derived from polling data and from analysis of demographic data and election statistics, has institutionalized a two-way communication link. If television commercials tend to encourage superficiality in politics, television is still the most efficient way and sometimes the only way for candidates to respond to voter concerns. The electorate's increasing dependence on television for news and information makes this expensive mode of communication an indispensable instrument for effective political speech. After all, the 30-second spot is still less superficial and more informative than shaking hands and kissing babies. A 45-minute campaign video imparts more of a candidate's personality than an eight to ten minute campaign appearance. The candidate cannot personally meet every voter, though television advertising and campaign videos are not a poor substitute. "It's the political equivalent of [candidate] cloning," concluded Jack Kemp's press secretary John Buckley.[28]

In summary, the political environment has shaped the modern methods of campaigning, and, like it or not, the players must play by the rules. Neither candidates nor consultants nor political pundits can ignore the current methods of electoral communication simply because they do not like them. In the campaigns of an era now past, candidates had to rely on the door-to-door canvassing by party workers and volunteers to keep somewhat abreast of voter attitudes. Now they commission pollsters to inform them of public opinion and hire media consultants to assist in message dissemination. Formerly, candidates depended on political bosses for advice, and political machines for turning out voters. Now they have expensive political consultants, with their intricate strategies for maximizing public support. Television and radio were once a luxury and a rarity in a political campaign. Now they are a necessity and commonplace.

Modern campaign technology has evolved and prospered because of the financial constraints found in current federal election laws. As long as legal political contributions are limited, and campaign expenditures limitless, those seeking public office will spend even more time fundraising, less time on the campaign trail, and will become more dependent on sophisticated election techniques. The race for new and better campaign technologies to market the overextended candidate will continue. But it is the candidates, not the technology or its practitioners, that will be responsible for the movement of American democracy toward or away from the American people. Technology is inherently neutral. Candidates and their campaigns are not.

The democratic political process depends on an interested and informed electorate. Campaigns of the 1980s have used modern technology effectively to provide voters with more information than otherwise would have been available. Failure to utilize the latest advances in communication would increasingly detach the elected representative from the voter, and eventually weaken the American political process. It is of particular importance that candidates be given the opportunity to make their views known to the electorate, permitting a thoughtful evaluation of the candidates' personal qualities and their positions on public issues. Whether by direct mail or television advertising, survey research or satellite transmission, modern campaign technology is providing the means to attain the ultimate democratic goal—an informed electorate.

NOTES

1. Quoted in *Washington Times* (5 November 1986)
2. Federal Election Commission Press Release, (10 May 1987)
3. Ibid.
4. *Campaigns & Elections* (March/April 1988), p.7.
5. Hearings before the Senate Committee on Rules and Administration, *Proposed Amendments to the Federal Election Campaign Act of 1971*, p. 3.
6. *New York Times* (14 November 1986)
7. Ibid., (7 November 1986)
8. Hearings before the Senate Committee on Rules and Administration, *Campaign Finance Reform Proposals of 1983*, (Washington, D.C., U.S. Government Printing Office, 1983), p. 46.
9. *New York Times* (14 November 1986)
10. *Campaigns & Elections* (January/February 1988), p. 48.
11. *Washington Post* (24 September 1986)
12. *USA Today* (27 October 1986)
13. *New York Times* (17 October 1987)
14. *Washington Post* (2 November 1986)
15. *New York Times* (14 November 1986)
16. *U.S. News & World Report* (7 March 1988), p. 29.
17. Ibid.
18. Ibid.
19. *Congressional Record* (23 February 1988), p. S 1260.
20. Ibid.
21. Ibid.
22. "The McLaughlin Group" (15 April 1988)
23. *Washington Post* (10 November 1986)
24. *Campaigns & Elections* (July/August 1986), p. 12.
25. *Washington Post* (2 November 1986)
26. *Baltimore Sun* (15 October 1986)
27. *Christian Science Monitor* (14 October 1986)
28. *Los Angeles Times* (8 December 1987)

Adapted with permission from *Candidates, Consultants and Campaigns* by Frank Luntz, published by Basil Blackwell, Oxford.

# MONEY, CONSULTANTS, TELEVISION AND CAMPAIGN TECHNOLOGY: Excerpts from the 1988 "Congressional Record"

*Frank Luntz*

Politics has got so expensive that it takes a lot of money even to get beat.

*Will Rogers*

Election reform legislation has been debated by every Congress since the passage of the last major election law amendments in 1979. The House and Senate have held endless hours of hearings each year into the problems of the American electoral system. Academics and scholars—and the occasional political consultant—are regularly invited to testify, offering their support or opposition to the "reform" proposals under consideration. Once a year, the debate reaches the floor of the Senate (and, on occasion, the House), only to be rejected or sent back to committee for further refinement—or an untimely death.

On Monday, February 22, 1988, the U.S. Senate began five straight days of debate, more than 65 hours, dedicated almost exclusively to S.2, the Senate Election Campaign Act. The legislation was an amendment to the Federal Election Campaign Act of 1971 and provided for a voluntary system of spending limits and partial public financing of Senate general election campaigns, a limit to the contributions by multi-candidate political committees (PACs), and other electoral reforms.

At one point during the deliberation, the Senate had been in session for more than 54 straight hours. The inability to break the stalemate (supporters of the legislation were unable to muster the 60 votes necessary to terminate a lengthy filibuster) and bring the Campaign Act to a vote contributed to the often heated debate between members. Nevertheless, the five days were not without lighter moments. Late in the evening of February 23, Senate Majority Leader Robert Byrd ordered the Sergeant at Arms to arrest and bring to the floor of the Senate any member deliberately absent from quorum votes. First accosted was Senator Lowell Weicker (R-Conn.), a rather bulky and temperamental individual, who warned his posse that they would need "a steel net and three tranquilizer guns" to force his presence on the Senate floor. The

Capitol guards then broke the lock to Senator Bob Packwood's (R-Ore.) outer office and physically carried the Senator into the Senate chamber. Packwood's hand was injured in the fray, requiring medical assistance.

Although the 1988 election legislation was primarily directed toward reducing overall campaign expenditures, much of the debate focused on two factors that have significantly contributed to the spiraling cost of running for federal office: television advertising and political consultants. Neither factor is new to American electoral politics. Every presidential nominee since 1952 has used television advertising. Professional political consultants have been advising presidential and statewide candidates for more than two decades. However, recent election cycles have witnessed a sharp increase in the dissatisfaction among candidates—and voters—toward both the techniques used by political consultants to market their clients, and the increasingly aggressive and negative tone of paid political advertising. Since it is the candidates who are most personally affected by changes in campaign environment, it is appropriate here to consider their opinions and concerns related to the current direction of the American electoral process.

The following *Congressional Record* excerpts were selected because they most closely focus on modern campaign technology, highlighting the impact of television advertising and the involvement of professional campaign advisors on the electoral process. The reader should note that the condemnation of political consultants and negative advertising included in this chapter are nearly unanimous—and are a fair representation of at-large Senate opinion. However, it must also be noted that *every* individual quoted maintained at least one political consultant on retainer during a recent Senate campaign, and a large majority were users of negative advertising as well.

*Senator Rudy Boschwitz* (R-Minn.)
(S1131,1136—23 February 1988)

In my judgment, winning votes is not just done by virtue of running a 30-second TV ad. As a matter of fact, many of our [Republican] candidates in the last election were defeated because they thought they could address their constituency in 30-second TV ads rather than addressing them in person and getting them involved in the political process.

When you put a limit on campaign spending, you also put a limit on grassroots involvement. The people who will consult and the people who will plan these campaigns will try to take the largest portion of campaign dollars and put it into even more expensive TV commercials. Then they will take large portions of the stipulated amount that can be spent on campaigns and make more and more complex TV commercials that will cost more and more.

*Senator Daniel Evans* (R-Wash.)
(S1287—25 February 1988)

There is going to be a lot of opportunity for [candidates] to get their message across to the voters. How do they get it across? They get it across in the ways that they believe are going to be most successful in electing them to political office. They have a whole new group of professionals that we did not have a generation ago. We did not even have them when I first ran for office, or in the second or third term. It is a brand new group that has now come along. They are the gurus of selling candidates.

Frankly, Mr. President, I think they have done more harm than good to the American political scene. They have crassly taken candidates and, in fact, told some candidates, "Look, we can take you and mold you and create you and sell you and, in fact, if we do it just right you do not even have to make much, if anything, in the way of personal appearance. We will just put [you] on the tube, carefully done in the right ways," and like a whole bunch of Max Headrooms we end up as nonpersons.

We are all two dimensional, flat on a television tube, instead of real people out there campaigning and talking and running campaigns in the way we used to. These gurus, who now take a lot of the money, have found that one of the best ways to ensure your candidate's success is to find that negative political advertising that will really skewer your opponent and convince the voter not that you are the best person for political office, but that the other guy is not good enough for public office. It seems to me, Mr. President, that that is one of the most evil things that has happened to our political scene as time has gone on.

It is not new. We have had negative political advertising in the whole 200 years of American political history. But negative political advertising in past years was at least mixed with the personal appearances of candidates, their speeches in front of hundreds, sometimes thousands, of people who would turn out to listen and to hear from a candidate as to where they stood and what they believed. It was harder for them than it is now. They had to get in their buggies or ride their horses and go distances to arrive at where the candidate was going to be. It took time and effort and they took that time and effort and they learned, and they ended up knowing a whole lot more about what that candidate stood for than most citizens know about candidates today in this time of instantaneous communication.

It should not be done that way, but it is, and it is because these gurus of political wisdom have told us that negative advertising is the way to political success.

*Senator Brock Adams* (D-Wash.)
(S1531—26 February 1988)

I faced an incumbent Senator in my campaign. He spent more money than I did but I was still able to win that race. The amount of money spent is not an indicator of the outcome. More is not necessarily better. But more is necessarily an invitation to excess.

Any political candidate can spend more money. We can always want to put on another 30-second TV spot or print another 100,000 copies of a brochure or hire a few more consultants and staffers. All of that spending may make sense in the context of the internal logic of the campaign; but that doesn't mean it makes any sense in terms of the larger logic of American democracy.

As a result of our ability to raise and spend so much money, the nature of campaigns has changed. Today's uncontrolled political spending has given rise to a professional group of people who have no interest in government, just in who governs. There is a whole industry which caters to the needs of campaigns. We have consultants who specialize in political functions which didn't even exist 10 years ago. There are the TV image makers, the direct mail fundraisers, the PAC solicitors, the computer specialists who manage lists, the pollsters, the Federal Election Commission specialists, the phone bank suppliers—the list goes on. There are even trade magazines for these people full of tips on techniques and notices of job openings.

These people play a crucial role in modern campaigns; but they didn't play an essential role. We can create a message even if we don't avail ourselves of all of their services; and we can take that message to voters without becoming overly dependent on them. Will our campaigns be as professional if we decrease our dependence on these specialists? Probably not. But they may be a little more meaningful.

*Senator Alan Simpson* (R-Wyo.)
(S1533—26 February 1988)

The reason we are all running around looking for money is because it costs so darned much to do television. It costs so darn much to get your message across. That is what is killing us all. We are a bunch of bagmen running all over the United States, and the reason for it is because our friends in television and the media have decided that the rate goes up whenever we decide to do this biennial or quadrennial exercise.

And then media consultants. All of us have to go to charm school. Then we go out and learn how to look at the camera and pay about 10 grand for that, and learn how to speak and elocute. That is what costs us the bucks. Let us not pretend that it is anything else.

*Senator Dan Quayle* (R-Ind.)
(S1249—23 February 1988)

During this debate, I have heard the amount of money we spend on congressional campaigns called a national embarrassment, a national disgrace, a corrupting influence. As a matter of fact, we have even heard worse. But, is there something inherently wrong about spending money in campaigns? The point has been made before but it bears repeating: The amount of money spent to elect the President and Congress in 1984 was less than the amount spent by the Nation's leading advertiser, Proctor & Gamble for its products that same year. Surely educating the electorate about those who make critical national decisions is at least as important as one company's annual advertising budget for soap and toothpaste.

Perhaps the greatest reason for the high cost of elections is something the Senate simply cannot control, the rapid growth in the cost of TV and radio advertising. Both media are central to Senate campaigns. Fifty percent of a typical Senate campaign budget goes toward broadcasting media advertising.

I also might add that another huge cost in campaigning comes from the so-called consultants. My wife happens to be one of my chief political consultants. Her advice, which I solicit a lot, is free. I do not have to pay for that. But there are a lot of other consultants that you do have to pay for. You have to have your media consultant. Sometimes people think you ought to have a [general] political consultant. And you also need a pollster. We always have to take polls. They are sort of like an addict that gets his fix. That is the way the politicians get their fix. They have to take polls. Those are expensive.

*Senator Dennis DeConcini* (D-Ariz.)
(S1527—26 February 1988)

Some have suggested that there is nothing wrong with these escalating costs—that in fact more is spent each year on selling dog food, and toothpaste than on selling Senators. But that is just the point; we are not selling Senators. The election process when the electorate must make an informed decision on who should run this country, should not be based on who has the snappiest ad campaign, the best hair dresser, or the best TV personality. Voter decisions should be made on the issues, on facts.

It is these very facts that have become obscured by expensive advertising campaigns and the pressures to raise money. The 100 Members of this body should not be packaged and sold like so much shampoo. But because Members must spend so much of their time raising money for multimillion dollar campaigns, they have less and less time to spend with the voters, and this is a tragedy.

*Senator John Kerry* (D-Mass.)
(S1524—26 February 1988)

The measure of a democracy and the measure of participation is not money and should not be money. The measure of an American's ability to be able to participate in our system is according to the first amendment. And the right to associate freely and organize and speak freely is, in the democratic process, best articulated through the vote, through the organizational ability, through the grass-

roots kind of politics that money has taken us away from.

The reason the cost of campaigns goes up each year is not that the cost of organizing goes up, but that the cost of media goes up. And the media costs are incessantly higher and higher because each candidate comes to the political trough believing that if they can just buy that extra ad, if they can just get an extra minute on television, they may win.

*Senator James Sasser* (D-Tenn.)
(S1059-1060—22 February 1988)

The pressure is there to raise huge amounts of money for the very simple reason that if you do not, your opponent certainly will, and you will be unable to compete on even terms with the well-financed, well-heeled opponent, and the result is this: Candidates spending too much time raising money and too little time talking to voters and letting the voters know what the views of the candidates are on the great issues of the day. This is not good for democracy, and it is not good for the United States of America.

Every election year we see the percentage of those citizens who participate going down, down, down. The result is there for all to see: A decline in individual contributors, 'debate' conducted in 30-second snatches, and wave on wave on wave of nasty and expensive TV commercials.

We saw in the last round of senatorial elections not candidates talking to voters but candidates running all across the country raising money to finance more television ads, with political reporters coming into States not talking to voters but simply looking at the television ads that were being run in those particular States and making their judgments on how the campaigns would turn out, because that is all there was to the campaigns in many States, just television and radio ads.

*Senator Frank Murkowski* (R-Alaska)
(S1328—25 February 1988)

Millions and millions of dollars that go to campaign committees each election do not end up in the candidate's pocket. The money is spent on the media throughout this country, the television, the newspapers, the brochures and the like. Candidates do not determine the price of a full-page ad or a 30-

second television advertisement. The media does that. Those large sums of money that are criticized are the amounts that candidates must raise in order to pay the media bills. . . . Paid advertising is one of the principal ways to get to tell our side of the story.

The news media does objectively inform the public about the candidates, about the positions, but we have all experienced the occasion when the media chooses to take a side, to promote a favored candidate or a political position. The only alternative for a candidate then is to purchase advertising if he or she wants to be very sure of getting his or her point of view across.

What options are available when the media decides to get involved in a campaign? There are no controls on how much campaigning they can do editorially for or against a candidate and rightfully so; our Constitution gives them that privilege. What we can do as candidates is to buy space to put in our side of the story. So advertising truly during a campaign is the principal option available to us to correct attacks on our record that we choose to respond to.

*Senator John Breaux* (D-La.)
(S1317—25 February 1988)

I know when I considered running for this seat . . . the first thing I had to consider and the very first thing that professionals in this business came to me and asked was, "Can you raise the money? Do you have access to huge amounts of money that it is going to take to run a Statewide campaign in the State of Louisiana."

I was told in some of my first meetings that, well, you are going to have to raise about $8,000 a day—I think that is what the figure was—in order to be a Member of the U.S. Senate. I said that is ridiculous. You do not have to do something like that. I cannot afford it. How am I in a State that is literally in a depression with 13 percent unemployment going to raise $8,000 a day in order to be a Member of the U.S. Senate? I was told, well, you have to get out of Louisiana and, of course, they were right.

So I found myself, Mr. President, during my early stages of our campaign in California, New York, Chicago, and Miami, and people would say, well, you are not going to get elected in those States, in those cities. What are you doing? Why are you all over

the United States when you are supposed to be running and tell the people of Louisiana why you could be a good U.S. Senator.

The reason I was in all of those cities was because I was not independently wealthy. I did not have access to millions and millions of dollars of funds. So I have to travel throughout the United States like a person with a tin cup. I really felt like a person who passes the collection basket in church.

*Senator David Durenberger* (R-Minn.)
(S1176—23 February 1988)

One of the unfortunate things that I have noticed over the years in this political fundraising business is that the cost of collecting the money, whether it is telemarketing, which is one of these latest inventions—everybody is on the phone at night catching you when you are trying to doze off or have a conversation with your spouse—or the direct mail campaign—mailing lists get run all around the country so everybody gets your mailing—whatever the case may be, the costs of spreading the base under the system are rising. So I said to the degree that somebody else can help in the collection process, all of us benefit. In other words, more money goes into the message than goes into the fundraiser.

*Senator Charles Grassley* (R-Iowa)
(S1051-1052—22 February 1988)

Challengers do not have to spend more money than incumbents to win. But challengers must spend *enough* money to win. They need to spend at least enough money to bring their case to the voters.

Political science research indicates that incumbents may actually do worse in elections if they spend too much money. Money, however, really is the 'make or break' component in the campaign of a challenger. . . . A challenger, however, cannot begin to launch a credible campaign without spending enough money to communicate effectively with the voters.

By allowing a challenger to raise enough money to deliver an election message, the better able the voter will be to make a clear-cut choice. A choice between candidates, between candidates of comparable visibility and credibility, is one of the most essential components of an electoral democracy.

# FRAGMENTATION OF THE ELECTORATE

"One danger in the new political technologies is that some of these technologies tend to work in tandem with the cultural fragmentation of the American people—and thus the American electorate—over the last few decades.

The new technologies enable politicians to direct different messages to segmented media cubicles.

We see this in cable satellite feeds, and in direct mail where they can classify you according to your nine-digit zip code and what mailing lists you appear on. Segmented media cubicles also exist on radio. There are radio stations in the United States where you can be guaranteed that virtually nobody who is white or nobody who is over 22 will be listening. And you can direct a message to that audience.

Thus, technologies are increasingly fragmenting our electorate. This is dangerous."

*Michael Barone*

"I was a member of the Illinois delegation to the Democratic National Convention some years ago. Mayor Daley was the leader of our delegation. We were seated opposite the California delegation. One time when not much was going on, one of the Chicago regulars got into a conversation with one of the California delegates who asked, "Isn't it terrible how unreliable the polls are?" Our Chicagoan replied, "I don't know what you are talking about, lady. We can always rely on the Poles." She responded, "Well, our experience in California is that you just can't depend on the polls." He answered, "Lady, I don't know what you're talking about. If there is anybody you can depend upon in Chicago it is the Poles." This went on for 15 minutes before they realized that each of them had a different conception of a poll."

*Newton N. Minow*

*Much of new communications technology—especially cable and targeted mass mailings—contributed to balkanizing the mass audiences. More than half of America's homes are now wired for cable, and interconnects among cable systems also encourage campaigns to create their own local, regional or national networks.*

*Increased storage capacity of microcomputers is permitting ever more highly sophisticated uses of mail. Campaigns can target television, radio and written messages neighborhood by neighborhood, minimizing waste and addressing appeals to specific groups such as voters who speak a particular language. Using demographic data for each area served by a cable headend, campaigns can address mail to certain types of cable viewers.*

*Such targeting will have significant effects, many of them positive. Social, ethnic and other groupings that give America much of its strength deserve to be addressed as separate entities. Breaking down mass-directed messages can improve political communications and move politicians beyond rhetoric that sounds like fast-food jingles.*

*But fragmentation is also troublesome. Are we isolating ourselves into cultural cubicles? Are demographic groupings replacing partisan background as the chief determinants of voter behavior? Does fragmentation cause voter volatility and contribute to non-voting? Is concern about demographic clusters changing the focus of campaign journalism? If the audience is too segmented, the content of the message will change, but in what direction?*

*Some of these concerns are not new, as shown by the 1964 novel excerpted here, The 480, with its talk of "a new underworld." Following The 480 are excerpts that show how political campaigns utilize demographic data, reinforcing—and causing— fragmentation of the electorate.*

*Public policy is closely tied to this fragmentation. Politicians and public officials, following the lead of advertisers promoting goods and services, now target messages at groups such as DINKS (double income, no kids). This is far different than addressing Democrats or Republicans or conservatives or liberals, and it is becoming the best way to mobilize voters in modern America.*

*Government action promises to enhance this process. As discussed in the Checco-Brace essay, the 1990 Census will link its data with local precinct boundaries. This will permit perfected targeting, and promises to heighten at least one constitutional clash. The U.S. Supreme Court has ruled that political redistricting that consistently excludes or degrades the influence of a group of voters may be unconstitutional. Given technologies and 1990 census data, however, high-tech gerrymandering will be a strong temptation.*

*One word of warning: While fragmentation and demographic targeting are real, party label is still the single most important predictor of voter behavior.*

---

## THE 480

*Eugene Burdick*

There is a benign underworld in American politics. It is not the underworld of cigar-chewing pot-bellied officials who mysteriously run "the machine." Such men are still around, but their power is waning. They are becoming obsolete though they have not yet learned that fact.

The new underworld is made up of innocent and well-intentioned people who work with slide rules and calculating machines and computers which can retain an almost infinite number of bits of information as well as sort, categorize, and reproduce this information at the press of a button. Most of these people are highly educated, many of them are PhD.s, and none that I have met have malignant political designs on the American public. They may, however, radically reconstruct the American political system, build a new politics, and even modify revered and venerable American institutions—facts of which they are blissfully innocent. They are technicians and artists; all of them want, desperately, to be scientists.

The American public believes that it "chooses" the Party candidates for the Presidency and then makes a free and sovereign choice between the two candidates. This is hardly an accurate description of what happens. The American public believes it is sovereign. It is not. The American public believes that its views "trickle up" to the halls of the congress and the White House and become law. This is rarely so. The American public believes in some vague and undefined way that its opinion is a fundament of our democracy. Too often this is not the case.

This situation is not evil. There is no conspiracy against the American public. There is only a great gap in knowledge. A few know a great deal, the great mass know very little. The few that know decide the shape and character of American politics.

The presidential candidate will say, publicly, often, and with a profound hypocrisy that he believes in the "common man" and is appealing to him. It is a form of Plato's Royal Sie: there are plenty of common men about and all the candidates know them well. They will vote out of habit for the party they voted for at the last election, and the one before. The "uncommon man" is the person the candidates are trying to find, identify, analyze and appeal to. The victorious presidential candidate is the one who is most successful in appealing to the uncommon voter.

The "uncommon voter" is not, alas always a superior person. His "uncommonness" sometimes consists of being bloody minded, hostile, ignorant, frightened and prejudiced.

The presidential candidate will make the form appearances before the "bosses" and the political rallies, but he knows these are not important. Political dinners at $100 a plate will not affect the election. The presidential candidates this year care very little whether the major newspapers or *Time* or *Newsweek* endorse them. They will be courteous to editors and publishers, but they know that newspapers and magazines comment significantly after an election, not before. Most of the newspapers opposed F.D.R. each time he ran and it did not hurt him. It would appear that the American voters do not necessarily trust the political views of their newspapers.

Who will the presidential candidates listen to? They will attend most carefully to the views of their invisible underworld usually quite small. There is every reason to believe that President Kennedy defeated Vice President Nixon in 1960 in great part because President Kennedy had put together a perceptive, quick, and "scientific" group from the new underworld. Nixon tried but was not as successful as Kennedy in his recruiting.

Every presidential aspirant must say "I believe that the American people when they have all the facts will make the right decision." But he knows it is not true. The average American voter has neither the interest nor the information to make a rational decision between the two major presidential candidates. The average voter votes the way his father did. He tells his wife to vote the way he does . . . and usually she obeys. Furthermore, these American voters are exposed to words and slogans which have been carefully researched to make sure they have exactly the desired effect. The candidates listen to these expert, apolitical, neutrals much more closely than to any boss from Boston or Chicago or the Far West.

Why the phrase "new underworld"? Because these people operate in happy anonymity. This underworld, made up of psychologists, sociologists, pollsters, social survey experts and statisticians, cares little about issues. That is one reason the candidates keep them invisible. The *romantic* heart of politics is partisan rather than neutral and deals with issues rather than statistics.

There is nothing un-American in all of this. On the contrary, it is in the best American tradition to use new facts, new discoveries, new insights. But there is a potential here which is ominous. First, the existence and mode of operation of the new underworld should be made known to the people. Much of the information given to President Kennedy in 1960 was handled at the time as if it were "top secret" classified information. Copies of reports were numbered and the information was seen only by those who had to see it. This was not casual reading, this was armament for a major battle.

Slavish adherence to such advice might mean the end of statesmanship. Candidates often do not say what they believe: they say what they know the people want to hear. And if farmers want to hear something which is contradictory to what trade unionists want to hear, two speeches will be written. One will be delivered in Des Moines and the other in Detroit. The new techniques could make a science out of this hypocrisy.

"The public temperature" is taken. If the pulse is feverish, the public is told "fever is good. I support it." The "public pulse" is taken and if it is low the public is told "passivity is good. I stand four-square behind it."

This may or may not result in evil. Certainly it will result in the end of politics as Americans have known it in the past. . . .

From *The 480*, by Eugene Burdick (New York: McGraw-Hill Book Company, 1964).

## A CASE STUDY: DEMOGRAPHICS AND CAMPAIGNS

*David B. Hill and Mary M. Kent*

Alaska is entitled to one Representative in the U.S. Congress, elected at large. The seat has been held since 1973 by Don Young, Republican of Fort Yukon, a teacher in winter and river boat captain in summer before embarking on a long career in local and state politics. Young was elected to the Alaska state legislature in 1966 and served there until his election to the U.S. House of Representatives.

Congressman Young has relied on Edmonds Associates, media consultants based in Alexandria, Virginia, to assist in each reelection bid since 1980, but he disagreed with Edmonds' approach to his 1984 campaign. At first.

Edmonds' discussions with politicians and political "pros" in Alaska highlighted the importance of migration for the state. As of 1980, two-thirds of the residents had moved there from another state or country. Young himself was born in Meridian, California. The general consensus was that a lot of Texans and other oil people were coming because of the North Slope oil fields.

For the 1984 campaign, Edmonds Associates ordered a demographic run-down from a subsidiary of the Population Reference Bureau, now established as Decision Demographics. Tom Edmonds says, "We knew it was

a 'transient' state, with a high population turnover. We needed to know the numbers. And what the numbers don't say. Who did we lose? Who did we gain? Who are the new people?

The demographic analysis described an influx of young, well-educated professionals from the West Coast into Alaska. Less than 6 percent of recent migrants had come from Texas; about a half had settled in Anchorage, Alaska's largest city.

The analysis documented a larger-than-expected turnover in population. Partly because of the completion of the oil pipeline and closing of military bases, over 100,000 people left Alaska between 1975 and 1980, slightly more than the number moving into the state during that period.

"What we learned from the demographers," says Tom Edmonds, "was that though Don Young had been the Representative from Alaska since 1973, while he had been around for quite a while, the 1984 voters hadn't. They didn't know who he was, or what he had done. They had to be educated." Edmonds recommended airing a 2-minute political biography, rather than the customary 30-second commercials, documenting all that Don Young had accomplished for Alaska. Congressman Young thought that was ridiculous: he had been in politics for over 20 years, everyone knew who he was and what he had done for the state. So Edmonds had to educate him, using figures from the demographic analysis.

The next major task was finding an issue. "You need an emotional issue without a downside; a win-win situation," advised Tom Edmonds. "It was also fairly easy to find an 'enemy' because of the Alaskan situation and character. Alaskans are anti-authority, even though so many of them work for the government; they resent the 'lower 48' making decisions concerning them. So the enemy was the blankety-blanks in the lower 48 who know nothing whatsoever about the special conditions of life in Alaska. And the hero is Don Young, who made the state into what drew the newcomers."

Their media spots stressed Young's role in making the Trans-Alaska Pipeline possible, overcoming "economic" objections to its construction and enriching the state. Young was also praised for supporting the 100-mile territorial limit on foreign fishing and controlling development on the 49 percent of Alaska that is "protected" land.

The result? Young received over 113,000

votes to his two opponents' 86,000 votes. "Only four times in Alaskan history has the vote total ever gone over 100,000. And three of those four times we've done it for Young," reports Tom Edmonds.

"The demographic data helped us discover who our target audience was, and what issue, what strategy would appeal to them. It told us where they were, and enough about them to help us determine who they were and what their interests were. And we won the election."

Reprinted with permission from David B. Hill and Mary Kent, *Election Demographics*, Population Trends and Public Policy Report No. 14 (Washington, D.C.: Population Reference Bureau, Inc., January 1988), p. 10.

## THE REAL ELECTORATE

*Norman J. Ornstein and Larry Hugick*

For the past several years, it has been apparent to political analysts that the existing, traditional typologies—Democrat/Independent/Republican; liberal/conservative—are simply not adequate either to predict political behavior or to classify voters. True, partisan identification has remained a powerful tool. But increasing defections, weaker identification and some signs of instability in the long-stable measures (temporary, sharp movements, for example, right after the 1980 and 1984 elections) have limited somewhat the utility of party alone, especially in the presidential election context.

At the same time, it has become clear that the terms liberal and conservative, in the Washington or elite context, do not easily apply to the mass electorate. Relatively few voters have the ideological constraint that Jesse Helms or Jesse Jackson, Howard Phillips or Howard Metzenbaum, do. Voters who are liberal on some subjects may be conservative on others, and vice versa—regardless of their self-identification on the ideological scale.

In the middle of an era of fluid politics, with the realignment/de-alignment debate in full force and approaching an open election, with no incumbent running, Times Mirror and Gallup decided to attempt to find a broader and more insightful typology to characterize the contemporary electorate.

Months of discussion led to a tentative decision to look at values, in addition to party, political involvement and issue positions. After a thorough literature review, we prepared a comprehensive set of questions eliciting responses on every value that had been mentioned in politically related studies. These questions (more than 70 in all) were asked, along with dozens of others, by Gallup interviewers in 70-minute, face-to-face interviews with 4,244 respondents in April and May of 1987.

Nine basic values [religious faith, tolerance/intolerance, social justice, militant anti-communism, alienating attitudes towards government, American exceptionalism, financial pressure, and attitudes towards business corporations] emerged in the factor analysis that followed; when the values were paired with party and political involvement, we discovered 11 separate and distinct voting groups that appeared to comprise the real electorate.

Are these groups stable and real? It appears so. Our approach has advantages and disadvantages, of course, but the typology seems to tap into real values and voter categories that should endure for some time, even if voters' political behavior changes. The values we elicited were not invented by us, or shaped by our preferences; they emerged from the respondents' own choices, grouped by factor analysis. Values should be more stable and deep-seated than simple issue positions; the typology, then, should have some inherent stability to it.

A look at the categories suggests the same; several groups have clear generational divisions (New Dealers, Sixties Democrats, Upbeats) based on formative generational experiences, not on ephemeral events. Other groups have ideological, partisan and socioeconomic links, which are also likely to be long-lasting. In several surveys we have done since the original, the types have all emerged intact, with few if any shifts suggesting an inherent instability in the categories.

Of course, 11 groups is an unwieldy number to keep in mind and to analyze, especially if one is used to dealing with three (Democrat, Independent, Republican; or liberal, moderate and conservative). But we have found that the number of groups is not a serious impediment. First, it suggests the greater complexity and sophistication in the electorate that in fact exists. Second, it enables one to view the two parties' electoral coalitions with more clarity—and to see the daunting tasks ahead for both the Democrats and Republicans as they seek to build enduring majorities.

The typology does not *replace* party as a key political measure; rather, it elaborates upon and clarifies party categories. There are actually two separate groups of Republicans; four separate and distinct groups of Democrats; and four groups of Independents, with two each leaning to the Democrats and the GOP. (The eleventh group, the Bystanders, is completely uninvolved in politics.) Working with the groups in this context for a short while leaves one readily conversant with the full range of them.

In fact, the typology becomes particularly useful when we narrow it down to focus on four key groups whose behavior is likely to determine the outcome of the 1988 presidential campaign. Two of the groups are Democratic-oriented, the New Dealers and the Seculars. The two others—the Upbeats and the Disaffecteds—lean to the GOP. Neither party can choose to ignore any of these four groups in attempting to put together a winning coalition.

### New Dealers

The largest of the four groups, and the one with the strongest tie to the Democratic Party is the New Dealers, people who find their roots in the old FDR coalition. These voters tend to be middle class, over 50 and to have been born into Democratic families. While they are pro-government and economically liberal, they are more conservative on social issues and defense.

The importance of the New Dealers to election '88 lies in their size, proven record of voting turnout, and past willingness to defect from Democratic ranks to support Republican presidential candidates. The Times Mirror studies have found that while the two voter groups who strongly identify with the GOP (Enterprisers and Moralists) have overwhelmingly stayed with their party's presidential candidates in recent contests, voters in the four core Democratic groups (New Dealers, Sixties Democrats, Partisan Poor and Passive Poor) have been much less loyal to their party. The New Dealers, who make up 15 percent of the voting public, are a particular problem: 30 percent of them report having voted for Ronald Reagan in 1984. Yet, they still identify strongly with the Democratic Party; an overwhelming 92 percent of them voted Democratic in the 1986 congressional elections. With New Dealers concentrated, strategically,

in the South and the Midwest—key electoral battlegrounds—the 1988 Democratic candidate must count on holding more of them than Walter Mondale did in 1984.

### Seculars

The second key swing group, the Seculars, has very different characteristics from the New Dealers. Seculars are white, well-educated and affluent. Disproportionately made up of members of the baby-boom generation, Seculars tend to live in large cities and suburbs on the East and West Coasts. In contrast to every other group in the Times Mirror typology, Seculars are characterized by their lack of belief in God. While very tolerant, socially liberal and dovish, they are not so liberal in economics, professing great concern about the deficit and no great enthusiasm for generous federal spending or higher taxes.

The Seculars represent a cultural elite whose potential political influence has been largely unrealized. Despite their upscale demography, they vote at levels just about at the national average. Perhaps this represents a hip cynicism about politics; part of it, though, comes from the tendency of baby boomers to settle down, have children, and form the voting habit later in life than previous generations. If Seculars come of age politically in 1988, and vote their political values rather than their pocketbooks, the Democrats will get a big lift.

Their recent voting history, however, has to give the party cause for concern. While Seculars side with the Democrats on most issues, less than half identify with the party. Even worse, the group shows a pattern of presidential defections; a full one-third voted for Reagan in 1984. Our Times Mirror/Gallup analysis found the strength of the economy was an important factor explaining Reagan's success with this group. So too was the Democratic Party's clear weakness in image when it comes to competence, either in governing or selecting candidates for office. A Democratic Party that looks indecisive and bumbling at the Atlanta convention would clearly have continuing problems keeping the Seculars in its camp.

### Upbeats

The third key group, the Upbeats, are young, optimistic and strongly pro-American. This voter group is largely under 40, middle income, and has little or no college training. Politically, Upbeats are a legacy of the Reagan presidency and era. While they are solidly pro-Reagan, their ties to the Republican Party are weak. Upbeats do not have sharply defined ideological views—they are relatively pro-government *and* pro-business, for example—and they are also largely tolerant of other people's lifestyles and beliefs.

As the youngest group in the electorate, Upbeats are forming voting habits they are likely to carry into the future. If this group, 9 percent of the voting public, can be brought firmly into the GOP fold, the Republican Party will be a major step closer to the realignment it has long sought. On the other hand, if the Democrats can break the GOP momentum among the Upbeats, stopping a Reagan enthusiasm before it becomes a Republican attachment, they can become more confident about maintaining their current edge among the voters.

President Reagan carried 86 percent of the Upbeat vote in 1984; he managed 78 percent in 1980. But in a survey we conducted last fall, only about half said they expected to vote Republican in 1988, while a quarter expected to support the Democratic candidate. George Bush's ties to Reagan will obviously help him with the Upbeats; Democrats must beware that they don't emphasize too negative and critical a message, or potential support among the Upbeats will melt away.

### Disaffecteds

The last key group is the Disaffecteds. This group contrasts sharply with the Upbeats in every way except political behavior. While also independent and Republican-leaning, Disaffecteds are middle-aged, middle-income, pessimistic, alienated and distrustful of business and political institutions. A disproportionately male group, many of them were likely Wallace voters in 1968 and Democrats for Nixon in 1972.

Their likelihood of voting is not high, but Disaffecteds make up a large enough proportion of the voting public to make a difference in a close election. Currently, many more Disaffecteds identify with the Republican Party (44 percent) than with the Democratic (26 percent), and 82 percent report having voted for Ronald Reagan in 1984, but they are more likely to have family links to the Democrats than to the GOP. Straddling the two parties, Disaffecteds seem to care less than any other typology group about which party a candidate

represents. And like the Upbeats, it is not just a question about how members of this group vote—but whether they vote at all . . .

Reprinted with permission from the April 11, 1988 edition of *The Polling Report*, a Washington, D.C.-based newsletter covering trends in public opinions.

## VOTERS GROUPED BY VALUES: THE TIMES MIRROR TYPOLOGY

*Norman Ornstein, Andrew Kohut and Larry McCarthy*

### Enterprise Republicans ("Enterprisers")

10 percent of adult population; 16 percent of likely electorate: Affluent, educated, 99 percent white, this group forms one of the two bedrocks of the Republican Party. As the name implies, Enterprisers are pro-business and anti-government. But what may surprise some is their tolerance and moderation on questions of personal freedom.

Who they are: 60 percent male, married, Northern European ancestry, suburban.

Key attitudes: Top concern is budget deficit, but overwhelmingly disapprove of tax increases to cut deficit. Oppose increased spending for health care, aid to homeless and programs for the elderly. Oppose more restrictions on abortion and quarantine for AIDS patients. Support "Star Wars" and aid to the Contras.

Lifestyle note: Group most likely to belong to a fraternal or civic organization; enjoy classical music.

Voting likelihood: High

Past vote: '86 Congressional—89% Republican

'84 Presidential—96% Reagan

'80 Presidential—93% Reagan

Information level: Very high

Heroes: Ronald Reagan, Lee Iacocca

Key events: Vietnam, the Reagan presidency

### Moral Republicans ("Moralists")

11 percent of adult population, 14 percent of likely electorate: Middle-aged, middle income, with a heavy concentration of Southerners, this group forms the second bedrock of the Republican Party. Moralists hold strong and very conservative views on social and foreign policy.

Who they are: 94 percent white, live in suburbs, small cities and rural areas, regular church-goers with a large number of "born-again" Christians.

Key attitudes: Strongly anti-abortion, pro-school prayer, favor death penalty and quarantine on AIDS patients, strongly anti-communist, pro-defense, favor social spending except when it is targeted to minorities. Deficit and unemployment cited as top concerns.

Voting likelihood: High

Past vote: '86 Congressional—95 percent Republican
'84 Presidential—97 percent Reagan
'80 Presidential—92 percent Reagan

Information level: Average

Heroes: Ronald Reagan, Billy Graham

Key events: Vietnam, the Reagan presidency

### Upbeats

9 percent of adult population, 9 percent of likely electorate: Young, optimistic and strong believers in America, this group leans solidly to the GOP. Unlike most groups (especially Republican-leaning groups), the Upbeats are *not* critical of the government's role in society.

Who they are: Middle income, little or no college, 94 percent white, under 40, strongly pro-Reagan.

Key attitudes: Identify the deficit and economic concerns as top problems, give moderate support to "Star Wars," but oppose Contra aid and fear it will lead to military involvement.

Lifestyle note: Enjoy rock 'n' roll, have highest readership of romance novels.

Voting likelihood: Average

Past vote: '86 Congressional— 64 percent Republican
'84 Presidential—86 percent Reagan
'80 Presidential—78 percent Reagan

Information level: Average

Heroes: Ronald Reagan, Lee Iacocca, John F. Kennedy

Key events: Vietnam, the Reagan presidency

### Disaffecteds

9 percent of adult population, 7 percent of likely electorate: Alienated, pessimistic, skeptical of both big government and big business,

this group leans Republican, but many of its members have historic ties to Democratic Party.

Who they are: Middle-aged, middle income, slightly more male than average, Disaffecteds live in higher numbers in the Midwest. Disaffecteds say they feel significant personal financial pressure.

Key attitudes: Strongly anti-government and anti-business, but pro-military, Disaffecteds strongly support capital punishment and oppose gun control. They are divided on abortion. Generally support social spending unless specifically targeted to minorities. Unemployment and budget deficit are top concerns.

Lifestyle note: Most Disaffecteds say Country and Western is their favorite music. Group with the highest number of hunters.

Voting likelihood: Slightly below average

Past vote: '86 Congressional—57 percent Republican
'84 Presidential—81 percent Reagan
'80 Presidential—69 percent Reagan

Information level: Average

Heroes: None

Key events: Vietnam, Watergate

### Bystanders

11 percent of adult population, 0 percent of likely electorate: Young, poorly educated and marked by an almost total lack of interest in current affairs, Bystanders are just that—non-participants in American democracy.

Who they are: Bystanders tend to be under 30, 82 percent white, 13 percent black, with a substantial number of unmarried individuals. When asked which party they prefer, Bystanders lean Democratic 34 percent to 29 percent.

Key attitudes: This is the only group that says they do not care who is elected president in 1988—57 percent hold this view. To the extent they hold positions on issues, Bystanders tend to hold fairly conventional views. Their top concerns are unemployment, poverty and the threat of nuclear war.

Lifestyle note: For many Bystanders, their favorite activity is going to clubs and discos.

Voting likelihood: Close to zero.

Past vote: —

Information level: Low

Heroes: John F. Kennedy

Key events: Vietnam, the Reagan presidency

### Followers

7 percent of adult population, 4 percent of likely electorate: With a very limited interest in politics, this group has little faith in America, but is surprisingly uncritical of both government and business. While they lean to the Democratic Party, Followers are very persuadable and unpredictable.

Who they are: Young, poorly educated, blue-collar, Eastern and Southern, little religious commitment, 18 percent Hispanic, 25 percent black (most of whom are under 30).

Key attitudes: Oppose "Star Wars" and favor increased spending to reduce unemployment. At the national midpoint on almost all other issues. While this group leans Democratic, it's divided on Reagan approval. Ted Kennedy receives strong support from this group.

Lifestyle note: Of all the groups, Followers are the least likely to exercise regularly or read for pleasure.

Voting likelihood: Low
Past vote: '86 Congressional—65 percent Democratic
'84 Presidential—54 percent Reagan
'80 Presidential—40 percent Reagan
Information level: Very low
Heroes: John F. Kennedy
Key events: Vietnam

### Seculars

8 percent of adult population, 9 percent of likely electorate: The only group in America that professes no religious belief. This well-educated, white, middle-aged group combines a strong commitment to personal freedom, moderate beliefs on social questions and a very low level of anti-communism. Despite their views, only a minority of Seculars think of themselves as Democrats and their political participation does not match their high level of knowledge and sophistication.

Who they are: Heavily concentrated on the East and West coasts, professional, 11 percent Jewish.

Key attitudes: Favor cuts in military spending, oppose "Star Wars," school prayer, anti-abortion legislation, relaxing environmental controls. Top concern is budget deficit. On social spending, Seculars differ from core Democratic groups in opposing increased aid for minorities and farmers.

Lifestyle note: Nearly one-half regularly attend theater, ballet or classical music concerts.

Voting likelihood: Slightly above average
Past vote: '86 Congressional— 72 percent Democratic
'84 Presidential—34 percent Reagan
'80 Presidential—29 percent Reagan
Information level: Very high
Heroes: Martin Luther King, Jr., John F. Kennedy, Franklin Delano Roosevelt
Key events: Vietnam, Watergate

### '60s Democrats

8 percent of adult population, 11 percent of likely electorate: This upper-middle-class, heavily female (60 percent) group of mainstream Democrats has a strong commitment to social justice and a very low militancy level. They strongly identify with the peace, civil rights and environmental movements that grew out of the 1960s. They combine church-going and religious beliefs with a very high degree of tolerance for views and lifestyles they do not share.

Who they are: Well-educated, married women with children, 16 percent black (most of whom are college educated).

Key attitudes: Favor increased spending on programs for minorities and most other forms of social spending. Strong opposition to "Star Wars". Feel U.S. is too suspicious of the Soviet Union. Although '60s Democrats support the Democratic agenda, they harbor doubts about some of the candidates the party nominates.

Lifestyle note: Heavy readers, exercise regularly, work with youth groups.

Voting likelihood: High
Past vote: '86 Congressional— 85 percent Democratic
'84 Presidential—25 percent Reagan
'80 Presidential—10 percent Reagan
Information level: Very high
Heroes: Martin Luther King, Jr., John F. Kennedy
Key events: Vietnam, civil rights movement, '60s assassinations

### New Deal Democrats ("New Dealers")

11 percent of adult population, 15 percent of likely electorate: The roots of this aging group of traditional Democrats can be found in the

New Deal Democratic coalition. Blue-collar, union members, moderate income with little financial pressure, religious, intolerant on questions of personal freedom, yet favor many social spending measures.

Who they are: Older (66 percent over 50), 29 percent Catholic, less likely to live in the West.

Key attitudes: The largest group of Democrats with significant defections to Reagan in '84, they came back to the Democratic Party in 1986. Favor most social spending except when specifically targeted to minorities. Favor more restrictions on abortions, school prayer, protectionism and "Star Wars." Less concerned about the environment.

Lifestyle note: Heavy television viewers, especially game shows, nighttime soaps and religious shows. Prefer Country and Western music.

Voting likelihood: High
Past vote: '86 Congressional—92 percent Democratic
'84 Presidential—30 percent Reagan
'80 Presidential—21 percent Reagan
Information level: Average
Heroes: Franklin Delano Roosevelt, John F. Kennedy
Key events: The Depression, the New Deal

### God and Country Democrats

7 percent of adult population, 6 percent of likely electorate: Older and poor, this solidly Democratic group has a strong faith in America and is uncritical of its institutions and leadership. Committed to social justice, the Passive Poor are also moderately anti-communist.

Who they are: Less well-educated, Southern, 31 percent black, poor, but feel only moderate financial pressure.

Key attitudes: Favor all forms of increased social spending, more supportive of tax increases than any other group. Favor "Star Wars" and oppose cuts in defense spending. Moderately anti-abortion. Favor relaxing environmental standards for economic growth.

Lifestyle note: Heavy television viewers.
Voting likelihood: Below average
Past vote: '86 Congressional— 83 percent Democratic
'84 Presidential—31 percent Reagan
'80 Presidential—21 percent Reagan

Information level: Low
Heroes: John F. Kennedy, Franklin Delano Roosevelt, Martin Luther King, Jr., Ted Kennedy
Key events: Vietnam, '60s assassinations, the Depression

### The Partisan Poor

9 percent of adult population, 9 percent of likely electorate: The most firmly Democratic group in the country—very low income, feel very high financial pressure. The Partisan Poor are very concerned with social justice issues and have a strong faith that the Democratic Party can achieve the social changes they want to see.

Who they are: 37 percent black, low income, Southern, urban, poorly educated.

Key attitudes: Strong advocates of all social spending, but oppose tax increases. Favor death penalty, school prayer amendment, but divided on abortion. Unemployment top issue. Little concern for budget deficit, but favor cutting defense spending.

Lifestyle note: Heavy television viewers, light readers.
Voting likelihood: Slightly above average
Past vote: '86 Congressional—95 percent Democratic
'84 Presidential—19 percent Reagan
'80 Presidential—16 percent Reagan
Information level: Low
Heroes: John F. Kennedy, Martin Luther King, Jr., Franklin Delano Roosevelt, Ted Kennedy
Key events: JFK presidency, '60s assassinations, civil rights movement.

Reprinted with permission from *The People, the Press, & Politics*, Reading, Mass., Addison-Wesley Publishing Company, Inc., 1988.

## COMPUTER-AIDED DIRECT MAIL DELIVERS THE 'PERSONAL' TOUCH

*Bill Peterson, The Washington Post, September 16, 1986*

ST. PETERSBURG, Fla.—The "invisible" part of Sen. Paula Hawkins' reelection campaign operates out of a sterile-looking room in an industrial park here. In the room is an IBM

4341 mainframe computer and a Storage Tech cold laser printer.

The printer, not much bigger than a kitchen dishwasher, can spit out 20,000 "personally" addressed letters per hour. It can make letters look as if they were typed in the White House, or scribbled in the senator's own handwriting from a hospital bed.

Hawkins, a first-term Republican facing a tough reelection battle against Democratic Gov. Bob Graham, has sent 900,000 such letters in recent months. Each personally addressed letter costs about 40 cents to produce and mail; each has brought an average of almost $1 in return.

Hawkins has mailed letters over the signatures of President Reagan, Senate Majority Leader Robert J. Dole (R-Kan.), Sen. Orrin G. Hatch (R-Utah), her husband Gene and herself.

But most of the letters were written by Mike Pachik, the creative director of Direct Mail Systems (DMS), a Florida-based direct mail firm. The politicians simply approved and revised them. This is a standard direct-mail practice.

Each letter uses a chatty, personal tone. The Dole letter, for example, was dated "Tuesday evening" and noted that "Paula told me she has already written to you for help . . . and she didn't want to bother you again."

But there is a clear sense of urgency in each letter, a new crisis to overcome. And each contains an urgent appeal for money. "Emergency campaign funds are needed immediately for use in media advertising, literature distribution and other programs," declared the most recent letter, mailed to 20,000 "very special supporters."

Most of the crises involve "the Washington pressure groups," the "special interests," "the liberal Democrats" and the news media. "The Democrats and the liberal news media have tried their best to keep me down," one Hawkins letter said.

"If I were to lose, the liberals could control the entire Senate and stonewall all of President Reagan's programs," her most recent letter said. "Together, you and I and President Reagan are an unbeatable team. Right now, he and I need your help, more than ever."

Included with the letter was a light blue certificate—"suitable for framing." Printed on the certificate was the name of the recipient, an American flag and the notation, "In appreciation, for your support of a stronger America and your commitment to better government."

Direct Mail Systems has raised $750,000 for Hawkins with such letters, or about one-eighth of her $6.5 million campaign budget. In addition, much of the $800,000 Hawkins is to get from the National Republican Senatorial Committee has been raised through the mail.

Graham, her opponent, has a smaller direct-mail effort designed to raise about $200,000. Like Hawkins, he too faces crisis after crisis, if one believes his letters.

Graham's crises, however, are caused by "the huge tide of national Republican money" and "all of the glamour, power and prestige the opposition can muster." "The list of individuals they have sent to protect her seat reads like a who's who of Washington politics," said Graham's most recent letter.

This kind of talk has become all too familiar to many Americans during the last 15 years. Direct mail, called the "Poisoned Pen of Politics," by University of Virginia Prof. Larry Sabato, has become a mainstay of fundraising for presidential candidates and scores of groups on the political left and right.

Senate and gubernatorial candidates have been slower to adopt direct mail. This year about three-fourths of all Republican Senate candidates and one-fourth of Democratic counterparts are using it.

The letters sent by Hawkins and Graham are shorter—to cut cost—and less emotional than many direct-mail appeals. "This company does not do hype and get-the-communists-out-from-under-the-bed letters," said DMS President Jack Latvala. "You could only say the sky is falling so many times," said Hal Malchow, whose firm does Graham's mailings.

One beauty of direct mail is that it allows a candidate to "target" a message at one group of voters without alienating another group.

The state of the art is such that a candidate can target one letter at single, white female Democrats age 25 to 30, stressing support of legalized abortion; another stressing "family values" can be targeted at independent married couples 35 to 45; and another about Social Security at Republicans over 65.

Jewish voters can be sent letters that talk solely about Israel, as did one Hawkins letter signed by Sen. Rudy Boschwitz (R-Minn.). Cuban Americans can get letters written in Spanish.

All it takes is some advanced computer technology and information readily available from voter rolls. But it takes time and money. Graham and Hawkins have chosen not to delve too deeply into such sophisticated targeting.

"The philosophy is that there are three ways

to win elections in Florida—media, media, media," said Jeff Brown, editor of *Campaigns & Elections*, a political journal. "I think that's a mistake."

Mainly, Hawkins and Graham use the mail to raise money to buy time for television ads. Almost every one of their letters talks about television.

One Hawkins letter warned that unless the senator could raise $900,000 for TV ads by July 1, her chances could become almost hopeless. A Graham letter mailed about the same time said, "We must counter her multimillion-dollar negative media campaign with our own message. If she goes on television with her attacks, we must go on to tell the truth."

Another Graham letter said: "Some people have suggested that we should run ads showing that Paula Hawkins has been an ineffective senator. Others say we should stick to a positive campaign. What is your opinion?"

The best-detailed letter of this type was a "Special TV Package" from the Hawkins camp, imploring "Keep Paula Hawkins on TV." It listed the price for airing 30-second ads in various markets and asked what television shows donors would like their money spent on: $45 for *Good Morning America*, $90 for *Donahue*, $965 for *Wheel of Fortune*, $50 for *People's Court*, $535 for *Jeopardy*, $1,025 for *The Cosby Show*, $1,200 for *Simon & Simon*, and so on.

Direct-mail firms use two kinds of mailings for fundraising—"prospecting" and "house."

A "prospect" mailing is a general, mass mailing to potential campaign contributors. These mailings are done early in campaigns, sometimes two years before an election. They go to people with demographic or ideological profiles that make them likely donors. The names come from lists that can be purchased by direct-mail firms for limited use.

Anyone in Florida who has given to the American Conservative Union, Young Americans for Freedom or the Conservative Victory Fund, subscribes to *Forbes, Business Week* or *Changing Times* magazine or has purchased anything from Harry and David's, a fruit marketing company, has received a prospecting letter from Hawkins. Anyone in Florida who has given to the Democratic National Committee will receive a prospecting letter this fall from Graham.

The idea behind prospecting is to build up the highly prized "house list." The name and address of any contributor goes on this list. They then will receive "house" mailings, which are far more profitable for a campaign

because they go only to people with a proven propensity to donate.

The two Senate candidates in Florida have taken vastly different approaches to direct mail and building house lists.

Direct mail was an important element of Hawkins' campaign plan from the beginning. When Hawkins' campaign team was put together in late 1984, DMS, a politically well-connected firm with clients in 10 states, was part of it. Pam Meacomes, a former Hawkins Senate aide, was picked to manage the account for DMS.

"We got an early start because we had to. Paula's appeal has always been to the average voter. She's never been a darling of the business community like Graham," said DMS President Latvala. "Direct-mail contributors aren't bankers or lawyers. In Florida, they are mostly retirees.

"The secret to direct mail is senior citizens. They don't complain about junk mail. One of the big events of their day is getting a letter from Paula Hawkins," Latvala added. "They are the major source of funds for most Republican and conservative candidates in Florida."

Direct mail has never been a big part of the Graham campaign. The governor didn't hire his direct mailer, Malchow, until this summer, although the National Committee for an Effective Congress, a liberal Washington-based group, had done some direct-mail fundraising for him earlier.

Graham said he had been advised against investing much effort in direct mail. Other Democrats have received the same advice, for the party was slow to realize the potential of direct mail and still has been unable to capitalize on it as much as the GOP has.

"Direct mail is a technician's game. The hard reality is that Republican technicians are better than Democratic technicians," Rodney Smith, finance director of the National Republican Senatorial Committee, has said.

Malchow, who managed the 1984 campaign of Sen. Albert Gore Jr. (D-Tenn.), got into the direct-mail business only a year ago with a computer on his kitchen table, but he now has as clients four candidates for the Senate and one for governor.

With the campaign in its final two months, Graham has a house list of 13,000 names. Each person on the list can expect to get three Graham letters before Nov. 4, according to Malchow. He estimates the mailings will net $62,000.

Hawkins has a house list of 25,000 stored

on a 10½-inch magnetic tape. DMS demonstrated how effectively it could use this list last April when Hawkins was hospitalized for neck and shoulder surgery.

At that time, the campaign was at a low point. Hawkins was doing badly in the polls, and her hospitalization had raised speculation that she would be unable to continue the race.

"We decided to make lemonade out of the lemons," Latvala said. After getting Hawkins' approval from her room at the Duke Medical Center in Durham, N.C., DMS drafted a letter in which Hawkins said the news media "insisted on creating their own mystery about my condition. And the unfounded rumors were further aggravated by a front-page story in *The Washington Post*. Some of my supporters point out that *The Washington Post* just happens to be owned by my opponent's family."

Graham's half-brother, Phillip L. Graham, was publisher of *The Washington Post* until his death in 1963. The *Post* did not publish a story on the front page about Hawkins' health problem; several stories did appear on inside pages.

Hawkins quickly approved the letter, which said, "the real story about my physical condition" is "I am back, working my normal 12-hour day and I feel great."

The letter was reproduced by DMS as if Hawkins had written it by hand from her hospital bed. Neither the handwriting nor the wording of the letter was Hawkins', according to Latvala.

Within weeks, the letter had raised $50,000.

Reprinted with permission from *The Washington Post*.

## COMPUTING AN AUDIENCE FOR A TAILORED MESSAGE

*Bill Peterson, The Washington Post, October 8, 1986*

The reelection campaign of Sen. Paula Hawkins (R-Fla.) recently produced a Social Security ad featuring Hawkins meeting with President Reagan, a commercial aimed at elderly voters. When, her strategists wondered, should the ad be shown on television?

They put that question not to any member of the campaign team, but to four small computers, in a new office building overlooking the Potomac River in Old Town Alexandria. The computers reported that 201,000 people older than 55 watch the 6 p.m. news on WTJV-TV in Miami, while 87,000 watch WPLG-TV and 69,000 see WSVN-TV.

After a few more buttons were pushed, the computer produced more useful information: The Social Security ad would be seen by 80 percent of the over-55 in greater Miami if it were shown simultaneously on all three stations—a "roadblock" ad that couldn't be missed, even by viewers switching channels. The Hawkins campaign bought that roadblock position on the three stations.

Those computers in Alexandria, using broadcast ratings and census data, can break down the audience for every program on every television and radio station in Florida into 50 categories according to age, sex, race, income, occupation and education.

They can tell how many 18- to 24-year-old men in Tampa will watch WTVT-TV's *Pulse News* at 5 p.m. Tuesday; how many unmarried women with two children will see *Wheel of Fortune* on Friday night in Jacksonville; or how many men over age 50 will tune in *Monday Night Football* between 10 and 11 p.m. in Orlando.

Such information is vital to Hawkins and her Democratic opponent, Gov. Bob Graham, as they decide how to spend millions of dollars on advertising in the frantic closing weeks of the campaigns.

In the world of megapolitics, candidates must be concerned not only with producing compelling commercials, but also with making sure that their ads are seen at the right time, by the right people—*i.e.*, those who will decide the election.

This is where computers, like those at National Media, Inc., which places ads for Hawkins, come into play.

If Hawkins wants to improve her standing among young voters in the Tampa-St. Petersburg area, the computers can tell her that she should advertise on TV shows such as *Moonlighting, Late Night With David Letterman, Perfect Strangers* or *Miami Vice*.

Or she can reach 60 percent of the 18- to 24-year-olds in the market with four "messages" each by purchasing 47 spots on five radio stations at a cost of $7,760, a fraction of what that exposure would cost on TV.

Some of this same information has been available for decades in rating books used by the A.C. Nielsen Co. and the American Research Bureau, Inc. (now called Arbitron).

### Finding the Target Audience

Commercial ad agencies use the books to help sell beer, soap and new cars; political ad agencies adopted them to sell candidates. The idea: You can't sell soap on programs watched mostly by beer drinkers, or sell politicians on shows watched by people who don't vote.

In the late 1970s, big commercial ad agencies began to turn to computers, which could supply more sophisticated demographic information, to target their "time buys."

Time-buying, however, remained a stepchild in politics—a highly technical, insider's game with its own confusing jargon such as HUTs (Homes Using Television), PUTs (People Using Television) and Gross Rating Points.

This has begun to change.

"We're all going into computers. We've had to because television costs have gotten so high and the potential for wasting money is so great," said Raymond Strother, a Democratic media consultant. "You just can't operate out of the hip pocket anymore."

National Media, Inc., a subsidiary of Black, Manafort, Stone & Atwater, a Republican consulting and lobbying firm, invested about $100,000 in a state-of-the-art computer network before the 1984 election. The Communications Co., Graham's media firm, bought less sophisticated computers for the 1986 election cycle, according to Bob Squier, president of the firm.

"I think our time-buying can make a 2 percent difference in a race," said Charles Black, Hawkins' chief political strategist. "That can make the difference between winning and losing in a lot of races."

### A Large Potential for Fees

But more than politics is involved here. There is big money in time-buying. Media consultants' fees are based on commissions, traditionally set at 15 percent by commercial ad agencies.

Squier charges 15 percent to all his clients; NMI, the subsidiary of Black's firm, charges 5 percent to 15 percent, depending on the contest. This means Squier's firm stands to earn about $490,000 in time-buying commissions alone in the Florida race; NMI may get as much as $600,000, because Hawkins is expected to spend more than her opponent on TV.

Time-buying is critical in Florida, one of the nation's fastest-growing states. It is populated by immigrants from other states and countries who have little sense of Florida's political traditions.

Elections there can be won or lost on the TV screen. The state has 4,480,100 homes with television sets and more than 40 TV stations. They are scattered in 10 media markets, located hundreds of miles apart. No single city, or media market, dominates.

Together Hawkins and Graham likely will spend more than $7 million on TV, or about 60 percent of their campaign war chests. About half of this money will be spent this month.

"It is in the closing weeks, frequently the closing days, that the most frantic, volatile and downright nasty things happen in a campaign," wrote John Witherspoon, a Texas political media consultant. "Frequently, the tracking [polls] are showing mixed trends, inconclusive results or confusing mixes of data. Rarely is anything sure at this point. . . . Timing is everything."

The Hawkins camp got an early taste of what to expect in mid-September.

### Investment Shows Results

For months, the race had been steady, with Graham maintaining a 10 percent to 15 percent lead over the incumbent Republican. Hawkins' campaign had tried to cut into this lead with a series of major advertising spurts, beginning in early October 1985. It had spent $1,029,239 on television by the end of January, when Graham aired his first ads.

Hawkins continued to outspend Graham on television throughout this year. Finally, in late summer, her investment began to pay off. According to polls taken for newspapers and television stations, Hawkins began to close the gap with Graham. In late August, after months off TV, Graham went on the air with two "positive" ads, which attempted to build him up, not tear down Hawkins.

That changed abruptly Sept. 16. Graham unexpectedly began airing a hard-hitting "negative" ad charging that Hawkins "voted to weaken Florida's front line on drugs by cutting the Coast Guard budget" and "even voted against drug education for children."

This caught the Hawkins camp by surprise. Drugs had been one of the handful of issues in which the senator could claim expertise. Her campaign considered the drug issue her turf and had proclaimed her "the Senate's general in the war on drugs."

### *"The Drug Issue Was Hot"*

Black concluded that "Graham saw he was slipping and we were gaining momentum. The drug issue was hot. I guess their strategy was to cut us off at the pass." The Graham camp denied that it was on the defensive, saying it just wanted to set Hawkins' record straight.

The events of the next few weeks give an instructive glimpse at the rat-a-tat-tat world of media politics:

—Wednesday morning, Sept. 17: Black, pollster Dick Morris and other strategists met with Hawkins in her Senate office. They debated three ads to respond to Graham, deciding on one that ridiculed the attack. "If Bob Graham is trying to make Paula Hawkins look soft on drugs, on *drugs*, what in the world will he do next?" it asked.

—Wednesday afternoon, Robert Goodman, Hawkins' media adviser, began preparing an ad in his suburban Baltimore headquarters. In Alexandria, NMI President Robin D. Roberts and his staff went to work with their computers.

"The computers give us the ability to fine-tune a buy overnight. We can do a buy in a matter of hours instead of a matter of days," said Roberts, a low-key South Carolinian and former administrative assistant to Sen. Strom Thurmond (R-S.C.) "We believe in a rifle, not a shotgun approach."

Graham's time buy was a big shotgun blast, aimed at a mass audience. In addition to major news shows, it included prime time spots on *The Cosby Show, Cheers* and *Golden Girls*, and fringe time spots on *Jeopardy* and *Wheel of Fortune*, popular game shows.

Hawkins had two other ads on the air, including the compelling Social Security spot. It was appearing on late afternoon reruns of *Quincy* and *Barnaby Jones*, game shows, and prime time spots on *Murder, She Wrote*, all popular among viewers 55 and older, station records indicate.

—Thursday, Sept. 18: Copies of Goodman's ad were produced, packaged and sent by Federal Express to about 35 Florida television stations. They began airing that night on news shows and programs before and after the news. "We wanted to make sure everyone who saw Graham's ad saw ours," Black said later.

—Tuesday, Sept. 23: Graham attacked for a second time, airing another negative spot criticizing Hawkins' votes on Coast Guard fund-ing. With the exception of a two-day break, he has been on television ever since.

—Saturday, Oct. 4: Hawkins went on the attack, again on the drug issue, with an ad that accused Graham of letting drug pushers out of prison early "to stalk our neighborhoods and kill our kids."

This one was targeted to younger white males, a group that is not enthusiastic about Hawkins, polls indicate. Roberts and company bought spots for the ad during several football games as well as *Hunter, Miami Vice, MacGyver* and *Hill Street Blues*.

The drug war was now three weeks old. Who had won?

"It was a wash," said Black. "We're both back to about where we were when it started."

But the Florida Senate race had turned an important corner. Graham was now matching Hawkins dollar for dollar on television. It would now be punch, counterpunch, punch again until Election Day.

The candidates themselves had been almost bit players in the change. The big roles were played by their hired strategists, media advisers and pollsters.

The time buyers for both camps, working in obscurity at computers hundreds of miles from Florida, had been preparing for this critical period for weeks. On Sept. 23, for example, Graham's campaign sent $60,180 to WTVJ-TV, the CBS affiliate in Miami, to lock in time for spots during the final week of the campaign on its news shows as well as *Dallas, 60 Minutes* and *Murder, She Wrote*, all among last year's top 10 rated shows, according to station records.

"We're looking for big ratings and sure things," said Squier. "We consider early buying to be a form of banking. We're buying the best stocks in the market and we're going to sit on them."

Much of the rest of time buying won't be so easy.

### *"Offensive" and "Defensive" Markets*

Sometimes a campaign may want to broadcast one ad, or "message," in one market and not another. Graham's base of support is in south Florida, where the two-term governor grew up. Hawkins' base is in central Florida, a heavily Republican area where she makes her home, and north Florida, an area populated by conservative Democrats.

"Tampa and Miami are defensive markets

for us. We will be trying to hold onto our base there," said Squier, Graham's media adviser. "Jacksonville and the rest of north Florida are offensive markets for us. We will be trying to break up her strength there. I can see us using very different ads there, although we haven't up to this point."

Other buys will be aimed at specific demographic groups. Polling information will guide them.

Hawkins, according to polls, does unusually well for a Republican among senior citizens, a group that makes up 17.2 percent of the state's population. As one of only two women in the Senate, she also does better than most members of her party among women. Yet she doesn't fare as well among younger voters as other GOP candidates.

Graham fares well among lower-income voters, blacks and Florida natives, a group that makes up one-fourth of the state voters. But he doesn't do as well as other Democrats among senior citizens and working women.

The buys will escalate each week as the election approaches. TV audiences are measured by Gross Rating Points. A rating point means an audience of 1 percent of the coverage area. If an advertiser buys 100 Gross Rating Points in an area, that means the average home should see one "message" a week.

This isn't enough to do politicians much good. "As a rule of thumb, a person has to see an ad 3½ or 4 times for it to sink in," Roberts said.

### Counting Points and Money

Campaigns typically buy 400 Gross Rating Points a week in September, then increase their buys to 500 in the first week of October, 600 in the second, 700 in the third and 800 in the week before the election.

But rating points tell only part of the story. Campaigns are concerned about how much money they spend and who sees their ads.

In Tampa, a 30-second spot on *The Cosby Show*, the nation's most viewed program last year, costs $6,500, and will be viewed by 383,000 women and 262,000 men. A 30-second spot on *St. Elsewhere*, a prime time show viewed by a smaller, better educated audience, costs $1,750; one on *Wheel of Fortune*, a game show that draws heavily among blue-collar families, $2,000; one on the daytime *Donahue*, popular among nonworking women, $600.

"Our problem is we want to appeal to both the people who watch *Wheel of Fortune* and *St. Elsewhere*," said Roberts, adding later, "We're a lot like the people who do buying for McDonald's, Hardee's, General Motors or Frito-Lay."

But there is one big difference between selling cars, hamburgers or soap and selling politicians.

A soap manufacturer may be hoping to capture 12 percent of the soap market over a two- or three-year period. A politician is aiming at capturing more than 50 percent of the political market.

Graham and Hawkins have only until Nov. 4 to do it.

Reprinted with permission from *The Washington Post*.

## WHEN AN ETHNIC NAME MAKES A VOTER FAIR GAME

*David Burnham, The New York Times, April 17, 1984*

WASHINGTON—What's in a name? Everything, if you are a candidate for political office and you buy the services of one of the small number of consulting companies that have gone into the business of compiling what are known in the trade as "ethnic dictionaries."

One of the acknowledged experts in the obscure but increasingly important technique of using the names of citizens to divine their probable political concerns is Frank L. Tobe. He is the president and founder of Below, Tobe & Associates, the largest computer service and direct-mail supplier to Democratic and liberal political candidates in the United States and Canada.

Mr. Tobe, who is 42 years old and has offices in a Washington suburb and in Los Angeles, discussed new techniques in computerized voter contact at a recent seminar in the capital organized by the Annenberg Schools of Communications. He enlarged on his presentation in an interview.

The point, Mr. Tobe said, is to use all available information, such as a person's occupation, age and ethnic background, to provide links between the recipient of a mailing and the candidate.

### *"Extra Fraction of Awareness"*

"The connections derived from these subtle personalizations may appear to be fleeting," Mr. Tobe told the seminar, "but they add that extra fraction of awareness to the candidate and his overall message that it takes to persuade voters to vote for the candidate and win elections."

An individual's occupation can be gleaned from a professional or union membership list, and a voter's age from a driver's license, but how does Mr. Tobe go about identifying the various ethnic backgrounds of each of the hundreds of thousands of potential voters that a candidate may want to send different messages? The example he gave involved one of his recent projects in Hawaii.

"Hawaii was a real challenge," he said. "We obtained a computerized list of the names of all the people living in the state. We then asked the computer to sift out those surnames that were very rare, like Aardvark.

"Then we sat down with a group of people from many different backgrounds and went through the list, assigning each name to the appropriate country. This one is a Chinese name, this one is Japanese, this is Korean, this is Tahitian, this is Hawaiian, this is Portuguese.

"It took a lot of time, but when we had finished we were quite certain that anyone with one of the 4,300 surnames was Korean, while those with 9,500 other surnames were Japanese."

When Mayor Tom Bradley of Los Angeles ran for Governor in 1982, he wanted a list of potential voters who were black.

"We took a list of all those living in several heavily black areas such as Watts," Mr. Tobe said. "Then we asked the computer to poll out any of the 14,000 Spanish surnames we already had identified in southern California, and the surnames that were Oriental. The remaining names almost certainly were black."

The consultants decided to use a second technique for the dictionary of black names, Mr. Tobe said. "We got lists of individuals who had driver's licenses from Kentucky and Louisiana, two states that identify by race," he said. "We pulled off all the black people and looked for first names uniquely used by black families. Willie, for example, in combination with certain surnames, almost always is black."

Mr. Tobe said the ability to identify black voters by name was especially important in states like California. "Every major city in the United States has areas that are predominantly black," he said. "But in the West, a relatively young part of the country, you find larger numbers of integrated areas where it is impossible to identify black voters by their neighborhood."

He said that by using the computer, he had also developed lists of "gay people for special mailings from politicians in San Francisco, Los Angeles and New York."

### *Narrowing the List*

Mr. Tobe said that the first step was to obtain a list, based on telephone books, of all the people living in areas that are believed to have a large number of homosexuals. "Then we start eliminating households," he said, "married couples, hetero couples living together and multiple male or female families with the same last name and two family households of the same sex but where the age spread is 20 or more years."

"The households that are left with two persons of the same sex but different last names may well be gay," he said. "Where the number is high in relation to hetero households, we encode the results as gays and we encode the single households as possibly gay in those areas where the ratio of gays to non-gays is the highest."

Mr. Tobe acknowledged that computer sorting could sometimes be wrong. "In the case of gays, however," he said, "we don't feel an occasional mistake is too serious because most of the heteros living in a known gay area probably are tolerant about gay issues."

He also said ethnic identification often required special geographic knowledge. "A good number of the 11,000 surnames we identified as being Jewish in Los Angeles," he said, "can be German in Wisconsin."

### *"Potentially Negative Aspect"*

Mr. Tobe said the "potentially negative aspect of ethnic dictionaries is that politicians can use the technique to send directly conflicting messages to different segments of the population. Because of the technology, this is possible. None of our clients has ever attempted to do so, however."

Mr. Tobe said he was the biggest critic and censor of this practice. "Sure," he said, "it is possible to send one message to Jewish voters another to those with an Arab background, one to a business owner and a contradictory one to a union member."

But he said the system tended to correct itself. To illustrate this point, he mentioned a company in California that specializes in what he called "desperate politics."

"This firm has been known to do outrageous things," he said, "hard ball tactics way beyond the normal and just barely legal, and had developed a reputation that now makes them an issue in the campaign."

Copyright 1984 by the New York Times Company. Reprinted by permission.

---

## POLITICIZING THE WIRE The Appeal of Cable as an Advertising Medium

*Peter Ainslie, Channels magazine, April 1988*

Four years ago, you couldn't give away advertising time on cable to politicians. "Selling cable ads in the political arena was kind of like being an elevator salesman in a world of two-story buildings," says Bob Williams, president of the eight-year-old cable rep firm National Cable Advertising (NCA). "There was no place for your product when you first started, and then, if you stayed with it, the landscape changed to fit your product."

But in this election year, candidates are discovering advantages to cable beyond lower rates. Why the big change? The reason is rising penetration and the availability of data bases that make cable increasingly efficient, and easy to buy. "Cable was an unknown quantity to political candidates," says Cable Advertising Bureau (CAB) president Bob Alter. "There wasn't much of a track record in '84. But over the past couple of years, it's become more apparent to political operatives that cable can play an important role in campaigns. We now have data to show them how it can be used nationally and locally."

Along those lines are two data bases that have been developed, one by the A.C. Nielsen company, called CODE, for Cable On-line Data Exchange, and another by Bob Williams' NCA, called CableTrack, both of which greatly facilitate the work of the political media planner. CableTrack was developed to help

Williams keep track of the vast inventory of advertising time available among the 1,400 or so cable systems that sell local inserts on ad-supported basic services. But because cable franchises coincide with political boundaries of one sort or another—county, ward, voting district—it was an obvious fit to put the data to work for politicians. Nielsen, says CODE's manager Julie Aquan, was collecting data on cable systems anyway, for metered and diary services and for phone coincidentals. "So we decided to turn it around," she says, "and make it available to ad agencies, cable networks, MSOs [multiple systems operators], cable reps and broadcast networks."

According to Williams, here's what cable can do for politicians: "It auto-pilots its way into the most desirable homes in America, for politicians and other advertisers. The facts bear out that cabled homes are more likely to vote, more likely to give money to a campaign, to work for a campaign. It selects out the homes you most want to talk to if you're a politician. Secondly, it helps target voting districts. The geography of politics is the geography of cable, and that's a tremendous benefit for a political campaign. Third, cable is a multimedia medium. If you're a politician, you can buy a half-hour show on cable in prime time to really tell your story, then promote that program with 30-second commercials on ESPN, CNN and USA, and you can also send a piece of mail to that same set of households, through the MSO's billing system or through an independent direct-mail approach. A TV station can tell you how many people are watching, but can't tell you where they live. It's a big advantage having the viewer's address."

Both CODE and CableTrack contain comprehensive information about which cable systems are in each television market, including, among other things, which programming services are carried; the cost for locally purchased ad time on each service; and information on cable interconnects. CODE also combines cable customers' zip codes with zip code demographic research from Donnelley Marketing and provides demographic profiles of a cable system's franchise area. One big difference in the two: CODE is for sale by Nielsen; CableTrack is available free to any politician (or advertiser) who buys cable ads through National Cable Advertising. (The company is compensated by the cable system.) Once a politician decides to buy, Williams places the time, monitors the schedules, gets notarized affidavits of performance and provides a single invoice.

If there's a vulnerability here, it's with cable's same old bugaboo: ratings. "For people who need broad reach," agrees Williams, "it's not the right service. When you get to the short strokes in a campaign, these people buy tonnage. Cable cannot compete in that war. So reach is something we concede. On the other hand, our strength is in frequency. We can reach the people they most want to reach with greater frequency because our commercials are less expensive. They can afford more of them."

Reprinted with permission from *Channels* magazine.

## THE 1990 U.S. CENSUS AND POLITICAL CAMPAIGNS

*Larry A. Checco and Kimball W. Brace*

What really distinguishes the [U.S.] census from other data sources and makes it the basic source of all demographics is the geographic detail. No other source attempts to—or can afford to—provide a comprehensive set of information for every city block and rural district in the country.

> *Demographics: People and Markets,*
> *by Thomas W. Merrick and Stephen*
> *J. Tordella [A publication of the*
> *Population Reference Bureau, Inc.,*
> *February, 1988]*

Demographic information is political fodder for both campaign strategists and many of the technology-oriented companies that supply campaigns with demographic-related products and services. For example, computerized direct-mailings, micro-mapping software, and audience-specific cable television programming masticate, ingest, and regurgitate demographic data to identify and target voters.

There are several sources from which demographic information can be obtained, including surveys, mailing houses, and companies that generate updated demographic data. However, the information these sources provide is too broad-stroked geographically—*i.e.*, demographics are broken down to the county level, at best—and, therefore, of limited use to campaigns, which require precinct-level data. Only the U.S. Census Bureau collects information from *nearly every household* in the country (and for 1990 will tally and publish it for every block in the nation.) Also, the type of information gathered by the Bureau is extremely relevant, politically. For example, age, income, level of education, occupation, marital status, whether someone rents or owns their own home indicate a lot about a voter's political persuasion and the kinds of issues that most concern him or her. Although this information is available from the Census Bureau only on an aggregate, not personal basis, it is the kind of information successful campaign strategists crave.

In the past, however, campaigns—especially those run in the latter part of the decade—overlooked the value of census data, believing that decennial census data was too outdated. (In many cases, this is a false perception. Although the number of people living in a particular area may change between census counts, the share of a demographic feature is likely to be similar from decade to decade. If for example, the 1980 Census indicated that left-handed Lithuanians comprised a goodly share of a particular block, it is likely that in 1988 the percentage of left-handed Lithuanians in that block will still be high.)

In addition to the perception that census data often is outdated, converting demographic information collected by the Census Bureau into political capital was too costly and difficult for campaigns. Campaign planners, for example, as well as most other people, had no idea where the boundaries of a Census Tract or Block Group were located. Even if they could figure out census boundaries, those boundaries usually did not fit easily on top of, or within, the type of geography that politicians are used to, namely political precincts. Census boundaries are defined by visible objects, such as roads, streams, rivers, and highways. Political precinct lines on the other hand, often take off across an open field or over a ridge line in rural areas. And despite the more orderly manner in which streets run in urban areas, in many instances precinct lines go along back lot lines or alley ways. The result is the same: census boundaries and political boundaries many times do not mesh.

The overwhelming majority of census data collected by the government, therefore, cannot be easily converted, if converted at all, into information campaigns could readily use.

The Bicentennial Census of 1990, however, has the potential to change that. For one thing, data collected in 1990 should be recent enough to make campaigns more comfortable about using it in 1992. But of even more consequence, for the first time in U.S. Census history most states will receive census data tabulated and broken down into political precincts. The compatibility of census geography with precinct lines will enable campaign strategists to link census-generated demographic information with voting districts. In addition, the Census Bureau's increased use of computer technology, combined with the vastly improved data-storage capability of microcomputers employed by most campaigns, portend greater use of census data in all areas of campaigning, including voter identification and fundraising.

How excited should campaign planners be about the 1990 Census? That remains to be seen. Although the potential is great, there are a number of issues still pending that will determine just how timely and useful 1990 census information will be for political campaigns.

The following briefly describes what makes the 1990 Census so much different from those of the past, and examines some of the census-related demographic issues campaign planners and strategists should be aware of.

### The Most Computerized Census Ever Taken

Given technological advances within the last ten years, it is not surprising that the 1990 Census will be the most automated ever. Computers will collect, "capture," tabulate and disseminate census data. In preparation for the 1990 census, the Census Bureau also has increased its use of computers for development, administrative, and evaluation purposes. However, the most innovative use of technology for this upcoming headcount, and one that should be of great interest to campaign planners, has been creation of the Topologically Integrated Geographic Encoding and Referencing system, or TIGER

Developed by the Census Bureau in conjunction with the U.S. Geological Survey, the TIGER system will provide computerized geographic products and services for the 1990 Census from a totally automated single source. In contrast to previous censuses, the TIGER system will enable all mapping and geoprocessing to be in complete agreement. For example, in the past, errors sometimes crept in when blocks appeared on Census Bureau maps but populations did not appear on

Census Bureau reports, and vice versa. In contrast, in 1990, all census geography required to conduct census field operations and to tabulate data will be contained within the TIGER system.

The computer-generated, digital maps created by the TIGER system are far superior to the hand-drawn maps used for previous census counts. These maps will make it easier for census data collectors (enumerators) to collect information from households that do not respond by mail. In addition, this improved system for collecting census information has the potential to directly assist those political campaigns that have the money, technology, experience, and savvy to use it.

For example, the new system will provide address ranges in urban areas that campaigns can use to link names of voters to census demographics. By address-matching the campaign names against the computerized TIGER files, political consultants will be able to pinpoint where contributions and support are coming from and identify the types of demographic groups and neighborhoods in which these supporters live. In addition, by integrating census data with information obtained from other sources such as mailing houses, surveys and past election returns, campaigns will be able to target new areas from which to seek support.

Paper copies of the computer-generated maps provided by the Census Bureau, however, may present a minor practical problem for campaign strategists grown accustomed to tacking maps side-by-side on a "war room" wall to show their entire district. Each county will be plotted separately on a different scale. There will also be inserts for more concentrated areas of habitation. It will be impossible, therefore, to place two county maps side-by-side and have them fit exactly.

On the other hand, the computer files that make up the TIGER system can generate customized maps of any given area of the country. While not cheap initially, these maps will give campaigns the option of presenting any given line or feature on the maps in a different color. In addition, these computerized Census Bureau files can also be manipulated to generate boundary files that will work in most commercially available mapping software packages. A campaign could then generate its own color-coded maps to indicate voting patterns or the location of different demographic groups in their district.

### The 1990 Census Questionnaire

Information requested in the various subject areas of the 1990 Census "long-form" questionnaire—to be sent to approximately one out of every six households—differs only slightly from those of the 1980 long-form. These differences should be of minimal consequence to most campaign strategists.

However, campaigns run in districts with large Asian populations may find it more difficult to identify specific Asian ancestry, *i.e.*, Japanese, Chinese, Filipinos, and so forth. The Census Bureau is attempting to limit the space given to recording Asian ethnicity. Instead of providing a check-off list of eight Asian subgroups—as it did on its 1980 questionnaire—the Census Bureau is requesting that "Asians/Pacific Islanders" write-in their specific ancestry in a place provided. Census Bureau officials claim that the write-in method would provide as good, and in some cases even more detailed information about ethnicity than the check-off method. Many in the Asian community, however, feel differently. They argue that recent immigrants with poor English language skills would have difficulty writing the information. If the latter proves true, campaigns run in states such as California—where it is estimated that Asians make up approximately 7.5 percent of the population and are beginning to flex their political muscles—may find it harder to identify areas containing critical swing votes among the various Asian subpopulations.

### Sample Size

While every person and household receives a form that asks several basic questions related to the census count, the more detailed or "long-form" demographic questionnaire, which requests detailed housing and other socio-economic information, is sent to only a sample of the nation's households.

Sample size is critical to any census. Since 1960, however, when the bulk of census data began being collected on a sample basis, the trend has been to reduce the census sample rate. This trend nearly reached disastrous proportions for the 1990 Census.

The Office of Management and Budget (OMB), which is entitled to review the census questionnaires under the Paperwork Reduction Act, originally recommended that the Census Bureau send its "long-form" sampling questionnaire to only one out of every 10 households in 1990. OMB's recommended sample size was down from the 1-in-5 overall sampling rate of the 1980 Census.

Census data users from around the nation, however, vehemently opposed OMB's recommendation, and in March of 1988, after much debate, OMB backed down. Under the compromise, the "long-form" questionnaire containing the short-form questions, plus several dozen others seeking detailed information about economic and social characteristics, will be sent to 17.7 million households, or about 1-in-6, of the nation's 106 million dwelling units. This is what the Census Bureau had originally proposed.

Had OMB gotten its way, the implications of the smaller sample on politically important data would have been enormous for campaigns. First, the availability and reliability of the socio-economic characteristics for small areas such as neighborhoods (block groups) and precincts would have been minimal, if existent at all. Without this small level data, such systems as the Cluster analysis that became popular in the 1970s and 1980s would have been impossible to conduct. In addition, the ability of large mailing houses, which integrate income and other demographic variables for campaign mailing lists, would have been in question.

### 1990 Census Deadlines

By law, the Secretary of Commerce must report counts for each state to the President within nine months of Census day, *i.e.*, by December 31, 1990. Also by law, the Secretary must report to each state its respective tabulations, by blocks and precincts, by April 1, 1991.

As we shall discuss later, if, for whatever reasons, the Census Bureau fails to meet these deadlines, redistricting may be delayed. Since candidates must meet their own district filing deadlines, many 1992 campaigns could be faced with not knowing the boundaries of the district in which their candidate is running.

### Redistricting Data Program

The 1990 Census will provide campaigns with more microscopic and politically relevant information than ever before.

For the first time, the Census Bureau plans to define small level blocks for the entire country and to have counts for each of these eight to 12 million blocks. This is in contrast to the 2.5 million blocks for which data was available after the 1980 Census. In addition, as a result of the 1990 Census Redistricting Data Program, a majority of states will receive census data for each voting district they (the states) specified, provided state-specified districts are made up of the same census blocks identified by the Bureau.

From a campaign standpoint, however, it is important to realize that the precinct program data will only contain total population counts and voting-age population (those 18 and over) for six ethnic/racial groups recognized by the Bureau. The precinct program will *not* report information on income, education, etc., by precinct. As in previous censuses, that information will only be available for the geographic units normally used by the Census Bureau, *i.e.*, census block groups. Therefore, 1991-92 campaigns wishing more detailed demographics by precinct will need to rely on the few companies that integrate other politically important data and reconfigure it for precinct geography.

The precinct program's evolutionary development, however, foreshadows increasing alignment of census data with political realities.

### Evolution of Precinct Program

The purpose of the precinct program is to provide state legislatures with small-area, or precinct level, census population totals for legislative redistricting. Possessing this information, legislatures would be able to move whole precincts between districts and still be in compliance with the redistricting laws that require balanced representation. The precinct program's origins date back more than 20 years.

Following the "one-person, one-vote" court decisions of the 1960s, state legislatures found 1970 census small geographic areas, *i.e.*, tracts, block groups and blocks, to have boundaries that did not coincide with voting district lines. This frustrated state efforts to merge local election returns with small-area census counts. These counts were necessary to create legislative districts that had not only balanced populations but also indicated the political make-up of the proposed district. The Census Bureau, National Conference of State Legislatures, and state officials began in 1972 to design a 1980 census program to meet this critical need.

As a result of their work, in 1975, Congress enacted Public Law 94-171, which amended the Census Law and mandated that:
—The Census Bureau inform state governments at least four years before each census of technical guidelines they must meet to obtain population counts for their locally defined voting districts.
—States wishing to participate in this voluntary program submit to the Census Bureau mapped boundaries of their voting districts no later than three years before the census.
—The Census Bureau provide small-area population counts to the legislature and governor of each participating state by one year after the census.

While the concept makes political sense, its application in 1980 was less than perfect. In fact, in many of the 23 states that agreed to participate, it was seen as a failure. Blocks were not put in the right precincts or were left out of precincts entirely. In essence, the data had to be extensively massaged and corrected before it was usable, something most legislatures did not have time for. Clearly, campaigns were not able to fill that need either. As a result, in most instances, district lines were created using census geography rather than precincts.

In the 1990 census, 47 states have indicated an interest in participating in the program. While this may be encouraging to many campaign planners, it is still too early to tell whether these states will in fact go through the tedious process of delineating precinct lines on census maps for their states. In addition, some states for reasons of time, money, manpower, or difficulty of the task, may opt to delineate precinct lines for only part of the state.

In addition, the program still has failed to designate such things as alleyways for block boundaries. So in some major urban areas, creating precincts out of whole blocks will be impossible for upwards of 20 percent of the precincts.

Despite these drawbacks, as a result of the 1990 Redistricting Program, in 1991:
—All state legislatures and governors will receive 1990 census counts broken down by major race group and Hispanic origin, for total population and for persons 18 years old and over.
—All states will receive these data for each

county, city, town and all census geography down to the block. In addition, states that participated in the precinct program will receive these data for each voting district they specified.

—These data will be delivered on computer tape, paper printouts, and perhaps computer compact disks. Census maps showing the boundaries of counties, cities, census statistical areas, blocks and voting districts will accompany these data.

From a political standpoint, campaigns will have more and finer data from which to work. From a technological standpoint, the need for computers to process this abundance of data will be greater than ever before.

### Undercounts and Aliens

Whether the 1990 Census will be adjusted for undercounts and whether illegal aliens will be included in the headcount also will have an impact on campaign strategy.

For campaign purposes, the two major issues related to adjustment of census counts are reliability of census data and the timing of the release of that data.

Every U.S. census since 1790 has experienced an undercount. The Census Bureau, for example, estimated the undercount in 1980 for the entire population to be 1.4 percent—or 3.2 million people. However, it acknowledged that it may have missed counting nearly six percent of all blacks, and as many as 15 percent of black males between the ages of 20 and 45. Thus, the majority of undercounting appears to occur in areas that are traditionally Democratic.

Most experts believe that adjusting the 1990 Census is technically and methodologically feasible and would generate more accurate data on the size, location, and demography of minority populations. The question from a campaign standpoint, therefore, becomes: if the census is *not* adjusted, how reliable will census data be for urban areas?

For example, if census data for an inner city area indicates 100 people living there, should a campaign target its resources to reach 115 people in making its own adjustment for a possible undercount? Given the limited resources of most campaigns, a potential 15 percent inaccuracy in population can make budgeting those resources much more difficult.

There is a corollary question to the adjustment issue. Even if adjusting the census is

feasible and would make the count more accurate, can the Census Bureau determine the extent of the undercount and make the necessary corrections down to the block level so that the redistricting counts can go to the states to meet the April 1, 1991 deadline?

Delays in reporting census figures would of course cause severe problems with the redistricting process in a large number of states. But it has even more fundamental consequences for anyone wishing to run for office in 1992: How will candidates know district boundaries if redistricting is not done in time to meet filing deadlines? Whatever demographic benefits 1992 campaigns may have reaped from the 1990 Census would mostly be negated if the Census Bureau cannot meet its reporting deadlines.

Some people claim the argument to exclude illegal aliens from the census count is the Republican response to the Democrats' desire to have the census readjusted for an undercount. Republicans reject the view and say they oppose a pending suit to exclude the aliens.

Based on its interpretation of the U.S. Constitution, the Census Bureau traditionally has included in its counts *all* people here as residents of the United States, whether or not they are legally admitted. Although the census does not ask anyone whether he or she has the proper papers to be in this country, the Bureau estimates that about two million illegal aliens, or less than one percent of the U.S. population, were included in the 1980 Census.

Under the theory that most illegal aliens are non-English speaking Hispanics with many social needs, whether or not they are included in the census has serious political implications. An attempt to exclude them would mean lower counts and representation for areas where the need for services and federal funds may be the greatest. From a campaign standpoint, however, whether illegal aliens are included in the census is moot. Illegals cannot vote. Since they are counted in the census, however, there is no way campaign planners are able to determine their exact numbers for any given district, and, therefore, may allocate more campaign targeting resources than necessary.

At presstime, the issues surrounding undercounts and aliens had not been resolved. Campaign planners should keep abreast of these two issues. Be aware, however, that at least one study has determined that adjusting for the undercount upwards, then deleting the illegal aliens for a downward count, would result in a wash.

### The True Purpose of the Census

Campaign needs aside, the primary purpose of the headcount taken in the United States every 10 years is to establish a truly representative government in Congress. How representation is apportioned to each state determines the influences each state has in Congress.

State representation in Congress is determined by the results of each decennial census. How that representation is "apportioned" to the states is based on : (1) the population base; (2) the number of seats in the U.S. House of Representatives to be divided; and (3) the method used to calculate apportionment.

Except for a temporary increase when Alaska and Hawaii became states in 1959, the number of seats in the House of Representatives—435—has not been changed since the apportionment following the 1910 census. And as complicated as it may be, the method for calculating apportionment among the states also has remained the same since enacted into law in 1941. Therefore, the major variable regarding apportionment is the population base.

For example, experts forecast that as a result of the 1990 Census, 18 congressional districts will shift between 18 different states, with northeastern states losing seats to those in the South and the West.

Once the census has been taken and the number of seats are assigned to the individual states, the states are required by law to "redistrict" those seats based on population counts. Historically, politicians were able to use redistricting as a form of discrimination. Certain groups of people, either because of their race, national origin, beliefs, income, or the way they voted, were divided up among several districts (to dilute their voting power) or were outnumbered by the people politicians wanted to favor.

For most of this century, many states established new districts with little or no attention to "population balance." They also failed to redistrict despite major population movements or elected "members at large" to avoid redistricting. The result was that some districts with large populations had no more political influence than those with few people. Each district still sent one representative to Congress. The "one-person, one-vote" court decisions of the 1960s eliminated this problem.

In addition, the Voting Rights Act of 1965 helped to end redistricting discrimination based on race. Today both race and population must be considered in redistricting at any level. Although the states themselves set the district boundaries, almost all states use Census Bureau data to redistrict.

### A Windfall of Data

The 1990 Census has the potential to provide political campaigns with a windfall of demographic information. For the first time, most states will receive census data (*i.e.*, voting age population by race) tabulated and broken down into political precincts and block-counts for the entire country. In addition, the Census Bureau's new computerized mapping system will make it easier for campaigns to address-match voter files to census data.

Much of the above, however, is predicated on how much the states do to delineate their precincts (so that precinct data can be made available to them), and how well the Census Bureau can deliver what it promises (its computerized mapping system, for example, has fallen behind schedule). Campaigns should also be aware that many district lines will change as a result of the 1990 Census, and they will have to make adjustments accordingly.

### BIBLIOGRAPHY

Hill, David R., Kent, Mary M. *Election Demographics*, Washington, D.C.: Population Reference Bureau, Inc., January 1988.

Kramer, Kevin L., Schneider, Edward J. "Innovations in Campaign Research: Finding the Voters in the 1980s." In *New Communication Technologies in Politics*. Edited by Robert Meadow. Washington, D.C.: Annenberg School of Communication, 1985.

Mathews, Jay. "California Asians Outnumber Blacks." *Washington Post*. April 24, 1988. A3.

Merrick, Thomas W., Tordella, Stephen J. *Demographics: People and Markets*, Washington, D.C.: Population Reference Bureau, Inc., February, 1988.

Moore, John W. "Head-Count Hot Potato." *National Journal*. December 12, 1987. 3143-3146.

*The Bicentennial Census: New Directions for Methodology in 1990*. Edited by Constance F. Citro and Michael L. Cohen, Washington, D.C.: National Academy Press, 1985.

*1990 Census Automation Committee Report*, Washington, D.C.: U.S. Department of Commerce. Census Bureau. November 10, 1983.

*Counting for Representation: The Census and the Constitution*. Washington, D.C.: U.S. Department of Commerce. Census Bureau.

*Larry A. Checco* is a Washington, D.C.-based writer/political analyst. He has reported on politics for a number of national publications. Mr. Checco received his M.A. in Journalism and Public Affairs from The American University, Washington, D.C.

*Kimball W. Brace* is President of Election Data Services, Inc. (E.D.S., Inc.), a Washington, D.C.-based political consulting firm that specializes in reapportionment, redistricting and campaign targeting. An expert witness in many of the key redistricting court cases of the 1980s, Mr. Brace is heavily involved in the planning for the 1990 round of redistricting in many states.

*E.D.S., Inc.* is one of the only companies in the nation that regularly manipulates and integrates census data and election results at the precinct level for campaigns. It collects precinct returns and maps from every county in the U.S. The firm is already heavily involved in the utilization of the Census Bureau's new TIGER mapping files for address matching purposes. E.D.S., Inc. is also nationally noted for its color-coded maps of election results.

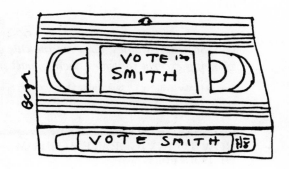

# THE CAMPAIGN VIDEO

"There are now nearly 40 million videocassette recorders in people's homes. These constitute a network within themselves.

Many campaigns are utilizing this new network in innovative and perhaps significant ways. They distribute videocassettes to voters to urge them to work for the candidate and to contribute money. The videos are seen in homes or in public places where people gather."

*Newton N. Minow*

"Certainly every campaign consultant sees the VCR as a great new marketplace. But most people want a VCR to escape from regular television or from commercials and the last thing they want is to sit and watch something from a candidate."

*Ed Rollins*

*One basic criticism of television is that programs cannot be repeated or reexamined. The videocassette recorder (VCR) changes this. VCRs can now be found in more than half of America's homes, and allow viewers to choose their own viewing time and to repeat a program as many times as desired.*

*In a political context this may help move us beyond journalist Robert MacNeil's observation that "fast food, fast ideas are the way to get to a fast, impatient public reared on television."[1] A wide variety of organizations are pumping out tapes that argue issues and present candidates. Candidates themselves produce videos, typically 10 minutes long, for fundraisers.*

*The accepted political wisdom is that the reach of such videos is limited, that most people willing to watch a cassette are already committed to a candidate, and that the cassette is a reinforcing mechanism or a fundraising device.*

*Scholarly studies, however, indicate a growing public interest in tapes, and, as the following excerpt indicates, their impact in campaigning could be significant.*

1. Robert MacNeil, "Is TV Shortening Our Attention Span?" *National Forum* 4(Fall 1981):21.

## HOW TO INVIGORATE BOTTOM-UP POLITICS

*Arthur B. Shostak*

Characterized at the outset by its very proud sponsor, the AFL-CIO, as "the most extensive education effort ever launched by any organization to involve voters in presidential politics," the *Democracy at Work* Project exceeded the robust goals of its designers, and then some![1] Throughout 1987 this two-part package (videotape and hard copy) set a record for bringing more grassroots unionists into greater-than-ever knowledge of the leading presidential candidates. And this educational feat allowed labor, in turn, to impact responsively and proudly on the '88 presidential contest. Bold in conception, polished in execution, and morale-boosting in every way, *Democracy at Work* could go into labor annals as an exemplary innovation!

### Background

Labor's political pros knew full well they could not galvanize voters any longer by simply endorsing a candidate. Those days were gone forever, as a "show me!" independent voter now dominated C.O.P.E.'s [Committee on Political Education] list of rank-and-filers worth phoning at election time. The way to win over this unionist was first to substantially *involve* him or her in the candidate selection process . . . or at least provide a plausible opportunity for such involvement:

"Traditional vote-churning organizations, such as the labor union and the urban machine, no longer function as they once did, largely because the electorate itself has changed. The American public increasingly seems to be made up of individuals with few deep political or organizational commitments, who form what ties they do have on the basis of information from the media, and who don't like to vote for a candidate just on some big shot's say so."[2]

An attention-getting and classy format was required to spotlight the 1988 presidential hopefuls, poll the responses of concerned unionists, and help guide the AFL-CIO endorsement policy.

### Doing It Better This Time Around

Despite its overall gains in the Congressional elections of '86, labor in '87 was still smarting from Mondale's defeat three years earlier. Labor's pre-convention endorsement of "Fritz," a robust move at the time, stirred much controversy then and since. Some political commentators allege it may have finally lost votes for the Democratic standard-bearer, a contention even certain unionists now accept; *e.g.*—

" 'Mondale had earned our support, and I think early endorsement is a good idea, but 1984 probably wasn't the best time to try it for the first time,' said Linda Rasmussen, president of a CWA local in Portland, Oregon. 'I don't think anybody was going to beat Reagan.'

K.W. Flanagan, a delegate (to the July '87 CWA convention) was even more vehement. 'We screwed up in 1984 by selecting so early,' he said. 'That turned a lot of my people off because it looked to them like the fix was in, and they were left out of it. I think a lot of them voted for Reagan as a result.' "[3]

While the AFL-CIO officially rejects this line of analysis, and will not apologize for its '84 political effort, the charges sting . . . and labor has been eager to get beyond them. (The AFL-CIO insists, nearly five of 13 million AFL-CIO members *were* polled *before* any endorsement was made).[4]

This time around it was going to be very different, or so AFL-CIO leadership resolved. This time the record would make unequivocally clear the ample and unfettered participation of *any* concerned rank-and-filer. Ordinary members would dominate the process by which their union would help the AFL-CIO General Board choose one or more presidential aspirants worth labor's unified backing. This time the pundits, the labor bashers, and the sore losers (among those seeking labor's endorsement) would look ridiculous if they dared charge "bossism," "special interest peonage," "back room deals," "membership puppetry," or any other such nonsense . . . as in '84 had Sen. Gary Hart, the Reagan election committee, and anti-Mondale types.

### Making It Happen

Sometime in 1986 the Federation cranked up one of the most efficient and effective political endorsement systems extant, and over 3.5 million direct-mail letters went to unionists explaining why labor backed or opposed candidates in key Senate and House races. Ably conducted by specialists working for C.O.P.E., the largely successful '86 effort relied on a steadily-improved computer program capable of providing political data (registration status; ward, precinct, congressional, and state legislative/senate district; etc.) on all but a handful of the AFL-CIO's 13.5 million members.

With this success as a motivator, C.O.P.E. was instructed to join forces with another Federation unit, the Labor Institute on Public Affairs (L.I.P.A.) to help the AFL-CIO make good on its participatory resolve. A special project tagged *Democracy at Work* (DAW) was soon working very long hours to meet a tight deadline of October, 1987, at which time the AFL-CIO General Board would meet to learn how membership polls had instructed affiliate unions to rank the presidential contenders.

DAW turned quickly to the option posed by a low-cost, readily produced, and easily distributed videotape, buttressed, perhaps, by an amplifying leaflet, booklet, or the like. What *kind* of a videotape, however, and what *kind* of hardcopy, was another question altogether.

In 1983, for example, C.O.P.E. had innovated in inviting Democratic Senators Cranston (CA.), Glenn (Ohio), and Hart (Col.) to come before a video-taped leadership group and answer tough and specific labor-related questions . . . one heck of a novel and exciting experience for all!

The '83 format, however, did not lack for constructive critics; *e.g.*—

" 'The last time, somebody went into a room with 32 people, and they all named their favorite bill. Are you for situs picketing? Are you for H.R. 22?' said Rachelle Horowitz, political director of the American Federation of Teachers (AFT).

Loretta A. Bowen, political director for the Communications Workers of America (CWA), said she was glad that Kirkland was changing the '83 format, which she said concentrated on 'purely parochial labor issues.' "[5]

Given the reluctance, as well, of major presidential candidates to subject themselves to the '83 style of testy and nettlesome grilling, the DAW team had little trouble abandoning that approach.

Instead, the DAW team sought a new format that would accomplish six goals for its '87 videotape:

—It would draw the largest possible number of announced candidates.

—It would give each a chance to put their best foot forward.

—It would attract Republicans as well as Democrats.

—It would demonstrate labor's responsible curiosity about the positions of *all* major contenders.

—It would avoid controversy and acrimony in favor of having a calm and reasoned presentation by a candidate.

—It would hold all speakers to the same very tight time limit, the better to retain the rapt attention of union viewers throughout.

In the early spring of 1987 the DAW team invited the leading candidates to submit written responses to four political questions, and come over thereafter to the AFL-CIO headquarters to make a 4½ minute videotaped presentation of their views on the "unique leadership role of the presidency." (Each was filmed standing at a white podium emblazoned with the clasped hands logo of the AFL-CIO.)

### Why Bother?

The candidates were told this unprecedented taping would give them "an opportunity to convince us you understand the aspirations of working-class people and will include our concerns in a leadership plan to serve all the people."[6] Each was asked to provide in writing their ideas for lowering the trade deficit. For reducing the federal budget deficit. For setting the government's role in domestic social policy. And for organized labor's role in the political process.

Cynics were quick to whisper this was a "party" few candidates, if any, would attend, and certainly not any Republicans. As well, in light of the lingering controversy over whether or not Mondale's endorsement by Big Labor in '84 had helped or hurt him, many Democratic candidates would be expected to cop out, discreetly apologizing that they had unavoidable schedule conflicts. C.O.P.E.'s *Democracy at Work* would bomb, and go into labor annals as just another revealing demonstration of labor's chronic inability to get its act together.

### Hail, Hail, the Gang's All Here!

In fact, however, *everybody* came! And labor's "party" was a huge success! Every announced presidential candidate accepted an invitation to pitch for the votes of 13 million trade unionists, the very fact of their cooperation as clear and firm a tribute to labor's political clout as unionists could wish!

Cynical forecasts to the contrary, a highly polished videotape made in the AFL-CIO building in April 1987, included 13 such "stars" as—

*Democrats*

Gov. Bruce Babbitt
Sen. Joseph R. Biden, Jr.
Gov. Michael S. Dukakis
Repr. Richard Gephardt
Sen Albert Gore, Jr.
Rev. Jesse Jackson
Sen. Paul Simon

*Republicans*

Vice President George Bush
Sen. Robert Dole
Gov. Pete du Pont
Mr. Alexander M. Haig, Jr.
Rep. Jack Kemp
Rev. Pat Robertson

In tandem, a special issue of the *American Federationist* offered the carefully worded, engaging, and cogent answers of 12 of the 13 presidential aspirants to labor's four overarching questions (Robertson passed this up).[7]

State federation bodies, city labor councils, and locals everywhere quickly discovered the "two-punch" package had genuine appeal, and higher-than-ever levels of turnout (members *and* spouses) became commonplace. (Impressed by the size and reaction of audiences they witnessed, reporters for the *Washington Post* told readers labor had put together "the hottest new video in politics—a sort of sneak preview of the 1988 campaign.")[8]

*Two Stars? Three? Four?* When I asked C.O.P.E. staffers how their 66-minute videotape was going over, I learned—
—demand was so good an unprecedented 10,000 copies had been created to meet urgent orders from all 50 states; and

—audiences stayed alert from beginning to end, despite the repetitions natural from 13 candidates held to less than five minutes each. Particular pleasure was taken in the fact that audience members felt *they* were being appealed to, that *their* approval and vote was being solicited in a cogent, focused, and adult manner: Many rank-and-filers told union film showers they could not recall ever being taken so seriously by the leading politicians in the land.

More subtle, though no less significant, was the appreciation expressed for the straightforward manner with which the videotape delivered its content—shorn of all the PR flim-flam and high tech razzle-dazzle the primary winners were likely to disappear behind as the November '88 showdown drew closer. Many rank-and-filers explained how bewildering they found high-powered political ads, and what a welcomed breath of fresh air was gimmick-less old-fashioned oratory on this AFL-CIO production.

Still more intriguing yet was a line of analysis I picked up from C.O.P.E. staffers, one I might not have gotten as readily from . . . laymen. The staffers were flattered by the use made by all the presidential hopefuls of greetings like "my friends of the AFL-CIO," ". . . women and men of labor," or even "My fellow unionists . . ." (in the case of Gov. Dukakis, Rep. Kemp, and Sen. Simon). Politicians generally take a very different tack, and use salutations like "My fellow citizens," or some other such labor-*distancing* expression. As Republican candidates, in particular, hesitate to use any salutation respectfully acknowledging labor's existence, let alone follow with an earnest plea for the votes of trade unionists, this was regarded as welcomed recognition of labor's political significance.

### Utilization Guidelines

Eager to assure the videotape and the hardcopy answers (the *American Federationist* special issue) were used correctly and with maximum effect, the DAW team established several thoughtful guidelines:

Audience members were to be encouraged to *react* vocally to all 13 presentations: A viewing was not regarded as successful *unless* rank-and-filers publicly shared their reactions to the candidates, the issues, and the importance of political participation by unionists and their families.

Audience members were to be urged to read the

special issue of the *Federationist* at home, and share their reactions with other rank-and-filers.

No discussions of candidate preference, or straw polls, were to follow a screening of the tape. The DAW program was the *educational* phase of the AFL-CIO political process. Later, before the October "choose-a-candidate(s)" meeting of the AFL-CIO General Board, members would get a chance to express their preferences through their unions, rather than through any arm of the AFL-CIO (city, state or national).[9]

Audiences were to be restricted to members of AFL-CIO unions and their families, as Federal election law forbade the Federation from distributing the written questions or showing the videotape to the general public.

Scrupulous impartiality was to be shown to all 13 speakers and to both parties: "The trust in the AFL-CIO displayed by the cooperation of the candidates must be reciprocated."[10]

Above all, unions were urged to assure that the views and preferences of members were determined in a manner that "leads to a bottom-up, rather than a top-down decision."[11]

### Extending the Project

So positive was rank-and-file response that two IUs [International Unions] created tag-on videos of their own to accompany the AFL-CIO item. The American Federation of Government Employees and the Union of Letter Carriers joined forces to produce their own tape of seven Democratic aspirants speaking about specific concerns of federal employees, such as "privatization" of federal programs and Hatch Act reform (all of the Republican hopefuls declined to participate).[12]

Getting into the spirit, the American Federation of State, County, and Municipal Employees (AFSCME) printed a poll in its newspaper that drew an average of 200 mail ballots from members throughout the Summer of '87. A similar mail-in poll in the Machinists' newspaper also earned a high response, with some 84 percent showing a preference for the Democrats.[13] Other major unions were not to be outdone; *e.g.*—

the July '87 issue of the Carpenter began a series on political action with the proposed solutions of the 13 candidates to the growing threat of foreign trade;

the July '87 convention of 700 delegates representing the 200,000 members of BRAC (the Brothers of Railway, Airline, and Steamship Clerks) filled out questionnaires on the candidates and issues, even as the union's magazine solicited a straw ballot vote from all BRAC members; and

the July '87 issue of *UFCW Action*, the magazine of the Food & Commercial Workers, focused on the views of candidates of the role of government in meeting human needs.

Publications of state federations and city labor councils also reprinted the views of the would-be presidents, and there soon was little excuse left for shrugging from ignorance when the name of one or the other came up in union political banter.

### Personal Reaction

When I saw the videotape with 15 Meany Center students, all of them local union officers or activists, on July 31, 1987, I was favorably struck by five impressions:

—The rhetoric was pitched at an adult and informed level, with no air of condescension or patronizing tone: Listeners were given credit for possessing a generalist's awareness of the key campaign issues.
—Republican candidates gave the union audience credit for possessing an open mind on the candidates and their positions; each complimented President Kirkland and the AFL-CIO for offering the G.O.P. a valuable opportunity to compare and contrast its front-runners with those of the Democratic Party.
—Democratic candidates gave the union audience credit for possessing an open mind on *the* major dilemma in front of that party—whether to go with the familiar FDR-Truman-Kennedy tradition (a la Dukakis, Jackson, and Simon), or take some upscale new tack (a la Babbitt, Biden, Gephardt and Gore).
—All of the speakers noted their varied efforts over the years to help the labor movement, with some, such as Gov. Babbitt, taking the opportunity to "set the record straight" where a seemingly anti-labor move was concerned (his use of the National Guard to end a major copper mine strike): The net impact was probably to swell the pride of union audiences in the significance their movement seemed to have to these 13 representative "big shots."
—The presence of the Republican candidates finessed the "special interest" charge that had long plagued labor: As CWA President Morton Bahr explained, ". . . we've taken the curse off what happened to Mondale. No one will be able to accuse someone else of being a 'captive' of labor."[14]

Overall, I found myself genuinely appreciative of the opportunity to ponder rhetoric custom-tailored for labor's support, and to "sense" the potential of the would-be presidents to further (or hamper) labor's political agenda.

In discussion with some unionists afterward, however, I raised three misgivings of my own:

I wondered if it would have helped to have had the C.O.P.E. rating of the voting record of each speaker, the better to sort our proven labor supporters from the others.

I wondered if it would have helped to have surprise questions posed to each, the better to expose their ability at spontaneous thinking (along with their capacity to deliver carefully prepared formal statements).

And I wondered if it would have helped to prepare and show a second videotape of revealing criticisms of the programs, policies, and voting record of all 13 politicians, the better to set their political record straight for videotape viewers.

While sympathetic with my goals, most of the unionists with whom I spoke faulted the means: Candidates who had not held federal legislative office had no C.O.P.E. voting record, I was told. And the use of different "surprise" questions would lay the tape open to a charge of bias or favoritism should some surprises appear tougher than others. As for a second tape of criticisms, many feared rank-and-file viewers might be overwhelmed by all the facts and figures: Some might turn away from political participation altogether, hardly a desirable outcome at all.

Satisfied by these sensitive rejoinders, I felt encouraged to raise one last nagging doubt. Could it be, I asked, that the entire project amounted to little more than "preaching to the converted"? Those rank-and-filers willing to give a precious evening to a union showing of the C.O.P.E. videotape were probably politically alert and relatively well-informed beforehand. The "no-shows," however, were probably a large plurality of the membership, a group indifferent to "egg-head" tools like this videotape. Could it be that *Democracy at Work* therefore demonstrated something else altogether, something more like how very taxing it actually was to get democracy to work at all?!

While quick to murmur "touche!" and to concede the limits of an all-talk, no-action 66-minute long presentation, the tape's proponents insisted I had missed a key point. The tape, alas, might appeal to few unionists otherwise turned off by such items. But it would complement the self-definition of local union *activists*—a type later strategic in manning election phone banks, stuffing envelopes, posting handbills, and in sundry other ways,

making concrete labor's political clout. The tape, in short, was something of a rallying cry, a call to arms, in effect. And this galvanizing of activists actually helped invigorate democracy in and outside of labor.

With these various qualms of mine now reasonably met, I was prepared to conclude with my fellow-viewers that it had been "one helluva fine experience, one damn good film!"

### Summary

A labor educator friend of mine and Meany Center colleague, Hig Roberts, on hearing of my interest in the DAW project, volunteered a judgment grounded in his 30-plus years in union affairs:

"It was a *brilliant* move. Not because of what was or wasn't said, almost all of which will be forgotten. But because they actually pulled it off! They actually got the front-runners together, and put the whole thing together . . . People like to feel they matter, like to believe their opinions count for something, and this goldarn film helps them feel good about themselves!"[15]

As his role has had him see the tape over and again with various audiences of grassroots unionists throughout the South, I attach special value to his assessment.

As of this writing (December 1987) it is by no means clear who will eventually emerge from the Iowa, New Hampshire, and other primaries as a likely candidate for AFL-CIO endorsement (or even for multi-candidate backing). Nor can it be known now, of course, if labor will wind up backing the November '88 winner, though its extraordinary voter-access apparatus almost guarantees it a significant role in determining the outcome.

Only this much presently seems clear: Regardless of the fate of labor's involvement in the '88 presidential campaign, labor is *already* something of a winner. Its videotape/hard-copy project has come off as designed, and has far exceeded expectations. (The media consensus, a proud *AFL-CIO News* boasts, is that the project has "dwarfed any education campaign ever undertaken to involve voters.")[16] It has enhanced labor's political respectability, and has boosted political sophistication and morale in the ranks. Above all, it has helped affirm labor's commitment to *bottom-up* politics, affirm and demonstrate it so clearly as to give a substantial lift to any—in and outside of labor—eager to believe democracy *works*!

## NOTES

1. Anon. " 'Democracy at Work' Project Draws Praise from News Media." *AFL-CIO News*, June 27, 1987. p. 2.

2. Anon. "See How They Run." *The New Republic*, May 4, 1987. p. 7.

3. As quoted in Dickenson, James R. "Early Labor Endorsement Not Expected for 1988." *Washington Post*, July 31, 1987. p. A-6.

4. The AFL-CIO relies here on a poll taken in late 1983 by the *N.Y. Times*, as cited in private correspondence to me from Ben Albert, Dir., Public Relations, Committee on Political Education, AFL-CIO (August 27, 1987).

5. As quoted in Barnes, James A. "Labor's Mixed Blessing." *National Journal*, March 28, 1987. p. 84.

6. As transcribed by me from the videotape, and as narrated by actor Ned Beatty.

7. Anon. " 'Democracy at Work' Project . . . ," *AFL-CIO News*, op. cit.

8. As quoted in Dickenson, "Early Labor Endorsement . . . ," *Washington Post*, op. cit.

9. So firm is this commitment that a C.O.P.E. officer, David Gregory, present at a film showing I attended, rose and left when a straw ballot was taken immediately after the screening. Seeing him outside patiently waiting in the hallway I joined him briefly to ask "why?," and smiled on hearing his whispered reply, "I am barred by my office from being present at *any* polling on the candidates."

10. C.O.P.E. "Presidential Candidate Education Program: Guidelines for State and Local Central Bodies." Washington, DC: AFL-CIO, 1987. p. 1.

11. AFL-CIO. "Statement by the AFL-CIO Executive Council on AFL-CIO Presidential Political Process Voluntary Guidelines."

12. Anon. "Government Unions Augment Videotapes on '88 Contenders." *AFL-CIO News*, June 13, 1987. p. 2.

13. Schwartz, Maralee and David S. Broder. "Labor May Split Support Among 1988 Contenders." *Washington Post*, July 23, 1982. p. A-4.

14. As quoted in Dickenson, "Early Labor Endorsement . . . ," *Washington Post*, op. cit.

15. Personal conversation; G. Meany Center, July 30, 1987. (Cited with permission.)

16. Anon. "Voter Education Drive Pays Dividends." *AFL-CIO News*, August 15, 1987. p. 2.

From a book-in-preparation, *Robust Unionism: Case Studies in Labor Creativity*, by Arthur B. Shostak (sociologist, Drexel University, Philadelphia; Adjunct Sociologist, AFL-CIO Antioch College Program, George Meany Center, Silver Spring, Md.).

# SETTING THE AGENDA

"In-depth commentary and analysis are rare commodities in television news, a medium which rations out information in small parcels so that it may be clearly grasped by an audience conditioned to passivity by sensory assault. But steady exposure to fleeting visuals and sound bytes—each reinforcing a common theme—can build powerfully fixed images in the public mind. Such propagandizing is so subliminal its full impact often escapes the consciousness of its own agents, allowing artful outsiders to manipulate the meduim's pervasive influence for their own advantage.

Such influence cannot be minimized, for the ability to engineer public perceptions confers the power to rule a democracy."

*David Beiler*

*Technological advances are now extending television's reach and are making its images far more visual and fast-paced. Quick cuts are common and argumentation is often packed into 15 seconds. In politics, a 60-second commercial is now "long-form."*

*The television audience, moreover, is increasingly what can be called the MTV generation, people who prefer images and sounds over words and analysis. An advertising executive explains: "What makes them unique is that they are children of the new technology—the first to grow up with a whole new audio and visual environment, from cable to VCRs to computers. . . . They are different in the way they process information."[1]*

*These developments have stimulated a new generation of researchers who take the impact of television for granted, no longer as something that must be proven. This frees them to explore television's non-verbal, visual impact, and to examine what Neil Postman calls the way "television's images penetrate and then shape public consciousness."[2]*

*One of the most exciting works in this area is <u>News That Matters</u> by political scientists Shanto Iyengar and Donald R. Kinder. This book demonstrates that "television* *news does indeed influence the priorities the American public assigns to national problems." Iyengar and Kinder then carry this one step further by demonstrating what they call "the priming effect." They argue that "by calling attention to some matters while ignoring others, television news influences the standards by which governments, presidents, policies and candidates for public office are judged." Priming, they say, "refers to changes in the standards that people use to make political evaluations."*

*The following excerpt from Iyengar and Kinder discusses priming in congressional campaigns. When reading it, keep in mind the authors' conclusion is based on over a dozen experiments not limited to congressional campaigns: "[Priming has] a robust effect; it occurs in coverage of various problems, for both Democrats and Republican presidents; in different experimental arrangements, and in analyses that remove the effects due to projection."*

*Following Iyengar and Kinder is material that discusses how issue-oriented groups, regardless of ideological or partisan background, are pursuing a form of priming. Issue-oriented groups build their efforts upon data from public opinion polls and focus group testing, which form the basis for "agenda packets"—press releases, flyers, videocassettes, television commercials and grassroots efforts designed to reshape political discussion.*

*Such long-term, opinion-molding efforts usually involve "soft" persuasive techniques, and have been common in the nonpolitical marketplace for years. National advertisers, for example, frequently prime their potential customers before introducing a new product or service.*

*Priming does not create public opinion; it locates, shapes and energizes pre-existing dispositions such as the desire for adequate health care.*

*Discussions of the impact of television must always remain in perspective. Thus, the last elements in this section—contributed by Jeff Greenfield and George Will—offer a useful reminder that television is far from all-powerful.*

1. Quoted in Margot Hornblower, "Madison Avenue Adapts to Generation of Skeptics," *Washington Post* 29 May 1986.

2. Neil Postman, "What You See Is How You Vote," *New York Times* Book Review Section, 7 February 1988, p. 9.

## ELECTORAL CONSEQUENCES OF PRIMING: VOTING IN U.S. HOUSE ELECTIONS

*Shanto Iyengar and Donald R. Kinder*

Candidates for public office go to extraordinary lengths in order to "make news" . . . In doing so, candidates hope to prime voters' choices to their own advantage. The experiments reported in this chapter provide a partial assessment of how realistic such hopes are. Here we extend our investigation of priming to elections—and therefore to the core of democracy—examining both a congressional

and a presidential campaign. In each instance our purpose is to illuminate the relationship between the preoccupations of television news and the decisions voters make on election day.

By the standards of presidential elections and certainly by the standards of civics textbooks, the votes citizens cast in House elections appear ill-informed and lightly-considered. No doubt . . . voters appear to follow simple rules of thumb. . . .

. . . Voting in House elections reflects a mix of partisanship, incumbency, national economic conditions, and the personal qualities of the candidates. We propose that the relative importance of these various considerations depends partly on how intensively each is primed. Voters exposed to local news broadcasts that focus on the national economy should be guided especially by their assessments of national economic conditions. Voters whose local news programs focus on the House candidates should be especially likely to choose according to their appraisals of the personal qualities of the candidates. Voters exposed to local newscasts that emphasize neither should rely especially on party and incumbency.

To test for priming effects in congressional elections, we embedded an experiment within the final days of the 1982 midterm House election in the third district of Connecticut.[1] The Third District spreads across south and central Connecticut and includes the city of New Haven. The 1982 contest pitted Lawrence DeNardis, the Republican first-term incumbent, against Bruce Morrison, the liberal Democratic challenger. Experiment 10, run in sequence style, began on October 25 and ended on October 30, three days prior to election day. Participants were recruited in the usual fashion with the additional stipulation that they be registered voters (91 percent of those recruited were in fact registered). Participants were randomly assigned to one of three treatment conditions, each offering a slightly different rendition of the evening *local* television news.

In the first, each day participants watched a half-hour newscast that included a 3-5 minute segment devoted to the candidates. These stories dealt with positions on public issues taken by DeNardis and Morrison, the groups that had endorsed them and their personal backgrounds. . . .

Participants in the second condition watched the identical news shows, except that stories about the candidates were replaced by stories about the economy. Most of these segments drew direct connections between the state of the economy, President Reagan's policies, and the midterm elections . . .

Participants assigned to the third condition constituted a neutral comparison group. They watched the same local broadcasts, but purged of any references to the candidates, the economy, or the impending election.

Our major interest here, of course, is in priming. We need to determine whether differences in the focus of local television news over the course of a week led to systematic differences in the criteria voters applied in selecting their representative. In the shadowy world of House elections, however, local television news may serve a more elementary function as well. Because voters typically know so little about the candidates who compete to represent them in Washington, a week's worth of campaign coverage may be quite instructive. Voters may become more informed about who the candidates are, which party they represent, the issues that divide them, and so forth. We will therefore assess whether television news coverage not only primes but also informs the voter.

### Informing Congressional Voters

One day after the last newscast, participants were asked to identify the party affiliations of the two candidates. Only 56 percent of the participants assigned to the control condition (who saw no stories about the candidates) knew that DeNardis was the Republican and that Morrison was the Democrat. Meanwhile, virtually *all* participants assigned to the candidate condition—94 percent—correctly associated DeNardis and Morrison with their parties.[2]

Participants were also asked whether there was anything in particular that they liked about each candidate, and, in a separate question, whether there was anything in particular they disliked about each. As expected, people assigned to the candidate condition had more to say in response to these questions than did those assigned to the control condition. This difference between conditions was somewhat greater in the case of viewers' comments about Morrison, the challenger, than about DeNardis, the incumbent.[3]

Participants were then asked the degree to which they agreed with first DeNardis and then Morrison on a series of five policy questions: nuclear arms control, social security, unemployment, defense spending, and federal aid to education. We expected the proportion of viewers who felt unable to say whether they agreed or not to be comparatively large in the control condition, and so it was: 44 percent of those assigned to the neutral condition could not indicate their level of agreement with DeNardis on all five policy questions, as compared to just 26 percent of those assigned to the candidate condition. This difference was somewhat sharper in participants' judgments of policy agreement with Morrison: the corresponding figures there were 44 percent and 16 percent.[4]

Finally, we examined the extent to which our participants had an impression of the candidates' personal qualities. Participants were asked how well each of eleven personality characteristics described DeNardis and then how well each described Morrison. As expected, participants who watched news broadcasts that paid attention to the candidates were more prepared to offer personality judgments than were those who watched news broadcasts that gave no attention to the candidates (although the differences were surprisingly small). Participants assigned to the candidate condition answered on average 65 percent of the trait questions posed to them about DeNardis and 61 percent of the trait questions posed to them about Morrison. Among participants assigned to the control condition, these averages fell off to 60 percent and 53 percent, respectively.[5]

In summary, we find modest but consistent differences in the anticipated direction. Voters assigned to local news that provided significant coverage of the House candidates knew more about them than did their counterparts whose broadcasts ignored the candidates: they were more able to identify (correctly) the candidates' party affiliation; they had more to say about each candidate and seemed to know more (or at least felt they knew more) about the candidates' policy stands and personal characteristics.[6] Although never decisively so, the differences were generally a bit sharper in participants' impressions of Morrison than of DeNardis. Since incumbents are typically much better known than challengers (Mann and Wolfinger 1980), our experimental intervention conveyed, in effect, more information about Morrison than DeNardis.

We also looked for differences in how much participants knew about the state of the national economy, the focus of the other experimental treatment, but in vain ... Evidently, our experimental manipulation regarding national economic conditions merely duplicated information participants had already gleaned from other sources—from newspapers, magazines, national television news, day-to-day conversations, and their own experiences.[7]

### Priming Congressional Voters

Another and quite separate question is whether the experimentally-induced emphasis upon the state of the economy affected the importance voters attached to the economy in deciding between DeNardis and Morrison ... We tested three separate propositions, each a specific incarnation of priming. First, do viewers exposed to news about the economy rely more heavily on their assessments of economic conditions when reaching their vote decision, in comparison to viewers exposed to news about the candidates or to no news of the election at all? Second, do viewers exposed to coverage of the candidates grant more importance to the qualities they admired in the candidates than do viewers in either of the other two treatments? And third, do viewers given no information about the campaign rely more heavily on partisanship and incumbency than do viewers in the economy and candidate treatments?

To answer these questions we obviously need to know how participants voted. Here we took an indirect route. Each participant was asked to evaluate both DeNardis and Morrison on a one hundred-point "thermometer" scale, on which zero degrees means a very negative evaluation (extremely cold), one hundred degrees means a very positive evaluation (extremely warm), and fifty degrees means a neutral or ambivalent evaluation. Previous election studies have demonstrated a close connection between the thermometer ratings citizens make of the contending candidates shortly before the election and the votes they eventually cast (*e.g.*, Brody and Page 1973; Mann 1978), and so it was in the Third District in 1982 ...

We presume that voters arrive at their ratings of the two candidates (and therefore their votes) by taking into account four considerations: their candidates' party affiliations,[8] their comparative visibility (a measure of the incumbent's advantage),[9] the candidates' personal qualities,[10] and national economic conditions.[11] ... If the priming hypothesis holds, then the impact of economic conditions should increase when local news focuses on the nation's economy, the impact of the personal qualities of candidates should increase when local news focuses on the candidates, and the impact of party and incumbency should increase, by default, when local news focuses on neither the economy nor the candidates.

Our analysis sustains the first two predictions but not the third ... judgments of national economic conditions predicted thermometer ratings powerfully, regardless of experimental condition. Even when not primed by economic news, voters who were more optimistic about national economic conditions preferred DeNardis over Morrison more often than did those who were more pessimistic about the economy ... When viewers were primed with economic news, the impact of economic assessments on evaluation of the candidates more than triples: a difference of four points on the index of economic optimism translated into a DeNardis advantage of over forty degrees.

An even stronger priming effect emerged with respect to candidate qualities. Unremarkably, viewers who saw more positive qualities in DeNardis than Morrison felt more warmly toward DeNardis, even when their local broadcasts ignored the candidates entirely. Such viewers who mentioned two positive qualities about DeNardis but who could think of nothing they liked about Morrison rated the former more warmly, on average, by some thirteen degrees. But among viewers primed with information about the candidates, the impact of this same difference increased nearly fivefold. Now viewers with nothing good to say about Morrison who cited two favorable qualities about DeNardis rated the latter more warmly on the thermometer by more than sixty degrees. This is a huge and politically consequential priming effect.

Contrary to expectation, we found no support for the prediction that incumbency and party would both grow more powerful when voters were not "distracted" by news about the economy or information about the candidates ... Party identification did have strong *indirect* effects, however, shaping both voters' assessments of national economic conditions and their impressions of the candidates. Democrats expressed more pessimistic opinions about the nation's economy than did Republicans; similarly, they said more nice things about Morrison than DeNardis. Thus, party identification did contribute to voters' thermometer ratings of the candidates, but indirectly. Furthermore, these indirect effects of party identification were strengthened by the focus of news coverage, just as the priming hypothesis would suggest. On the one hand, the impact of party identification on views of national economic conditions increased among viewers assigned to local news devoted to the national economy. That is, compared to Republicans, Democrats were more pessimistic in their economic assessments and more critical of the Reagan administration's economic performance when local news focused on national economic conditions.[12] On the other hand, the impact of party identification on appraisals of the two candidates increased among viewers assigned to local news devoted to the candidates. That is, compared to Republicans, Democrats had more nice things to say about Morrison than about DeNardis when the local news focused on the candidates.[13]

The electoral consequence of the kinds of priming effects we have detected here can be very substantial. Depending upon the mixture of other forces at work in a campaign, they may even be decisive. For illustrative purposes, consider voters in Connecticut's Third District who recognized both DeNardis and Morrison and were ambivalent toward them (*i.e.*, they named as many positive qualities for DeNardis as for Morrison). Such voters who were also modestly upbeat about the national economy, according to our analysis, would tend to support DeNardis. But DeNardis could count on their support to a much greater degree if the voters received news about the nation's economy than if they watched news that emphasized the candidates ...

These projections from our experimental results suggest that voters can be moved from indecision to strong preference depending only on the coverage that television news provides. It is not unreasonable to conclude that priming may sometimes determine who wins and who loses. In the Third District in 1982, Lawrence DeNardis spent over $300,000 and received more than 88,000 votes. It was not quite enough. With 50.5 percent of the vote, Morrison was elected; DeNardis was sent home.[14]

### Summary and Conclusion

Our election experiments show that priming operates on the choices voters make. The priorities that are uppermost in voters' minds as they go to the polls to select a president or a U.S. Representative appear to be powerfully shaped by the last-minute preoccupations of television news.

NOTES

1. This experiment was conceived and conducted by Roy Behr, as part of his Ph.D. dissertation research in the Department of Political Science at Yale University.
2. Corrected Chi-square = 5.33 with 1 degree of freedom, p = .021.
3. For DeNardis, 1.42 replies on average versus 1.06: p = .37 by F-test. For Morrison, 1.32 replies on average versus .89: p = .17.
4. For DeNardis, Chi-square with 5 degrees of freedom = 3.96, p = .56; for Morrison, Chi-square with 5 degrees of freedom = 4.94, p = .42. Participants assigned to candidate coverage were also more likely

to agree or disagree strongly with the candidates. For DeNardis, p = .17 by F-test; for Morrison, p = .08

5. For DeNardis, p = .68 by F-test; for Morrison, p = .53.

6. These results are corroborated by Goldenberg and Traugott's survey-based analysis of incumbents and challengers running for Congress in 1978 (Goldenberg and Traugott 1984).

7. On average, participants in the control treatment expressed opinions on the economy 98 percent of the time while participants in the economy treatment did so 96 percent of the time.

8. Participants were asked if they generally thought of themselves as Democrats, Republicans, Independents, or something else.

9. Participants were asked to name the two candidates. Those who correctly identified DeNardis but were unable to name Morrison received a score of +1; those unable to name either candidate or who named both candidates got scores of 0; and those who named Morrison but not DeNardis received scores of −1. Thus the higher the score, the greater the relative visibility of the incumbent.

10. Participants were asked "Is there anything in particular you like about Larry DeNardis? What?" They were permitted to list up to three characteristics. The identical question was asked with respect to Morrison. We subtracted the number of positive qualities ascribed to Morrison from the number ascribed to DeNardis. This measure thus ranges from −3 (three likes mentioned for Morrison, none for DeNardis) to +3 (three likes mentioned for DeNardis, none for Morrison).

11. We constructed an index of economic pessimism based on answers to four separate questions. First, participants indicated whether they thought the economy had improved, stayed the same, or worsened over the past year. They also indicated whether the economy would improve, stay the same, or deteriorate during the coming year. Participants then evaluated President Reagan's performance in "handling the economy" on a scale from "very poor job" to "very good job." Finally, participants indicated whether problems of the economy would be handled better by the Republicans or the Democrats. Responses to these questions were then added together (the index ranges from four to fourteen). Low scores indicate pessimism about the economy, negative evaluations of Reagan's economic record, and the perception that Democrats deal with economic problems more effectively than Republicans do. Conversely, high scores indicate upbeat perceptions of the economy, favorable evaluations of Reagan's economic performance, and the perception that Republicans are better than Democrats in solving economic problems.

12. This effect is represented in statistical terms by the interaction between party identification and assignment to the economy treatment. In an equation predicting assessments of economic conditions, this interaction approaches statistical significance: B = 1.68, se = 1.69, t = 0.99, p .18.

13. In statistical terms, this effect is represented by the interaction between party identification and assignment to the candidate treatment. In an equation predicting the difference between positive qualities mentioned about DeNardis and positive qualities mentioned about Morrison, this interaction is marginally significant: B = 1.09, se = .87, t = 1.27, p .10.

14. These figures are taken from *The Almanac of American Politics, 1984.* Vote percentage reflects division of the two-party totals.

---

# AFSCME TAKES TO TELEVISION TO PROMOTE ACTIVIST ROLE OF GOVERNMENT IN 1988 PRESIDENTIAL CAMPAIGN

*Press release issued January 18, 1988*

WASHINGTON—As part of a year-long, $1.2 million television advertising campaign designed to insure that Democratic and Republican Presidential candidates view government and government services in a more positive light the 1.1 million member American Federation of State, County and Municipal Employees (AFSCME) is spending $250,000 in four of the first caucus and primary states on two 30-second campaign-style TV commercials to be carried on nearly two dozen stations.

The AFSCME commercials begin airing on Iowa stations today, three weeks before that state's Presidential caucuses. The commercials will also run in the New Hampshire, Maine and Minnesota markets several weeks prior to elections there.

"We want to see prospective Presidential candidates talking about using government as a problem-solver to improve the quality of life in local communities," said Gerald W. McEntee, President of AFSCME. "Our own polls show that the average taxpayer wants an activist government to protect our environment, educate our children, care for the elderly and increase economic opportunity for all Americans."

The AFSCME TV spots, with the tagline "America, It's Time for New Priorities," focus on the lack of government programs to insure clean drinking water and the lack of adequate government services to care for the elderly.

"The 1988 Presidential campaign will address emerging issues in which government can play a vital, sometimes pivotal role," said McEntee. "The ads are the antithesis of President Reagan's 1980 campaign slogan that 'government is part of the problem and not part of the solution.' AFSCME believes that the public will support government programs which have a direct, positive impact on their own local community."

AFSCME's TV advertising is the largest "issues" campaign undertaken so far for the upcoming Presidential elections. In May and June of last year, AFSCME placed similar advertising in numerous primary and caucus states, plus the hometowns of all the declared Democratic Presidential candidates.

---

BIRTH OF AN ISSUE: Older People's Lobby Gets a Message Across to All the Candidates; Need for Long-Term Care Mobilizes the Retired, and Politicians Take Note

*Joe Davidson, The Wall Street Journal, March 8, 1988*

DEERFIELD BEACH, Fla.—Few of life's horrors instill more dread—particularly in the elderly—than to be very sick for a long time without the money to pay for doctors, hospitals and nursing homes. And few groups have more clout with politicians than the *28 million* members of the American Association of Retired Persons. Put the two together—deep concern and voting power—and, boom, a political issue is born.

At a fancy retirement village here two weeks ago, Democratic presidential aspirants Richard Gephardt and Michael Dukakis videotaped a one-hour discussion on the sole subject of providing affordable long-term care for the sick, the frail, the injured and the handicapped. Their only real disagreement was over which man, once in the White House, would do more about it.

The talk, which has been broadcast in states with Super Tuesday primary elections and caucuses today, is a case study in issue creation in a presidential race. The candidates got free TV time, thanks to local stations and a $46,000 grant by the Villers Foundation, which, with the AARP, is an organizer of an ad hoc coalition called Long Term Care '88.

### Rare Success

Paying for television is but part of a million-dollar effort begun nearly 18 months ago to gain commitments from Republican as well as Democratic presidential hopefuls. Few lobbies have been so successful at generating support.

Joshua Wiener, a senior fellow at the Brookings Institution in Washington, says he is flabbergasted at how long-term health care has moved from the "political backwater," as he puts it, to the forefront of this year's election. Floyd Fithian, a former Indiana congressman who now is the chief of staff for Democrat Paul Simon, thinks it may well be a "decisive issue in the campaign."

The coalition isn't pushing a specific program; it just wants to be sure that long-term care is a priority of whoever is elected. Ronald Pollack, the executive director of the Villers Foundation, says he wants "this issue to come up over and over again in the campaign." He wants the candidates to be on record making promises.

The backers use many different tools. One is a powerful videotape produced by the coalition, which has been shown to most of the men running for president. Among the cases depicted is that of Mary Hill of Des Moines, Iowa, who describes with great anguish how she had to divorce her paralyzed husband of 33 years. Without her income, he could then be declared indigent and thus qualify for government assistance in paying huge nursing-home bills that the couple couldn't afford.

### Making an Impression

Four days after seeing the tape, Robert Dole used some of his time during an NBC-TV debate to bring up the problem. "It seems to me that must be a priority in the next Republican administration," the Kansas senator said. The videotape helped crystallize Mr. Dole's views, said Marie Maseng, his press secretary. "He does cite the tape in many of his speeches."

So does Gov. Dukakis. He said in one speech: "We need a president who understands what the failure to provide for adequate and affordable long-term care . . . is doing to our families—the pain it causes, the impossible choices it forces many of our citizens to make. Ask the Hills of Des Moines. . . ."

The free TV time Long Term Care '88 has been providing, in cooperation with local broadcasters, is irresistible to politicians. In New Hampshire, the candidates each had a one-hour forum to discuss the subject with a studio audience after viewing the coalition's tape. In Iowa, the candidates did five-minute, televised interviews.

### Cagey George Bush

The first two questions asked each candidate were clearly designed to elicit commitments: Would you mention long-term care in your inaugural address, and would you introduce a comprehensive policy during the first year of your administration? Most of the current candidates said yes to both; nobody said no. Vice President George Bush declined to say what he would deal with in his inaugural, but he still promised: "I will give long-term care the priority that it deserves."

The subject was raised again on Feb. 27 in Atlanta in a televised debate among the Democrats, a debate the coalition didn't sponsor. The Democrats generally favor an approach to providing care that emphasizes federal financing. Legislation of that sort has been proposed by Rep. Claude Pepper, the 87-year-old Florida Democrat. His bill would provide for a self-financing home-care program, financed by an extension of the Medicare payroll tax. Republicans, as usual, put more stress on governmental incentives for the purchase of private insurance and tax-deferred savings plans similar to Individual Retirement Accounts.

The AARP conducted workshops in several Super Tuesday states—Florida, Alabama, Missouri and Washington. Voters were briefed, told how to draw specific answers from candidates. The group also ran spots on cable TV in 16 Southern Super Tuesday states. The AARP has given out nearly 800,000 copies of its "Presidential Voters Guide."

### Using the Campaign

Planning for the national drive began in the fall of 1986 when John Rother, the AARP's legislative director, and Villers' Mr. Pollack got together over lunch to discuss how to sue the presidential campaign to promote action.

As Mr. Rother describes it, they devised a plan similar to what a company might use to launch a new car or breakfast cereal. The effort called for market research, product development and a sales force. Starting last fall, the groups used survey results to try to influence campaign issue and research directors, and provided their staffs a steady flow of slick propaganda. Because research showed that long-term care is an issue that grabs many voters, not just old people, they strategically broadened the issue: It's not just that many adults are burdened with aged parents needing nursing home care at an average cost of $22,000 a year: anybody of any age could be struck down in an accident and need medical help, perhaps for the rest of his life.

The AARP/Villers-sponsored poll indicates that 86% of the public believes some government action should be taken to provide for long-term care of Americans; 68% of respondents would be willing to pay higher taxes to get it.

After examining the "very, very powerful evidence" of the poll results, Sen. Simon's campaign manager, Mr. Fithian, says he urged the senator to stress long-term care, an issue the senator had already embraced. The coalition, he says, "made it easy for candidates to get involved."

### Smut and Acid Rain

Other groups espousing causes have had considerably less luck in getting to the top of the candidates' agendas. And it isn't because they don't try. The Vietnam Veterans of America wants candidates to back legislation to compensate victims of Agent Orange. The National Coalition Against Pornography wants government action against smut. Others push their views on acid rain, space and water policy.

But "it's a real uphill battle," says Jerry Herman, the national coordinator of the American Friends Service Committee's Southern Africa program. He led a delegation through Iowa and New Hampshire seeking support for tougher sanctions against South Africa. Because the self-interest of the average American doesn't seem to be directly involved the issue can't turn out voters the way health care can, says Mr. Herman.

An obvious reason long-term care attracts politicians' attention is that the elderly are a particularly powerful voting bloc. The AARP estimates that twice as many older voters participated in the Iowa caucuses this year as in 1984. And more than 50% of the Iowa participants were older than 50.

Another reason for the attention is that Long Term Care '88 has used a $500,000 budget and 115 coalition groups to spread the word. Most of the groups sent packets of information to the candidates, says Steve Mc-Connell, the campaign's national coordinator. In addition, members of those groups were encouraged to write letters to the candidates. (The AARP and the Villers Foundation, on their own, are expected to spend at least another $500,000.)

### The Glut

"We've really been bombarded" with data, says Gregory Mermelstein, the issues director for Rep. Gephardt. He says long-term-care advocates have been particularly effective, "simply because of the volume of the material."

The issue caught on in part because several of the men who would be president, including Messrs. Dole, Simon and Gephardt, have supported the cause all along. "You can't manufacture an issue," says Mr. McConnell. When the Reagan administration introduced legislation last year to cover catastrophic illnesses, many Americans became aware of just how poorly they are covered now. The bills passed by both houses and now awaiting action in conference committee don't cover long-term care, but they do provide increased acute-care coverage for elderly and disabled people covered by Medicare. Private insurers are just beginning to get into long-term care, and most Americans are still not covered. Medicare currently provides poor coverage.

Medicaid covers costs only if the recipient is poor, which is why some couples—the Hills of Des Moines for example—get expedient divorces after decades of marriage.

"Here's the person who said she would" take care of her husband, "and now she's getting a divorce," said Mrs. Hill on the videotape. "It's pretty upsetting."

Reprinted with permission from *The Wall Street Journal*.

---

## INJECTING AN ISSUE INTO THE '88 CAMPAIGN

*Julie Kosterlitz, National Journal, August 29, 1987*

As America ages, new issues inexorably find their way onto the political agenda. The 1988 presidential campaign could well mark the

first time candidates grapple with how to pay for long-term health care for the elderly.

The situation is as follows: Next year, public expenditure for nursing and home health care for the elderly will top $20 billion. By the year 2040, the number of people in nursing homes is expected to be four times the number reported in 1980. Medicare pays only about 2 percent of these costs, and Medicaid, which picks up 41 percent, requires that individuals first bankrupt themselves to be eligible. As a result of the tight restrictions on, and low compensation for, such care, nursing homes are in short supply, with occupancy levels at 92 percent. In this seller's market, quality homes are overbooked, and Medicaid patients are often turned away.

Long neglected but potentially explosive, the issue is now coming to center stage as the result of a confluence of legislative events and demographic trends.

This year's introduction of catastrophic health care legislation, it seems, has had the added effect of hastening the day of reckoning on long-term care. While President Reagan and Congress had hoped to defuse concern over the vulnerability of senior citizens to high health-care costs, the bills now working their way through Congress deal mainly with short-term, acute illnesses, which immediately affect a relatively small number of the aged. Rep. Claude Pepper, D-Fla., dropped his bid to tack on a long-term-care amendment with a five-year price tag of $28 billion (which most believed would doom the bill) only after extracting a promise from House Speaker Jim Wright, D-Texas, that long-term care would get full consideration at a later date.

Furthermore, many Members touting the catastrophic bill back home have found constituents more concerned with what it fails to do. Worried about the possible backlash if seniors learn the hard way that Medicare still won't cover their nursing home bills, several Members have raised the red flag. Senate Finance Committee member Donald W. Riegle Jr., D-Mich., for example, who is up for reelection next year, has held four hearings around his state to explain the bill and has pointedly included discussions of long-term care.

At the same time, senior citizens' groups are launching a sophisticated campaign to get the issue before the presidential candidates. Led by the American Association of Retired Persons (AARP) and the private, nonprofit advocacy group for low-income elderly known as the Villers Foundation, a group of six organizations, including nursing and religious groups, has launched "Long Term Care '88." It has hired Stephen R. McConnell (former minority staff director of the Senate Special Committee on Aging), commissioned an extensive public opinion poll and enlisted experts to help with a long-term-care proposal. It hopes to launch an advertising campaign in key primary states. The AARP plans to make long-term care one of three issues to be addressed at its Iowa candidate forums as well as a key part of its voter education drive. Villers has made a grant to a New Hampshire public radio station working with a local television station to hold a series of candidate forums this fall and winter exclusively on the issue of long-term care.

The goal isn't merely to get the issue on the agenda. The proposal of Republican presidential candidate and former Delaware Gov. Pierre S. (Pete) du Pont IV for tax-exempt individual medical savings accounts, for example, is anathema to most seniors' groups, who view it as ineffective and inequitable. Instead, they're hoping to get candidates to do what Sen. Paul Simon, D-Ill., has already done—endorse the concept of a federally run, universal social insurance program offering a range of long-term-care services, including nursing home and home care.

Besides seniors, the baby boom generation that so many of the candidates are courting is likely to add impetus to the issue. As their cohort begins to enter middle age, many boomers are being called upon to help out parents—and even grandparents—who have trouble paying for care. Watching parents run through their savings to end up on a medical welfare program is not only a wrenching experience, it means that even with two incomes, some struggling families can't expect much of an inheritance and serves as a foretaste of what they themselves can look forward to.

The downside for politicians, however, in the era of record federal deficits, is talking about financing. The private sector probably can't solve the problem. While new private long-term-care insurance policies show promise, the 30 to 40 percent of seniors who could afford them aren't the ones pushing Medicaid costs up anyway, said Brookings Institution senior fellow Joshua M. Wiener. "Unless you wanted a very minimal program, you're going to need a broad-based tax" to finance it, he said. Adding long-term-care insurance benefits to the Medicare program, Wiener estimates, could require a 2.5 percent payroll tax (to be split between employers and employees and levied with no cap on the amount subject to the tax), compared with a 1.6 percent payroll tax required to finance current Medicare and Medicaid programs.

Keeping proposed benefits modest could trim the estimate a bit, and the finance burdens could be spread around by charging the elderly premiums, increasing "sin taxes" on alcohol or tobacco, or raising inheritance taxes. But the remaining costs would still be large, and meeting them would raise sticky political questions.

Difficult as these issues are, the fact remains that the costs will have to be covered somehow. Expenses for existing programs are growing, and their inadequacies, in turn, are exacting social costs. With wives, the traditional care givers, as well as husbands now in the work force, employers are starting to encounter losses in productivity when employees take time off or burn out from caring for and worrying about elderly parents.

Are people willing to shell out for an overhaul of the system? Villers public policy coordinator Ed Howard said that the still-unreleased poll conducted for Long Term Care '88 indicates that they are, and that the issue draws concern among all age groups. If activists have their way, candidates on the trail will find the long-term-care issue marching along beside them.

From the "Health Focus" section, "HealthCare '88," *National Journal*, August 29, 1987.

---

# THEY WERE WRONG ABOUT TELEVISION

*Jeff Greenfield*

Everyone knows that television is the most important—maybe the only important—factor in a Presidential campaign. The candidates know it; that's why they turn themselves into a collection of walking sound bites for the evening news.

The campaign operators know it; that's why they act as if they would barter their families into slavery for five minutes of air time for their candidates. The insiders and the pundits know it; that's why they solemnly proclaim a set of axioms about the medium's irresistible impact.

So why doesn't the American electorate seem to know it? Why do they cheerfully march to the polls every four years and ignore the conventional wisdom about the power of television?

Consider what all the experts *knew* about this power going into 1988—and consider what has actually happened so far. Everyone *knew* that the mass media's obsession with Iowa made that state critical. A win, or at least a surprisingly good showing, was essential because of the "Iowa bounce." With 3,000 journalists descending on Iowa, the first axiom of 1988 was "the road to the White House leads through Des Moines."

Well, what happened this year to the Iowa success stories? What happened to Bob Dole, Pat Robertson, Richard A. Gephardt and Paul Simon? Nothing. By contrast, what happened to Iowa's big loser, George Bush? What happened to the lagging Democrats: Michael S. Dukakis, the Rev. Jesse Jackson and the non-candidate, Albert Gore Jr.?

It turned out that an early campaign success puts a candidate to an intense test of consistency and substance. A lack of one or the other—as Mr. Gephardt and Mr. Dole discovered—can be a fatal flaw.

Consider another "certainty" of campaigning: that without the resources to produce high-powered TV advertising, a successful campaign is impossible.

So what happened to the biggest media success story of 1988, Mr. Gephardt's "$48,000 Hyundai" ad? Yes, it crystallized the anger over foreign competition and helped him win Iowa. But it also raised a drum beat of skeptical inquiries: How could this consummate Washington insider suddenly cast himself as a firebrand populist? The image did not withstand the test of reality.

Similarly, primary after primary witnessed huge TV expenditures by candidates who found that their expensive messages simply found no resonance among the voters. For example, Senator Gore spent well over $200,000 on TV in one week in Illinois—and received a little more than 5 percent of the vote.

By contrast, the least well-financed candidate among the Democrats, Mr. Jackson, turned out to have not simply passion but something that has historically been crucial to a candidate: a constituency.

Just as Ronald Reagan was able in 1980 to withstand critical media scrutiny because of decades of service to the conservative cause, so Mr. Jackson managed to rally to the polls those who saw in him a tribune of black affirmation and those who saw in him the most forceful embodiment of the populism that has long played well in Democratic campaigns.

Even the old chestnut that a candidate must be a good television performer has gone by the wayside this year. Neither Vice President Bush nor Governor Dukakis set hearts aflutter on the tube.

Fundamentally, 1988 has been shaped far less by media images than by political forces far older than television:

—By the fact that a candidate linked to a President unpopular in one state is likely to do poorly there (Mr. Bush in Iowa).

—By the fact that this same candidate, linked to a President who is popular in a region is likely to do very well (Mr. Bush in New Hampshire and the South).

—By the fact that primary voters respond more enthusiastically to a political vision than to arguments about electability and inevitability, however well-financed (the current dilemma for Mr. Dukakis).

These facts won't stop the assertions that our presidential process is dictated by the tube. Every once in a while, though, it might help if the experts ran this bit of wisdom against a reality check. It might surprise them.

From *The New York Times*, April 5, 1988. Copyright 1988 by the New York Times Company. Reprinted by permission.

---

## VOTERS ARE LIKE THAT

*George F. Will*

. . . In politics especially, there comes a point at which the dollars spent have sharply declining utility. Republicans learned that in the dismal (for Republicans) experience of the 1986 Senate elections. In the 34 races, Republican candidates spent $122 million, $33 million more than did Democratic candidates ($89 million). Republican candidates outspent Democratic candidates in 23 of the 34 races. But Democrats won 20 of the 34. In the 13 closest races, those decided by 6 percentage points or less, Democrats won 10 and Republicans won 3. Of those, Republican candidates outspent Democratic candidates in 11 out of 13.

The guy in Idaho was joking when he said it would have been less expensive in 1986 if, instead of strafing the state with television commercials, the two Senate candidates had just taken the undecided voters out to dinner. But the guy was right. About 70 percent of Idaho's 515,000 registered voters were expected to vote that Tuesday. Since Labor Day only about 7 percent of those likely voters had been undecided. The two candidates threw more than $5 million at the 25,000 undecided, or $200 per voter. That would buy a feast in Boise.

By election day Idaho knew how veal scaloppine feel. Many states were pounded flat by the merciless attentions of people seeking admission to the Senate. The pounding hammers were negative television commercials that rarely rose to the level of lowbrow.

The most expensive 1986 race was California's. The two Senate candidates spent $20 million. But on a per capita basis, that was a bargain-basement campaign. California's race involved $1.55 for each of the 12.8 million registered voters. Next door in Nevada, the $3.5 million race involved about $10 for each of the 356,384 registered voters.

What money made possible in 1986 was a mass conversion of candidates to the Dick Butkus Doctrine of Political Manners. Butkus, a maiming linebacker for the Chicago Bears, once said, "I wouldn't ever set out to hurt anybody deliberately unless it was, you know, important—like a league game or something." In 1986 "going negative"—doing unto your opponent before he could do unto you—was the preferred style.

There are always excuses for going too far in any contest. When Sugar Ray Robinson landed a punch after the bell had ended a round, the ringside broadcaster explained, "It's hard to hear the bell up there. There's a tremendous amount of smoke here in the Boston Garden." In 1986 three excuses were offered for negative campaigning. "The other guy started it." And "I'm not being negative, I'm just alerting the electorate to my loathsome opponent's squalid record." And "Negative campaigning is as American as apple pie—and, by the way, did I mention that my opponent hates apple pie."

True, American politics has always had a bare knuckle side. "Ma, Ma, where's my Pa?" was a Republican reference to Democrat Grover Cleveland's illegitimate child. Demo-crats added the defiant line, "Gone to the White House, ha, ha, ha." Cleveland's 1884 opponent was James G. Blaine.

"Blaine, Blaine, James G. Blaine, continental liar from the state of Maine." Somewhat negative, that. But television has unique immediacy. Today voters do not venture out to experience negativism at torchlight rallies. Today negativism comes to voters in their living rooms.

In 1986 Congressman Bob Edgar was criticized for negative ads he used against Pennsylvania's Republican Senator, Arlen Specter. Edgar's response was that the 1986 campaigns were not much, if any, more negative than many campaigns have been. The difference, he said, is that the gusher of political money has made the negativism more audible. That is, candidates have always said beastly things about one another in speeches at union halls or lodge meetings, but now that there is so much cash sloshing around in the system, candidates can afford to broadcast their attacks.

There is a lot of money around, and it goes a long way in some states. Horace Busby notes that four of the fiercest contests in 1986 were for Republican-held seats in four of the least populous states: Idaho, Nevada, South Dakota and North Dakota, ranked 41st, 43rd, 45th and 46th respectively. They have a combined population of 2.7 million, about half the population of Cook County, Illinois. Television time is cheap out where the deer and the antelope outnumber the voters. In Dakota Territory you can buy 30 seconds of time on *The Cosby Show* for just $800.

What is new is not just the amount of negativism, it is the niggling tendentiousness of it. Only a candidate sitting on a large and solid lead feels he can be too principled to run negative ads. (New York's Republican Senator Al D'Amato was always so far ahead in 1986 he felt no need for negative ads. Too bad. His campaign manager's name was Rick Nasti.) And there is nothing wrong with criticizing the public record of public people. What is tiresome is the reckless use of a candidate's votes to characterize the candidate. A vote for less-than-maximum funding for a program for the handicapped or against the most stringent sanctions against South Africa becomes grounds for 30 seconds of rubbish about the candidate "voting against the handicapped" or "supporting apartheid."

One reason for the recourse to negative ads is that in recent years they have worked. Another reason is that in 1986 the issues were so unsatisfying. The top 10 issues were: drugs, drugs, drugs, drugs, drugs, drugs, drugs, drugs, drugs and the deficit. Drugs is the conservatives' money-throwing issue: "Don't just stand there, Hoss, throw some money at the problem!" But after Congress has denounced drugs and the deficit, and has made the latter worse by throwing money at the former, the situation remains as follows. No one really knows what the federal government can do effectively against drugs. Everyone knows what it can do about the deficit (cut spending or increase taxes, or both) and no one wants to do anything.

So grown men with too much money, too few ideas and too little respect for the voters get into slanging matches, such as the one in South Dakota in 1986. There the Republican incumbent Senator accused his opponent of accepting a contribution from Jane Fonda. And that sin was made scarlet by the fact—so said the Senator—that Fonda hates a South Dakota export, red meat. However, the Democrat did not personally get a contribution from Fonda. She attended a fundraiser for all Democratic Senate candidates. And South Dakotans were assured that on a recent trip she pulled into a McDonald's and devoured two Big Macs. It seems somehow right that the 1986 political season ended with a Senate contest and perhaps the fate of the free world hinged on voters' reactions to the news that Jane Fonda suffered a Big Mac attack.

Negative advertising sometimes succeeds, in part because people tend to confuse rudeness with sincerity and to equate sincerity with high principle. However, if negative advertising worked most of the time, then most of the time we would be governed by the richest and nastiest. We are not. The electorate is not a debased, manipulated mob. They are serious about what is serious in politics. The serious stuff is not advertising and is not any other nut or bolt.

America has a surplus of people who know everything about the nuts and bolts of politics. They can name all the county chairmen in Indiana and tell you the cost of 30 seconds of drive-time radio in Denver. But they do not have a clue as to why Americans pull one voting lever rather than another. So let us say something for a reason Saul Bellow gave in *Mr. Sammler's Planet:* ". . . it is sometimes necessary to repeat what all know. All mapmakers should place the Mississippi in the same location, and avoid originality. It may be boring, but one has to know where he is. We cannot have the Mississippi flowing toward the Rockies for a change."[1] So let's just blurt out this truth: Americans vote for candidates they think they agree with.

In 1980, to the despair of many advisers and creative advertisers, Reagan insisted on relying heavily on "talking head" ads. There were no fancy production values. But it turned out the candidate knew something. Americans want to hear what is in a candidate's head. In 1984 Reagan could rely on gooey "feel good" ads filmed in orange sunsets because by then people knew what was in his head. Even so, he paid the price for the vacuousness of the 1984 campaign. Even before the Iran-contra affair blew his administration's transmission, his second term had been sputtering along on too few cylinders. The 1984 landslide was shaped by a campaign too themeless to impart the momentum that comes from a practical, specific mandate.

Here is a fact that should be printed on both parties' brains with letters of brass: The candidate who has received more votes for President than anyone in American history is that telegenic charmer Richard Nixon. He got the votes because—I apologize for the banality— lots of voters liked what he said, and took what he said more seriously than his manner of saying it. The best politicians understand that voters are like that. . . .

Reprinted with permission from *The New Season: A Spectator's Guide to the 1988 Election*, by George F. Will, New York, Simon & Schuster, 1987.

# FOCUS GROUPS

"Focus groups and instant readings of reactions can probe in more detail and elicit extensive qualitative data and unstructured responses that are unavailable using public opinion polling. The danger, however, is that campaigns sometimes make basic thematic decisions using pseudo-science. Why do I call it pseudo-science? Because, they are a shallow unidimensional gauging of a very complex set of reactions in public opinion. These results can be purely impulsive. It is unrepresentative of the much more important opinion that is reached later on after reflection and after the mediation of the press. They are also absolutely not random samples, but are often treated as such—not just by the campaigns, but also by the media reporting on them. Unfortunately, it is an applause meter approach to politics and it is proliferating.

It is an attempt to quantify the unquantifiable."

*Larry Sabato*

*"For those of us who spend two man-hours closeted in our campaign offices," a top presidential strategist said in 1988, "[focus groups] represent a window into the real world and keep us in touch with average people."[1]*

*The emerging role of focus groups—whose influence has been magnified by communications technologies—is a hot topic among campaign scholars and professionals. Focus groups provide real and useful data. Abuse of this data should be blamed, not on focus groups as a technique, but on how particular users may apply the technique. Focus group advocates point out that public opinion polls with statistically "valid" sample sizes are also prone to abuse. Polls, they say, are only true at the moment; they may or may not indicate something meaningful about the future. Polls taken far in advance of an election, or polls whose sampling error is misinterpreted or misreported can also seriously mislead voters and campaign decision-makers.*

*But do focus group data permit generalization? What opportunities and dangers come with linking focus group participants to computers? Scholarly literature has yet to answer such questions, while real-world utilization of focus groups—as indicated by the following excerpts—is constantly generating new ideas and data.*

1. Lloyd Grove, "Focus Groups: Politicians' version of taste-testing," *Washington Post*, 6 July 1988, p. A5.

## INSTANT COMPUTER POLLS EYEBALL CANDIDATES AT THE SPEED OF SIGHT

*Jeff Mapes, The Oregonian, October 30, 1987*

Vice President George Bush was in trouble. He was explaining how he would hang President Reagan's picture in the White House Cabinet Room when he took over, and the 45 Portland Republicans attentively watching Bush on television in the darkened research room of Columbia Information Systems were not buying any of it.

Their reactions were instantly turned into a graph on a computer screen, and Bush's approval rating was dropping faster than the stock market on Black Monday.

"See, that tells you right there he has to distance himself from Reagan," said Mike Malone, Columbia president, excitedly pointing at the computer.

Welcome to the world of high-tech politics.

It no longer may be enough for candidates to judge how they're doing by listening to the audience or to wait for a telephone survey. Research companies such as Columbia think they have come up with a way to judge the visceral reactions of voters—instantly—as they sit and watch the presidential hopefuls on television.

In fact, Malone predicts the day when candidates in a debate could actually find out how they were doing during the debate itself—and react accordingly—in the same fashion a football coach sitting in the press box sends his quarterback information on what the defense is doing.

Malone's company entered this brave new world Wednesday night when it and affiliates in Atlanta and Des Moines, Iowa, invited small groups of Republicans to watch the six GOP presidential candidates debate in Houston on a public broadcasting show hosted by commentator William F. Buckley, Jr.

Each Republican was given a dial that could be twisted from zero to 100. Fifty was neutral. If they liked what they heard and saw, they were asked to turn their dial toward 100. If they had a negative reaction, they moved their dial toward zero.

"This isn't a matter of how articulate you are," said Malone as he explained his system. "All you have to do is turn a dial."

With the ease of Roman spectators turning thumbs up or down, the Portland Republicans sent the graphic lines shooting up, for example, when Rep. Jack Kemp of New York talked about supply-side economics and dropping down when former Delaware Gov. Pete du Pont directly criticized Bush.

For the most part this was a shakedown cruise, although Malone said one of the presidential candidates—whom he would not identify—had agreed to purchase data from the Iowa portion of the test.

The Portland group, selected with the help of the Multnomah County Republican Party, turned out to be a less-than-representative sampling of Republican voters as a whole. Before the debate, 31 percent of the group said they supported former television evangelist Pat Robertson while only 11 percent were for Bush. However, national surveys consistently have shown Bush leading the Republican pack with Robertson having less than 10 percent support.

The firm's computer showed five different lines on the graph, representing the group as a whole, men only, women only, a group who described themselves as conservatives and a group describing themselves as moderates.

The lines most sharply diverged whenever Robertson spoke.

As soon as he opened his mouth, the conservative, men and total group lines would head upward. The lines representing women and moderates would head downward.

Of course, there were exceptions. During a

segment showing filmed biographies of each candidate, the women suddenly started showing their approval when Robertson's wife, Dede, spoke of her concern for single mothers.

Not surprisingly, the Portland Republicans also showed a tendency to turn thumbs up whenever the candidates denounced higher taxes and Democrats and praised President Reagan's foreign policy.

They also seemed influenced to some degree by the audience at the Houston debate. When du Pont's direct attacks on Bush were greeted with scattered boos, his approval rating started falling.

But Alexander Haig, former secretary of state, won loud applause when he said that none of the Democratic candidates were fit to tie the bootstraps of the GOP presidential hopefuls, and the Portland watchers sent their dials spinning toward 100.

Haig and du Pont—the two darkest horses in the GOP presidential race—seemed to benefit the most from the debate, at least judging from the reactions of the Portland audience.

Each was favored by 13 percent of the group, compared to only 2 percent before the debate. Robertson dropped slightly, to just under 27 percent while Sen. Robert Dole of Kansas took the biggest plunge—from nearly 29 percent beforehand to 13 percent afterward.

Dole didn't seem to say anything that sent his computer ratings tumbling—but he also rarely sent the graph shooting sharply upward. Bush finished with about 9 percent support and Kemp stayed about steady by finishing as the favorite of about 24 percent of the group.

Malone Thursday pronounced himself satisfied with the first test, saying he intends to refine and expand the procedure for future debates, hoping his firm can grab hold of a share of the gigantic $40 million market in political research during the next two years.

Columbia already has used what Malone calls his "perception analyzer" for a number of commercial accounts to judge customer reaction to a variety of new products. And Malone, along with two other competing companies nationally, believes what works in judging a brand of deodorant can work in judging a politician.

Does this mean that style will triumph over substance in the political arena as candidates learn voters don't like the way they are shaking their jowls?

"That happened as far back as the Nixon-Kennedy debate," said Malone, when Nixon's poor makeup and shifty eyes didn't go over well with the television audience.

As for the participants, they seemed excited to have a way of letting the world know what they think about the presidential candidates.

"If we can pinpoint our feelings with electronics, so be it," said Landon Thompson, a Northeast Portland real estate agent.

---

## THE PEOPLE SPEAK: ASSESSING AMERICA'S FUTURE

*Press release on the 1987 AFSCME Focus Group Sessions*

Between March 23-25, 1987 the political and marketing research firm of Bernard Engelhard & Associates of New York conducted a series of six focus group sessions in Boston, St. Louis, and Denver among community opinion leaders to assess their feelings about emerging domestic issues facing the country.

Each focus group consisted of officers of Parent-Teacher Associations, civic associations, and local Democratic and Republican Party committees, plus newspaper editors, business leaders, and educators. Often, focus groups like these presage changes in public opinion.

The focus group information was used to help AFSCME in developing a $1 million television ad campaign airing in May and June of this year advocating a more activist government role in addressing domestic problems.

The focus groups voiced worries about the condition of our economy, concerns about the environment, support for increased funds for public education and fears that recent government budget cuts in programs to assist the elderly, the poor, the handicapped, and so on have gone too far.

This report summarizes the focus group findings, quoting participants on how they feel about the issues facing America today.

### Discussion of America's Domestic Problems

In opening the discussion about life in America today, the moderator asked, "How are we doing domestically?" Despite this neutral approach responses were almost uniformly negative, emphasizing problems that face the country.

Perception of these problems can be summarized as follows:

—*A weak economy which imperils not only our current way of life, but especially that of our children.* We're on borrowed time; the economy is in bad shape and getting worse. No balanced budget, so our grandchildren will have to pay. It's in terrible shape. We'll be owing. We're selling more of our real estate to foreign countries, borrowing more. We owe more than we are getting. What if interest rates improve abroad and people take their money out? We're spending less on education and technology, and the Japanese and Germans are pouring money right and left into this. Senior citizens are scared to death about how they're going to live tomorrow. Kids are worried about how they're going to be able to buy homes. We all have to decide how to live and be happy with less, because that's coming. The pie is getting smaller. We can't spend money left and right any more.

—*The breakdown of the family* as more and more households are headed by a single parent, or even by two parents whose workday responsibilities leave them with little time or energy to concern themselves with their children.

If I were President, my number one priority would be stabilizing the family, whatever it is. That includes money and health.

The whole family unit, the whole parental guidance, care, children growing up. . . . I do a lot of work in the inner cities and it scares the living daylights out of me. A breakdown of parental responsibility. Spending time with kids, talking with them, communicating with them. The whole problem of substance abuse with adolescents. In St. Louis, if you're poor, have a drug problem and are under the age of 17, you can't get any help; it's not there. It comes back to caring for kids, spending time, taking the time. In any public place kids are running wild. Whatever happened to the days when parents took the kid's hand and walked together?

The family unit and the whole social structure have changed: The support services, with the grandparents and aunts and uncles. Now people are spread out across the country. In St. Louis, we're dealing with 50 percent one-parent families in Girl Scouts. We need support programs for drug abuse, pregnancy, preventative programs. We have to adapt other services to make up for the lack of family support.

I serve on two school board committees. We beg people to serve on these committees, and parents are so involved in just trying to make the mortgage payment, $1700 a month on a $175,000 house, and they just don't have time. Mom works, dad works, baby is in day camp. They don't have a clue as to whether or not the kids are succeeding. By the time they get to be sophomores in high school it's too late.

—*The decline of the educational system.* I worked many years ago as a probation officer, and I don't think things have changed a lot in kids' behavior. One of my big concerns is the move away from striving for excellence in education, high school and elementary level. We've seen a definite move away from the support of education. People who have knowledge, education and care can get along in spite of some pretty lousy parents. But others can't.

The quality of education has really changed from when I was in school. So many come out and don't even know how to read and write. They're not prepared to work, to live in the world. I'm getting into educating them, sending them back.

I see it mostly in engineering. The educational system has changed from producing engineers and scientists to producing technocrats. They don't know how to solve problems. I think the educators have switched their philosophy on how to develop these people. The college I went to had a very structured curriculum; most courses were required. The same school allows a lot more electives now.

They can't spell, they can't write, they can't communicate. The basic skills are not there. They get by too easily, are promoted too easily.

—*A widening gap between rich and poor,* with more and more individuals and families struggling at the bottom end of the scale. The plight of the homeless and the unemployed are elements of this problem.

I think the poor are doing worse. There are lots more people who are poor or destitute.

The poor and homeless, that's a pretty sad commentary on where we're going.

There's a tendency for people to deny problems in general, to sweep them under the carpet. Whether it's homelessness or drugs and alcohol. It seems like there's an awful lot of street people lately—the homeless.

I would like to say something positive, but it's difficult. People's expectations are a lot different from what they were 20 years ago. Our standard of living is higher, but there is a shrinking middle class.

Some people are doing just terribly. Some people who thought they would never be out of work are out of work. A widening gap with the poor, and the middle class is being shrunk. A small group of people is very visible, people really making it.

—A related problem mentioned loudly in St. Louis is *lack of support for health care* for those who need it and who cannot afford it.

What we're seeing nationally is infant mortality rates which were going down. Now they're flattened out and going up. They are a chief indicator of the status of health. More babies are dying. St. Louis city has had an incredible increase, even in the county which is considered more affluent.

Federal money was taken out of St. Louis county, and all that money was in the health budget. There are definite cutbacks on the federal level that relate back to how things are going.

We say we have a doctor shortage, but not in St. Louis, just outside. Doctors here won't take young, pregnant women because they're on Medicaid.

—Another related problem emphasized in St. Louis and also in Denver is the reported *lack of opportunity for "pulling oneself up by the bootstraps."* This used to be possible in the past, but with today's technologically advanced workplace and the high cost of living, respondents say even hard work doesn't necessarily result in economic security.

It's too easy to look back at the old times and say I pulled myself up. There's been a big change since then. We've been through a long inflationary period. A lot of damage was done . . . when someone has to work for three forty-five an hour and has to pay some of the rents that are charged these people in the inner city. . . . Utilities are incredible.

My mother raised three children by herself and she worked as a clerical person, a secretary. I can tell you there's no way she could do that now.

I think all of us here have probably pulled ourselves up by our bootstraps. The situation, the economy, has changed over the years. There are fewer and fewer resources and opportunities to take advantage of.

We're into technology. You can't get an entry-level job like before. You've got to have all kinds of skills.

Lack of opportunity to develop your potential. Education, job training. I worked myself through college, but when I consider my daughter who will start next year, starting out at Washington University. . . .

—*The lack of inspiring leadership on the national level* directed at solving our domestic problems. President Reagan is seen as unconcerned with domestic social and economic problems, leaving state and local communities without the resources to help themselves.

What I would do as President would be what Iacocca did to the local dealerships; give us back some integrity. Force us to take a look at ourselves, at the point of losing everything. I would say get together folks, you CAN do it. I will support, help, motivate.

As President, you have the power to establish the values, pick the issues you attack. Do you sacrifice the homeless for another battleship?

Take the bureaucracy that's causing the deficit and pump that into education and the drug fights. Cut back on bureaucracy. But the President is basically powerless.

I think we *are* making progress, but our problem is that we look for solutions to problems in the same ways we always have and we can't solve problems like that. . . . There are lots of people out there who are poor and we have tried and tried to have the bureaucracy serve their needs, and you can't do it. The money never filters down to the people who need it; they're still in the streets. We can't go into the next generation of leaders and approach problems the same way. My children won't be able to pay the bills; we'll be bankrupt.

There's been a lot of slippage in the last few years; that starts at the top. There's no leadership trying to get people to extend beyond themselves. In the Kennedy years, the message was to try to reach out and help the less fortunate. The message seems to be mostly help yourself. If the rich get along better, the poor will also rise. That's a different message.

—*Toxic waste and the environment.* This is perceived as an extremely important problem. Almost all agreed that toxic waste and the environment is a real, even frightening problem.

We're not spending enough of our resources dealing with those things that if you live on top of it long enough, eat it long enough. . . .

Hazardous waste in this community is scary. We're sitting on top of it, and sticking our heads in the ground. This burning to get rid of it is also scary. We don't know what it will do.

Water quality, too. People have a right to live and raise their children, but Boston is located in an unusual geological area where we have reason to downplay the water users, because of the aquifer recharge characteristics and trying to hammer out a balance of needs now and the responsible management of these resources for the future. . . .

That's what keeps us in business. No one wants to take responsibility for it. Where does the buck stop?

Hazardous waste? Very important. It can destroy the whole environment, how we dispose of it.

### Conclusion

In 1980 President Reagan campaigned saying that "government was part of the problem, not part of the solution." For the first time in almost 50 years the central role of government in the country's economic and social development was questioned. Now, more than six years into the Reagan presidency, opinion leaders in the AFSCME focus group sessions are beginning to seriously question this central premise of the Reagan Administration.

The focus group participants are worried about the fragile state of the economy. They want government to play a more activist role in reviving public education, cleaning up the environment and caring for the elderly and the disadvantaged. The 1987 AFSCME advertising campaign is designed to alert the public and the policymakers to the choices the American electorate will have in the 1988 Presidential elections.

In a very real sense, the AFSCME tagline "America, It's Time for New Priorities" is echoed in the focus group sessions which formed the basis for the union's unprecedented public education campaign aimed at influencing next year's presidential election agenda.

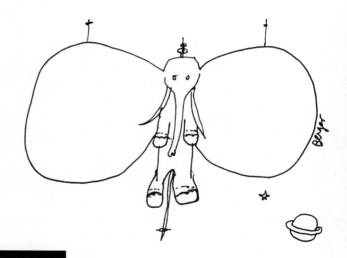

# POLITICAL PARTIES

"While communications technologies have been and are anti-party, they can be marshalled for the parties if used in the right way.

A good example would be for both parties to undertake an 'ombudsman' scheme—Ombudsman is Norwegian for red tape cutter. The parties should establish ombudsmen, paid agents of the party who will do what the old ward heelers used to do, that is simply get to know their neighbors, find out their problems, and use networking and the new technology to solve those problems—all in a way that reflects well on the party. The parties could thus build themselves in the only way that is durable and sustainable, from the ground up."

*Larry Sabato*

"In general, technologies have served to weaken the parties. Whether the parties will learn to be something more than money-raising and service shells remains an open question."

*Curtis Gans*

"Parties used to be a voluntary agency that enabled you to do something like get a job with Cook County Sanitation District. Parties in that sense are a thing of the past. They are now businesses that need to generate money and perhaps learn to spend it a little more intelligently."

*Michael Barone*

*Political parties are essential to the functioning of a democracy. James Bryce's* <u>The American Commonwealth</u>*, written in the late 19th century, notes that: "In a country so full of change and movement as America, new questions are always coming up, and must be answered. New troubles surround a government, and a way must be found to escape them; new diseases attack a nation, and have to be cured. The duty of a great party is to find answers and remedies."*

*In 1950, at the dawn of the television era, the committee on political parties of the American Political Science Association published a study entitled, "Toward a More Responsible Two-Party System." This study concluded that in the face of challenges such as the rise of mass media, the key to party survival would be responsiveness. Since then, academics, scholars and journalists have debated whether political parties can meet this challenge.*

*Communications technologies have been at the heart of the debate. Experts agree that to survive—and perhaps flourish—parties must become "technocratic," i.e., reliant on communications technologies.*

*The first six of the following excerpts provide a sampling of this debate as it has spanned the last two decades. These arguments are still fresh and timely—a reminder that key issues remain unresolved.*

*In reading these excerpts one must discard some misleading historic images. The good old days of political parties were not necessarily better than what we have today. "The late 19th century was a golden age for the party as an institution," Arthur Schlesinger, Jr. notes in* <u>The Cycles of American History</u>*. "It was not a golden age for presidents or for public policy or for politics as a profession."*

*The last two excerpts, Stephen Frantzich's and Rob Stoddard's, focus on political parties as service providers. This is what* <u>Via Satellite</u> *magazine calls "cosmic politics,"[1] state-of-the-art services trickling down from national and state party headquarters to state and local campaigns.*

*One of the most fascinating prospective services—a party-controlled cable channel devoted solely to party affairs and appeals—has not materialized. In the mid- and late 1970s, when cable began to blossom, many observers thought such a channel was inevitable. It would offer great possibilities. If only one percent of the voters in any community regularly watched a party cable channel, for example, local parties would have a grassroots base unmatched in the history of any democracy.*

*Parties have survived, but they are changing. Does reliance on technology restrict the role of parties? Can parties be centralized and responsive at the same time? Can communications technologies foster a regeneration of party-citizen contact? How will continued campaign finance reform affect parties? Should government regulate political databanks to protect citizen privacy? And ultimately, will parties meet the test posed by the American Political Science Association in 1950?*

---

1. Scott Chase, "Up Close and Personal: Candidates, Congressmen, Campaigns and Satellites," *Via Satellite* (November 1987):10.

# PARTIES: THE REAL OPPORTUNITY FOR EFFECTIVE CITIZEN POLITICS

*John S. Saloma III and Frederick H. Sontag*

*Recommendation: To balance the trend toward greater professionalization of parties, citizen groups and private individuals and organizations should develop ways to encourage citizen involvement and participation in the use of the new political technology.*

Lack of public information and public misunderstanding of polls, computers and the technology of the new politics only serve to increase the influence and mystique of the pollster or consultant. Many of the applications of computers to politics, for example, are straightforward and easily understandable if intelligently presented to the interested citizen. A public guide to polling and the new technology of politics could be prepared and published as a paperback book presenting in non-technical language the various new techniques being developed and applied to politics.

A new mechanism and motivation for introducing such innovations as the modern digital computer, cable television and interactive media into citizen-oriented politics will have to be found that parallels the close relationship between profit-oriented consulting firms and managerially oriented party professionals. Research and development of information systems that would encourage citizen involvement in politics should receive priority attention by foundations, private contributors and possibly government sources.

Another way to encourage citizen involvement and participation in professionalized politics would be for major reform-oriented contributors to contract directly with consulting firms for specific innovations or studies they would like to see made available to the parties or citizens or cause groups. Individuals and citizen groups could also invest in the stock of a consulting firm. A group of such investors could, perhaps through an annual meeting of stockholders, help to offset any tendency toward the development of a closed party-consultant relationship.

Library and other reference facilities should be encouraged to develop their collections on the new political technology to serve both the general public and interested citizen groups. One private collection of political TV spot advertisements, begun by Julian Kanter in 1952, now includes spots from 206 candidates in 154 races, a unique and invaluable resource for students of the evolution of the new politics.

All public polls could be collected by an institute of politics or other independent body which could publish periodic comprehensive reports of poll results for the use of party leaders, the media, and interested citizens.

*Recommendation: Political consultants should take initiatives to increase public understanding of their role in politics and to continue to improve and upgrade their profession.*

Political consultants bear the principal responsibility for increasing public understanding of their role in politics and for improving and upgrading their profession. The adoption by the American Association of Political Consultants in March 1971 of a Statement of Purposes and Code of Ethics was a first step. The new political quarterly of the association, *Polite'ia*, should also increase public understanding of the profession.

Consultants could work to upgrade the parties and the political process. They could develop, through seminars and publications, greater professional and public awareness of the relationship between politics and government and party responsibility for governmental performance.

Political consultants ought to follow the example of the legal profession in performing pro bono or public interest work. They might also become affiliates of such firms or specific cause groups. The announced educational and research programs of the AAPC could be expanded and formal resolutions could be adopted to further such activities. The profession could devote attention to the participatory as well as the managerial aspects of politics, sponsoring research, for example, on the reasons for nonvoting. Political consultants could also exert a constructive discipline on the parties by investigating complaints of unfair party practices and suits against clients filed by firms or individual consultants and encouraging new and constructive party procedures.

From John S. Saloma and Frederick H. Sontag, *Parties: The Real Opportunity for Effective Citizen Politics.* Copyright 1972 by Knopf, reprinted with permission of the Twentieth Century Fund, New York.

# THE "NEW POLITICS" AND PARTY RESPONSIBILITY

*David S. Broder*

A growing danger to the prospects for responsible party government is the technological revolution that has affected campaigning in the past decade. With the regular use of sophisticated public opinion polling, computer simulations of the electorate, automated and highly selective direct mail techniques, exploitation of the communications potential of telephone service, and, of course, the controlled use of mass media, particularly television, the makeup and organization of campaign staffs is changing . . . .

What is significant is that the "technocratic" tendencies often work against the direction of responsible party government. It is true that party headquarters are being professionalized. Indeed, in 1970, the Republicans opened the first permanent headquarters building either party has ever owned in Washington, D.C. That step, long recommended by reformers interested in responsible party government, seemed to symbolize the coming of age of the political party. But Saloma and Sontag argued in a paper presented to the American Political Science Association convention in 1970 that what has occurred is a professionalization of technical experts, rather than political leaders.

Instead of treating elections as periodic tests of party programs before the public (the objective of responsible party reformers), the parties have further narrowed electoral politics to a contest of political skill and technique between teams of "non-ideological" professionals. Politics is reduced to a problem-solving strategy of wining elections. The mobilization and rational allocation of resources is the primary objective of the "political managers." Government is treated as a separate and incidental activity distinct from the politics of elections.

Often, those political managers are not even party officials or staff members but independent political consultants, doing their work for a fee. The business of campaign management has flourished in the past decade; frequently, the first step an aspiring candidate will take is to hire a pollster, an ad agency, and a campaign manager, or sign a contract with one of the many firms offering to package a whole campaign for him. While some of the managers specialize in candidates of one party or the other, essentially, as James M. Perry said in his book *The New Politics*, "they are mercenaries; they are willing to go almost anywhere for a buck." Conservative or liberal, high tax or low, the campaign managers must treat their client-candidates essentially as commodities to be merchandised to the voters. There are exceptions, of course, but the professional campaign managers tend to be as anti-party as they are non-ideological. They talk with scorn (often well-merited) of the bumbling incompetence of the old-fashioned "political pros," who rely on their intuitions or their experience to guide campaign decisions. They have an over-developed sense of their own power and prowess. I remember the man from the New York agency that handled Lyndon Johnson's 1964 television campaign saying smugly over lunch, "The only thing that worries me is that some year an outfit as good as ours might go to work for the *wrong* candidate."

The "hired guns" have scored their biggest successes over the old-line party organizations in primary elections, where the ability to "sell a candidate," to establish his name identification with a small and largely indifferent electorate, makes their commercial approach to politics pay off. In general elections, where issues and party loyalties play more of a part and where the resources of competing candidates tend to be more equal, their success has been more limited.

But, of course, from the viewpoint of responsible party government, it is the nomination process that is particularly important. One of the major determinants of the degree of responsibility in a party system is the extent to which the party controls the nomination of the candidates who run under its name. In the last five years, all the major states—California, New York, Illinois, Pennsylvania, Ohio, Florida—have seen wealthy or well-financed men, with little background in party activity, little support among the party cadre, and little allegiance to the party or its programs, come in and beat the formally or informally designated organization favorite with expensive campaigns managed by outside political consultants. To the extent that the technocratic "new politics" means the separation of governmental problems from the content of the campaign and the separation of campaign management from the jurisdiction of the political party, it represents a twin threat to responsible party government. Obviously, many decent, able and well-motivated candidates are using the "new politics" techniques to gain public office. But, if the goal is responsible party government, then these techniques, and the ways they are being employed, must be a cause of concern.

Reprinted with permission of David S. Broder, from *The Party's Over: The Failure of Politics in America*, New York, Harper & Row, 1971, 1972.

## CAMPAIGNING OUTSIDE THE PARTY APPARATUS

*The American Assembly, Columbia University*

Achieving a preeminent role in campaigns has always been difficult for American parties. Federalism has not only fragmented the party organizations, it also has meant that literally thousands of party candidates run for public office. The sheer size of the campaign enterprise plus the frequency of American elections imposes an almost impossible campaign burden upon even the most efficient of party organizations. Furthermore, parties are not the only actors in the campaign process. They have always had to compete with other forces—candidate organizations, campaign managers, and interest groups. In recent years, the ability of the parties to compete for a place in the campaign process has been adversely affected by the growth of a professional corps of campaign experts and consultants skilled in the latest campaign techniques and technology. These professionals operate largely outside the party organizations, are closely tied to individual candidates, and pose a mounting threat to the influence of the parties.

Robert Agranoff, a political scientist who has studied changes in campaign styles and is himself one of the new breed of campaign professionals, points out four important distinctions between the "old" style of campaigning and the "new" style. First, the candidate, rather than the party, tends to be the major focus of modern campaigns. A well-financed candidate can build an organization devoted almost exclusively to his own election, while the traditional party support was usually divided between many candidates for many offices. Even though there are campaigns which are still run by party organizations, most have

given way to candidate-directed campaigns, often carried out by professional managers outside the party apparatus.

Second, in the new modes of campaigning that have emerged in the past three decades, the use of party professionals has given way to the technical professional—the management specialist, the pollster, the direct mail expert, and the media consultant. As it became evident that the traditional party organizations usually did not have personnel trained in these new campaign techniques, candidates turned more and more to those who did have such skills.

A third distinction between the "old" and "new" styles of campaign management stems from improvements in technology. The new campaign manager uses information gathered systematically from public opinion surveys, census tracts, precinct voting records, and poll lists and processes this data through a computer. As a result, the traditional reliance on precinct captains and party officials for needed information has been substantially reduced.

The fourth change has emerged from the communications revolution. In earlier times information was distributed to the voters through speeches, rallies, and handouts organized by the political party. Services and favors were the staples of the precinct captain. The party leader cut through government bureaucracy, found jobs, and performed favors. The payoff was on election day when the voters were asked to reciprocate for past favors. Now, the candidate-oriented campaign is often guided by outside experts who have mastered the use of telephone banks, computer-printed direct mail letters, and radio and television advertising. The key to all of these changes, Agranoff notes, is the transfer of campaign emphasis from political party organization to candidate organization. The transfer was made possible by the development of modern communications and computer technology.

The "old" politics of party-directed campaigns still occupies a place in the contests for offices below the congressional and state-wide levels, in a few major cities, and some sparsely populated areas. Candidates for major office, however, wishing to maximize their chances for election, increasingly embrace the new technology and professional management even though this has undercut the traditional campaign role of the party.

A second major aspect of the new politics is that the mass media, particularly television, have become important determinants as to the kinds of campaigns that will be waged. Candidates now gauge their campaign activities to media opportunities and concentrate attention on press conferences and photo opportunities. Public appearances and press releases are timed to meet television and press deadlines for the evening news. When it became apparent in 1976 that the Iowa caucuses were going to be heavily covered by the media, candidates who had previously shown no interest in Iowa hastily rearranged their schedules so that they could hopefully make a good showing in that state.

Candidates who are not good public speakers are scheduled and filmed with small groups of voters with whom they can interact. Others, who are unable to attract media attention, stage events which they hope will gain them air time and column inches. Visiting the factory gate, walking across the state, working for a day as an ordinary laborer, going up in a balloon or down in a diving suit, have all become staples of the media campaign. They are particularly important to non-incumbents who must scramble for attention and do not have the built-in advantages offered to incumbent officeholders.

Finally, the third major impact of the media on politics has been the decline in influence of the political parties, particularly in elections for Presidents. Professor Doris Graber has noted that when social scientists first studied the impact of the mass media on the outcome of 1940s presidential elections they concluded that party allegiance was the most important determining factor in the vote, followed by group allegiance, the candidate's personality, and the consideration of issues. With the advent of the television age, however, the order has been reversed with the personality of the candidate becoming the principal determinant, and issues, party affiliation, and group membership following in order. As she notes, when the voters base their decisions on candidate personality and issues, the media, particularly television, become more important because they represent the chief source of information about such matters. Correspondingly, since this has been a traditional role of the political parties, they become less important in the voter equation. Even so, party affiliation remains an important determinant of voting behavior in state and local elections where the large number of candidates makes it more likely the voters will rely on the electronic and print media in making candidate and issue choices.

All in all, therefore, the emergence of the electronic media has brought with it a different type of candidate, a new style of campaigning, and an erosion of influence for the political parties. Television in particular has assumed an important place in the kinds of decisions made by the electorate. It is an awesome power, but it is one that concentrates on major candidates—Presidents, governors, senators, and, on occasion, members of Congress. It is no wonder that the professional media adviser and the experienced campaign consultant have assumed roles of such importance in major political campaigns.

### The Impact of Technology on Politics

Not long after the invention of the computer some far-sighted political leaders sensed the value of automatic data processing in party organizational activities and campaigns. As early as 1966, the Republican National Committee authorized a study of centralized data processing and produced and distributed a handbook to explain computer technology in lay terms. It also undertook a pilot program based on test precincts and sponsored some training conferences designed to familiarize state party leaders with the use of such equipment.

Decision-makers in a political campaign need to know the economic, social, and political composition of the electorate to whom they are directing their appeal. They need to be able to pinpoint what issues are important and where their significance lies within their constituency. Up-to-date precinct lists, which in many states can be purchased from voter registrars, are important to "get-out-the-vote" drives and to direct mail fundraising. Campaign strategists know that there is no effective way to reach all of the voters. Information on selected voter groups, however, is available through computer technology, and it has become commonplace in major campaigns for a voter profile to be constructed based on census data, past voting records, and various economic indicators. All of these are suitable for computerization and, in fact, could not efficiently be provided in any other way.

The wide array of campaign uses for data processing has caused an increasing number of candidates for major office to use this technology as a matter of course. Since data processing services are normally provided not by state and local party organizations but by campaign consultants, these professionals have gained prominence in campaigns . . .

which are likely to be staffed by personnel who will have to learn these skills through on-the-job training.

. . . The increasing use of the combination of the electronic media, automatic data processing, and professional campaign consultants has undercut the traditional campaign role of political parties and affected our institutions of government. Reliance on campaign consultants and media campaigns, with their direct appeals to the voters over the heads of party and group leaders, is not geared toward negotiation, compromise, and coalition building. Rather, media campaigns are often heavily symbolic, necessarily superficial in the handling of issues, and often confrontational in character. But governing requires more than symbolic appeals and confrontations. It demands coalition building—the traditional function of political parties. However, to the extent that changes in campaign practices bypass parties and result in candidates with less experience in this art, our governing institutions are likely to be staffed by personnel who will have to learn these skills through on-the-job training.

Reprinted with permission from "State Parties in an Era of Political Change" in The American Assembly, *The Future of American Political Parties* (Englewood Cliffs, N.J., Prentice-Hall, 1982). The American Assembly is a nonpartisan group, affiliated with Columbia University, that holds meetings and prepares books on public issues.

# THE PARTY OF THE FUTURE
*Xandra Kayden and Eddie Mahe, Jr.*

. . . One critical question the parties and their campaign organizations must resolve is how to motivate support, and once motivated, how to apply it in a meaningful way for both the participant and the organization. It goes back to the question of incentives and rewards, which is the basis of all organizations. It goes back to the constant theme of would-be party leaders that they want to "rebuild the grass-roots."

It is our contention that the part of motivation dependent upon communication—upon reaching the minds (and maybe hearts) of party supporters—is very much within the sphere of party control. If anything, it has improved in quality and in quantity. Some of that communication has been in the form of direct mail solicitation which provides the re-

cipient the opportunity to act on it, and as many fundraisers know, commitment tends to follow money: once you invest money in a cause, you come to believe in it more strongly. In that regard, then, it is likely that millions of Americans have a more firmly rooted commitment to their party.

But what of those who want to come out and contribute their spare time and energy? One reality everyone must face (including those who would like to contribute their time) is that there is less of it around these days. Seventy percent of the women under 35 work. Both women and men want to spend more time with their families and more time in health-related activities. The question is what can an organization do with individuals who want to make a contribution but have limited time and, usually, little to offer beyond their enthusiasm?

There will undoubtedly be many efforts made by both parties to find satisfying useful tasks. The probability remains, however, that the only elections to rely entirely on that sort of grassroots efforts will be local elections. Even state legislative races have become more expensive and more dependent on the sophisticated campaign technologies available, as PAC money moves increasingly in that direction.

Politics appears to be becoming a more passive activity, but it should be borne in mind that the percentage of the population who used to be active was always small and not always representative of the population as a whole. The legitimacy and acceptance of the entire system depended and continues to depend not on this small elite but on the proportion of the population who vote. They are being reached; they are better informed; they may be more committed in the future. More of them are contributing money to the parties, and they may feel that their participation is anything but passive, given that it was more than they did before, and they are engaged in more communication with the party as a result of their donation.

## Communications and the New Party System

By the end of the 1980s, both parties will probably have their own cable networks reaching out to the party faithful, educating them to the party's principles and the skills required for running campaigns. The lists of registered voters maintained by the parties and their affiliates will be more extensive, and the communication between the party and the voters will increase accordingly in the mails, by telephone, probably even by computer. More people will have access to more information than ever before and that, we believe, will lead to an increase in partisan intensity. The capacity to communicate so much so easily will make our politics much less labor-intensive, not unlike many of the activities in the rest of our lives.

The increased communication may mean that politics becomes more passive because so much of the former activity had to do with reaching out to voters. Certainly many of the old tasks are no longer relevant, and the campaign finance law has added to the passivity by requiring a centralization of the process in order to keep track of the income and expenditures. The general election of the president makes that point most dramatically because it is the one most likely to generate the greatest amount of enthusiasm. But the public financing law prohibits contributions directly to the campaigns, and the spending limitations (combined with the uncertain relations between the presidential campaign staff and state and local parties) encourage even more centralization. It is a time when many people want to do more and find that there is less to do. The fact that there is less for the volunteer to do and the fact that, presidential elections aside, there are fewer volunteers is both cause and effect of the new circumstances.

Someday, someone may solve the problem of what to do with volunteers in a way that is both satisfying to the volunteer and productive to the party and the campaign. Organizations must find a way of making themselves efficient if they are to survive, and it is not likely that irrelevant work, or unsatisfying participation, will sustain anything for very long, even if campaigns are temporary phenomena. It is likely that the solution will have less to do with communication and more with other organizational tasks, such as decision making, unless we begin training more individuals in the technology of tomorrow's communication systems—not an unlikely prospect.

The professionalization of politics has its strengths and its weaknesses. It is part and parcel of the new system, however, and it brings us back to the focus of this book. We have been writing principally about the people who actively participate: the party structure and the individuals who make it work. It has been our view that the parties lost ground with the voters because they did not mean

very much. One reason they lost control of their destiny was because most of the reforms in this century effectively weakened the structure—the ability of party leaders to make their organizations do very much at all. The strength of the new party system rests on the capability of these new professionals to make decisions about candidates and issues, and to reach out to the citizenry and make those decisions known.

## WHERE PARTY WORKS AT THE LOCAL LEVEL

*Larry J. Sabato*

When Americans think of local political parties, most quickly cite New York's Tammany Hall or Chicago's Daley Machine. But Tammany died before mid-century, and the Daley Machine has gradually faded since Mayor Richard J. Daley's passing in 1977, decimated by fratricide, by court rulings striking at the heart of the patronage system, and by opponents that one long-time machine alderman characterized as "intellectuals, troublemakers and know-hows." ("When you give them a $10 bill, they can't even get a dog out of the dog pound for you!" he noted.)[1] That all local party organizations have gone the way of New York's and Chicago's is a commonly held belief, even among journalists and political observers.

Commonly held—and perhaps also mistaken. A recent study of the 7,300 county-level party organizations in the United States revealed that many local parties—Democratic as well as Republican—are surprisingly active, and have not really become less so over the past two decades.[2] While party organizational atrophy is unmistakable in many cities and counties and most county parties have no paid staff, central party headquarters, or even a telephone listing,[3] some local parties appear to have a life of their own, aided by substantial help from the state and (on the GOP side) national committees. These local organizations seem to endure and sometimes prosper despite party reversals at state or national levels.[4] In the most successful cases, that is due to one of two sources of strength: either a well-nourished grassroots organization fed by a patronage or a technologically advanced party with a solid base of ideologically attuned contributors and supporters.

While in a decade's time there may well be more examples of the latter than the former, it is the big-city machine prototype that is still more common among vital local parties. One example is found in St. Clair County (East St. Louis), Illinois, where an electorally weighty Democratic organization holds sway. In a testament to old-time politics, the organization managed in 1986 to reelect Congressman Melvin Price, an 81-year-old who had been ousted as chairman of the House Armed Services Committee in 1985 because of advanced age and debilitating frailty. Despite the efforts of an energetic, young, and attractive opponent, Price won a 52 percent to 39 percent victory by riding the back of the organization, which resented his opponent's attempt to secure office without having "paid his dues" to the machine.[5]

Another potent local organization, which many believe to have eclipsed Chicago's as the nation's most effective, is found in the Republican party of Nassau County, New York. No doubt Mayor Daley would have found much to like about this rigid and hierarchical machine that controls more than 20,000 jobs and features an elaborate superstructure of ward chairpersons, precinct committee members, and block captains who turn out the vote on election day.[6] Originally built on New York City's out-migration of blue-collar Irish and Italian ethnics who wanted to disassociate themselves from the city's liberal politics, the machine now takes great care to recruit young people, in part by distributing plum summer jobs, and many of these youths go on to base their whole careers on service to the party. In the best tradition of machine politics, aspiring officeholders are expected to work their way up the ladder slowly, toiling for years in the backrooms and the neighborhoods, delivering votes for the party candidates and dollars for the party war chest. Party chiefs encourage competition among committee members to see who can attract the most new registrants or sell the most tickets to a fundraiser. (About $2 million annually is raised in this single county for party activities.) The machine is not without its problems, of course. Corruption charges against some of its leaders have been proven, for instance, and its command of so many patronage positions is under attack. Yet electoral success keeps the organization humming, and it regularly wins a large majority of the area's county, state legislative, and congressional posts. The machine has even produced one of New York's United States senators, Alfonse D'Amato, first elected in 1980. D'Amato was a supervisor of Nassau's Hempstead township and a top leader of the party organization prior to his Senate bid. The conservative Republican learned constituency service politics well in the county machine, and he attended assiduously to the state's interests just as he had done for his township, earning a landslide reelection in 1986 that even included an endorsement from the liberal *New York Times.*

This description of the Nassau machine would once have seemed unremarkable or even tame, but with each passing year there appear to be fewer truly vibrant, grassroots, neighborhood-based parties. Indiana's local parties, especially on the Republican side, are often cited when the subject of strong organizations is raised. Yet there, too, parties have suffered recent body blows. Fundamentalist Christian congressional candidates embarrassed the local parties in two 1986 House primaries by defeating the party consensus choices by substantial margins.[7] (The GOP suffered for it in November; both nominees lost, including one from a reliably Republican district.) And the governor and state legislature, egged on by the news media and anti-patronage public sentiment, voted to phase out the most unique and sustaining form of public financing in the nation.[8] In each Indiana county, the organization run by the governor's political party[9] had traditionally been allowed to retain a portion of the revenue from the state's motor vehicle licensing system. This delightful arrangement produced about $400,000 a year for the local parties. Moreover, another $400,000 or so derived from the sale of personalized license plates was split between the two major parties. But no longer: as of 1987 the profits are going to the state.[10]

If Chicago, Nassau County, and Indiana represent the old-style party organization, then the Waxman-Berman machine in California may suggest the future directions of strong local parties.[11] Named after its founders, liberal Democratic Congressmen Henry A. Waxman and Howard L. Berman, this Los Angeles-based machine has built its success on direct mail and new campaign technologies rather than patronage and ward committee members. In many ways Waxman-Berman is the polar opposite of the Nassau County organization: informal, candidate (not party) centered, impersonal in the communication media it chooses, and a creation of California's basically anti-party environment. Also unlike their Nassau brethren, who virtually ignore national politics and concentrate on local offices, Waxman, Berman, and their allies care little about local politics; most of their energies are devoted to electing congressional candidates and influencing national and international policy. Yet a fundamental link between the two machines remains: they accumulate power by helping friends win elective and appointive office.

The Waxman-Berman machine (which prefers to call itself an "alliance") combines entertainment industry money and a firm liberal base in Los Angeles with the direct mail skills of Howard Berman's brother Michael (a well-known Democratic party consultant). Sophisticated fundraising and persuasive mail campaigns have enabled the machine principals to elect several dozen allies to congressional, state legislative, and major local posts. Moreover, the machine funnels money to a political action committee controlled mainly by Waxman. In the 1983-1984 election cycle Waxman gave about $140,000 from the PAC and his own campaign treasury to House and Senate candidates across the country.[12] Such gifts do not go unnoticed and unrewarded. After Waxman made similar contributions in 1979 to eight of his fellow members on the House Commerce Committee, he was able to win a key subcommittee chair over another, more senior member.[13]

If Waxman-Berman is the best example of the new technologically based party on the left, Senator Jesse Helms's (R-NC) Congressional Club may symbolize a similar development on the right.[14] Helms has built a formidable PAC, one of the nation's largest, on direct mail solicitation of right-wing Republican supporters. The Club has been a powerhouse in North Carolina politics, recruiting, training, and financing dozens of congressional and state legislative candidates. Though considered a divisive element by much of the state's GOP leadership and despite having suffered many setbacks over the years, the Club is still a force to be reckoned with in and out of North Carolina.

As I have already suggested, the newer technologically advanced model of strong local parties probably has more of a future than the older ethnically based or patronage-fed machine. Yet the latter should not be dismissed so easily, not only because it has proven hardier in some places than many expected but also because there is a great deal to be said for such personalized, neighborhood-oriented, "bottom-up" parties. The ideal self-sustaining and advancing party might well be a carefully crafted combination of modern technology and community service-centered organization . . .

### Implications for Politics and Government

If this extended discussion of the strengthening of party organizations has proven anything, it is that the new technologies of politics, which have so often been used to weaken the parties by liberating individual candidates from party influence, are now being employed to build more vital political parties. No technology, after all, is inherently good or evil; the uses to which it is put determine its morality. Party advocates can only be delighted that these techniques are enabling parties to rebuild and fortify themselves at a time when either an anti-party mood prevails or people simply do not care very much about the parties' fate.

The consequences of reinvigorated party organization and financing are many. First of all, an obvious result is that parties are in a much better position to help their nominees win elections—a fact that does not escape the notice of candidates and officeholders. Already, it is apparent that elected officials are devoting more time and energy to party affairs in many states, as a recent survey of party chairpersons by the Advisory Commission on Inter-governmental Relations determined.[15] The ACIR also found that the more campaign assistance state parties provided to their candidates, the more likely it was that those candidates would take part in party activities.[16]

More importantly, the parties' new recruitment efforts, financial contributions, and provision of campaign services are bearing fruit in another way. The evolving ties between the parties and their elected decision makers may be helping to enact the party agenda and to increase cohesion among the party's officeholders. Gary Jacobson, among others, has suggested that the Republican party has been able to impose greater discipline on some policy matters through appropriate distribution of its campaign services.[17] For example, the large GOP Senate class of 1980, which owed its election in good measure to Ronald Reagan's presidential coattails and the lavish expenditures of the national party committees, showed unusual cohesion throughout the six-year term of its members. As a *National Journal* analysis of Senate voting records demonstrated, the members of the class of 1980 (with just a couple of exceptions) consistently voted with each other and with their party majority on almost all key domestic and foreign policy issues during their tenure.[18]

Interestingly, *both* congressional parties are displaying greater solidarity in the pattern of their floor votes in the 1980s compared to the 1950s. . . . There are many reasons for this, of course, including the dwindling of the ranks of both Southern conservative Democrats and Northern liberal Republicans, which makes each party more ideologically and internally consistent. But the influence of party label seems to be an increasingly important aspect of the congressional voting calculus. The national parties' institutional advertising campaigns have made legislators accept basic party themes and realize that any single candidate's electoral fate is unavoidably bound up with that of his or her party. The parties have also created "chits" in exchange for their gifts of money and services that party leaders are able to "call in" on crucial matters. Thus, for perhaps the first time in decades, the parties have been able to counteract to some small degree the individualistic, atomizing forces that favor personalized, candidate-centered, interest group-responsive politics and legislative voting. There is even some evidence that the same phenomenon is occurring on the state level. Andrew Aoki and Mark Rom were able to conclude a study of Wisconsin party campaign contributions and the subsequent voting records compiled by state legislators by suggesting that "those candidates receiving more money may indeed be more likely to support the party in the following session than the candidates receiving less money."[19]

Nonetheless, there are considerable limitations on the influence American parties can exert on legislators under even the most favorable of conditions. Parties are certainly a more substantial source of cash and campaign technology than ever before, but they are not the only source by any means. While a legislator will not wish to offend any major benefactor, he or she will do so when necessary so long as other alternative support is available. Then, too, parties are hardly inclined at elec-tion time to discipline their incumbents—almost any incumbent, however uncooperative or obnoxious. Since the overriding objective is victory, the parties will normally choose the pragmatic course and aid any party candidate, rather than reward only some while punishing others and risking their defeat. After all, a candidate completely deprived of party assistance will be less pliable and even more hostile in the future. Still, it cannot be denied that the parties' influence has grown legislatively because of their enhanced electoral capabilities. This is potentially of great significance, even though in most votes, the effect may be minor. As Aoki and Rom conclude: "The changes are understandably small, but small changes can have big political effects, if they mean the difference between passing programs and indefinitely postponing them."[20]

There is another consequence of strengthened party organization that deserves mention. To this point, at least, party development has extended from the top down, from national to state party organizations. All politics may be local, but more and more, the key political decisions and allocations are being made nationally. Economies of scale and the new campaign finance rules have so far encouraged the centralization of electoral services and technology in the national party committees. While the national organizations were at one time financed by the state parties, the opposite pattern is closer to the truth today, and the national parties frequently also intervene to recruit state and local candidates.[21] This reversal of the flow of party power disturbs some federalists. As the Advisory Commission on Inter-governmental Relations expressed it:

Throughout much of American history, the strongly decentralized structure of the political parties helped maintain a balance between national, state, and local authority. . . . To the extent that the decentralized party system once contributed significantly to maintaining political balance in the federal system, that capacity has to some extent declined.[22]

Yet the health of federalism is also dependent on the vitality of the parties as a whole. The fact that the national party organizations have been revivified can only help the parties perform their linkage role in the federal configuration. If nothing else, the centralization of party resources permits the national parties to target weak state and local parties for special remedial help, freeing them from the demoralizing cycle of inbred defeat. By infusing money and services to anemic parties that otherwise might not have been competitive, vigorous two-party competition is spread in sometimes unlikely places. Surely, the federal division of power is fortified under such an arrangement. Beyond that, we must remember that the national parties are slowly but surely transferring the means and methods of the campaign technologies to the state and local parties themselves. Indisputably, centralization is probably a permanent feature of the new party system, but the dependency of state parties on their national counterparts will likely lessen somewhat as they develop quasi-independent capabilities. This process ought to be accelerated as much as possible, . . . a goal that will serve the purposes of both parties and federalism. Then, too, the degree of centralization in party activity that has actually taken place can be exaggerated. The parties remain firmly rooted in the states both because the vast majority of party leaders and officeholders are elected and reside there and because the states, far more than the national government, regulate and control the parties.

Politically, there are the other results of the parties' gain in campaign power, some of them almost universally recognized as beneficial. For instance, as the parties' clout rises, the influence of PACs and special interest groups is indirectly limited both in campaigns and in governing. The alternate source of financing provided by the parties is especially potent in checking PACs.[23] Furthermore, the expanding role of the parties as providers of campaign information to PACs and interest groups has gathered these organizations under the party umbrellas to a greater degree; many millions of dollars are contributed each year from PACs and interest groups to the party (not just candidate) coffers,[24] and many of the organizations, especially labor and education groups on the Democratic side and business and conservative religious interests on the Republican side, are participating in party activities more substantially.[25]

The mushrooming of party organizational strength has come at a crucial moment. All of the forces arrayed against the parties have weakened them, and would have continued to do so except for the parties' self-initiated innovations. Now instead of continuing a slide into disfavor and oblivion, parties are battling those forces, using their expanded capacities to aid their candidates and to contact more voters—and thereby *perhaps* to develop

stronger bonds with both groups. The parties may even have become, in the words of Cotter et al., "effective counter-de-aligning agents" combating "the departisanization of the electorate" and "counteracting anti-party trends."[26]

## NOTES

1. Alderman Vito Marzullo as quoted in the *Washington Post*, November 2, 1985, A3. Marzullo won 23 elections as a machine candidate and served for more than three decades on Chicago's city council before being forced to retire after unfavorable court-ordered redistricting in 1986. He spurned all offers of higher office over the years, explaining, "I just want to stay where I am . . . where I can help my friends and shaft my enemies."

2. Cotter, Gibson, Bibby, Huckshorn, *Party Organizations in American Politics*, 57. See also Epstein, *Political Parties in the American Mold*, 152.

3. Cotter, Gibson, Bibby, Huckshorn, 57.

4. See William Crotty, ed., *Political Parties in Local Areas* (Nashville: University of Tennessee Press, 1987); and Mayhew, *Placing Parties in American Politics*.

5. See *Congressional Quarterly Weekly* 44 (March 22, 1986): 660.

6. See Tom Watson, "All-Powerful Machine of Yore Endures in New York's Nassau," *Congressional Quarterly Weekly* 43 (August 17, 1985): 1623-1625.

7. See *Congressional Quarterly Weekly* 44 (April 26, 1986): 931-932, and (May 10, 1986): 1046.

8. *Washington Post*, September 23, 1985, A14. Also, it was an election issue in the 1984 gubernatorial race. While the Democratic candidate who opposed the patronage system lost, he seemed to gain support based on the issue. The successfully reelected governor, Republican Robert Orr, received the electorate's message, and proposed abolition of the funding scheme in 1985.

9. The Republicans have been the major beneficiaries since they have controlled the Indiana governorship continuously since 1969.

10. Information supplied by Indiana Legislative Services. The bill that passed in 1986 was House Bill No. 1400 (IC 510-372).

11. See Rob Gurwitt, "Waxman, Berman and Allies Aim to Shape National Policy," *Congressional Quarterly Weekly* 43 (August 17, 1986): 1620-1623.

12. Ibid.

13. *Wall Street Journal*, November 10, 1983, 58; and *Congressional Quarterly Weekly* 41 (March 12, 1983): 505.

14. See Sabato, *PAC Power*. See also Irwin B. Arieff, Nadine Cohodes, and Richard Whittle, "Senator Helms Builds a Machine of Interlinked Organizations to Shape Both Politics, Policy," *Congressional Quarterly Weekly* 40 (March 4, 1982): 479-505; and Paul Taylor, "Helms Modernizes GOP Political Machine for the Electronic Age," *Washington Post*, October 15, 1982, A2.

15. ACIR, *The Transformation in American Politics*, 116-118.

16. Ibid. This relationship was especially strong for Democratic candidates at all levels, but also was valid for the GOP in the case of congressional candidates.

17. Gary C. Jacobson, "Republican Advantage in Campaign Finance," in John Chubb and Paul

Peterson, eds., *The New Direction in American Politics* (Washington, D.C.: The Brookings Institution, 1985), 169.

18. *National Journal* 18 (April 12, 1986): 866-868.
19. Andrew L. Aoki and Mark Rom, "Financing a Comeback: Campaign Finance Laws and Prospects for Political Party Resurgence," paper prepared for delivery at the annual meeting of the American Political Science Association, New Orleans, La., August 29-September 1, 1985, 14. In five of the six cases examined by the authors, the representatives who received the most money from the party during a campaign were more likely to support the party in the next legislative session than the group of representatives that received the least amount of money. However, the difference between the means of the two groups was never statistically significant.
20. Ibid., 17.
21. Kayden and Mahe, *The Party Goes On*.
22. ACIR, *The Transformation in American Politics*, 332, 360.
23. Sabato, *PAC Power*, 141-159, 176-177.
24. Ibid.
25. ACIR, *The Transformation in American Politics*, 234.
26. Cotter, Gibson, Bibby, and Huckshorn, *Party Organizations in American Politics*, 989-991.

# PROSPECTS FOR THE PARTIES

*Paul S. Herrnson*

The influence of political parties has waxed and waned throughout American history. During the late nineteenth and early twentieth centuries party organizations exerted tremendous influence over the electoral process. They often controlled virtually every facet of election campaigning, from recruiting candidates to mobilizing voters. By the 1960s, however, the old-fashioned political machines had withered and a new era in election politics had begun. The widespread adoption of the direct primary, the enactment of civil service reforms, the restriction of immigration, and the assimilation of ethnic neighborhoods greatly weakened the political machines. The emergence of the candidate-centered system, along with its plebiscitary nominations process and sophisticated methods of campaigning, left the nation's declining political parties on the periphery of the electoral process. Party organizations not only lost control over candidate nominations; they also lost their ability to play a dominant role in election campaigns. The proliferation of PACs that occurred after the enactment of the FECAs further hastened the decline of parties. To some political observers, the PAC phenomenon sounded the death-knell of America's political parties.

This study rejects the belief that legal reforms, new campaign technologies, the development of rival political organizations, and other transformations in the political environment have been so hostile to political parties that they can no longer play an important role in elections. It also rejects the contention that these transformations will result in the parties' ultimate demise. Rather, it demonstrates support for the thesis that parties are malleable institutions that are continually adapting, albeit slowly, to their environment.

The old-fashioned political machines' failure to develop a mass-membership base and their inability to amass substantial financial and technical resources left them unequipped to adjust to the reforms in early twentieth-century American politics. Stripped of their control over government jobs and contracts, deprived of the power to hand-pick candidates for election, no longer possessing a monopoly over the resources needed to wage election campaigns, and without a mass of largely uneducated, easily mobilized immigrants, most local party bosses and machines declined rapidly. The national and state party organizations of the period also lacked the money, professional staff, and centralized authority to take over the electoral functions formerly conducted by the local parties. As a result, the party organizations of the 1960s through 1970s were pushed to the periphery of the election process.

By the 1970s merchandised, new-style political campaigning had become widely practiced in House and Senate elections, increasing their complexity and the resources needed to get elected to Congress. At this time, first the Republican and then the Democratic national party organizations began experimenting with modern fundraising, communications, and research techniques. Once on the right path, the national parties were on their way to becoming the major repositories of many of the campaign services and resources needed by congressional candidates, state and local party committees, and other electoral actors. This transformation ushered in a new era of party politics whose debut went unnoticed by political observers unaccustomed to thinking in terms of strong national party organizations and whose analyses of legislative behavior, voting patterns, and local party activity reinforced their preconceptions that parties were caught in an irreversible decline.

In contrast to predictions for the imminent collapse of political parties, this study demonstrates that national party organizations have successfully adapted to contemporary politics. The parties' national, congressional, and senatorial campaign committees are now wealthier, more stable, better organized, and better staffed than ever before. They are also playing an important role in congressional elections. The growing importance of national party activity is confirmed by those who are its principal beneficiaries—those actually competing in the 1984 House and 1984 and 1986 Senate general elections. Data collected from interviews with House and Senate campaigners and from a mail survey of a much larger and more representative sample of congressional contestants support what interviews with party staff suggest. National party organizations, especially the congressional and senatorial campaign committees, are providing candidates with valuable assistance in campaign management, campaign communications, fundraising, and gauging public opinion. State and local committees are providing many candidates with assistance in mobilizing voters and recruiting volunteer workers. Party organizations in general are having a greater influence in nearly every area of campaigning than are PACs, unions, or any other political organizations besides the candidates' own campaign committees.

The findings also demonstrate that the national parties strategically target their election services and other resources in an effort to maximize the number of seats they hold in each chamber of Congress. They provide more campaign services and resources to competitive House and Senate candidates than to noncompetitive ones. Competitive challengers and open seat contestants also receive more campaign assistance than do incumbents in competitive races. In addition, Republican candidates typically receive more campaign assistance than do Democrats, and House candidates of both parties derive greater benefits from party assistance than do candidates for the Senate. The partisan differences can be attributed to the financial, technological, and organizational advantages

of the Republican national party. The House and Senate differences, on the other hand, reflect . . . dissimilarities between congressional and senatorial campaigns . . .

The principal goals of this study were to address two questions about the roles of political parties in the electoral process. First, are party organizations capable of adapting to the changing nature of American electoral politics? Yes, they are. Signs of their adaptability include the recent institutionalization of the national party organizations, their integration into the networks of PACs and political consulting agencies that largely make up the new corps of congressional campaigners, and the expansion of the services they provide to their congressional candidates. The national parties now assist in campaign functions requiring technical expertise, in-depth research, or connections with campaign elites that possess many of the skills and resources needed to communicate with the electorate. They help many of their candidates, and especially those running in competitive races, run more professional and sophisticated campaigns that are well suited to the electoral conditions of the contemporary United States. Although the parties will probably never enjoy the level of electoral influence attributed to the old-fashioned political machines, the evidence suggests that party organizations have and will continue to develop structures and processes that are well suited to the current system of cash-oriented, "high tech" campaign politics.

The second question is: do parties make a difference in contemporary congressional elections? The answer is a little more complicated than a simple yes or no. From the perspective of the national parties' staffs, their organizations surely make an important difference. The parties, and particularly the Washington committees, do furnish valuable campaign services directly to their candidates. In this sense, they function as important appendages and accessories to campaign organizations, especially those of candidates running in close elections. The national parties also assist their competitive candidates in obtaining various resources and services by facilitating contacts and agreements between the candidates, PACs, campaign consultants, and other important electoral organizations. In this sense, the parties have assumed a useful brokerage role.

From the perspective of PACs and other non-party electoral groups, party organizations also make a difference. When national party organizations designate some elections as competitive races and make large contributions to candidates running in them, that helps to clarify the picture for PACs, unions, and other interest groups, enabling them to pick out and support candidates running for competitive seats. PAC directors and other interest group leaders likewise stress the importance of the parties' brokerage role. The national parties' ability to channel the resources of other electoral organizations to competitive candidates has made them the most important intermediaries in contemporary congressional elections.

From the perspective of the candidates, the difference that party activity made in their races depends upon their particular situation. Many non-incumbents have little chance of getting elected and many incumbents are in safe seats. These candidates typically receive some help from their local party organizations and small amounts of services and assistance from their parties' national, congressional, and senatorial campaign committees. For these candidates, parties generally do not make a very big difference. However, approximately 25 percent of major party House and Senate candidates are involved in competitive contests and have a strong chance of winning or losing a congressional seat. Most of them, and especially those who belong to the Republican party, consider the national parties to be important sources of advice, connections, and valuable campaign services and assistance. For these candidates, parties make a very big difference—sometimes enough of a difference to change the course of a campaign and affect the outcome of an election. . . .

It is clear that the institutionalization of their national organizations has strengthened the parties' role in congressional elections. Electing candidates to public office has always been the primary concern of American political parties, and electoral success has traditionally been the dominant standard for assessing party strength. According to this standard, the political parties are alive and well, and the parties' national organizations are more powerful than ever before. The United States may be embarking on a new era of party politics, one characterized by strong and highly active national parties.

Excerpted with permission from *Party Campaigning in the 1980s* (Cambridge, Mass.: Harvard University Press, 1988).

## THE PARTY AS CONSULTANT

*Robert Blaemire, Campaigns & Elections magazine, July/August 1987*

The 1986 election post-mortems that described new trends and effective campaign techniques missed at least one important development that suggests a revitalized future for state Democratic parties. Many of the professional services campaigns ordinarily purchase through consultants now are available to candidates at a lower cost through state parties.

Although the Democratic party often is depicted as the party favoring big government and centralized power, as a political institution it has moved in a different direction in the 1980s. It has strengthened its state parties, increased their respective power and influence, and has done so without concentrating additional functions or authority in Washington, D.C. . . .

As an employee of Senator Birch Bayh (D-Ind.) for 13 years, and now as a consultant specializing in computer work and direct mail with Below, Tobe & Associates, I have witnessed the takeover by some Democratic state parties of many of the functions previously reserved to consulting firms. As a result, many more campaigns at all levels are able to take advantage of modern campaign techniques.

### New Party Role

. . . Since the breakdown of the patronage system and the advent of modern communications (especially television), the power of political parties to influence elections has diminished to the point that it now is confined almost exclusively to contributing money to candidates. This role has led to a perception that the Democratic party is outgunned and impotent.

. . . The last few years have seen a change, however, instigated by a few strong individuals within the Democratic National Committee (DNC) and by one or two imaginative consultants. They have redefined the role in campaigns for state parties, largely by encouraging state party officials to help coordinate aspects of various campaigns and to help them share computer technology. As a result, many of the services campaigns relied on consultants to perform now are available to greater numbers of candidates at a far lower cost.

... For those elections in 1986 that were determined by the way the campaign was waged, the strategic contributions of a few progressive Democratic state parties were important factors.

### Creating a Voter File

In 1979, I was working toward the development of a campaign plan for Birch Bayh's 1980 Senate campaign. Always interested in seeing that we compiled the best lists for direct mail and other voter contact, my colleagues and I looked into the possibility of creating a statewide voter file in Indiana. Not knowing much about it, we went at the project like many amateurs do and quickly were discouraged by the potential costs.

... We knew we wanted to use targeted, repetitive direct mail and phone banks but not necessarily how best to attain that goal on our own without exorbitant cost. Although we had played a significant role in installing the new state Democratic leadership and could count on their desire to provide services to the Bayh campaign, we simply never tied the two pieces together. We never believed or even considered that they really could provide meaningful services to us or even organize a project of that magnitude in which we would share costs and benefits with other Indiana candidates.

... State parties now have grasped this important concept that cooperation is key. Undertaking coordinated efforts means parties not only have a renewed role in helping candidates win elections, but that they can develop a profit center as well, thus augmenting their ability to assist candidates in tangible ways.

Let's look at a few examples, specifically the six state parties of Alabama, Florida, Indiana, Maryland, North Carolina, and Tennessee, and see how this has worked. Our firm is one of a number of computer-services and direct-mail companies that, working with Democratic parties and candidates, has been involved in helping make these coordinated efforts work for candidates.

The concept is fairly simple. ...

A growing area of modern campaigning is the use of computers to create large databases of registered voters and to be able to communicate specific messages to only those voters who need to receive those messages. The computer is used to amass these voter databases and to append as much data to the names as possible, so the targeting can be as precise as possible. The more you know about a specific voter, the better you can communicate with him or her...

Creating these enhanced voter databases, as we found out in Indiana, is expensive. The high costs are a function of the difficulty in compiling the lists, the numbers of voters involved and the various pieces of information required to enhance the database. By coordinating the various needs of campaigns for voter files, the party can make sure the files are built only once and that several candidates are able to use them.

Our firm had contracts with six state parties to create these databases. Candidates, in turn, paid fees to their respective state parties to gain access to the voter files. This joint-financing approach means each candidate has access to a voter file for a relatively small sum. Consequently, candidates who never might have considered the venture have access to the files. ...

In Florida, it costs more than $14,000 to purchase the necessary computer tapes from each of the 67 counties. For a cost far less than that, statewide candidates have access to a standardized voter file that includes all registered voters with information on their party identification, age, race, sex, address, telephone number, voting history, ethnicity, place of birth, date of registration, and composite data based on the household in which each voter resides.

Candidates for congressional and other offices have the same access for lower prices, based on the size of their electoral jurisdiction. In 1986, the Florida Democratic party sold access to its lists to 99 candidates, who then ordered computer and direct-mail products from the statewide voter file. Because of these sales, accumulated access fees paid for the startup costs of the project and made a profit for the party. These funds were used for staff support to help manage the project, for updating the files, and for the party's own use on behalf of Democratic nominees ...

Other examples of successful ventures between state parties and candidates are worthwhile to examine:

—During the 1984 campaign, then-Congressman Albert Gore, Jr. (D-Tenn.) was the motivating force behind the Tennessee Democratic party's project to create a voter file. Potential participants were asked to pool their financial resources in advance, and the party was able to organize the creation of the voter file without spending any of its own funds up front. During 1986, a similar pooling of resources enabled the file to be updated. It was used for voter-contact programs by all three candidates for governor.

—Last fall, Steve Pajcic, coming off a close Florida gubernatorial primary campaign and entering a runoff, decided that the four-week campaign would be decided by a narrow universe of voters who cast ballots in runoff elections. There would have been no time to create such a file on such short notice. Consequently, Pajcic paid an access fee to the party, which updated the file with primary information and implemented an aggressive voter-contact effort. They waged a campaign that targeted 300,000 likely voters who were mailed twice and phoned twice during the last week of the campaign. Pajcic won the runoff by less than 10,000 votes.

—The North Carolina Democratic party instituted a statewide get-out-the-vote campaign on behalf of Terry Sanford's senatorial campaign and several congressional campaigns. The cost of each piece of mail was considerably less than what it would have cost each candidate to mail the pieces individually; I believe several close campaigns were won as the result of the last-minute mailings.

—The Indiana campaign of Jim Jontz for a long-held Republican congressional seat used the party's voter file effectively to find, target, and repeatedly contact the persuadable voters in a way never before seen in the state. The mail was noticed, had its impact, and Jontz was elected.

—In Alabama, which allows access to voter lists only by the two political parties, the state party created the only available voter database for Democratic candidates. Dozens of candidates used the file for state and federal offices, most using a computer in their campaigns for the very first time.

—The Maryland Democratic party expanded its services for candidates not only by creating a voter file but by managing polling and fundraising projects for candidates. The fundraising efforts that used the voter file on behalf of candidates have led the party to use the file to raise money for itself . . .

### Profit Possibilities

State parties can operate similar projects as profit centers:

—Access fees or other participatory costs, based on the electoral jurisdiction of the candidate and the candidate's proportion of the file's cost, can cover most or all of the costs of creating the master file. . . .

—The state party can mark up products ordered by candidates to cover handling costs and as a share in the management costs of the project.

—The parties can take advantage of batch ordering on behalf of multiple candidates ordering the same products at the same time . . .

—Other organizations or candidates outside the state, should they be interested in using the file, also pay access fees and costs that are commissionable to the parties. On some occasions, commercial opportunities for generating revenue from the voter file also exist.

These projects are no different from the way vendors deal with candidates now except in one respect: The party serves as an agency that manages the project . . .

Candidates have access to the data and technology at a low cost (some possibly for the first time), and they can save money simply by following party procedures. On occasion, candidates benefit simply because they no longer are mailing untargeted and wasteful direct mail. Vendors, on the other hand, while charging less money per product than they would to individual candidates, end up working for many, many more candidates through the parties, and gain long-term institutional clients. The projects make sense for everyone involved.

Does it make a difference? Who knows what factors in a campaign tilt the final scales. But if you believe the key to winning elections is communicating the right messages to the right voters and moving people to vote, then the ability to do this is enhanced by your state party's voter files.

Reprinted with permission from *Campaigns & Elections*.

## THE RISE OF THE SERVICE-VENDOR PARTY

*Stephen E. Frantzich*

. . . The national Republican party was first out of the gate with new fundraising techniques and a willingness to invest resources in building a solid financial base . . .

With increased resources, the Republicans

could turn to organization building. On the national level, the Republicans built a permanent party headquarters conveniently located on Capitol Hill more than a decade before the Democrats. In an attempt to recruit and train experienced political professionals, the Republicans expanded the staff and made it permanent while the Democrats were still going through the process of swelling numbers during campaign years and a paring down to a skeleton crew during the non-election period. A large number of the increased Republican employees supported the increases in the production and delivery of campaign services . . .

As significant as strengthening the national organization structure was the early Republican attempt to rebuild the state and local structures who had fallen on hard times. During the late 1970s, the RNC [Republican National Committee] began sending field staff members at no cost to most states giving them organizational advice and access to national party resources such as mailing lists, computer programs, research training and expertise . . .

Aside from providing staff and services to build (rebuild) party organizations, in 1978, the national Republicans started providing a more indirect service—partisan advertising designed to create a positive image for the party as a whole . . .

### Campaign Services

Since winning elections serves as the chief litmus test for party effectiveness, it is not surprising that the Republicans have expended considerable effort in regaining the initiative in campaigns. After suffering through decades where independent candidates were lured away by campaign consultants offering useful services, the Republicans struck back by becoming a provider of services at lower cost and higher quality than that available on the open market. For anything consultants had been charging for, the party attempted to become the "vendor of choice."

#### TRAINING

The first step was training. The Republicans pioneered offering a wide range of campaign related seminars for almost all kinds of campaign functionaries (from the candidate and finance director to candidate spouses) . . .

#### CANDIDATE RECRUITMENT

With the advent of the direct primary, political parties became more and more timid about "choosing the wrong horse" and ending up offending the winner of the primary. . . .

In the late 1970s, the RNC began a new selective tactic: having its field representatives seek out the most viable candidates, clear them with the local party, discourage potential opponents and favor them with campaign services. While the risks were great, and national party support did not always guarantee primary victory, when it did the winners owed a great deal to the party.

#### VOTER LISTS

. . . Through grants and technical help to state parties, the national Republican party encouraged the building of computerized lists, often enhanced with demographic and public opinion polling data . . .

#### VOTER REGISTRATION

. . . The RNC and particular state Republican parties have shown significant creativity and committed major resources to the time-honored party function of registering voters . . .

#### OPPOSITION RESEARCH

. . . For many years the Republicans have been ahead in clippings services, developing data banks of elections, statistics and quotes, and have continued to apply new techniques . . .

The Republicans have also led the pack in funding and coordinating campaign polling, as well as carrying out polls directly . . .

#### CAMPAIGN ADVERTISING

Using in-house advertising, the national Republicans saved candidates a significant amount on their advertising costs by producing and distributing radio and television spots. Through a coordinated approach, one stock advertisement could be revised for use with a number of different candidates.

Going well beyond traditional television advertising, the Republicans were first to use the potential of narrow-casting (rather than broadcasting) via satellite and cable systems . . .

#### GET-OUT-THE-VOTE DRIVES

Political parties traditionally took on the responsibility of getting out the vote on election day. As the parties weakened, candidate organizations began taking up the slack in this area. With the advent of up to date statewide voting lists and the efficiency of telemarketing systems, the parties again seemed like the best source for this service. Above and beyond reminding potential supporters who had been identified on the basis of party registration, and/or polling, many get out the vote drives used demographic targeting to communicate with and activate potential supporters . . .

. . . The Republican congressional committees took the lead in the 1960s providing help to incumbents for creating radio and television spots and distributing them efficiently to the local media. With each enhancement of technology, the Republicans have been at the forefront using satellites and electronic mail to get the message out.

Focusing on the often forgotten state legislative races, the Colorado Republicans took the lead in providing services to their elected officials in the hope of not only getting them in office, but keeping them there . . .

As the above litany of activity should reveal, the national Republican party, and many of its state and local affiliates have fought back into the political game by becoming super service vendors. Eschewing most of the procedural reforms which busied their Democratic opponents, the Republicans took on the consultants and the PACs directly by trying to beat them at their own game. . . .

### The Democratic Response

If imitation is the sincerest form of flattery, the Democratic party has consistently flattered its Republican counterpart to the degree that most recipients would get an overinflated ego. It would hardly be an exaggeration to conclude each of the above paragraphs describing new party services with the phrase, "and the Democrats followed . . . years later providing the same service. . . ." The Democrats copied Republican targeted mailing approaches, opened a media center, stimulated state and local party organizations with field staff and consultants, opened a permanent party headquarters—all essentially for the first time since 1980 . . .

A similar pattern of Republican leadership in providing services applies on the state party level . . .

The Democratic Party is clearly playing a game of "catch up" when it comes to becoming a service-vendor party. Their slow start places them at a disadvantage, but certainly has not placed a damper on their ardor in transforming their efforts . . .

### Consequences of the Rise of the Service-Vendor Party

. . . We seem to be well into a new age for the parties in which party image, ideology, labor intensive human resources, and party decision-making procedures (expressive goals) have largely given way to competitive goals largely dominated by the ability of the parties to provide services to their candidates and subordinate organizational units. These service-vendor parties have taken the largely technologically based services which once dramatically weakened their role in contemporary politics, and began to use these services to rebuild the party organization . . .

While accepting the admonition that there is no necessarily simple cause and effect relationship, the following sections will attempt to assess the effect of the rise of the service-vendor party on the party-in-the-campaign, the party-in-the-electorate, the party-in-office, and the party organization.

### The Party-in-the-Campaign

WINNING ELECTIONS

While there is consensus that the increased services offered by the Republican Party partially explain presidential victories, taking over the Senate in 1980, a domination of special election contests where all the resources can be focused, and an increase in Republican officeholders at all levels of government even in areas of traditional Republican weakness (i.e., the South), the mechanism is less clear. To a large degree, campaign services help win elections directly by more efficiently communicating messages to receptive recipients. A more indirect contribution is made by the parties' ability to register and activate their voters using the new service and even more indirectly because the lure of available services allowed the recruitment of stronger candidates who might have bypassed the race under different conditions . . .

The perceived importance of new technology for winning campaigns has driven up the cost. . . . Through group buying, screening of charlatans, and direct grants to candidates, most candidates find the party to be the vendor of choice if cost is the criterion.

### The Party-in-the-Electorate

The use of party-based service directly affects the way in which parties and their campaigns reach out to voters, and may indirectly affect the way in which voters relate to the parties.

PARTY APPEALS TO VOTERS

. . . Many of the services such as voter list creation, demographic analysis and polling serve as initial steps for targeted communications which work on the basis of sending different messages (and presumably more effective ones) to different groups of voters . . .

Such targeting strategies raise some serious questions such as the citizen's right to privacy which often falls victim to sophisticated computer-matching techniques (see Arterton, 1983, p. 78). From the perspective of the political system, such targeting contributes to if not causes political fragmentation. Whereas political parties were once seen as "interest aggregators" bringing about compromise under the party banner, they may now (perhaps unwittingly) be contributing to societal fragmentation (See Arterton, 1983, p. 44) . . .

### LINKING VOTERS TO THE PARTY

. . . The reversal of declining voter participation in the 1984 election can be at least partially attributed to massive registration and activation programs by the parties . . .

A logical, although at this point not empirically verified speculation, furthermore, could be that Republican superiority in the realm of targeted communications and constituency mobilization is at least partially responsible for the increases in party identification. Recent surveys show a decline in the percentage of independents and a closed gap in party identification between Republicans and Democrats to the narrowest margin in recent history.

### The Party-in-Office

The ultimate goal of reestablishing the party's campaign role and success with the electorate lies in having some influence over the policy process. The rise of the service-vendor party sets up conditions increasing such influence by helping the party affect the issue agenda and facilitate compliance from newly dependent elected officials.

### CONTROLLING THE ISSUE AGENDA

. . . Campaign schools present tested models for choosing issue stands and promote a party agenda among candidates from across the country (Hershey, 1984, p. 143) . . .

Through the skillful use of new technology, the Republican party got an early start in reintroducing some party instigated coherence in campaign themes. The party uses its polling capabilities to identify the kinds of candidates to recruit. It trains candidates in campaign schools both in the technique and substance of politics. There is a coordinated effort to share poll results during the campaign. The national committee provides issue memos and draft speeches with the latest in-

formation and data, often distributed instantaneously through computer-based electronic mail. Since candidates will focus on areas in which they are informed, this provides a subtle push toward presenting a party position . . .

In 1982, the party directed congressional campaigns toward the emphasis on Reagan economic policy through these methods. More directly, the GOP has encouraged party members and voters alike to write their congressmen supporting administration policies (see Kayden and Mahe, 1985, p. 189).

### BUILDING DEPENDENCY AMONG ELECTED OFFICIALS

To the degree that elected officials credit the party for their electoral success, and to the degree that the party links the provision of services to party support, the rise of the service-vendor party promises the party organization an enhanced role in the policy process . . .

### The Changing Party Structure

Thirty years ago, two experts on American politics boldly asserted:

There is perhaps no point on which writers on American politics are so . . . agreed as that our state and local party organizations, taken collectively, are far more powerful than our national organizations (Ranney and Kendall, 1956, pp. 160-161).

Little could be further from the truth today.

Both reform initiatives, the Democratic commitment to expressive procedural reform and the Republican lead in building a service-vendor party, contributed to a nationalization and centralization of the parties. Democratic procedural reforms were originated from the top and enforced centrally . . .

The Republican lead toward the development of service-vendor parties came as the second of a "one, two punch" to redefine the organizational influence within the parties. Since strong national parties require active state and local parties, the national parties worked hard to keep them in the game, but constantly reminded them of their status. While local party activity has increased dramatically in recent years (see Gibson), national party activity increases make it pale in comparison, and have often been the stimulus for state and local party change . . .

The nationalization of the political parties during the second half of the 20th century should come as little surprise to those who have observed the nationalization of other political and social institutions. Many of the same pressures which have led to the "age of executive ascendency" which placed the president in a predominant power position relative to the Congress, and the domination of local media by the national mass media are also at work within the parties . . .

### Organizational Strength

. . . Without strong party organizations, the benefit of a party mediated democracy will not be reached. Although there is little agreement on precise measures of organizational strength, the American political parties seem to have turned the corner . . .

The party organizations, particularly at the national level, are alive and well . . .

While Democratic party procedural initiatives showed the power of the national parties over the rules, the Republican Party led in developing a service-vendor party ready and able to support candidates with the newest technology. The Republican approach portends the future . . . For the foreseeable future, the well being of American parties will depend on their ability to compete with their counterparts in providing services.

### A Note on the Future

. . . There is little probability that technological opportunities will stand still waiting for party activists to catch their breath. A whole new wave of applications are already being tried, from telemarketing to cable TV and satellite transmission (American Assembly, 1982, p. 7). The potential for communicating with party activists and supporters is significant . . .

A bit less developed but equally applicable is the use of teletext and videotext . . .

There is no reason that communications have to be one-way. Interactive television could be used to poll voters or party activists and set campaign or party agendas. A whole raft of new technologies and applications are well beyond the horizon, but surely they will arrive.

The challenge for the parties lies in being adaptive enough and having the resources to sort through the potential new services, test them and apply the most promising. For once the parties have become locked into the service-vendor mode, relative success or failure will lie in maintaining a competitive advantage over the opposing parties in efficiently applying new services. Having once lost the initiative in this area, wise party leaders will fight to avoid being superseded once again.

*Stephen Frantzich* teaches in the Department of Political Science, U.S. Naval Academy. Presented at the 1986 Meeting of the Midwest Political Science Association, April 10-12, 1986, Chicago, Illinois. An expanded version of the paper can be found in: Stephen Frantzich, *Political Parties in the Technological Age* (New York: Longman Publishers, 1989).

---

## TAKING POLITICS TO THE SKIES

*Rob Stoddard, Satellite Communications magazine, April 1988*

A U.S. senator, conservative in both style and politics, accepts an invitation to address a large crowd at a prestigious Midwestern university. Plans are set in motion, arrangements are made, and invitations are extended to guests. But hours before the event is to begin, crucial developments arise that force the senator to remain in Washington.

A decade ago, the situation would have resulted in embarrassment for the senator, disappointment for university officials, and a public relations nightmare. But thanks to satellite technology, this story has a happy ending.

The senator's press secretary contacts the Senate Republican Conference, a policy arm and umbrella organization of Republican senators. Whipping into motion, the conference staff readies its production studio in the Hart Senate Office Building in Washington, activates its microwave path to the Washington International Teleport, and brings the senator—live—to the large and expectant crowd at the university.

The use of the sophisticated and slick technology actually enhances the senator's appearance, bringing a standing ovation and earning yet another convert—the senator—to the believers in satellite technology.

This anecdote is no longer unique. Satellite applications that have become commonplace in business are making a belated splash in American politics and government.

Most of the publicity this year has gone to the dozen or so campaigns of the presidential contenders. Those who could afford it have become adept at using ad-hoc satellite feeds to campaign simultaneously in several states, to raise money and to increase their accessibility to the media and their own supporters.

Among members of Congress, too, there has been a gradual and growing awareness of the political advantages offered by satellite communications.

Two organization have risen to prominence in the provision of satellite services for Republican office holders. More than three years ago, [the Republican Party] initiated regular satellite feeds from modest production facilities for Republican senators needing to address policy issues for constituents and home-state media.

More recently, the Democratic Party has increased its commitment to satellite technology with the addition of full-time satellite capability to the Harriman Communications Center, a modern production facility at Democratic National Headquarters. It offers video and audio services to political and commercial clients.

The mission of each group differs somewhat: the Democrats' Center is largely used for unabashedly political ends, while the Republicans say their Senate facility is limited to non-political material, designed to forward policy goals.

### C-SPAN—The Leader

The dawning of the satellite era came to the U.S. Congress eight years ago, when the Cable-Satellite Public Affairs Network (C-SPAN) began beaming live coverage of U.S. House floor action to cable systems across the country. Several years later, C-SPAN leased a second transponder and added Senate floor proceedings to its coverage, offering C-SPAN II to cable operators who had the channel capacity.

Although C-SPAN signed on in virtual obscurity, it was only a short time before members of Congress realized the power of the satellite-fed programming. Letters poured in from voters who had observed their congressman's actions on the floor or in an important hearing. And it wasn't long before House members began emphasizing issues important to them in speeches before an empty House chamber, merely to gain the exposure that C-SPAN offered.

In 1984, the Senate Republican Conference began leasing transponder space on Westar

IV several times a week for any Republican senator interested in making use of it. The conference also acquired some video equipment and sent a camera crew to public hearings, senators' offices and even to other locations around Washington.

With this capability, a senator could request that a portion of his or her activities—be it a speech, comments at a committee hearing, or responses to questions submitted by home-state news reporters—be edited and transmitted to any group capable of receiving the signal. The tapes were delivered to a nearby post-production company that fed them to a suburban uplink.

The video feeds were part of a broad-based effort by the group to provide a variety of communications services for senators, including dissemination of opinion columns to newspapers and magazines, feeds of taped "actualities" to radio stations, production of custom-made art work and graphics for publications, and the development of a variety of in-house newsletters and activities.

The Conference leadership was taken over by Sen. John Chafee (R-R.I.) at the start of the 99th Congress in January 1985. Robert Vastine, a long-time Chafee aide who was appointed Conference staff director, recalls an intense re-evaluation of Conference activities.

### One Basket

"I can remember (Sen. Chafee) asking, 'What can we do that's unique?'" Vastine says. "Our answer was, 'let's put all our eggs in one basket.'" And that basket was video production with satellite distribution. Many of the print-related communications projects were phased out, and satellite broadcasting was beefed up.

The Conference went to daily, 30-minute feeds to provide additional satellite time for senators. It added a second camera crew and began refurbishing its technical facilities. Significantly, a microwave path was established from the roof of the Hart Senate Office Building to a downtown high-rise office building, which in turn relayed the signal to the Washington International Teleport.

Today, the Conference headquarters in the Hart building boasts two editing suites and a refurbished studio that can accommodate a variety of live and taped video productions. A staff of 12 coordinates a news assignment desk, production and editing tasks, and all the jobs intrinsic to a video news and production routine.

"We consider ourselves to be just a communications service," says Vastine. "I think that for a lot of the senators, it's an indispensable part of their communications program."

Usage figures assembled by the Conference indicated that there were about 2,000 separate video segments transmitted on behalf of Republican senators in 1987, aboard Galaxy III and Westar V satellites. Vastine says about 25 senators use the satellite facilities four times a week, and 10 more use them two or three times weekly. The average use for a Republican senator is about 58 to 65 times per year.

Those figures highlight the significance of satellite communications to Republican senators. "This facility gives them state-of-the-art access to local video and television markets. I don't think there is anything more valuable than that," Vastine says.

He estimates that about $250,000 from the Senate budget has been spent on the Conference's video and satellite facilities over the years, which he believes is "an amazingly low figure" for its results. Senators pay for use of the services from their office budgets.

"I believe we are head and shoulders above anybody on the House or Senate side, in terms of what we do," adds Vastine. The Republican efforts in the Senate recently have been emulated by Democratic senators, whose Democratic Policy Committee also has hopped aboard the satellite bandwagon.

But if Vastine claims to hold the high ground on dissemination of policy-related information, he concedes it to the Democrats in the area of satellite usage for campaign-related information. That's due largely to recent strides made by the Democrats' Harriman Communications Center.

### Full Service Facility

Housed in Democratic National Headquarters just a few blocks from the Capitol building, and operated by the Democratic Congressional Campaign Committee, the Harriman Center is somewhat similar to the facility at the Senate Republican Conference. However, it is larger, better funded, has a larger staff, and operates as a full-service video production facility that is competitive with other such companies in Washington.

Last September, the Center added a microwave unit, establishing satellite capability with a path to Washington International Teleport. The satellite addition was one result of a campaign by party fundraiser Pamela Harriman,

which netted nearly $400,000 for the Center. Democratic Congressional Campaign Committee leadership says it sees satellite capability as a political necessity.

"This is another step for the Democratic Party in using technology available to more effectively communicate the Democratic message to constituents and voters," says Committee Chairman Beryl Anthony, an Arkansas congressman. Adds Sen. John Kerry (D-Mass.), chairman of the Democratic Senatorial Campaign Committee, "Satellite capability will be the single most important innovation in the 1988 campaigns."

"It really puts us on the map," agrees Ginny Kontnik, the deputy director of the Committee responsible for Communications Center operations.

The Center consists of a 25- by 35-foot television studio, a radio studio, two post-production suites and assorted control rooms and off-line editing equipment. It also can provide a camera crew to follow Democratic congressmen and candidates, who are offered the Center's services at discounted rates.

Kontnik reports that as of mid-January, the Center had produced about 10 events that called for satellite transmission. These included videoconferences with congressmen, via-satellite appearances by Democractic lawmakers on college campuses, and live statements from party officials in Washington to a number of gatherings around the country.

David Potasznik, operations manager for the center, says use of Washington International Teleport provides complete flexibility in transmitting material. It might be via C band, Ku band, or a combination, and the teleport makes all arrangements for setting up transponder time on available satellites.

### Technological Edge

How important is the satellite capability to the Democratic party?

"At this point in time, it's invaluable," comments Howard Schloss, assistant communications director for the Democratic Congressional Campaign Committee. Schloss says committee leadership has recognized "how important it is to be technologically competitive with the Republicans."

Despite these advantages, staff of both the Democratic Committee and the Senate Republican Conference report they often are required to educate politicians and office holders about the benefits of satellite technology—

and to encourage them to take advantage of it.

"We've had to acquaint all sorts of Democrats on how to use satellite technology to assist them in their campaigns and political needs," confirms the Center's Kontnik.

The Center's marketing director, Elizabeth Moore, is up to the challenge. "We have this (satellite) technology, and now it's a matter of marketing," Moore says.

At the Senate Republican Conference, Robert Vastine agrees that some senators have had to be educated about the communications potential of satellites. He says his staff has "pushed very hard" to spread the word, and that usage has steadily increased as more and more senators have had favorable experiences with the technology.

Reprinted with permission of *Satellite Communications* magazine, 6300 S. Syracuse Way, Suite 650, Englewood, Colo. 80111.

# CONSULTANTS

"None of these new technologies are worse than existing technologies. Or more precisely, they are but refinements of existing technologies—most notably the campaign consultant system and its reliance on spot political advertising. It is the consultant system and the use and abuse of political advertising which represent the true danger to American politics."

*Curtis Gans*

"I am a consultant and let me defend my profession. I see a consultant only as a sort of jockey. Horses running by themselves can do extremely well. But horses by themselves in all probability will not go around the circle or hop over the steeplechases or what have you that they have to without a rider. So all campaign consultants really should think of themselves as jockeys. If you got Secretariat all you got to do is not fall off. If you got some nag from the county fair obviously you have to be a little more clever and a little more effective. But you've never seen the horse on the back of a jockey."

*Ed Rollins*

*Many people equate new communications technology with consultants because those entrepreneurs make the most use of them. New communications technologies, moreover, have made specialization necessary. The same people who know how to make intelligent cable buys, for example, cannot be expected to remain <u>au courant</u> with the latest computer software.*

*Every piece of campaign reform legislation and every change in party rules seem to spawn more consultants. Larry Sabato's <u>The Rise of Political Consultants</u> was published in 1981, and yet remains definitive.*

*"There has been no greater change in American politics in recent years," Sabato*

writes, "than the manner in which candidates run for public office. Political consultants and the new campaign technology may well be producing a whole generation of officeholder far more skilled in the art of running for office than in the art of governing. Who can forget Robert Redford as a newly elected, media-produced U.S. Senator at the end of the film *The Candidate* asking pathetically, 'Now what do I do?' "

While current reliance on consultants raises what Sabato calls "democratic concerns," he also argues that "the very technologies that once enabled candidates to run independent of their parties are creating immense opportunities for the parties to bring candidates and voters back to their moorings."

As could be expected in such a pervasive and fast-changing field, fundamental questions remain far from answered. Indeed scholars and journalists have just started to address them. Are consultants taking functions once reserved for the parties? What are consultants' responsibilities to the broader governing process? Has their importance been exaggerated?

## CONSULTANT SERVICE: THE NEW CAMPAIGN TECHNOLOGY

*Larry J. Sabato*

Generalist consultants offer an especially wide range of service packages to prospective clients. They will do as much, or as little, as the campaign organization desires. Generalist Joseph Cerrell occasionally has done little more than let his firm's name (and, by implication, its successful reputation) be used in a campaign's directory or roster. "Selling your name," as Cerrell calls it, is done almost as an endorsement—in exchange for payment, of course. Cerrell and his associates will also sell their time on a *per-diem* or other basis, for which "we don't do a thing except be a critic." But the firm is also an "A-to-Z shop" where "we'll sit in the back room and make all of the radio spots right here" and attend to the details of a multitude of other campaign chores . . .

Specialist consultants usually provide more restrictive services. But those who have been in the business for a long time seem inevitably to diversify their offerings, both because they become more familiar with other technological specialties the longer they are associated with campaigns and because there is a good deal of additional money in it and candidates often request other services. (Having been "sold" on a consultant's product in one area, candidates are often eager to thrust even more

responsibility on to a "trusted expert.") Thus it is quite common to find established media consultants such as Douglas Bailey and John Deardourff being hired to write a "soup to nuts" campaign plan or to give *per-diem* strategy advice. Whether the candidate actually benefits from this sort of arrangement is another question. Some consultants, such as Bailey and Deardourff, clearly have the background to be a bit expansive, but many others learn one specialty well and then offer a series of "add-on" services that are cheap imitations of the work done by competent professionals.

A consultant is undeniably at his best when concentrating on his specialty, and the new campaign technology has become advanced enough in several areas to be well worth having. Yet some political participants emphatically deny that this is so. "Campaign technology hasn't changed since the three-by-five card,"[1] claims the executive director of a liberal political action committee. While it is true that the new campaign technology (like all technologies) builds upon older, established principles of political communication and organization, Matt Reese, a generalist consultant, has the weight of evidence behind his assertion that "the whole political world has changed. . . . It's unbelievable what is available to Ted Kennedy in 1980 as opposed to what was available to his brother in 1960."[2]

Most political technicians trace the advances in political polling, direct mail, demographic precinct targeting, and most media innovations to the private sector, whose marketing needs financed volumes of research and much trial-and-error experimentation. The development of computers for government and business purposes also had major impact on the political sphere.

Not only did consultants borrow heavily from business technology, but they also found each other's work a tempting cookie jar from which to snatch a sweet or two. As a consequence, no new item of campaign technology stays dazzling very long. All consultants in the field grab hold of it, and it becomes standard. One campaign professional saw the process as a kind of political detente: "Everything neutralizes out. It's just like the U.S. versus Russia: They get a new missile, then we get it, and on and on." Standard though the techniques may be generally, a good number of technology-deficient campaigns (lacking the necessary financing or with an overconfident incumbent) serve as convincing case studies of the difference technology can make. U.S. Senator Clifford Case's defeat for re-nomination in New Jersey's 1978 Republican primary is a classic example.[3] Case's opponent was Jeffrey Bell, a young and unknown right-wing activist who targeted Case's liberal record with devastatingly effective direct-mail pieces produced by Eberle and Associates, conservative direct-mail consultants. Bell's extensive use of telephone banks with excellent Republican voter lists was in pointed contrast to the absence of any on Case's behalf. The senator had also used a quickly produced, $3,000 poll whose methodology was questionable.

Still, the importance of campaign technology to electoral success can easily be overstated (and usually is). Elections, and the choices voters make among candidates, are too complex and involve too many variables to be determined by a single element. In most elections the new campaign techniques, and the consultants themselves, probably do not make the difference between winning and losing, although they make some difference and in at least a few cases can convincingly be given credit or blame for the margin of victory or defeat. This alone would serve to make consultants modestly influential in the conduct of the campaign. But due in good measure to journalist "hype" and consultants' own superb sense of self-promotion, the *perception* is that consultants and technology make the difference in a greater percentage of elections than they likely do. This perception among the press and political people simply means that consultants and the new campaign techniques are even more important than their actual electoral effect would justify—more important, certainly, than they deserve to be.

This is not to say that consultants and their technologies are worthless. In general, the new techniques are more effective than many "old-fashioned" methods. Moreover, consultants and the new techniques can and do influence virtually every significant part of a campaign, and the campaign certainly makes some difference in the outcome of an election. While it is still true that most voters make their choices in good part on the basis of party loyalty and many if not most have their minds almost made up before the campaign even begins, it is also true that in just about every election as much as a third or even more of the electorate is honestly uncommitted or switchable, and that number may be growing as the strength of party identification declines. Voter turnout is also variable. Even if persuasive action is fruitless, a campaign's success depends heavily on its ability to stimulate those favorable to it to vote and, alas, to encourage those unfavorable to it to stay at home, mainly through negative advertising directed almost solely at the opponent's weaknesses.

Technology provides the means to both these ends: New organizational techniques . . . have been developed to stimulate turnout, and a disturbing proportion of the innovative modern media is negative. Also, for all practical purposes campaigning is now continuous, and voters can be influenced by television, direct mail, and other campaign aids long before the outset of the official campaign season. There is some evidence that at state as well as national levels, campaign technology is being employed increasingly early.

Still another situation in which campaign technology is especially influential is during primary elections, where party identification (absent a pre-primary party endorsement) can play no role at all. Many political consultants love to work in primaries, where they believe relatively low turnouts and the lack of party ties give the new campaign technology its broadest potential use. Finally, it should be noted that campaigns have other functions besides winning, which a European would acknowledge sooner than an American. Party building for future elections (or candidate building within the personality-centered American system) is a perfectly legitimate and useful campaign goal.[4]

Inevitably, anyone who attempts to assess the effectiveness of modern campaign techniques is humbled by the scarcity of empirical evidence to support any hard and fast conclusions. There have been few solid election-day and post-election surveys, for example, and, compared to the extensive privately supported research in product advertising, little thorough testing of the impact of political media advertisements during campaigns. The impact of any consultant or any technology, then, can usually only be guessed at. No one has the foggiest notion of what percentage of the vote a consultant or a piece of new campaign technology can or does add to a candidate in any given set of circumstances. Campaign observers rarely even have a precise idea of what event or series of events produced the election result. Campaigning remains a complex, unpredictable, and very unscientific process, and one may expect and be grateful that it always will be.

Consultants' understanding of the new campaign technology is often just as inexact. Most political consultants, even some of the best, "don't know why they are doing what they're doing. They just mechanically learn some new technique, but they don't really understand it," says media professional Tony Schwartz. Matt Reese admits that after 187 campaigns at every level, "I know more what not to do than what to do."[5] Even with other professionals in their own specialty, consultants rarely seem to agree on anything. They disagree violently about the most basic of campaign questions (such as the allocation of the budget between media and organization). They delight in deriding the "rules" of the political game—the origin of the rules is never disclosed—and relish telling an interviewer of their most recent successful rulebendings. Yet they create much of the currently accepted political wisdom and generalize about campaigning and electioneering with abandon "because they like to believe they have the answer, and everyone expects them to have some handle on the truth." But, continues Charles Guggenheim, a respected Democratic media professional, "none of us has *the answer*, and every race is so different that the generalizations are either obvious or not useful."

If we can be grateful that campaigning cannot be completely quantified, we can also give thanks that the profession of consulting is still far more of an art than a science. As Bob Goodman sees himself and his fellows:

We are still artists, trying to develop a dramatic way of capturing the attention and then inspiring resolve. The new technology is in its infant stage for those who practice the media arts. What we learn is what doesn't work, by trial and error. My value to a candidate right now is that after ten years of doing media, I won't try an idea that I had five years ago and I found bombed. We're becoming a little more error free. But we really don't know a great deal. If we knew more we would be dangerous. . . .

NOTES

1. Personal interview with Russell Hemenway, Executive Director of the National Committee for an Effective Congress.
2. Ironically, it was Ted Kennedy's opponent in 1980, Jimmy Carter, who marshalled all the up-to-date techniques in support of his candidacy, while Kennedy's operatives ran a campaign whose technology was, except for direct mail, vastly inferior.
3. *Campaign Insights*, vol. 9, no. 13 (July 1, 1988): 14.
4. See [Dan] Nimmo, *The Political Persuaders*, pp. 3-5.
5. Remarks delivered at the annual meeting of the American Association of Political Consultants.

From *The Rise of Political Consultants: New Ways of Winning Elections*. Copyright by Larry J. Sabato. Reprinted by permission of Basic Books, Inc.

---

## THE MYTH OF POLITICAL CONSULTANTS

*Fred Barnes, The New Republic, June 16, 1986*

Political consultants have sex in the shower with their buxom assistants. They fly around the country in plush jets, which they own. They cleverly manipulate the political system. They strip candidate after candidate of their real personalities and viewpoints, and impose phony but politically appealing new ones on them. Political consultants are almost always successful. Any candidate they're behind has a very high probability of winning, the odds being something like seven to one. Pity the poor candidate whose consultant quits on him. Forsaken by his guru, he is high and dry, and all but certain to lose.

This is the Hollywood version of political consulting in a recent film called *Power*. The consultant is played by Richard Gere, and power is what he has lots of. He is a political Svengali. Campaigns turn on his plots and ploys. Candidates are empty vessels, which he fills. Of course, Hollywood has pushed this line about political consultants before. But in *The Candidate*, a 1972 movie, the omnipotent consultant was crass, dumpy, and played by

Allen Garfield, no matinee idol. The candidate was Robert Redford. By the end of the picture he'd become so dependent on his consultant that, having won the election, he asked plaintively, "What do I do now?"

Ordinarily no one believes Hollywood. But with consultants, conventional wisdom imitates art. Serious political writers exalt them just as Hollywood does. O.K., they leave out sex in the shower and the private jets. But the rest is practically the same: consultant chic. "Television and polling have bred a new profession of electronic manipulators," Arthur Schlesinger Jr. warns. Sidney Blumenthal writes in *The Permanent Campaign*, a book about the "elite" corps of operatives, that consultants "have supplanted the old party bosses" and "superseded" the parties themselves. In the May issue of *GQ*, Randall Rothenberg hails "a new breed of political insiders [who] understand the nuances and influence of their overpopulated generation [and] may well change the way American politics is conducted for decades to come." Not to be outdone, David Chagall says in *The New Kingmakers*, which should have been titled "The New Gods," that since the 1960s "a brigade of consultant superstars developed and assumed positions of unparalleled power and influence in the political structure of America." More breathless yet, Roland Perry declares in *Hidden Power*, still another book puffing up consultants, that "with their control over politicians and understanding of the new technology, it is the strategist who, more and more, will dictate the direction of nations and the world."

Wow! This takeover poses a new peril, not only to democracy but to the entire world. Don't believe a word of this. It is pure myth. Political consultants have not even seized control of American elections. They now work in every national and statewide campaign, and in many smaller races, but their effect on the outcome of elections is marginal at best. And they screw up as often as they do well. Consultants can't turn nerds into U.S. senators. They can't elect people. They can't overturn the laws of politics.

If they can't do that, what can consultants do? Lots of things. They come in four basic types—pollsters, media consultants, direct-mail experts, and strategists. The mail experts limit themselves to fundraising. But pollsters and media consultants often double as strategists. In fact, strategists who don't offer other services—Republican Stuart Spencer

is the most famous—are a dying breed. There's not enough money in it. To bring in big bucks, you've got to supply the TV spots. For statewide races, topflight consultants charge $30,000 to $50,000, but that's just for starters. They get reimbursed for their production costs, with ten to 15 percent extra tacked on. But the real money comes from the usual 15 percent of the media buy that they get. If a candidate spends three million dollars on TV, that means $450,000 for his media consultant. Small wonder more and more consultants are getting into media work.

There's a catch in signing up one of the two dozen big-name consultants, most of whom work out of Washington. You don't get their full-time attention, since they hire out to numerous campaigns at the same time. This causes trouble. Candidates want to talk to their consultants more than their consultants want to talk to them. But often consultants' aides are fobbed off on them. Lynn Cutler, running for Congress in Iowa in 1982, fired her media consultant when she couldn't get him on the phone for two weeks. But while they can't guarantee victory, consultants have their specialties. Spencer rode the campaign plane with Ronald Reagan in 1980, advising him over and over how to avert gaffes (usually by saying nothing of substance at all). Pollster Robert Teeter is adept at gauging what undecided voters want. Another pollster, Arthur Finckelstein, can tell you how to get out the hard-core conservative vote.

Consultants can help, but not much. If all goes extraordinarily well, they might add one or two percentage points. Of the factors that decide elections, consultants rank a distant fifth. What's most important, not surprisingly, is the candidate himself. Personal assets matter—a message, skill in communicating it, the ability to keep cool under stress, attractive looks, and so on. If the candidate's an ugly dope, there's nothing a consultant can do to change that. The second factor is the political environment. Republicans don't win in Chicago. It's Democratic turf, no matter what GOP consultants do. Next, there's the political mood. A liberal finds the going tougher in a conservative era. Then there's money, the more the better. Finally, consultants come into play. It's certainly nice to have a shrewd strategist, a clever media consultant, and a perceptive pollster. In many races they are indispensable. But so is the guy who handles the campaign schedule, and no one says he's a genius.

Nicholas Lemann agrees with Sidney Blumenthal about the powers of consultants. "They are the new political bosses," he says. "They have put more important politicians into power than Boss Tweed or Mayor Daley ever dreamed of." There's a fundamental misunderstanding here. The old bosses had real power. If you were a Democrat running for president and didn't get the support of Mayor Daley, you were out of luck in Illinois. There was nowhere else to turn in hopes of getting the convention votes of the Illinois delegation. But consultants are interchangeable, and there are many good ones. If you don't get Robert Squier to produce your television spots, then you can turn to Ray Strother or Neil Oxman or Michael Kaye. If you find that Patrick Caddell has been hired to do the polling for a rival, you can sign up Peter Hart or Paul Maslin or William Hamilton.

Consultants feed their own mystique. They love to discuss their work, and crave press attention, knowing all the while that this detracts from their candidate. "I was guilty," admits Gerald Rafshoon, Jimmy Carter's media consultant. "I enjoyed the attention." Consultants can be counted on to chat up winning campaigns, and little else. Losers? Mum's the word. Consultants are especially talkative about long shots who got elected. True, there are cases where a consultant catapulted a candidate from obscurity to victory. This happened in the Florida governor's race in 1978, when Squier's TV commercial showed state senator Bob Graham "working for governor" at a different job every day (ditch-digger, bellhop, etc.). Graham was distinguished from the pack of candidates, and won. But cases like that are few and far between. And there were factors peculiar to the Florida race that made Graham's emergence possible. It's a transient state with weak political parties, which makes TV all the more important. Besides, Graham's opponents were duds.

Political reporters, including me, are suckers for tales of consultants' legerdemain. By ascribing election victories to consultants, they explain the secret, behind-the-scenes reality of politics. The uninitiated may think the candidate won. The reporter knows better. The consultants, who happen to be his best sources, were responsible. But there's something overlooked in the puffery about hot consultants and winning streaks. For every consultant on the winning side, there's one (in general elections) or more (in primaries) that worked for losers. If consultants get credit for victories, shouldn't they be blamed for defeats? In some cases, they should. But the press never picks up on this. If stories have appeared about consultants who've lost the knack and are mired in a slump, I've missed them. I know I've never written one like that myself.

In 1979 Squier was lionized in the *Washington Post* as "the kingmaker of the 30-second spot." He was described as "a political image-maker riding a hot streak, the hottest streak in his career. Of the last 14 primary and general election campaigns he has worked in, Squier has lost only one." Not only had Squier put Graham in the Florida statehouse, he'd elected a bland fellow named William Winter governor of Mississippi. Winter's chief opponent in the Democratic primary was a 58-year-old spinster, and Squier's television ads played up Winter's closeness to his wife and daughter. Another spot showed Winter on military maneuvers, and noted that "the governor is the commander in chief of the National Guard." These were effective commercials. But the question is whether Squier was pivotal.

Probably not. If he were, Squier could be expected to produce winners in other Mississippi contests. In 1983 he was back—same consultant, same state, same race, but this time his candidate for governor was Michael Sturdivant. Despite spending the most money, much of it to air Squier-created ads, Sturdivant came in third in the primary. The spinster Winter had beaten four years earlier made the runoff, but she wound up losing again, even without Squier's aiding her opponent. More telling still was what happened in 1984, when Winter hired Squier in his bid for the Senate—same consultant, same candidate, same state. Winter was humiliated. In a Democratic state, he lost to incumbent Republican Thad Cochran by 58 to 42 percent. Squier now says the contest was lost before Winter announced. "We probably all did Winter a disservice by continuing to argue that he run way past the point where he had a chance to win," Squier says.

Squier may be explaining away an embarrassing defeat, but he's right. He couldn't make Winter a winner in 1984. And it points up the limitations on his ability, or any consultant's, to affect a race. Winter had hurt his own reputation by lobbying to become chancellor of the University of Mississippi, then rashly rejecting the job when it was offered and announcing for the Senate. There was also a strong conservative and Republican tide in the state in 1984. (Reagan beat Mondale 62 to 37 percent in Mississippi.) Nothing Squier provided in TV spots could erase these factors. Nor in the 1983 governor's race could he transform Sturdivant into as appealing a candidate as Winter had been in 1979. The difference wasn't Squier's work, which is always skillful, but the quality of the candidates. Winter was a better candidate than Sturdivant. He wasn't good enough, though, to overcome an unfavorable political environment and ideological mood in 1984. But how many stories did you read about Squier's losing streak?

In 1984 the hot consultant was Roger Ailes, a Republican, who got credit for Mitch McConnell's victory over incumbent Democrat Dee Huddleston in the Kentucky Senate race. What did Ailes do? He produced a very funny television commercial that showed a bloodhound in pursuit of Huddleston, who was away from his Washington duties making speeches for money. When McConnell won, surprised political analysts needed a reason. So they latched onto the commercial. This was only natural. The largest chunk of money spent in campaigns goes to buy TV time. That must mean that the TV spots are the most important ingredient, right? Rarely. Getting on television just happens to be expensive. That's why it takes such a hefty percentage of campaign funds. In publishing a newspaper, the biggest expenditure is for paper. But that doesn't make paper a major factor in the success or failure of the newspaper. Anyway, Ailes got a notch in his gun for supposedly electing McConnell.

Yet the reasons had little to do with Ailes, good as his spots were. Pollsters for Huddleston went back after the race to find out why he lost. They asked which commercials voters remembered. "There was a very, very low remembrance of [the bloodhound spot], like 15 percent," said Harrison Hickman. Three times as many people recalled an ad that nicked Huddleston for poor Senate attendance and junkets. Even that ad had little to do with Huddleston's defeat. He was simply an overconfident incumbent with a mediocre record who was engulfed by the Reagan tide. Huddleston was a bad candidate running in a bad year for a Democrat.

Ailes, meanwhile gets credit for electing McConnell, but no blame for his work on behalf of Charles Percy. A month before election day, the Percy campaign put a strong tax-cutting ad on TV. His Democratic opponent, Paul Simon, dropped ten points in surveys done by his pollster. He was in deep trouble. But the tax ad was yanked. It had "run its cycle," an Ailes aide said. Percy went with another Ailes commercial that attacked Simon for having written a letter to the Ayatollah Khomeini. That ad backfired, and Simon won.

Blunders like the Khomeini ad in Percy's campaign are a lot more common than consultants care to admit. In the 1981 governor's race in Virginia, Republicans nominated a moderate named Marshall Coleman. Virginia is a very conservative state, and Reagan is wildly popular there. Thus Coleman, guided by consultants Douglas Bailey and John Deardourff, tried to run as a Reaganite right-winger. It didn't fly. He lost, the first time since 1966 that a Republican had lost a major statewide race in Virginia.

Pollsters also make mistakes. Polls taken for both Coleman and his Democratic opponent, Charles Robb, pegged Coleman as the winner. In 1976 a survey in North Carolina by Robert Teeter persuaded President Gerald Ford that the Republican nomination was already his. He relaxed his campaign. This allowed Ronald Reagan to pull an upset in the North Carolina primary and revive his candidacy. In 1978 a poll by Patrick Caddell's firm showed Democratic senator Thomas McIntyre of New Hampshire with a solid two-to-one lead over Republican Gordon Humphrey. Nor was there any trend toward Humphrey. This was a few weeks before the election—which Humphrey won. In Iowa that year a poll by Peter Hart a month before the election showed Democratic senator Dick Clark leading 57 to 27 percent. He lost. In 1982 Republicans were delirious about the prospects of winning the Alabama governorship. A late poll by Lance Tarrance showed a dead heat between George Wallace and Republican Emory Folmar. But Folmar lost 60 to 40 percent.

The conceit of many national political consultants is that they have expertise that local consultants haven't mastered. Sometimes they do, sometimes they don't. The 1979 Louisiana governor's race was a laboratory for the national crew. There were six candidates, and five hired nationally known consultants. Squier worked for Louis Lambert, then Ray Strother did. Charles Guggenheim, who had worked for Bobby Kennedy in 1968, was hired by Bubba Henry. Sonny Mouton brought in David Garth. Jimmy Fitzmorris and Paul Hardy also got out-of-state help. But the winner was David Treen, the lone Republican in the race. He used a local ad agency of no national renown. His TV spots were spare and inoffensive.

Another conceit of some consultants is the eye-popping win-loss record. In *Power*, Gere boasted of an 85 percent winning percentage. No big deal, says Strother, who produced the TV spots for Gary Hart's presidential campaign in 1984. Strother quotes the advice of rodeo rider Casey Tibbs: "You get on the back of a good horse and hold on." In other words, consultants pad their percentage by taking on the right clients. "I represent a lot of incumbents," Strother says. "Incumbents tend to win." And winning is everything. Consultants rarely are praised for making the most out of a lackluster or otherwise flawed candidate, as Bailey and Deardourff did with Gerald Ford in 1976 and Rafshoon did with Carter in 1980. A loss is a loss in the consultant's world. On his list of clients, Squier names senators who won, but no Senate candidate who lost.

At the core of the myth of political consultants is the notion that they can elect presidents. Nothing could be further from the truth. Consultants actually have less influence on presidential races than any other. The higher the visibility of the race—and presidential contests are the most visible of all—the less impact consultants have. Consultants do best when voters have few sources of information about candidates. In such cases, what is conveyed in campaign advertising fills a vacuum. But in presidential races, voters are bombarded with information. There is no vacuum. The news media cover presidential campaigns in lavish detail. All a media consultant can do is produce ads that go with the general news flow. These may help marginally, but no more. In 1984 there was nothing any consultant could have done to save Walter Mondale from defeat. There was nothing any could have done to cause Reagan to lose.

The legend was started in 1968 by Joe McGinniss' *The Selling of the President*. McGinniss attributed Richard Nixon's election to slick handling by consultants, who closeted him except for staged sessions with voters. On the contrary, this strategy was a spectacular flop. Nixon won in spite of it. His mammoth lead over Hubert Humphrey dissolved as election day approached. If the election had occurred a week later, he would have lost. McGinniss was flatly wrong, but his book appealed to Nixonphobia and became a best seller.

The legend grew in 1976 with Jimmy Carter's advance to the White House. In Carter's case, the myth holds that he did whatever pollsters said he should, and that his media message was shaped accordingly. Well, not quite. Pollster Caddell was a late addition to the campaign, arriving after the TV commercials had been produced by Rafshoon. The media effort was "90 percent Carter and ten percent technique," says Rafshoon, who has given up political consulting to make movies. "We followed him around for two years and we gave you what he was saying. No political consultant would come up with these lines: 'I'll never lie to you,' or 'I want to have a country that's as good and decent and honest and competent and compassionate and as full of love as the American people.' We looked at the footage we had and these were the lines that were capturing audiences. Who came up with it? Jimmy Carter the candidate. It worked for those times."

In 1980 the legend was bolstered by Reagan's election. Here was putty in the hands of consultants. Except for the fact that the more they handled, the worse he did. Kept under wraps by campaign manager John Sears, Reagan lost the Iowa caucuses to George Bush. Unleashed, he won the New Hampshire primary. When Sears was replaced by William Casey, a political hack, Reagan's fortunes suffered not at all. In the fall campaign against Carter, Reagan's TV ads were mushy, pointless, and dull. His California governorship was described in a spot in the vaguest possible terms. Carter's ads were riveting, far better than the spots that had allegedly carried him to victory four years earlier. The most effective one showed Carter burning the midnight oil at the White House. But commercials were irrelevant. So were all the consultants on both sides.

The same was true in 1984, except when consultants hogged the spotlight from the candidates. Just as White House reporters cover presidential aides as much as they do the president, political reporters concentrate on the ebb and flow of consultants. This diminishes candidates, who are seen as puppets. Their political message gets less attention. Patrick Caddell's rocky forays into the Hart and Mondale campaigns were widely reported. There's a quip in the political community about Caddell: if you want the consultant to get more ink than the candidate, hire Caddell. A critical moment in Hart's campaign for the Democratic presidential nomination came when his consultants, notably Caddell, put an ad on TV in Illinois without his approval. He tried to yank the spot off the air just before the primary, failed to do so, and ended up looking silly. He lost the primary, and his decline began.

Nothing like the Illinois glitch happens in the literature about the awesome power of consultants. The puffery about the big-name national consultants has created a whole new role for them. No, they aren't bosses, but they are able to make candidates look credible—just by being hired. If a candidate has a team of well-known consultants on board, he gains instant credibility. Political action committees are more likely to supply money. The press takes the candidate more seriously. When Stewart Bainum Jr., a Maryland businessman, hired Patrick Caddell last year to take a Senate race poll for him, it warranted a full story in the *Washington Post*. Bainum had gotten all he could have wanted from Caddell. So he moved on to another pollster.

The fundraising role is a critical one. Mark Siegel, the chairman of the National Bipartisan Political Action Committee, a Jewish PAC, says consultants are "an indication of the seriousness of a campaign." If a candidate looking for money drops by with a consultant Siegel respects, that improves his chances. Siegel's PAC sends out a critique of every Senate race, which includes the names of each candidate's consultants. Even in House races, consultants can bring money. "If a challenger has been able to attract big-name consultants, it raises eyebrows," says Joseph Gaylord, executive director of the National Republican Congressional Committee. "People are going to pay more attention. PACs are." But sometimes it doesn't work that way. When Linda Chavez left the White House Staff to run for the Senate in Maryland, she hired Ed Rollins, who ran Reagan's 1984 campaign. Her expectation was that he would bring in the big donors. However, Rollins hasn't made fundraising calls for her—he's a strategist, after all—and Chavez has been forced to shave back on his spending plans.

With so many requests for their services, consultants spread themselves thinly. "They're getting away from what makes a good consultant: personal attention to a candidate," says Todd Domke, a Massachusetts consultant. Consultants have a limited number of fresh ideas. The same campaign plans and TV gimmicks show up again and again. "Candidates think they're getting a fresh, 150-page campaign plan, and it's been around for 20 years," says Siegel. Candidates who want to

demonstrate they they're tough on crime are shown slamming a jail door shut, a crude image that has little impact. In the Alabama governor's race this year, state attorney general Charles Graddick got nowhere until he dropped the jail-door ad in favor of one calling for improved schools. David Garth uses roughly the same style in every campaign spot—cinema verite episodes with information crawling across the bottom of the screen. It worked in the 1970s, less so in the 1980s.

It's partly fear that keeps consultants in demand, fear that your opponent will get a leg up. If one candidate hires a famous pollster or media consultant, the other candidates have to get expensive consultants of their own. In the end, the consultants nullify each other in most races. But the problem for a candidate is that he's got to hire consultants to achieve this. If a candidate goes to the trouble of running in the first place, he doesn't want to give his opponents even the small edge that consultants might bestow. So he takes on a squad of them as a defensive maneuver. But who knows? The race might be close, and one of his consultants might come up with the one-in-a-million gimmick that gets him elected. It happened once in Florida.

---

# THE BOOM IN POLITICAL CONSULTING

*Randall Rothenberg, <u>The New York Times</u>, May 24, 1987*

Scott Miller proudly displayed his company's new headquarters on 60th Street just off Fifth Avenue in Manhattan, and the contrast with days past could not have been more striking. Where once the Sawyer/Miller Group, Inc.'s 30 employees had toiled in cramped, windowless rooms, the new offices—replete with sleek black furniture and fresh maroon carpeting—abound with light, space and air.

"Our corporate clients expect something like this," said Mr. Miller, the firm's senior partner, as he glided past the glass-fronted office of its new director of international business. As he talked it was hard, too, not to notice the change in Mr. Miller. Just two years

ago, the youthful, crew-cut, six-foot-tall former college athlete plotted strategy dressed in
jeans and a sweatshirt; this day Mr. Miller, 41
years old, was draped in an impeccably tailored blue pin striped suit.

Former Senator Gary Hart's withdrawal
from the Democratic presidential nominating
contest cast attention on the critical importance of image in American politics. As the
trappings of Scott Miller's success indicate,
the image makers—political consultants—are
playing a more prominent and lucrative role
than ever. And the business of political consulting is not only booming, it is changing in
some significant ways.

Only 15 years ago, this firmament's stars
were a small constellation who provided a limited set of services for candidates for national
office. Today, political consulting is an industry, with thousands of highly competitive players offering increasingly specialized assistance to clients inside and outside of the
political arena.

"We've entered an era where a campaign
involves a consortium of consultants—in media, polling, fundraising, strategizing and
other disciplines—all under the guidance of a
general manager who can coordinate all aspects of the message," said Mr. Miller, who
along with his partner, David H. Sawyer, has
represented such candidates as Ohio Senator
John Glenn and Israeli Labor Party leader Shi-
mon Peres.

Money—surprise!—is the driving force behind the industry's growth. In 1976, the average winner in a United States Senate campaign spent $609,000; in 1986, the winners
spent, on average, $3.1 million, according to
Herbert E. Alexander, director of the Citizens'
Research Foundation at the University of
Southern California. During the same period,
the average cost of a successful House of Representatives campaign increased from
$87,200 to around $355,000.

"More money and more complication mean
more consultants," said Bradley F. O'Leary,
the president of the American Association of
Political Consultants, whose membership has
grown from 43 to 600 in only six years. Or, as
Mr. Alexander put it, "The profusion of consultants is an exercise in supply-side economics."

Mr. O'Leary believes that "there are probably 2,000 to 5,000 firms involved in the political industry at some level." Larry J. Sabato,
a professor of government at the University of

Virginia and the author of "The Rise of Political Consultants," said that "if you include staffers at all levels, then the crew would have to
number 50,000." Both Professor Sabato and
Mr. O'Leary agree that approximately $100
million of the estimated $1.8 billion spent an-
nually on party and elective politics finds its
way to political strategists.

Two firms run by political tacticians are
now among the 30 largest research companies
in America. Decision/Making/ Information of
McLean, Va., founded by President Reagan's
longtime pollster Richard B. Wirthlin,
boasted revenues of $10.4 million last year,
making it bigger than the better known Gallup Organization of Princeton. Market Opinion Research of Detroit, whose president, Robert N. Teeter, is a key cog in Vice President
George Bush's presidential campaign, had
1986 revenues of $9.4 million.

The crowding of the marketplace has
forced consultants to focus on narrower areas
of specialization. "You can be a paid media
specialist or a free media specialist," noted
Joseph Cerrell, 52, of Cerrell Associates, Inc.
in Los Angeles, a longtime Democratic strategist. "If you're in paid media, you can specialize in electronic or print. If electronic, you
can do radio or TV. We may be reaching the
time when guys specialize in either 30-second
or 60-second spots."

The growth of the political consulting industry has not been confined to the domestic
market. So lucrative is the overseas market
that *Campaigns & Elections*, a trade publication
for political professionals, is sponsoring a seminar in June for American consultants in Ar-
gentina, which is holding 23 state elections this
fall. "Democracy," said James M. Dwinnell, the
magazine's publisher, "is a growth business."

There has also been a proliferation of consultants operating strictly at the local and regional level to handle a growing number of
candidates for the nation's half-million elective offices. Clinton Reilly Campaigns of San
Francisco is, perhaps, the most successful. In
1986, the 15-person firm netted more than $3
million for work on 18 campaigns. One client
spent more than $500,000 to become the sher-
iff of Santa Clara County.

"The consulting business is like the morti-
cian business," said Yvonne Ryzak of San
Francisco, whose specialty is county supervi-
sor races. "Someone is always dying, and
someone is always running for office."

Most significantly, perhaps, a growing

number of tacticians who made their reputations in politics are now adapting their expertise to serve corporate clients, from United Parcel Service to Coca-Cola. Ever since the publication of Joe McGinniss' book, *The Selling of the President, 1968*, critics have scored political consultants for using slick, empty "Madison Avenue" techniques to sell politicians and policies. Now, in a classic reversal, many consultants claim that they can employ political marketing techniques to sell products.

While there is no doubt that the political consulting industry has expanded, these "mercenaries of American politics," as California State Treasurer Jesse M. Unruh once called them, continue to cloak much of their work in an atmosphere of magic, making it difficult to determine what, if anything, they add to a campaign besides cost. Those who have mastery over video technology, who claim to divine public attitudes, who devise political "thematics" have conveyed the idea that a campaign is a magical mystery tour—and only they can drive the bus.

Many of the "gurus," the handful of stars at the top of the profession, have distinguished themselves by their "signatures." The television ads of Republican producer Robert Goodman, for example, are known for their emotionalism and stirring musical cadences, while David Garth pioneered the use of "talking heads" and man-in-the-street testimonials for his clients, primarily Democrats like New York's mayor Edward I. Koch.

Some strategists and pollsters, whose work is not as visible as that of the media gurus, also market themselves by their tactical strengths. Roger Stone, 33 years old, who learned the trade as a junior "dirty trickster" during President Richard Nixon's 1972 re-election campaign, is credited by many experts with having devised ways to attract traditionally Democratic urban ethnic voters to the Republican Party. Patrick Caddell, who wielded Svengali-like influence over the George McGovern, Jimmy Carter and Gary Hart presidential campaigns, is known as the clarion of the Baby Boom generation, and is now trying to attract young voters to the presidential candidacy of Democratic Senator Joseph R. Biden Jr. of Delaware.

Still, consistent styles are not as valuable to political consultants as connections. "Much of the marketing is done by gossip," said Paul Bograd, the assistant director of the Institute of Politics at Harvard's John F. Kennedy School of Government, who has managed several Democratic campaigns. "It's working the cocktail party circuit in Washington. It's who hangs out with whom."

For the most part, the longevity of most of the gurus is based simply on success. "The biggest single selling point is record," said Mr. Bograd. "If you win campaigns, you get the business." Big wins have catapulted Republican media producer Roger Ailes and Democrat Robert Squier to the pinnacle of their profession; so admired is the Ailes touch that all the candidates for the Republican presidential nomination are wooing the sometime Broadway producer.

Few of those top-level media producers will admit it, but business has been getting easier. Political media consultants garner a commission, usually 15 percent, on every television spot they place, although aggressive competition among media consultants has allowed some candidates to negotiate commissions as low as 7 percent. Increased television advertising rates—up 44 percent for spot time between 1982 and 1986, according to the Television Bureau of Advertising—have given media consultants a revenue windfall.

The Robert Goodman Agency, for example, which handled as many as 18 campaigns in a single season from its base in Baltimore in the mid-1970s, took on only six statewide and two Congressional campaigns in 1986. Yet the firm earned between $150,000 and $275,000 for each contest, a 25 percent increase over 1984, according to Adam Goodman, the 32-year-old son of the agency's founder, and its vice president-political director.

The agency's fees have remained constant, in the range between $3,000 and $5,000 a month, for the past five to 10 years, said Mr. Goodman. "But our commissions have gone up because of the increased costs of television and the increasing emphasis on TV" as a campaign tool, he said.

Both strategists and observers ascribe the explosion in television campaigning to the development of video and polling technology that allows candidates to respond overnight to televised attacks by their opponents, rather than simply repeat bland, non-combative "issues" spots shot at the campaign's start. "It's like the arms race," said Prof. Sabato of the University of Virginia. "You need this missile because the other guy has that missile."

The emphasis on what Mr. Goodman calls "confrontational" advertising has led to more commercials in most statewide campaigns. It has also led to earlier starts, with candidates trying to present their messages in the calm, pre-election atmosphere, before the "confrontational" period begins. Democratic presidential candidate Bruce Babbitt, the former Governor of Arizona, premiered his television spots in Iowa in April, a full 11 months before that state's caucuses—the earliest start ever for presidential advertising.

The growth of the consulting industry also stems from consultants' ingenuity in devising new products and services to peddle. The most fertile area for innovation has been "voter contact," which, because of advances in computer-targeting technology, is now the keystone of modern campaigning. Voter-contact specialists claim they can aim fundraising appeals and political missives to specific voter groups via direct mail, door-to-door canvassing, even targeted television advertising.

The buzzword here is "geodemographic clustering"—essentially, the use of computerized mailing lists keyed to zip codes, which allows candidates to target their appeals to increasingly narrow demographic groups. Others have managed to direct their pitch to specific homes.

Mr. O'Leary's P/M Corporation has a master list of 140 million separate households that it has cross-referenced against 200 other lists, allowing it to target people for fund raising based on economic, social or behavioral characteristics. The company discovered, for example, that 90 percent of Volvo owners are wealthy liberals, while 80 percent of Jaguar owners are conservatives with incomes above $50,000.

By combining those lists with the computerized telephoning technique known as telemarketing, "we have the ability to contact 35,000 people in one hour," said Mr. O'Leary.

For all the fancy terminology, some of these purported advances haven't added anything but cost to the modern political campaign, according to some political professionals. "There's a lot of hot air being blown on this voter contact stuff," said Lawrence C. McCarthy, a fellow at the Institute of Politics at Harvard's Kennedy School, and the former head of Ailes Communications' political division.

"You hear a lot like, 'My new computer software will make it possible for you to target only the right people watching the right shows,'" said Mr. McCarthy. "In the real world, it doesn't really work the way they say."

Political advertisers cannot always buy the time they need. Broadcasters, who by law can charge candidates only their lowest unit rate, naturally prefer higher-paying commercial customers. Politicians who purchase information from voter-contact experts are thus often unable to use it, said Mr. McCarthy.

Nevertheless, the trend toward finer and finer specialization in political consulting seems inexorable. Some experts suggest that the industry is following in the historical path of its parent industry, advertising. "There was a time when J. Walter Thompson sat at his typewriter and batted out ads," said Ralph D. Murphine of Murphine & Walsh, a Democratic firm in Washington. "The ad agencies eventually developed a whole superstructure of very highly skilled specialists." Unsurprising, then, that many political consultants find it natural to sell their expertise to private-sector clients.

Political professionals have long taken on business clients to solve what they call the "off-year problem." But in recent years, strategists have begun to market themselves more aggressively in the corporate arena, blurring the lines between political consulting, advertising, public relations and lobbying.

"Corporations face an election every day," said Mr. Miller of the Sawyer/Miller Group, whose corporate clients have included the Coca-Cola Company, Apple Computer Inc. and KYW-Television in Philadelphia.

Black, Manafort & Stone was taking on so many ostensibly nonpolitical clients that in 1985 it divided itself into two distinct (albeit overlapping) entities. Campaign Consultants Inc., a seven-person operation, handles only domestic Republican clients; two of its partners, Roger Stone and Charles R. Black, Jr., are personally "volunteering" their services to Rep. Jack Kemp's presidential campaign, according to Mr. Stone, and partner Lee Atwater is managing Vice President George Bush's presidential race as an individual project. The principals of Black, Manafort, Stone & Kelly, on the other hand, include both Democrats and Republicans, and they do consulting and lobbying for corporations, trade associations and foreign governments.

Critics, and some consultants, claim that the only thing these strategists have to offer corporate clients is access to their political clients. The New Republic, noting the Stone firm's political contacts as well as their $100,000-per-year representation of Kamen Aerospace and $6,000-a-month contract for Salomon Brothers, labeled Roger Stone "the state-of-the-art Washington sleazeball."

Others say that the consultants' access is overrated. "They sell themselves to corporations based on their political portfolios," said Professor Sabato of the University of Virginia, "but a lot of what they do is blue smoke and mirrors." He said he believes that many private-sector clients have dropped their political strategists.

Some clients maintain that they have profited from the political experts' advice. KYW-Television in Philadelphia hired the Sawyer/Miller Group in 1985, to help broaden the audience for its "Eyewitness News" broadcasts. The station hired a political firm, said Allan Lafferty, KYW's marketing director, "because they are experts in strategic positioning. They could help us understand how people were making choices in a competitive situation and develop an overall strategy so that people will choose us over the competition."

Sawyer/Miller recommended repositioning the local news "as a commodity, as an item that serves the viewer," according to Mr. Lafferty. The consultants suggested the advertising line, "Eyewitness News. We're there for you." While Mr. Lafferty concedes that "any agency with expertise in strategic positioning"

could have provided similar services, he credits Sawyer/Miller with helping KYW's news jump from third place to second in the market.

Not that there aren't embarrassments. When the Coca-Cola Company changed the formula of Coke in 1985 and then had to reintroduce the old formula as Classic Coke, much of the blame fell on political pollster Patrick Caddell. The company had hired Mr. Caddell and Scott Miller to do some "sacrilegious thinking" about the marketing of New Coke, Mr. Miller said. Perhaps it was too heretical. Some marketing professionals criticized Mr. Caddell because his surveys on the public's attitude toward a possible new soft drink failed to ask about the impact of removing the original soft-drink formula.

Mr. Miller, who escaped public censure, was not discouraged, and he may be vindicated after all. Coca-Cola, with its two Cokes, again dominates the soft-drink market. And Sergio Zyman—the Coca-Cola Company's director of marketing during the New Coke episode—recently joined the Sawyer/Miller Group as a partner. He will help to bring corporate clients into the agency.

# NONVOTING

"That television and the television campaign may be a principal cause of declining turnout is likely but the evidence is not as clear-cut. But what evidence we do have indicates that it is no coincidence that turnout has declined as expenditures have gone up. Since 1974, the percentage spent on media in the average budget for a senatorial campaign has increased from 30 percent to 55 percent in 1986, exclusive of campaign costs. In 1986, Sen. Alan Cranston spent more ($12 million) than had ever been spent on a senatorial campaign. Of that amount 55 percent went to media and 28 percent went to fundraising to pay for that media. That left only 17 percent of the campaign budget for candidate travel, staff and next to nothing for any activities involving citizen participation.

Citizens thus find themselves invited by the modern campaign to be spectators and consumers of politics rather than participants and stockholders."

*Curtis Gans*

"Through the technology of the tracking poll, campaign consultants can gauge the relative standing of the candidates. Should a consultant's candidate be behind, that consultant will not hesitate to recommend a generous dosage of demogogic attack ads. The opponent's consultant, seeing the gap closing, will recommend an equal dose of attack ads. The result is an arms race of tit-for-tat negative ads which cannot help but give the citizen a negative view of both candidates and of the political enterprise as a whole. Is it any wonder that there was in 1986 a 10 percent increase in negative attitudes towards candidates and a 10 percent decline in voter turnout?"

*Ed Rollins*

"George Orwell, in *1984,* had a vision of high technology being a tool used by rulers to control the ruled. I think that what we are seeing now is a little better. We don't—or we can't—use technology to effectively control people the way Orwell feared. In fact, voters and non-voters are using it to stay away from politics. In large part, campaigns are now an effort to find voters and catch them wherever they may be."

*Michael Barone*

"Over the last 20 years we have made it easier to vote and yet a smaller proportion of Americans are voting, election by election. We have a population that is not terribly interested in politics."

*Michael Barone*

"Is the demography going to be used ever increasingly to target likely voters and therefore make the non-voter someone who never gets contacted by anybody? Is the message honing going to be used in ever more sophisticated demagogic commercials that will turn more and more voters off—some of it by intent?"

*Curtis Gans*

*Journalist Jonathan Schell decided to cover the 1984 presidential election by living with a "typical" American family. His observations and conclusions are troubling.*

*"Each election year," Schell writes in his book, <u>History in Sherman Park</u>, "the politicians and others in and around politics and government campaign and, as required by the Constitution, hold elections, and everyone involved gives every sign of believing that the drama is as engrossing to the country as it ever was; but the evidence grows steadily that the public at large is becoming less and less interested. It's said that recently politics is being treated more and more as if it were an entertainment. If so, the performance is a failure. . . .*

*"There is little evidence," Schell writes, "that anyone who does not have a professional interest in politics in this country takes a very passionate interest in it. Is the American public becoming not so much de-aligned as de-politicized?"*

*Of all the complaints against new communications technologies, the most pervasive is that they foster such depoliticization by encouraging a passive sit-in-front-of-the-set attitude, and by machine-gunning negative images at voters. Much of this negativism, critics say, is derived from computer on-line opposition research services, and is based upon poll and focus-group data that allow targeting to voters' fears and misconceptions.*

*Such charges do not capture the entire truth. The same communications capabilities that allow effective targeting can improve communication between candidate and voter. Much blame for political alienation, furthermore, belongs to other causes including events such as Vietnam and Watergate. A recent Rolling Stone magazine poll of 18-to-44-year-olds, for example, found an entire generation that "hangs back from politics."[1] Young people are the only group of Americans whose participation has declined since it received the franchise. This cannot be blamed entirely on computers or television.*

*At the other end of the spectrum, furthermore, are "supervoters," people who take advantage of communications technologies, keep well-informed, and vote at every opportunity. Such people now constitute a highly-politicized minority, but nothing prevents the majority from joining in.*

*Beyond voting, there is a broader definition of political participation that includes working as a campaign volunteer, contributing money, writing letters to the newspaper or to public officials, attending political meetings or rallies, and circulating petitions. By such measures, participation is up. A 1988 Times Mirror/Gallup study, for example, found that more than half the respondents had signed a petition; one-third had contacted a public official; nearly a quarter had attended a public meeting; and one in 20 had spoken out at a public meeting or forum. Here, however, scholars argue about whether voting is a threshold activity—many studies indicate that people who do not vote also do none of the above.*

*The extent of nonvoting screams for attention. In the 1986 congressional race, for example, non-southern states experienced their lowest turnout in history. More than 104 million people chose not to vote.*

*The best source for such data is the Committee for the Study of the American Electorate, some of whose tables are excerpted below with an analysis by the Committee's director, Curtis Gans. Following that comes a unique perspective on nonvoting from Jonathan Schell.*

*These excerpts remind us that we must somehow make voting more attractive. Public policies such as changes in registration laws offer only a small part of the answer. The larger answer lies in an understanding of the demography and psychology of nonvoting, in government policies that are honest and responsive, in what we teach our children, and in what we ourselves believe about our government.*

1. William Greider, "The Rolling Stone Survey," *Rolling Stone* (7 April 1988):34.

---

# NONVOTING: THE NATURE OF THE PROBLEM, ITS IMPORTANCE TO AMERICAN DEMOCRACY AND SOME APPROACHES TO ITS SOLUTION

*Curtis B. Gans*

. . . The United States is now, in its congressional elections, the lowest participating democracy of any in the world and, in its presidential elections, only equaled occasionally for dearth of turnout by Switzerland and India.

### The Scope and Nature of the Problem

While these figures in and of themselves would appear appalling in a nation which prides itself on being the foremost democracy in the world, there are those, largely in the academic community, who question the scope and severity of the problem.

Those who take a minimalist view of the problem tend to do so on two bases:

—That the substantial decline in voter participation since 1960 can largely be explained by the enfranchisement of 18-20-year-olds in 1971—adding a low voting cohort to a moderate voting electorate, and/or

—That nonvoting is not a significant problem in the United States or that while it may be a significant problem, it could largely and readily be resolved by revisions in registration and voting law to make voting, for the citizen, a one-step act as it is in most of the world's advanced democracies. (In the United States, one must vote in two steps—register and vote. In most other democracies, the business of registration is conducted, in whole or in part, by the state. All the citizen has to do is vote.)

While both of these analyses are misperceptions of the problem, they are sufficiently widely held misperceptions that they deserve discussion . . .

There have been no fewer than five academic attempts at estimating the impact of enfranchising those aged 18-20, including one study by Thomas Cavanagh, commissioned by the Committee for the Study of the American Electorate. Those quantifications agree that the portion of the decline in voter participation that can be attributed to the enfranchisement of 18-20-year-olds is between 1.5 and 3 percentage points, far less than the nearly ten percentage point decline in voter participation in presidential elections since 1960 and the more than 11 percentage point decline since 1962 in even year non-presidential elections[1] . . .

### Non-voting and Registration

Similarly those who argue that non-voting is not a major problem or is largely a problem caused by the American system of voter registration do so on the basis best illustrated by Table 1:

That table shows, in column one, that when voting is seen as the percentage of eligible voters (that is age-eligible Americans as defined by the U.S. Bureau of the Census), turnout in the United States ranks 19 among the world's major democracies. (And if truth be told, if you factor in turnout in non-presidential years, which reached 37.1 percent in 1986, U.S. turnout is the lowest.)

On the other hand, when turnout is measured as a percentage of *registered* citizens, the turnout rate is 89 percent and the U.S. ranks seventh among the world's democracies and all those who have higher rates of turnout of registered voters either have compulsory or automatic registration. Thus, in the view of many academics the problem of voter participation in the United States is primarily a problem of registration and that were registration and voting laws revised participation rates would be comparable with other democracies.[2]

There are a number of problems with this analysis, four of which will be detailed here:

1. *The estimate of 89 percent of registered voters voting is based on survey response and is both misleading and inaccurate . . .*

In 1984, in connection with a project to evaluate the efficacy of the various and massive voter registration campaigns of that year, the Committee for the Study of the American Electorate commissioned Peter D. Hart Research Associates to conduct a survey of new registrants, but included in the sample a small number of in-person interviews for those without telephones. The Committee and Hart also conducted a validation study on its respondents. That validation study showed that of those who responded to the survey by phone, 90 percent said that they voted and very nearly 88 percent of those for which the Committee could get validation data actually voted. (Some states did not permit access to the records and the Committee did not have the resources for a lawsuit.) On the other hand, when the Committee and Hart attempted to validate the equally high reported voting figures for those without phones, they found that actual voting dropped down more than 20 percentage points.[3]

Thus, the only things that can be said about the survey responses to Michigan, Census and the Committee is that for those people with telephones, who are willing and capable of responding to a survey, 88 percent of registered voters vote.

2. *The survey responses do not square with actual voting performance.* Table 2 shows the actual percentage of registered voters with regard to voting in both presidential and non-presidential general elections.

This table is based on the actual votes cast for President in presidential years and the highest vote cast for statewide office in non-presidential years (usually Senator or Governor, but in 1986 included was the aggregate vote for U.S. House of Representatives in Indiana which was higher than the votes cast for statewide offices) . . .

Leaving aside for the time being, the exact percentage of registered voters who vote, it is clear that the percentage is, in presidential

Table 1    Voter Turnout in 20 Democracies in the 1970s

| Country | Average Turnout As Percent Eligible | Average Turnout As Percent Registered | Compulsory Voting | Eligible Required to Register |
|---|---|---|---|---|
| Australia | 86 | 95 | Yes | Yes |
| Austria | 88 | 92 | No | Automatic |
| Belgium | 88 | 93 | Yes | Automatic |
| Canada | 68 | 73 | No | Automatic |
| Denmark | 85 | 87 | No | Automatic |
| Finland | 82 | 82 | No | Automatic |
| France (Presidential) | 78 | 86 | No | No |
| West Germany | 85 | 90 | No | Automatic |
| Ireland | 77 | 77 | No | Automatic |
| Israel | 80 | 80 | No | Automatic |
| Italy | 94 | 94 | Yes | Automatic |
| Japan | 72 | 72 | No | Automatic |
| Netherlands | 82 | 84 | No | Automatic |
| New Zealand | 83 | 87 | No | Yes |
| Norway | 82 | 82 | No | Automatic |
| Sweden | 88 | 91 | No | Automatic |
| Switzerland | 44 | 52 | No | Automatic |
| U.K. | 75 | 75 | No | No |
| United States (Presidential) | 54 (19/20) | 89 (7/20) | No | No |
| Spain | 78 | 78 | No | Automatic |

From G. Bingham Powell Jr., "American Voter Turnout in Comparative Perspective," *American Political Science Review* 80:17-43 (1986).

Table 2    Percentage of Registered Voters Voting in Presidential and Non-Presidential General Elections

| Year | % Registered Voters Voting |
|---|---|
| 1960 | 85.3% |
| 1964 | 81.9 |
| 1968 | 80.5 |
| 1972 | 74.6 |
| 1976 | 75.5 |
| 1980 | 74.9 |
| 1984 | 72.6 |
| 1962 | 69.3 |
| 1966 | 66.5 |
| 1970 | 57.9 |
| 1974 | 56.0 |
| 1978 | 56.5 |
| 1982 | 60.7 |
| 1986 | 54.0 |

years, at least ten percent less than the survey responses and at least 25 percent less in non-presidential years; that it has been declining steadily since 1960 and that in presidential years the United States ranks about 15th among the 20 democracies in turnout of registered voters and in non-presidential years it ranks 19th.

3. *Registration law is not the principal impediment to increased turnout and enhancements in registration will not necessarily produce higher turnout.* If registration law were the principal impediment to high turnout then one would have expected turnout to have increased during the last two decades (absent the votes of those aged 18-20). It has not . . .

Increasingly, registration is no longer a good barometer of voter turnout. Table 3 shows the changes in the level of registration since 1976 in both presidential and non-presidential elections and the actual turnout during those years.

As can be seen from Table 3, in only one election cycle—between 1976 and 1980, did voter turnout correlate with voter registration, both going down at relatively the expected percentages. In every other year, either turnout and registration followed diametrically opposite patterns or, in the case of 1980-84, the turnout increase was miniscule compared

Table 3   National Registration and Voter Turnout (As Percentage of Voting Age Population) 1976-86

| Year | Registered as % VAP | Turnout |
|------|---------------------|---------|
| 1976 | 71.0% | 53.5% |
| 1980 | 69.8 | 52.6 |
| 1984 | 73.0 | 53.1 |
| 1978 | 66.7 | 37.5 |
| 1982 | 66.6 | 41.1 |
| 1986 | 67.9 | 37.0 |

to the registration increase, indicating nothing near a 90 percent correlation between registration and turnout.

4. *Registration barriers do not account for the overwhelming majority of the nonvoting problem in the United States.* . . . A longitudinal study of actual turnout conducted by the Committee for the Study of the American Electorate under a grant from the Ford Foundation completed this year, estimates that if every state would remove all . . . barriers to registration and enact election day registration, base level voter turnout would increase by 6 million voters.

But the range of between 6 million and 13 million voters who might turn out if all the remaining impediments to participation were removed represents only a small fraction of the nonvoting problem in the Unites States. . . . In plain terms, more and more people are losing faith in the efficacy of their vote and the will to participate and the faith that such participation will be meaningful is atrophying . . .

### The Impact of the Problem

. . . Low and declining turnout poses a series of specific threats to this democracy . . .

1. *The threat of government by elites, of, for, and by the interested few* . . .

2. *The threat to policy formation in the general interest.* If some groups vote more heavily than others, in a declining electorate they wield more influence . . .

3. *The threat of decreased voluntarism.* If . . . voting is the lowest common denominator political act, then the will to participate in other forms of societal activity declines as the will to vote declines . . .

4. *The threat of a bleak future.* Perhaps the most striking set of statistics to emerge from the 1986 election is that in California, according to a Mervyn Field Survey, only 15 percent of those aged 18-24 voted; and nationally, according to exit polls, only 16.6 percent of those aged 18-24 voted.[4] If interest in politics

and participation among the young stays at such a low level, the future for American politics is bleak indeed.

5. *The threat to cohesion.* If strong political parties are necessary for political cohesion and effective governance insofar as they define priorities, plot national direction, provide some element of discipline to the political process, and mobilize political resources for the constructive use of power, then one cannot be happy that in two of the last three congressional elections each of the major parties had less than a 20 percent share of the eligible vote and that there is an increasing tendency among the few who continue voting to split their tickets.

6. *The threat of demogoguery and authoritarianism.* To deal with the problem of nonvoting in America, we must address both problems— low and declining voter participation. We must address low voting by dealing with the unfinished agenda that will help create the opportunity for all Americans to participate. And we must deal with the factors that affect voluntary nonvoting and recreate the will to participate.

### Addressing Low Turnout: Creating the Opportunity

During 1986-87, the Committee for the Study of the American Electorate, which I direct, conducted a study to find out what portion of the problem of low voter participation could be ameliorated by changes in voting and registration laws and procedures and which changes offered the most promise for substantial effect. The methodology of this study was to test the impact on turnout of similar types of changes in laws in several states by comparing turnout before and after changes were made. The study, carried out with help from the Ford Foundation, arrived at three major findings and a number of questions.

The first of these findings is that there has been a dramatic change in the nonvoting community. Historically, it has been almost axiomatic that the nonvoting community was less educated, poorer, more minority and more urban and rural underclass than the rest of the population. . . . In 1984, however, the percentage of non-voters who were white and had completed a high school education had climbed to 54.4 percent.[5] This indicates two things: (1) that previous changes in voting law such as the Voting Rights Act of 1965 have helped enfranchise many persons previously excluded; and (2) that nonvoting should begin to be seen, not as primarily a problem of exclusion of some previously disenfranchised groups, but rather as a growing national phenomenon in which all elements of the population can claim their increasingly equal share.[6]

The second major finding is that even in this era of declining voter participation certain changes in voting law can be expected to have a substantial effect on base level turnout. This study shows that if election day registration was adopted in all states (as it has been in Maine, Minnesota, Wisconsin and Oregon—but since rescinded in Oregon), turnout in presidential elections, all other things being equal would increase by more than six million voters. It also indicated that certain less sweeping changes could have the effect of increasing normal turnout by more than two million voters. The most promising of these more modest reforms are programs of voter outreach through door-to-door registration, an open deputy registration program and abandonment of the practice of purging people from registration lists for failing to vote.

The third major finding is that there is no certainty that adding people to the rolls of the registered will actually produce higher turnout.

NOTES

1. Thomas Cavanagh, *Changes in American Voter Turnout, 1964-76, Political Science Quarterly*, Vol. 96, Spring 1981, pp 53-65. See also: Richard Boyd, *Decline of U.S. Voter Turnout, American Politics Quarterly*, Vol. 9, No. 2, April 1981; Steven D. Shaffer, *A Multivariate Explanation of Decreasing Turnout in Presidential Elections, Political Science*, Vol. 25, February 1981, pp. 68-95; Howard L. Reiter, *Why Is Turnout Down, Public Opinion Quarterly*, Vol. 43, Fall 1979, pp. 297-311. Also, in connection with this paper, Walter Dean Burnham did an estimate of the turnout decline attributed to 18-20-year-olds, using the P-20 series Current Population Survey of the U.S. Bureau of Census, an estimate which attributes 1.5 percentage points of the 10 percentage point drop in turnout to youth enfranchisement.

2. One of the clearest statements of this position is by Peverill Squire, Raymond E. Wolfinger and David Glass, *Residential Mobility and Voter Turnout, American Political Science Review*, Vol. 81, No. 1, March 1987, p. 45: "... nor that this country's dismal showing in international comparisons of turnout is due in large measure to our registration system, in which the individual, not the government, bears the responsibility for establishing one's eligibility to vote."

3. Committee for the Study of the American Electorate, *A Study of 1984 Registration Mobilization Drives*, April 1987.

4. This is an interpolated figure. According to the ABC-*Washington Post* exit poll of November 1986, 6 percent of the voting electorate consisted of those in the age group 18-24. According to the CBS-*New York Times* survey, 7 percent of the voting electorate was between the ages of 18-24. According to the pre-election projection of the voting age population of the U.S. Bureau of the Census (op. cit.), the percentage of the voting age population aged 18-24 was 17 percent—thus, those aged 18-24 voted at a 41 percent rate of the total population, which voted at a rate of 37.1 percent.

5. U.S. Bureau of the Census, *Current Population Survey, Series P. 20*, Nos. 192 and 405.

6. It should be noted that the gap has not fully closed. Of those who vote, 73.7 percent are among the white middle class, as defined in this paper.

Reprinted with permission from Curtis B. Gans, Director, The Committee for the Study of the American Electorate.

---

## FACT SHEET

*Compiled from reports by the Committee for the Study of the American Electorate, 1988*

A. *Presidential Turnout Trend:* The percentages below represent the percentages of eligible Americans who voted. Eligible voters, or Voting Age Population (VAP), are estimates from the U.S. Bureau of the Census. Vote counts are final and official and certified by the Secretaries of State of the respective states.

| Year | VAP | Total Presidential Vote | % VAP Voted |
|------|------|-------------------------|-------------|
| 1984* | 174,447,000 | 92,659,600 | 53.1 |
| 1980 | 164,595,000 | 86,515,221 | 52.6 |
| 1976 | 152,308,000 | 81,559,889 | 53.5 |
| 1972 | 140,777,000 | 77,718,554 | 55.2 |
| 1968 | 120,285,000 | 74,211,875 | 60.9 |
| 1964 | 114,090,000 | 70,644,592 | 61.9 |
| 1960 | 109,159,000 | 68,838,219 | 62.8 |

* There are seven states—Arkansas (G), North Dakota(G), Washington(G), West Virginia(G), Colorado(S), Mississippi(S) and North Carolina(S)—in which the Governor or Senator vote (as indicated) exceeds the presidential vote. The total vote for the highest race in every state is 92,756,504, or 53.3 percent of the eligibles.

| Year | Republican | Democrat | Other | Non-Voters |
|------|-----------|----------|-------|-----------|
| 1984 | 31.3% | 21.6% | 0.4% | 46.7% |
| 1980 | 26.7% | 21.6% | 4.3% | 47.4% |
| 1976 | 25.7% | 26.8% | 1.0% | 46.5% |
| 1972 | 33.5% | 20.7% | 1.0% | 44.8% |
| 1968 | 26.4% | 26.0% | 8.4% | 39.1% |
| 1964 | 23.8% | 37.8% | 0.3% | 38.1% |
| 1960 | 31.2% | 31.4% | 0.5% | 37.2% |

B. *Partisan Presidential Turnout Trend:* The percentages above represent the percentage of eligible voters who voted Republican, Democratic, or for other parties, or did not vote in the presidential election.

C. *Partisan Percentage of Total Presidential Vote:* The percentages below are the Republican and Democratic percentages of the total vote for President.

| Year | Republican | Democrat |
|------|-----------|----------|
| 1984 | 58.7% | 40.5% |

D. *Registration Trend (Estimates):* The following are estimates of total registration for all states and the District of Columbia based on the actual registration statistics from the states which keep registration records. The estimates are derived by applying that percentage to the national voting age population figure. In 1984, for instance, in the 49 states which had actual registration figures (North Dakota and Wisconsin did not), 124,122,167 persons registered to vote—73.0 percent of the eligible voters. Applying that percentage to the national voting age population figure (which includes North Dakota and Wisconsin) results in a national registration estimate of 127,029,586. (Note: actual registration figures in these two high-turnout states may have been slightly higher than the national average).

| Year* | Registration (estimates) | % VAP Registered |
|-------|-------------------------|------------------|
| 1984 | 127,029,586 | 73.0% |
| 1980 | 114,743,711 | 69.8% |
| 1976 | 108,132,655 | 71.0% |
| 1972 | 103,123,862 | 73.3% |
| 1968 | 89,919,744 | 74.8% |
| 1964 | 87,517,061 | 76.7% |
| 1960 | 82,350,245 | 75.4% |

* These registration figures are based on the final and official registration statistics provided by Secretaries of State and State registrars. The accuracy of these figures vary according to the stringency of purges conducted in each state and locality. There is, therefore, some inflation in these figures, although the trends between years are likely to be accurate.

E. *Registration Trend:* The following figures are the actual numbers of registered voters in the states which keep registration records (the number of such states is indicated in parentheses next to the year).

| Year | Registration | % VAP Registered |
|------|-------------|------------------|
| 1984(49) | 124,122,167 | 73.0% |
| 1980(49) | 112,064,058 | 69.8% |
| 1976(49) | 106,680,785 | 71.0% |
| 1972(44) | 93,778,200 | 73.3% |
| 1968(44) | 78,887,316 | 74.8% |
| 1964(36) | 65,227,022 | 76.7% |
| 1960(34) | 59,245,795 | 75.4% |

F. *Registration Trend:* The following figures are the actual numbers of registered voters in the 34 states which kept constant registration records from the years 1960 to 1984. (The 34 states are: Arizona, Arkansas, California, Colorado, Connecticut, Delaware, Florida, Georgia, Hawaii, Idaho, Illinois, Indiana, Louisiana, Maine, Maryland, Massachusetts, Michigan, Montana, Nevada, New Hampshire, New Jersey, New Mexico, New York, North Carolina, Oklahoma, Oregon, Pennsylvania, Rhode Island, South Carolina, Utah, Vermont, Virginia, Washington, and West Virginia).

| Year | Registration | % VAP Registered |
|------|-------------|------------------|
| 1984 | 90,200,460 | 71.4% |
| 1980 | 81,740,240 | 68.5% |
| 1976 | 77,480,736 | 70.2% |
| 1972 | 76,009,684 | 74.4% |
| 1968 | 65,550,813 | 75.3% |
| 1964 | 63,378,510 | 77.0% |
| 1960 | 59,245,795 | 75.4% |

G. *Turnout of Registered Voters Trend:* The percentages below represent the percentage of registered voters who voted for President in the states which keep registration records (number of such states is indicated in parentheses next to year).

| | |
|---|---|
| 1984 (49) | 72.6% |
| 1980 (49) | 74.9% |
| 1976 (49) | 75.5% |
| 1972 (44) | 74.6% |
| 1968 (44) | 80.5% |
| 1964 (36) | 81.9% |
| 1960 (34) | 85.3% |

H. *Turnout of Registered Voters Trend:* The percentages below represent the percentage of registered voters who voted for President in states which kept constant registration records from the years 1960 to 1984 (see F for listing of states).

| | |
|---|---|
| 1984 | 73.8% |
| 1980 | 75.9% |
| 1976 | 76.0% |
| 1972 | 75.0% |
| 1968 | 81.7% |
| 1964 | 82.2% |
| 1960 | 85.3% |

I. *Senator/Governor Partisan Turnout Trend:* The following are percentages of eligible voters who voted Democratic, Republican, or for other parties in senatorial and gubernatorial elections. (Figures represent the results of whichever office received the highest vote).

| Year | Republican | Democrat | Other |
|---|---|---|---|
| 1984 | 26.9% | 25.7% | 0.4% |
| 1980 | 23.1% | 26.0% | 1.5% |
| 1976 | 22.8% | 27.5% | 1.6% |
| 1972 | 27.6% | 25.5% | 0.7% |
| 1968 | 27.5% | 28.6% | 1.8% |
| 1964 | 28.4% | 33.2% | 0.5% |
| 1960 | 26.6% | 31.5% | 0.4% |

J. *Congressional Turnout Trend:* The following are percentages of eligible voters who voted in the U.S. House of Representatives races.

| | |
|---|---|
| 1984 | 48.3% |
| 1980 | 47.1% |
| 1976 | 48.9% |
| 1972 | 50.2% |
| 1968 | 52.4% |
| 1964 | 59.0% |
| 1960 | 58.8% |

K. *Partisan Congressional Turnout Trend:* The following are percentages of eligible voters who voted Republican, Democratic, or for other parties in the U.S. House of Representatives races.

| Year | Republican | Democrat | Other |
|---|---|---|---|
| 1984 | 22.6% | 25.0% | 0.6% |
| 1980 | 22.6% | 23.8% | 0.8% |
| 1976 | 20.6% | 27.5% | 0.8% |
| 1972 | 23.4% | 26.1% | 0.7% |
| 1968 | 25.3% | 26.4% | 0.7% |
| 1964 | 25.4% | 33.2% | 0.3% |
| 1960 | 26.4% | 32.2% | 0.2% |

L. *Turnout Trend in Non-Presidential General Elections* —Percentage of registered voters voting.

| Year | % Registered Voters Voting |
|---|---|
| 1962 | 69.3% |
| 1966 | 66.5 |
| 1970 | 57.9 |
| 1974 | 56.0 |
| 1978 | 56.5 |
| 1982 | 60.7 |
| 1986 | 54.0 |

*Primary Turnout Trend*: Trend in overall turnout, as a percentage of VAP. (Note: Republicans did not have meaningful contests in 1972 and 1984.)

| | Overall Turnout | Republican Turnout | Democratic Turnout |
|---|---|---|---|
| 1960 | 20.53 | 11.23 | 15.41 |
| 1964 | 21.83 | 11.11 | 12.09 |
| 1968 | 18.12 | 6.00 | 14.62 |
| 1972 | 27.60 | 8.11 | 20.18 |
| 1976 | 28.15 | 11.11 | 17.10 |
| 1980 | 22.94 | 10.34 | 13.90 |
| 1984 | 20.56 | 6.62 | 15.23 |
| 1988 | 22.52 | 8.51 | 15.04 |

# HISTORY IN SHERMAN PARK
## An American Family and the Reagan-Mondale Election

*Jonathan Schell*

. . . Wherever I went in Milwaukee, I talked to people about politics, but I found little evidence that people talked about politics among themselves. The day after the Mondale-Reagan debate, none of the salesmen that Bill worked with in the supermarkets brought the subject up. Nor did many people seem to discuss politics within their families. Family members very often did not know how other family members were voting. Gina had thought that Harry would vote Democratic and that Art would vote Republican, but just the reverse seemed to be the case, and Harry had mistakenly thought that his "Yuppie" sister meant to vote Republican. Even Fred Skoretsky, who took a lively interest in politics, was surprised to learn that his wife had voted for Reagan in the 1980 election. (However, the Skoretsky's did discuss political matters with some of their neighbors.) Friends were not necessarily better informed about one another's views. Gina regarded Paul and Betty Toruncyk as quintessential highly educated young Democrats when in fact they were leaning toward Reagan.

If this lack of discussion reflected lack of interest, it also reflected, I felt, fear of dissension. Often, other people's political views were not merely unsought but actively avoided, or held secret. On occasion, I heard a political discussion begin only to be abruptly dropped when it became clear that there was disagreement among the participants. Once, at a family gathering at Gina and Bill's house, the conversation turned, at my instigation, to the election, and one cousin, who worked in a car factory, expressed the view that only two categories of people voted Republican—either "the very rich, who are going to profit, or the very stupid, who don't know any better." After he had said this three or four times, another cousin's husband, who was a business executive, replied testily that this view displayed an ignorance of how Reagan's policies were helping the economy, by providing incentives for business to expand. A silence fell, and the subject was dropped. Those present seemed to feel that the gulf between the two views was too wide to be bridged, or even further exposed, without a serious quarrel, which might

ruin the occasion. Often, I felt that in their conversations people were ready to go to great lengths to avoid dispute. Sensing that the realm of political views could be a battlefield, they shunned it. It was never quite clear, therefore, when people were steering clear of political discussions whether they did so because they were bored with politics or because they were afraid of it, or both. Gina and Bill were the great exceptions. They not only were unafraid of political disagreement, but seemed to enjoy it. Yet they rarely discussed politics, they told me, when I wasn't asking them to.

Spontaneous political discussions were only one of many things that were notable by their absence in my conversations in Milwaukee. Bill and Gina were the grandchildren of immigrants from Poland and Italy, but neither of them ever mentioned either of these countries or seemed to be influenced by their national traditions. Once, when Gina saw a documentary about the Solidarity movement in Poland, she was amazed. "They all looked like Bill," she said to me. Nor did anyone else I met seem to attach importance to his or her ethnic past. Milwaukee has one of the most unusual political histories of any city in America. For 38 years between 1910 and 1960 it was run by the Socialist Party, whose roots went back to immigrants from Germany who had participated in the revolution of 1848 there. But no voter I met ever mentioned this piece of history. With the exception of Kate and Pete, no one mentioned that his or her political views had been influenced by a book. And, again with the exception of Kate and Pete, and of the Skoretsky's, who paid close attention to the views of several Catholic publications, no one mentioned being influenced by anything read in a magazine. . . .

From *History in Sherman Park* by Jonathan Schell. Copyright 1987 by Jonathan Schell. Reprinted by permission of Alfred A. Knopf, Inc.

# JOURNALISM

"The free media—the 22-second sound bite—is probably more important than any other element of the campaign today. You must know how to utilize the free media effectively. You must get your spin across. That's the shooting match. This is true for presidential primaries and several elections, statewide races, and local contests."

*Michael Barone*

"People have not gotten very much information from the news media. In large part, this is because they are not seeking it."

*Michael Barone*

"Satellite feeds permit candidates more direct access to local media markets at a reasonable cost. This enables candidates to bypass a bulky or unresponsive national media, and it gives campaigns some control over news coverage.

This campaign control over news coverage, however, should disturb all of us. Satellite feeds may also encourage laziness in media outlets, less aggressive reporting, fewer station-generated segments, and more instances in which broadcast stations simply take feeds directly from the campaign. There is a basic ethical question involved here."

*Larry Sabato*

"The new technologies increasingly allow politicians to direct different—and conflicting—messages to different population segments without anyone catching on."

*Michael Barone*

*Journalists have always been part of the political process, but the pervasiveness of electronic media and the decline of political parties give them unprecedented influence. Thus, journalists today worry about wandering on stage rather than reporting news, and about reporting on a campaign "reality" created just so they can report it. Candidates, in turn, have picked up new skills. It is not unusual to hear them respond to a question by saying, "I can answer that in a 15-second sound bite."*

*Most journalism-related issues that attract public attention—the focus on the Iowa caucuses and the New Hampshire primary, exit polls, and an emphasis on personalities—fail to address the ways technology is changing campaign journalism. The following excerpts demonstrate, however, that new and significant changes have emerged. These changes, in turn, raise questions related to:*

*—Campaign mastery of "unfiltered messages" such as candidate-initiated television programs made available to local stations via satellite.*

*—"Fast pack" journalism, in which computer hotlines feed groupthink.*

*—A flood of poll and focus-group findings, some with complicated or questionable methodology, and others overtly designed to manipulate the news.*

*—A trend toward technology-based, punch-counterpunch dialogues that encourage negativism.*

*—A fascination with technology and with the techniques of politics that diverts attention from issues.*

*—Campaign targeting of messages to disparate groups, making it difficult—and often impossible—for journalists to cover what each campaign is saying.*

*—Video press releases that resemble television news stories.*

*—Campaign control over access to candidates so strict that live appearances become high-stakes drama.*

*—Pervasiveness of coverage that robs campaigns of spontaneity and threatens to transform human foibles into front-page news.*

*—General dissatisfaction with network news.*

*—Belief that stories with "pictures that wiggle" are the most newsworthy.*

---

## C-SPAN'S SPOTLIGHT BRINGS QUIET CORNERS OF CAMPAIGNING INTO VIEW

*Andrew Rosenthal, New York Times, October 22, 1987*

WASHINGTON—Bruce Babbitt subscribed to it to help him learn how to look better on television. Tom Rath, adviser to Senator Bob Dole in New Hampshire, uses it to observe campaign rivals with a degree of intimacy unheard of in previous elections. And it played an important role in the disintegration of Senator Joseph R. Biden Jr.'s campaign.

The Washington-based Cable Satellite Public Affairs Network, once known primarily as "the network that dares to be boring," has found new prominence and respect in the 1988 Presidential election season.

C-SPAN still is not considered so influential on the course of the campaign as newspapers and the major networks. But some political operatives believe its blanket coverage has started to change the rules of campaigning, bringing television into areas once shielded from general view and exposing candidates to minute analysis by their opponents and the press.

"The electronic presence in politics is becoming more pervasive, and C-SPAN is paving that road, for better or for worse," said Richard Bond, deputy campaign manager for Vice President Bush.

### Role in the Biden Episode

The power of C-SPAN was dramatized last month toward the end of Mr. Biden's campaign. Nan Gibson, C-SPAN's press coordinator, says that after publication of newspaper articles about a speech in which the Senator had lifted the family history of a British politician, she received scores of calls from reporters interested in the network's tape of Mr. Biden's remarks.

The major networks' news programs televised the C-SPAN tape in their coverage of the story, and another C-SPAN tape contributed to a subsequent Newsweek article that told how Mr. Biden, at a New Hampshire campaign event, had misstated his academic record.

"Reporters are using us as a video archive," Ms. Gibson said. "They can't be everywhere at once, so they can watch from here."

### Now Eight Years Old

Since beginning operations in 1979, C-SPAN, the public affairs service for cable television, has specialized in live programs in which a dispassionate camera records the action, or lack of it on the floors of the Senate and the House of Representatives.

But that is hardly the limit of its efforts. The network provided gavel-to-gavel coverage of the two party conventions in 1984, and this time it has greatly expanded its campaign reporting, mostly through a weekly program, "Road to the White House," on which C-SPAN's political editor, Carl M. Rutan, is host.

It also has morning call-in programs on which every major candidate has appeared at least once, for a grilling by viewers, and it broadcasts debates, speeches and other campaign appearances. But its most innovative efforts have been in bringing cameras into small events like coffee gatherings in New Hampshire and dessert parties in Iowa.

### "High-Tech Retail Politics"

"C-SPAN brings everything that the candidates are doing into the people's living rooms," said Phil Roeder, executive director of the Iowa Democratic Party. "It's the high-tech version of retail politics," the style of one-on-one personalized campaigning deemed man-

datory for success in Iowa and New Hampshire.

With an annual budget of about $12 million, as against hundreds of millions for the major networks, C-SPAN is hardly a challenge to them. Nor can its officials estimate how many of the 35.1 million households that subscribe to its programming are regular viewers. But those officials agree with the conventional wisdom that a large part of the audience is composed of political junkies: politicians, their aides, party officials, consultants and journalists.

"It's a godsend to press secretaries because reporters watch it, editors watch it, and the political activists watch it," said John Buckley, spokesman for Representative Jack F. Kemp of New York, a Republican candidate.

### Every Word and Gesture

At small campaign events, C-SPAN crews attach a wireless microphone to the candidate's clothing and use a shotgun microphone to reach everyone else. The object, Mr. Rutan said, is to record every word the candidate says and every gesture he makes as he shakes hands, kisses babies and drinks coffee.

Mr. Rath, of the Dole campaign, said he was startled by the evident popularity of a Republican rival, Pat Robertson, when Mr. Robertson made a C-SPAN appearance early in the campaign. "I was watching him sign books," Mr. Rath said. "What impressed me was not just that there was a crowd, but that they had all brought the books. There's a message there."

Vada Manager, assistant press secretary for Mr. Babbitt, said that after the candidate's shaky performance at a televised debate in Houston on July 1, the campaign installed C-SPAN in his home.

"That was part of our plan for recovery," Mr. Manager said. "We wanted to show him how members of Congress and other candidates use television."

But the presence of C-SPAN cameras, political operatives said, also forces candidates to be more careful about such things as efforts to tailor their remarks for different parts of the country. Mr. Rutan, C-SPAN's political editor, said that after Mr. Biden's experience, campaign aides were more wary.

"In the past, candidates have been able to go where they want and maybe stretch the truth just a little bit," he said. "Suddenly what they say in a small Iowa town is on the record, just as if they had said it at the National Press Club in Washington."

---

## C-SPAN PLAYS A PIVOTAL ROLE IN 1988 PRESIDENTIAL ELECTION

*Thomas P. Southwick, Multichannel News, November 30, 1987*

. . . Members of the press also follow the campaign via C-SPAN. In the pre-C-SPAN era, nationally syndicated columnists such as Mary McGrory or David Broder would be able to spend only a few hours a month with each campaign. They would make their judgments about a candidate based on spending a day or less with the campaign. If the candidate happened to stumble through a speech on the afternoon that James Reston was aboard the press bus, his candidacy could be severely damaged even if he had been tearing down the house at every other stop along the way.

This year every political writer in the country has been able to watch every debate and important speech in full. And journalists use the network. In 1984 far more reporters followed the convention proceedings via C-SPAN than via personal reporting from the convention floor.

The broadcast networks have focused too much of the voters' attention on the horse-race aspects of politics—the polls and the tactics— and on relatively minor but easy-to-understand incidents—such as President Ford's slip on Poland in 1976.

Now the voters will have the ability to see the candidates in depth, to place a mistake in context and to view the would-be leaders for longer periods of time in a variety of circumstances. Citizens will have the option to make their own judgments about what is important about a speech or a debate without having to rely on some TV reporter or anchor to pick out the 45 seconds that the viewer should watch.

Voters who rely on broadcast networks for their information are given the most emotional, simplistic view of the campaign, both through the truncated, sensationalized news reports and through the candidates' advertising campaigns. They are forced to base their decisions on their gut instincts.

C-SPAN gives voters the option to use their minds in deciding which candidate to support. And that has to be a step forward for the nation.

---

## PRESIDENTIAL PITCHES BY SATELLITE, VIDEOTAPE

*Thomas A. Fogarty, The Des Moines Register, June 7, 1987*

Richard Gephardt, the Missouri Democrat who wants to be president, made electioneering history on a recent campaign trip to Iowa.

For $7,000, Gephardt hired a camera crew and a satellite uplink truck to trail him on April 24, a day he planned stops in Cedar Falls, Des Moines and Marshalltown.

At mid-afternoon, technicians beamed three minutes of videotape from the day's campaign events to a satellite 22,000 miles above the equator. The satellite then deflected the signal back to 700 television stations across the country.

### Three TV Advancements

Political professionals cite three television-related advancements since 1984 that are altering how candidates run, how journalists cover and how caucus-goers and voters will make their selections in the 1988 election:

—The availability of mobile satellite trucks like that used by Gephardt. The vehicles, about the size of bread trucks and equipped with retractable satellite dishes on top, make videotape editing and television transmission available anywhere.

—The widespread use of videocassette recorders, or VCRs. The recording devices now are in 37 million American homes—2 1/2 times more than in 1984 and 26 times more than in 1980. Assuming Iowa reflects the nation, more than 400,000 households in the state have VCRs.

—The rapid growth of C-SPAN, or Cable Satellite Public Affairs Network, which now reaches about 30 million households nationally, including 350,000 in Iowa. Political professionals say the cable network is gaining influence in the Iowa caucus process because of its heavy coverage, and because its viewers, though small in number, are politically motivated.

### Local Media Power

"It gives local television stations more control over the news," says Ann Brackbill, deputy press secretary for Republican Pierre S. du Pont. "The Iowa caucuses will be worked and won through the local media."

Michael McCurry, Democrat Bruce Babbitt's press secretary, agrees. "Campaign aides used to sidle up to network correspondents like butter on bread," says McCurry. "Now the local news director in Sioux Falls is more important than some of the news executives from New York."

Local television news people seem less impressed than campaign aides with their new role in presidential politics.

Gary Griffith, political editor at WCVB-TV in Boston, whose crews have made six trips to Iowa recently for political stories, says his basic news judgments are unchanged by the new technology.

"You can cover the story better because you can stay with it longer," says Griffith. No longer do reporters need time to ship their videotapes for transmission.

Some say the new ability of candidates to provide visually appealing interviews via satellite on a timely basis raises ethical questions for television news organizations.

The du Pont and Babbitt campaigns, for example, paid about $6,000 to produce and transmit the candidates' May 29 debate at Drake University. The broadcast was free to television news departments.

Rather than broadcast the candidate-sponsored program, C-SPAN spent $2,500 for its own production and satellite transmission of the debate. "There is an ethical problem in taking a free feed from a campaign," says Carl Rutan, C-SPAN political editor. "It's nothing more than a one-hour press release from the candidates."

Other broadcast journalists see nothing wrong with it precisely because they view it as the equivalent of an old-fashioned press release delivered on paper.

### Like a Hand-Out

"It's just a hand-out in a different medium," says Griffith, of Boston's WCVB. "We've had hand-outs from politicians for decades. If you use it, all you need to do is say that's where it came from."

Steve Murphy, news director at WOWT-TV in Omaha, says news makers in politics, government and business increasingly make themselves available for satellite interviews. He rarely accepts the offers.

The proposed interviews usually consist of low-grade news stories that are unable to compete for air time with other stories, he says. In the rare instance when they can be justified, the interviewer must be unrestricted in questioning and viewers told the subject is paying for the satellite link.

C-SPAN's Rutan says stations do such interviews more to make their news readers look important, giving the appearance that they have exclusive interviews, than to obtain information.

### C-SPAN

The number of Iowa households receiving C-SPAN, a non-profit network supported mainly by the cable industry, has increased by 75 percent since the last presidential election, according to network figures.

Since 1979, C-SPAN has been feeding the habit of political junkies around the country with its 24-hour fare of congressional sessions, public policy conferences and the like. The network provides heavy coverage of presidential campaign events, including the Midwest Republican Leadership Conference last weekend in Des Moines.

By the end of the year, the network will have a satellite uplink truck in Iowa devoted exclusively to caucus coverage, says Rutan.

"C-SPAN's viewership is not wide," says David Oman, a Des Moines cable television executive, local C-SPAN director, and co-chairman of the state Republican Party, "but those who do watch it are very loyal, and they watch it very intensely."

Although C-SPAN creates hardly a blip in the viewer ratings, politicians crave exposure on the network, partly because a 1985 network study showed 93 percent of its viewers had voted in the 1984 general election.

That suggests that those who watch C-SPAN are exactly the kind of people who attend the Iowa precinct caucuses.

## DID POLLSTERS GIVE BUSH HIS N.H. WIN? Super-Modern Surveys and Strategic Voting Might Account for the Veep's Big Comeback

*Paul Taylor, The Washington Post, February 28, 1988*

Have we reached the point where the media's use of super-modern polling techniques—and the public's reaction to them—are skewing the outcome of campaigns? Take a look at the recent example of New Hampshire.

For seven days this month, the state of New Hampshire was transformed into a hothouse of polling, punditry and politicking, the elements of which have never before been comingled quite so explosively in a presidential campaign.

By night the pollsters queried the voters; by day they reported back the latest reading on their shifts in sentiment, like so many blips on an EKG machine. In the end, this orgy of observation did not keep pace with the object under study—perhaps, several analysts now speculate, because the act of measurement itself kept changing the object under study.

The size of Vice President Bush's 38-29 percent victory over Sen. Robert Dole in the Feb. 16 primary wasn't foreseen by any of the news organizations that had been conducting nightly tracking polls for a week. Measured against the 20-point gap he had enjoyed in New Hampshire polls throughout 1987 and January of 1988, his winning margin was hardly remarkable. It's how he got there that caught nearly everyone by surprise.

In the days immediately before and after his third-place "humiliation" (that's how it was widely reported in the media) in the Feb. 8 Iowa caucuses, Bush lost all of that 20-point New Hampshire advantage, according to nightly tracking polls, and actually fell behind Dole. Then, in the last 72 hours before the New Hampshire vote, he recouped much of his lost support.

Tracking polls—repeating the same set of questions to a small sample on successive days—monitor shifts in voter sentiment, typically in the last days before an election. They've been used by well-financed campaigns for nearly two decades to guide last-minute tactical decisions. This year many media organizations began using them as well.

The various tracking polls in New Hampshire all caught the last-minute shift in momentum, but not its magnitude. Even now, pollsters are mystified that sentiment could have moved so sharply in one direction then doubled back just as sharply in the other—without the intervention of a major news event. "I've studied data from thousands of elections," said one pollster, who asked not to be identified. "This is the most unique finish I've ever seen."

What happened? With hindsight, there's no shortage of explanations: the Bush campaign's far superior get-out-the-vote operation (a factor that, experts say, could account for three to five points of his margin); a well-conceived late attack ad against Dole; an 11th-hour boost from Sen. Barry Goldwater, and an almost plaintive "warts and all" appeal from the candidate himself.

The Dole campaign, on the other hand, started the week flush with the Iowa victory and determined to "act presidential" so as to bury once and for all the "mean Bob Dole" stereotype. It never wavered from that strategy, even in the face of tough television ads depicting Dole as a "straddler" and a taxraiser. Dole now says he regrets his week spent above-the-fray, attributing it to overconfidence spawned in part by tracking polls. "I felt pretty good there for about 24 hours," he said, ruefully, last week. "I was writing my inaugural address."

Beyond the second-guessing over tactics, however, there is an emerging line of analysis which argues that the heavy publicity surrounding the Bush "collapse" in the early part of the week created a counter-trend almost in and of itself.

Dole's New Hampshire coordinator, Thomas Rath, argues that the media, in their eagerness to bury Bush, may have set the stage for his comeback. "The press was focusing on 'the death of George Bush story'—you almost think they already had the leads written in their typewriters—and I think that it dramatically altered the stakes of the race," he said. "It created a 'poor George Bush' phenomenon, and allowed him to come back and say, 'Don't throw this good and decent man out.'"

Rath is correct that the media—emboldened by tracking polls showing a massive hemorrhaging of Bush support in New Hampshire—captured and, in retrospect, over-dramatized the peril of his situation. The night after Iowa, NBC had him suffering a "humiliating" defeat and quoted a senior Bush aide saying that unless he won New Hampshire, "the race may be all over." On CBS, the Bush campaign was depicted as "desperate." *The Washington Post* chronicled the Dole surge all week, as did *The Boston Globe, The Manchester Union Leader* and virtually all of the smaller papers that New Hampshirites read.

"Just as voters in New Hampshire started thinking about the race," said Henry Brady, a University of Chicago political scientist, "they may very well have started saying to themselves, 'My God, if I vote for Dole I might knock Bush out of the race.' "

"This gets into an area psychologists would call 'framing' the way you think of your choice," said Samuel Popkin, a political scientist at the University of California at San Diego. Popkin drew a contrast between what happened to Bush in New Hampshire this year and what happened to Walter Mondale in the same state in 1984. In January of 1984, a *Washington Post*/ABC poll showed Mondale with a lopsided 50-4 percent New Hampshire lead over Gary Hart. Then came the Iowa vote. Hart got only 16 percent. But, by coming in second in a crowded field, he established himself as the clear alternative to Mondale, who was an unpopular frontrunner with many Democrats. The next week, Hart zoomed past Mondale in New Hampshire, 37-28 percent.

Why couldn't Mondale reverse the collapse, as Bush did in 1988? One difference is that in 1984, the electorate was not so heavily bombarded with daily poll evidence of its own abandonment of Mondale—the *Washington Post* and ABC were the only news organizations doing tracking polls that year. So in 1984, the counterforce had less of a chance to set in.

Popkin is one of many academicians who believe that primary voters often engage in "strategic voting"; that is, they take into account factors other than the simple question of preference. Until this year, however, the prevailing evidence has been that strategic voting creates bandwagons in the early phase of the nomination season, and impedes them only in the late phases. In the early primaries, voters who are attracted to longshots or protest candidates may not vote for them, because they don't think they can win. "The overwhelming evidence is that voters' expectations of who they think is going to win correlates in a positive way with who they vote for," said Larry Bartels, a political scientist at the University of Rochester who has written a book about the dynamics of primaries. "The only example of a negative correlation comes late in the process, and it tends to be weaker."

The Rath explanation of the "strategic" vote to save Bush would break that pattern, and Bartels is skeptical of it. "It seems unlikely to me that 10,000 or 15,000 voters came to the spontaneous conclusion that Bush was on the verge of being eliminated, and they all reacted the same way. You are talking about telescoping into a couple of days a process that usually unfolds over months."

But Dole's media adviser, Larry McCarthy, thinks that's exactly what happened. "If it hadn't been for the tracking polls, Dole would have won," he said. A tracking poll question asked by Dole's pollster, Richard Wirthlin, showed that on Sunday, Feb. 14, and Monday, Feb. 15, more Republicans—by a margin of nearly 20 percent—thought Dole was going to be the winner over Bush. Wirthlin's post-election survey also showed that voters who said they were undecided on Sunday and Monday wound up breaking 7-3 for Bush on election day (although network exit polls show a more even break among late deciders). Lots of people appear to have decided "in the last 12 hours," Wirthlin says, to vote for a candidate they thought was going to lose.

Bush's pollster, Robert Teeter, said he believed that what ultimately saved Bush was not so much better execution in the last 72 hours as his larger base of support going in to the final week. "Our polls showed us running at about a 40 percent support level for a year—and, of that, 30 percent was hard-core support. The Iowa loss stripped us right down to our hard-core. But we knew exactly who the 10 percent were, and we were able to go right back after them in a targeted way."

The Dole camp, meantime, was a step behind the curve all week. On the Wednesday after Iowa, it filmed an "innoculation" ad on taxes, in which Dole uttered the phrase, "I pledge to veto any tax increase which. . . ." But because of production and delivery glitches, the ad never showed, except for a few hours on one Boston station.

A rule of thumb in the closing days of a campaign is never to let an attack go unchallenged—and all week Dole had been accused of being a tax-hiker by his opponents. Many in the campaign now concede their failure to respond contributed to the margin of defeat. But all also say that larger forces—not the least of them their early-week surge and the media reaction to it—were at play. It's a suspicion that can neither be proved nor disproved—but one that is sure to crop up again in this age of non-stop polling.

Reprinted with permission from the *Washington Post.*

---

## WHO WON THE GEORGE BUSH-DAN RATHER DEBATE?

*Michael Robinson and Margaret Patrella, Public Opinion, March/April 1988*

Will you always remember where you were and what you were doing at 7:00 p.m. EST on Monday, January 25—the night George Bush took on Dan Rather? Maybe not. But you may remember the Bush-Rather debate as the only one to make real *news* in election year 1988.

The Bush-Rather imbroglio took place the evening President Reagan delivered his final State of the Union address, but the next night it was Bush-Rather, not Reagan, who led ABC and NBC news. "Nightline" devoted its entire broadcast to the exchange. CBS sheepishly treated the great debate story as a secondary piece, a backgrounder to its top story: that Bush still hadn't come clean on Iran-Contra.

Brawling live on the evening news ensures one thing—people will find out about it. Within forty-eight hours of the Bush-Rather interview, 78 percent of adults surveyed by Gallup for the Times Mirror Company had heard about it—a level of penetration usually reserved for national disasters, military combat, or terrorist acts.

Millions of Americans felt the need to say they'd seen this historic interview, whether they had or not. According to the Times Mirror/Gallup survey, 29 percent of the population said they saw the actual interview; the Nielsen ratings indicate that two-thirds of them were mistaken or had confused news coverage of the interview with the interview itself. While the event was taking place, only the cognoscenti realized anything was happening.

Public reaction to the Bush-Rather fracas mimicked the reaction to President Gerald Ford's legendary blunder in his foreign policy debate with Jimmy Carter. Ford had insisted that the Soviet Union doesn't dominate Eastern Europe or, particularly, Poland. Yet, few viewers recognized this as the political gaffe of the decade until the press told them it was.

In the Bush-Rather debate on January 25, the CBS viewing public may have had little inkling that they were watching television news history in the making. In fact, the audience for CBS News *fell* during the interview, while the audience for NBC rose slightly. Even in Washington, D.C. (!), according to Nielsen, the CBS audience fell by 18,000 homes during the interview; NBC's audience picked up 15,000 homes during the same 15-minute period.

It is possible that anger with Rather drove away CBS viewers, but it's more likely that most left because they were bored or confused and wanted real network news, not talking heads. Think not? Consider this: CBS lost about a tenth of its audience the night of the interview: it gained two million the next night, as viewers learned (via the media) that what had happened was worth following.

### Was Rather "Bushwhacked?"

The vice president insists that he did not know CBS planned to make the Iran-Contra affair the sole basis for its Bush profile or for the subsequent interview with Rather. CBS insists that Bush knew what was coming and that Bush attacked Rather as part of a cynical ploy to make the vice president look tough. As far as the public was concerned, opinions split just about evenly on questions of performance, blame, and justification.

A slim majority (51 percent) thought that Dan Rather was rude (*Time*/Yankelovich). But a slightly larger majority (59 percent) thought Rather was right to push Bush on his role in Iran-Contra (*Time*/Yankelovich). The Times Mirror survey asked whether Rather had been fair or unfair in the way he conducted the interview: 44 percent said fair; 44 percent said unfair. *Newsweek*/Gallup found that 37 percent felt that Rather had done a good, tough job in the interview, but 37 percent also said he had been too aggressive. *Time's* poll pitted Rather against Bush directly in what is probably the only trial-heat ever conducted between a legitimate presidential candidate and a news anchor. Bush "won" the head-to-head. Forty-two percent felt he had done a better job in the interview; 27 percent said Rather had. But that finding is muddied by others in the same *Time* survey. According to *Time's* data, the public is still twice as likely to trust Rather to tell the truth as to trust Bush.

Given all the polls, either Bush or Rather can claim that he didn't lose to the other. That's probably a better outcome than CBS expected. Initial phone call response to the interview ran overwhelmingly in favor of Bush and against Rather. On Tuesday night ABC and NBC both noted that public response had gone decidedly for the vice president. Only Bruce Morton at CBS said that by the end of the following day phone calls in Iowa were running much more evenly—seven to six in favor of Bush.

Consider the debate itself to have been a public opinion draw, or at best, a split decision with a slight tilt toward the vice president.

### The Iowa Target Audience: No Measurable Impact

One immediate and reasonable assumption was that Bush's performance would help the vice president's standing in his party and possibly in the election contests to come. Republicans were most likely to blame Rather and to applaud Bush. But in Iowa, where the caucuses were about to take place, Bush gained next to no real support for his on-camera bravura. Gallup data indicate that Bush may actually have *lost* support among likely Republican caucus-goers and among Republican identifiers.

Among all registered voters in Iowa, 13 percent said the CBS incident made them feel more favorably toward Bush; 22 percent said less. Even among Republicans Bush did only so-so, with 22 percent saying they felt worse. The rest—66 percent of the Republican sample—didn't know about the interview, didn't care about the interview, or stood pat in their attitudes toward the vice president.

The only group in Iowa that expressed *unequivocal* improvement in its overall attitude toward Bush as a consequence of his attack on Rather was made up of people who supported him anyway. Not since ABC's *The Day After* has a televised political event produced so much controversy and so little real effect.

### The Story CBS Failed to Mention

Four days after the Bush-Rather incident, CBS's Bob Schieffer used results from the Times Mirror/Gallup survey for a news story. He began with the results that made Bush

look bad—those that dealt with the public's lingering doubts about Iran-Contra. Schieffer then used the data that showed the public evenly divided about Rather's fairness during the interview.

Schieffer's presentation was consistent with the way CBS played the story all week—emphasizing whatever made Bush appear to be the loser in all this. In fact, Schieffer failed to mention some of the other major findings from that Times Mirror/Gallup survey: that Rather had dropped seven points in overall favorability from three months before the interview to two days after; that Rather had fallen eighteen points in overall favorability between April 1987 and late January 1988—an unprecedented decline in anchorman image in the four-year history of the "People and the Press" polls. Almost all of Rather's January decline was partisan, from Republicans. Beyond that hint, there is no way to know how much the interview cost Rather.

But we do know this: Rather's rapid decline in public approval coincides with a significant weakening of support for news organizations in general, and most particularly for network news. While overall favorability ratings of network news have not declined significantly, the proportion of those expressing "very favorable" opinions has fallen by more than 50 percent. In June 1985, 25 percent of the public expressed "very favorable" opinions of network news. This figure had climbed to 30 percent by August of 1985, and it was still there in July 1986. But by early 1987, the figure had dropped to 19 percent, and it was consistently low when measured in the spring and fall of 1987 (21 and 19 percent respectively). Following the Bush-Rather interview, it slid further to 12 percent, an all-time low in the "People and the Press" surveys.

Newspapers have not suffered from this erosion, but news organizations have. In fact, on a central question of credibility, there has been a marked shift downward. As of January 1988, 44 percent of the public felt that "news organizations get the facts straight"—down eleven points from two and a half years ago.

There are some interesting anomalies here. While Rather has been sliding, ABC's Peter Jennings' image has been holding fairly constant (74 percent favorable in autumn 1987, 78 percent favorable this January), and Tom Brokaw over at NBC has been on a roll. What with his interview of Gorbachev and his starring role in the first televised debate ever to include all candidates for both parties, Brokaw jumped ten points between autumn 1987 (69 percent) and late January this year (79 percent).

But the general pattern for broadcast news is down in 1987-1988, and Rather may be more than a symbol of its decline. He may be part of the cause. During the earliest rounds of "People and the Press," Rather used to run ahead of the networks and the other anchors. Now he's running behind his peers and the industry.

In 1985 the Gallup data suggested that Rather produced a positive coattail effect for broadcast journalism and CBS. Now he may be leading public opinion away from the news media and becoming something of a public opinion liability, regardless of the quality of his journalism. And his negative coattail started at least a year before his fight with Bush.

### Blaming the Messenger

Slippage in network image and credibility raises the specter of the kill-the-messenger syndrome. Is the public blaming the networks or Rather for their behavior, or for the behavior of the politicians they cover?

Press history during the last two decades suggests that the public blames the bearer of bad news under some conditions, but credits him under others. What Bush-Rather suggests is that we're in an era in which it's bury-the-messenger, not praise him.

The only scientific evidence on this question comes to us from the research of Seymour Martin Lipset and William Schneider. Their work during the sixties and seventies indicates that public support for the press *improves* when the press takes on the government, acts like a watchdog, and reports bad news. Watergate is, of course, the best example of bad news enhancing perceived media credibility.

But what's happened recently suggests the contrary. Since Iran-Contra and during Campaign 1988, bad news and tough reporting on network television have correlated with *declining* credibility. For the last year and a half at least, the messenger has been blamed, not credited.

The explanation for this is fairly straightforward, and the Bush-Rather affair is a useful illustration. The severity of a politician's "crime" proves to be the determining factor. In Watergate, for example, the Nixon White House's missteps came to be almost universally regarded as serious. The press helped uncover violations of law and of political norms that were fundamental, and the public applauded. That was then; this is now. Setting aside Iran-Contra for a moment, consider the kinds of "crimes" the watchdog has warned us about during the last campaign year. How about Joe Biden? Biden didn't violate the basic political culture. He violated an academic convention—a prohibition against plagiarism. And he violated a social norm; he lied about his grades in law school and college. Nothing in that attacks the heart of democracy. And how about Senator Hart? He violated his marriage vows. But again he never broke the law or flouted the Constitution or betrayed his oath of office. During the last year, then, the metaphor for the press is not so much "watchdog" as "peeping Tom." Watchdogs get credit; peeping Toms get something else. The "severity of crime" interpretation does not accommodate news about Iran-Contra as easily, however. These issues are serious, and the Democrats, at least, insist that laws were broken by this government since at least 1985. But press scores *fell* during the initial revelations about Iran-Contra in late 1986. How come? There are three possibilities. First, the case is still open on who did what in Iran-Contra. The jury is still out and may be deadlocked. Second, this was less a crime than a stupid blunder. The public gives less credit to the press for revealing idiocy than it does for exposing a felony. Third, Reagan was exceptionally popular when all this began to break open. So the press really had a tough time gaining credit for tainting a political hero.

So, in short, the watchdog gets credit when the crime against the community is palpable, certain, and committed by somebody with a so-so image and credibility. The messenger gets the blame when the crime is seen as farce, politics as usual, or still to be proven.

The Bush-Rather affair, then, is a perfect instance where the press has failed to show the public a crime serious enough and certain enough to merit the kind of behavior Rather displayed. In essence, Rather barked too loudly and rudely, given the issue at stake and the uncertainty of Bush's guilt. In the end this sort of thing hurts the networks as much as the politicians.

From *Public Opinion*, March/April 1988, pp. 43-45. Reprinted with permission from the American Enterprise Institute for Public Policy Research.

# CAPITAL LETTER

*William Boot, Columbia Journalism Review,
March/April 1988*

DAQ Enterprises
1300 Conduit Street, N.W.
Washington, D.C. 20005

November 15, 1989

Dear X:

This letter may pose the most important question you have ever been asked.

Our researchers have compiled a list of skilled professionals—including advertising executives, professors, poets, board game designers, scriptwriters for daytime television— who have made employment agency inquiries about less mentally taxing work.

Your name, X, is on that list.

Our question is this—have you ever considered journalism?

We at DAQ Enterprises feel you have a strong aptitude for analyzing major news events in Washington—a job in which, paradoxically perhaps, you must never reveal that you have any thoughts, ideas, or opinions of your own.

Judging by your background, we are confident we could place you in a Washington news operation, perhaps in one of our own rapidly expanding DAQ news franchises.

Once you are on the job, DAQ will, for an affordable subscription fee, provide all the support and backup you'll need to flourish . . .

December 18, 1989

Dear X:

Congratulations on your new job in Washington! As promised, we are writing to offer advice, help, and professional support services. . . .

Bear in mind, X, that the unwritten rules of journalistic objectivity require you to behave as if you are intellectually helpless. The Washington news analyst's role is not unlike Ingrid Bergman's in *Casablanca*, when she falls into a swoon and murmurs to Humphrey Bogart, "Oh, I don't know what's right any longer. You have to do the thinking for both of us, for all of us."

Bogart, playing tough and decisive Rick,

replies: "All right, I *will*. Here's looking at you, kid."

In much the same spirit, Washington pundits (think-tank scholars, political consultants, etc.) do the thinking for the press corps. DAQ is the world's largest clearinghouse for punditry.

Put us at your service. Our easy-to-understand political and foreign policy analyses will place the day's conventional wisdom at your fingertips almost instantaneously.

And that's not all. Suppose (for the sake of argument) that you come up with an idea or news interpretation of your own. We will express it for you (assuming, of course, that it is not too extreme and does not contradict the conventional wisdom). You simply quote us, thereby preserving your aura of objectivity.

You won't often find yourself catching flak from an editor for using too many sources "who spoke on condition that they not be identified." At DAQ Enterprises (formerly Dial-a-Quote), we speak only on condition that we be *conspicuously* identified. Our sole purpose is to be quoted in the news media.

Here are just a few of the top experts you'll be talking to:

—William Schneider (middle-aged, centrist political scientist, American Enterprise Institute). Quoted some 300 times in major U.S. newspapers in 1987, and the trend has been upward. Designated "Aristotle of American politics" by *Boston Globe* (1/12/87) in 287-line piece lauding his insight.

Sample quote: "Bush is . . . riding on Reagan's coattails" (*Los Angeles Times*, 1/4/88).

—Stephen Hess (middle-aged, centrist political scientist, Brookings Institution). Cited roughly 100 times by major U.S. papers in 1987 (typical newspaper reference: "Presidential scholar Stephen Hess . . . notes that Bush has one of the most impressive resumes of anyone ever to seek the White House"—*Christian Science Monitor*, 12/28/87). Hess says that in 1987 he fielded about twelve reporters' calls per workday. That made for a rough annual average of 2,880, if you factor in a two-week vacation and ten public holidays. As Hess says, "Answering reporters' questions can be very time-consuming."

—Norman J. Ornstein, (middle-aged, centrist political scientist, American Enterprise Institute—but he really needs no introduction). Dubbed "King of Quotes" in *Washington Monthly*. Known for energetic efforts to return reporters' calls. Reassuring nickname, Norm, neatly describes middle-of-road position. *Washington Monthly* reporter Steven Waldman called him living embodiment of the conventional wisdom (12/86).

Ornstein quote: "People want a hard-nosed, knowledgeable chief executive" (States News Service, 12/29/87).

From a scant two dozen major newspaper references in 1981, Ornstein blossomed until in 1986-87 he was quoted some 600 times in media outlets ranging from *The New York Times* to *Ladies' Home Journal*, *Sport* magazine, and *700 Club*. He has addressed subjects ranging from the trade deficit to tax reform, abortion, pizza, and professional football. Entirely conceivable but as yet untapped Ornstein subject areas include investment strategies, household tips, medical diagnoses, advice to the lovelorn, and best opening lines in singles' bars.

Others in DAQ's stable of experts include former secretaries of state and defense, ex-United Nations ambassadors, and a host of independent consultants, all with steel-trap minds.

To enliven your copy, you can turn to any one of them for a deftly revamped cliche ("A lot of these [campaign-spending] loopholes are large enough to drive a rental car through"—political consultant Bob Beckel, *New York Times*, 12/19/87) or a spicy analogy ("In playing for small potatoes with Kuwait we risk losing the big enchilada, Iran"—foreign policy expert Robert Hunter, Reuters, 6/11/87; "It is the big enchilada"—Hunter on the INF treaty, Reuters, 12/27/87).

Now, you may be thinking that some of the sample quotes we have repeated above are a bit, well, self-evident. The truth, X, is that in Washington you can't do without glaringly obvious quotes. Your editors will insist that even straightforward points be bolstered by authorities to enhance the credibility of your articles. It doesn't matter so much what the experts say—it's who they are that counts.

In the era of the sound bite and the 20-second news analysis, expertise has taken on an entirely new meaning. The more a person is quoted, the more of an expert he or she by definition becomes; the more he or she is defined as an expert, the more that person will be quoted. Not to take advantage of this perpetual motion machine would be folly for a fledgling Washington journalist. So step aboard, sit back, and enjoy the ride.

Certain nay-sayers have taken pot-shots at the press corps for relying too exclusively on Schneider, Ornstein, Georgetown U's Michael

Robinson, political consultants Bob Beckel, John Sears, Frank Greer, etc. *New York Times* reporter R.W. Apple, for instance, has accused these experts of purveying "pseudo-facts" that masquerade as reality in the pre-campaign period.

But guess to whom reporters turned for help in assessing the significance of this sort of anti-pundit critique? To the pundits themselves, of course—William Schneider (*Boston Globe*, 1/12/87), Michael Robinson, and Frank Greer (both, *Atlanta Journal* and *Constitution*, 1/2/88), none of whom seemed to think the Republic was in grave danger.

Our experts have staying power. They won't let you down.

According to *The Washington Monthly*, some busybodies in the higher reaches of the *Los Angeles Times* once got the idea that their paper was quoting Norm Ornstein too often—sixteen times in 1985—and imposed an Ornstein moratorium. It didn't stick. In 1986, the paper used him twenty-four times; in 1987, some twenty-five.

To repeat, our experts have staying power. In fact, for a while their very popularity became a problem.

By mid-1989, Norm Ornstein's name recognition as measured in the Gallup poll exceed that of all politicians he was commenting about, including the president. After he began substituting for Pat Sajak as host of *Wheel of Fortune*, further expanding his news appeal, Ornstein was logging 100,000 journalists' calls per month. Access became difficult. Other leading pundits were swamped as well. This put Washington reporters into one hell of a bind.

Luckily, the seeds of a solution were visible as early as October 1987, when an electronic newsletter called *Presidential Campaign Hotline* made its appearance. Each morning reporters could call up that day's edition of *Hotline* on their office computer consoles and read the comments of the pundit of the day. The service enabled journalists to lift quotes without making a call—a blessing when the line was busy, although asking follow-up questions was a mite difficult.

*Hotline* was an inspiration to us, but it was primitive. DAQ took the basic idea and expanded it exponentially. The result is INSTA-QUOTE, a computerized answer to your every news need. Our software specialists have closely studied the writings and utterances of Ornstein, Schneider, and all the others. They have come up with data programs that capture the mindset, the quirks, and sense of humor, and we think the essential spirit of each expert.

Subscribers to INSTAQUOTE (Visa and MasterCard accepted) can call and conduct actual give-and-take conversations with our electronic savants. A 3-D hologram service is available for on-camera sessions. (Each flesh-and-blood expert is a DAQ stockholder and owns the copyright to his or her software personality.)

Our data programming technique provides an extra dimension which you might not have considered. The passage of time is no barrier to INSTAQUOTE, which relies solely on the written, audio tape, and video record of human thought. Subscribe now and, at no extra charge, you can conduct in-depth interviews with long-silent authorities, among them:

—Walter Lippmann (all topics)
—Colonel Edward House (the fourteen points, Woodrow Wilson)
—Thomas "Tommy the Cork" Corcoran (life as an FDR brain-truster)
—Field Marshall Erwin Rommel (strategy and tactics)
—James Madison (the intent of the framers)
This special offer is for a limited time only, so sign up today. Don't shortchange your future. Welcome to the perpetual motion machine and good luck in Washington!

Sincerely,

Bob Keister, C.E.O.

William Boot is the pseudonym of a Washington reporter "who writes for newspapers around the world." Reprinted with permission from the *Columbia Journalism Review*, March/April, 1988.

---

## THE OUTSIDE STORY

*Richard Brookhiser*

In the last days of the 1960 presidential election, a party of New York's finest, led by a deputy chief inspector of police—there were no Secret Service phalanxes then—boarded the upper deck of the old Brooklyn-Staten Island ferry, swept the lone passenger, a teenage kid, into a corner, and made way for the entourage of John Kennedy. The race was tight, the state was crucial, Kennedy looked exhausted. During the ferry ride, the Senator's aides readied him for the debarkation. One helped him into a fresh shirt. One passed a windup shaver over his face (where was *he* when Richard Nixon needed him?). One read through a sheaf of greetings, notes, messages, to which Kennedy responded with number-coded answers (as, give him a three, he gets a seven). A fourth aide, the most important, squatted in front of the candidate and flashed a series of photos, accompanied by biographical patter: *This is Mike O'Brien [say], Seventeenth Precinct, his son plays basketball for Villanova. Joe Antonelli, Twenty-third AD, his wife works with the deaf* . . . and so on, through the whole Brooklyn Democratic machine. By the time the boat touched Bay Ridge, the candidate was refreshed, rejuvenated, and rewired. When the gangway lowered, Kennedy didn't wait for it to fall completely into place, but gave a little hop ashore (so youthful was he). There to greet him were all the pols he had just been briefed on; back it all came. *Mike, hear good things about your son. Joe, it's great what your wife is doing. . . .*They loved it; there were even damp eyes . . .

There was a lot in that glimpse: a shot of the Kennedy apparatus in action; a sense of the grinding routine we exact from all candidates; a sense of the even more grinding zeal with which they perform it. Only a glimpse, but a thousand make a picture. The only trouble with this small story is that no one ever reported it. The inside view never made it outside. Kennedy's ferry ride did not appear in *The Making of the President: 1960*, still less in the court histories. It doesn't even appear in the revisionist trashings. It reaches print here, 26 years later, only because the kid on the upper deck became a colleague of my wife's.

That is the trouble with inside stories generally. There is no omnipresence, and hence, no omniscience. You see one vignette, you miss 50. The candidates themselves are not privy to everything worth seeing; how can observers be?

What is true of inside events is still more true of less concrete actions. Who is rising, and who supports him? Who is out, and who gave him the shove? What was the motive? What was the intention (not always the same thing)? Where will the next backstage maneuver come from? The answers to these questions can only come from the principals, which in the short run means they do not come at all. Either the parties don't talk, or they talk, self-servingly, all over the front page of tomorrow's *Washington Post*. When there is no consensus of testimony, there is only judgment. When there is consensus, there may be deception, and self-deception. Historians, with time and patience, can sift the conflicting accounts, and politicians must judge them by the seat of their pants every day. But the elusiveness of inside stories is an insurmountable problem of instant histories.

There is another way of looking at American presidential elections. That is to focus on what the candidates and their supporters say and do in public; to leave the green room and the wings and go out front, and attend, with respect, to the performance. In the course of the 1984 campaign, eight men sought the nomination of one of the major parties. The winner and his running mate then took on the incumbents, the nominees of the other major party. In the last year of the campaign alone, they spoke millions of words and made thousands of appearances. Surely they meant something by it? There were plenty of inside stories, too many; what of the outside story?

In looking at the outside story, several things emerge. Elections take on a deep calm. They are no longer brawls, marathons, endless aimless scrums. All the chaos and bawdry remains, enough for the most avid connoisseur, but it falls into simpler forms. Politicians, it turns out, are actually saying something; their antics have a purpose.

The voters, it seems, pay attention. There are good structural reasons why this should be so. Politics must be public wherever there are voters. In hermetic, totalitarian societies, where politics consists entirely of secret backstabbing, all stories are inside stories. The only source in Sofia is Deep Throat. In a democracy, however, where power is achieved only through presenting oneself to the public, politicians are obliged to be demonstrative. Since most politicians who aspire to be President have presented themselves repeatedly over a substantial career, they are also obliged to be moderately sincere. They cannot lie promiscuously, and mere razzle-dazzle wears thin. So it is that an outside story exists, and that voters do well to take note of it.

That is theory; the outside story can also be tested in practice. Jimmy Carter's 1976 rise from nowhere was the epitome of modern political technique. Four years later, George Bush (evidently assuming that technique had been decisive) alone of the Republican hopefuls studied the Carter game plan. He, like Carter, was rewarded with an Iowa Surprise. Suddenly Big Mo—the phrase Bush used to describe his momentum—was inevitable, unstoppable; Ronald Reagan was washed up, burned out. But only a month later, Bush perished like a bug on a windshield. Inside-story specialists came up with appropriate explanations for his collapse—Bush talked too much about his sudden prospects (but wasn't the image of snowballing success part of the plan?); Reagan's staff got its act together (why not before?); Reagan began showing spunk, particularly at a pre-primary debate in Nashua, New Hampshire, where Bush appeared stiff and indecisive. Yet would spunk have done Reagan any good if he hadn't also had forceful themes? Would dithering have done Bush any harm if he had had any? Isn't it possible that Reagan's 1980 campaign had a clear message while Bush's was murky?

The 1940 presidential race, though ancient history, figures in a clutch of recent biographies of some of the principals in a way that makes it even more suggestive. The Republican contest that year was honeycombed with inside stories. The campaign of Wendell Wilkie had more cheerleaders than the Dallas Cowboys. *Time, Life, Look, The Saturday Evening Post* all puffed him shamelessly. The editor of *Fortune* became his campaign manager; the book review editor of the New York *Herald Tribune* ghosted his speeches (she was also his mistress—an early instance of user-friendliness). Wilkie also profited from old-fashioned dirty tricks. The chairman of the Republican convention's committee on arrangements, a Wilkie man, aborted a rival's speech by slipping in a dead mike. He also packed the galleries of the hall, so that the hapless delegates were battered by unceasing roars of "We Want Wilkie"—the Big Mo of 1940. For the race against Franklin Roosevelt, Wilkie was armed with copies of crackpot letters that FDR's running mate, Henry Wallace, had sent to a Russian theosophist.

I have been thinking of you holding the casket [wrote the man who wanted to be a heartbeat away]—the sacred, most precious casket. And I have thought of the new country going forth, to meet the seven stars under the sign of the three stars. And I have thought of the admonition, "Await the stones."

The Wallace letters were never used, perhaps because Roosevelt had copies of letters from Wilkie to his ghost writer.

But there was also an issue. Germany invaded Norway and Denmark in April and the Low Countries in May. France collapsed the week before the Republican convention opened. Of all the GOP hopefuls, Wilkie was the only one forthrightly committed to helping embattled England. His rise in the esteem of Republicans tracked Europe's fall. The election offered a less clear-cut choice, partly because Wilkie and Roosevelt both were internationalists at heart, partly because they both lied and waffled as the fall wore on. But the issue remained, and the electorate remained concerned. What did the majority finally place its trust in—Roosevelt's ability to steer through a period of international havoc, or his Teflon quality? Were the voters more affected by Hitler, or by the wheelings and dealings of *Fortune*?

This doesn't mean that politicians, or voters, choose wisely—that they always hit on the right remedies for the country's problems, or even the right ones for the problems they see. I do believe, though, that most presidential candidates are trying to offer something, and that most voters are trying to judge.

A few things the outside story is not. One approach to elections, which is superficially similar to it, in that it also seems to take into account public appeals, is the analysis of imagery. The cut of hair, the tone of voice, the subliminal cues—all these are indeed fashioned for public consumption. The most successful shapers of imagery—Ronald Reagan comes to mind—do not even exert their power consciously: the charm flows out of them, without thought or effort. Yet "How the Image Makers Do It" is in fact another inside story, reducing the relation between the candidates and the electorate to another set of inexplicit maneuvers and manipulations. The disposition to keep one's eye on imagery may derive from a larger social theory, that advertising controls markets. Fifties economists, brooding on tail fins, concluded that Detroit, allied with Madison Avenue, could get anything it wanted. Three decades later, Washington was bailing out Chrysler. The look-so-fine school of political science has had its own Chryslers, as mediagenic candidates falter and uncomely ones (Nixon, even shaven) endure.

The outside story is also more than a simple rundown of policy proposals. The kinds of promises that find their way into party platforms and political speeches are worth reading, and when they are broken, as they often are, the fact should be pondered for its political significance. But candidates are also judged on more than their promises—for a promise is always more than itself. Who makes a promise and how it is made materially affect the pledge. Candidates define their promises by the records they have fashioned, by the supporters they tolerate, by the rhetoric they use. Of the three, rhetoric can mean the most. What a politician would like to do, even if only in an ideal world, is important because it gives a clue to what he is likely to attempt in this world. "A man's arguments," wrote G.K. Chesterton, "show what he is up to."

The outside story, finally, never explains just one contest. We are always "up to" more than one election at a time. The only thing politicians care about as much as the next election is the one after that. They plan for it in all the "inside" ways—buying friends, buying off competitors, blocking enemies. But their most important preparation is their performance. Rhetoric opens all the little trails and wagon tracks which become the interstates of the future. A politician shows, by what he says and does, where he thinks the electorate is headed (and how only he can lead them there). The voters show, by their response, where at least they might be willing to go.

## TELEVISION: OBSESSION OF THE ERA

*George F. Will*

. . . Paradoxically, this penchant for simple, not to say simple-minded, explanations may be a result of new sophistication and complexity of campaigning. As the machinery of politics—polling, direct mail, and all the rest—has become more elaborate, there have been more nuts and bolts for political journalists to know about. Political journalism has become more preoccupied with mechanisms and cosmetics. Television, especially, has encouraged the notion that a vivid gesture or memorable "sound bite" seen by millions of people at a dramatic juncture of a campaign must be as consequential as it is conspicuous.

Theodore White had a reporter's tendency to believe that vivid events are as important as they are vivid. He wrote, wrongly, that Ronald Reagan won the 1980 New Hampshire primary by seizing the microphone at the Nashua debate. Actually, Reagan had surged ahead well before that. Perhaps journalistic narcissism makes journalists think that communications technologies are the levers that move history—hence White's obsession with television. He called it "the most unsettling event in Western Society since the invention of printing."[1] However it is easy to make too much—and White did—of the Republican delegate in 1968 who said he could not switch from Nixon to Reagan because, "I told CBS that I'm voting for Nixon. I'm pledged to CBS."[2]

O! Television! It is the obsession of the era. It is time to say something about what it does, and what it does not do.

It has been said that once when Disraeli was canvassing for votes door to door, a woman opened the door and Disraeli paused, then, explaining his pause, exclaimed: "I was overcome by the resemblance to my sainted mother—and she was a very beautiful woman." Candidates no longer win by canvassing door to door, dispensing charm like Disraeli. (His gallantry was all the more gallant because it was politically wasted: the woman could not vote.) They stomp into our living rooms via television. They get on television because they are newsworthy, and because they are products that pay to advertise themselves.

Suppose in the campaign's final 60 days each candidate averages two minutes on the evening news. In that case the period after Labor Day is the final 240 minutes of the campaign. True, there also are paid media, but their job is to amplify themes established on the evening newscasts. However, paid media mesmerize political journalists and reformers. . . .

NOTES

1. Theodore H. White, *America in Search of Itself: The Making of the President 1956-1980* (New York: Harper & Row, 1982), "Interpassage: Ideas in Motion," p. 101.
2. Ibid., "The Reign of Television," p. 185.

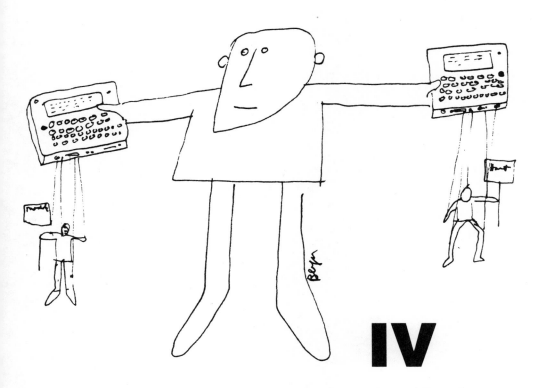

# IV

## RESOURCE
## MATERIAL

# ANNOTATED BIBILOGRAPHY ON NEW TECHNOLOGY AND POLITICS

*Marcus Matthews*

The literature on communication technologies in politics has expanded along with utilization of these technologies. Following is a discussion of the most representative. This is a continuation of work started by Anthony Fellow in *New Communication Technologies in Politics* (Washington, D.C., Annenberg Washington Program, 1985).

## General Works

The definitive account of the modern practice of politics in the age of computer consultants and their technological tools is Sabato's (1981) *The Rise of Political Consultants: New Ways of Winning Elections*. Among the topics discussed are polling, political action committees and ethical questions. Sabato also describes the Claritas Clustering System in detail and includes comments from political consultants on what their work involves.

One of the first books that addressed the takeover of political campaigning by technology was Perry's (1968) *The New Politics*. This "new politics" included the utilization of computers, professional campaign consultants, television commercials and pollsters. Another early manual that highlights electronic campaign technology is Napolitan's (1972) *The Election Game and How to Win It*. He presents case studies from presidential, gubernatorial and congressional campaigns, and the lessons he outlines are still insightful and revealing.

In their informative and entertaining *The Spot*, which chronicles the rise of political advertising on television, Diamond and Bates (1984) describe a new form of political communication that has appeared in the last few decades, one that depends on high technology and big dollars: television advertising. They argue that elections and campaigns might be turning into a type of spectator sport via television— something to watch and enjoy as entertainment, but not necessarily participate in by voting.

In the same vein, Wilson's "Presidential Advertising in 1988" (1987) shows the new technologies available to candidates with regard to their political advertising. His chronology of the history of political advertising is especially informative.

Blumenthal (1982) in *The Permanent Campaign* describes how consultants package and then sell candidates before, during and after elections. He argues that the permanent campaign is part of a profound technological revolution based on computers and telecommunications. In *Teledemocracy*, Arterton (1987) takes a comprehensive look at the impact of new communication technologies on democratic political life. His study raises disturbing questions about the future of democracy in a world continually facing rapid technological changes.

Goldberg (1984) in his article "Political Campaigns and New Technology: Winning Elections with a Computer" provides examples of how to use computers for targeting, direct mail, campaign organization and election day strategies. He also discusses computer and software costs.

A more academic work is *Political Communication in America*. Denton and Woodward (1985) present a well-researched look at the professionalization of political communication by the political consulting industry. They also discuss communication patterns within American political institutions.

The best work on nonvoting is *Why Americans Don't Vote* by Ruy A. Teixeira.

In addition, a number of journals and magazines are useful. Among the most helpful are *Campaigns & Elections*, *Election Politics*, *Congressional Quarterly*, *National Journal*, *The Journal of Communication*, *PC World* and *Computerworld*.

### Developments in Targeting Research

In "Geodemographics: The New Magic," Robbin (1980) faults previous targeting procedures since at most only a few variables were considered. He develops a multivariate approach which allows him to consider multiple variables in a single analysis. By utilizing United States Census data, Robbin's approach locates voters most responsive to political candidates or issue-oriented referenda.

Mockus (1980) relates in "Geodemographics II: Targeting Your Turnout" how Robbin's techniques were successfully used to defeat a 1978 "Right-to-Work" proposition in Missouri.

Schneider (1983) in "Geodemographics Refined: An Alternative to Standardized Clustering," discusses a refinement of geodemographic targeting methods. He incorporates certain types of census information along with political data. Also, instead of standardized clusters, survey-driven clusters are used. In his series of articles on "Electoral Targeting," Fishel (1983) demonstrates how to do electoral targeting at home, how to process and analyze data, and how to build an electoral targeting database.

In "Innovations in Campaign Research: Finding the Voters in the 1980s" Kramer and Schneider (1985) discuss the various applications of geodemographics and the implications of new technologies on further professionalization of campaigning. They also question whether demographic stereotyping will further de-individualize political views and whether these new technologies are driving politics, rather than vice-versa.

Power (1987) in "Plug in to Cable TV" asserts that cable television is an efficient way for any candidate to reach a target audience with a specifically constructed message. He discusses a powerful cartography service which is being developed that will merge demographic and geographic information. He also speculates on how in the future candidates will target precise groups of voters on local stations.

In "Direct Mail on Target," Reilly (1987) presents a case study which shows how a targeted direct-mail strategy helped win a California state senate seat. He shows how the integration of computers and campaign dollars allowed targeted individualized messages to be directed to a splintered electorate.

### Reaching Voters

Paley and Moffett (1984) in "The New Electronic Media— Instant Action and Reaction" point out the advantages of cable television for reaching the electorate. They also highlight the abilities of computerized telemarketing and two-way interactive communications, such as interactive cable and personal computer networks. Paley and Moffett say that these new technologies are underutilized because many advertisers are reluctant to experiment with new media and worry about their effectiveness.

Tobe (1985) in "New Techniques in Computerized Voter Contact" examines how political databases enable targeting of direct mail to be more precise. According to Tobe, these databases enable candidates to personalize direct mail, enabling the candidate to treat each voter as an individual. He argues that in the best databases social stereotyping is minimized by having as much information on the voter as possible.

In "From Telephone to Telelobby: Two Decades of Targeted Communications" Reese (1985) describes his use of modern geodemographic techniques to move voters, but says that despite the use of more sophisticated technologies, the core of a successful campaign is organization at the grass roots level. Personal contact through the new technologies makes these contact methods more efficient.

Tkach (1982) in "Microcomputers: Their Use in Small-Scale Political Campaigning" discusses how he used an inexpensive microcomputer in an annual school board election in Montana. In a related article, "Micros: How to Buy and

Use Them in Campaigns," Tkach (1983) shows that microcomputers allow more cost-effective campaign spending if used properly.

In "Voter Registration Tapes: Mining for New Votes, New Voters & New Money," Getter and Titus (1984) contend that only about ten percent of the potential of voter registration data is applied in most campaigns. They present a step-by-step approach to getting the most out of voter registration data, and demonstrate how to solve problems that may develop from this data.

In *The Party's Just Begun* Sabato (1988) argues that while the two major political parties have never been organizationally stronger at the national level, they have never been weaker at the grassroots level than they are today. He states that diminishing party strength is likely to lead to further declines in voter turnout, but finds that the new technologies of politics are being employed to reach voters and build more vital political parties.

### Effective Campaign Management

Steinberg's (1976) *The Political Campaign Handbook: Media, Scheduling and Advance* and *Campaign Management: A Systems Approach* are classics. Unlike most campaign manuals, Steinberg's discuss campaign management within the framework of management theory by referring to the basic management tools, techniques and principles for running a campaign.

Schwartzman's (1984) *Political Campaign Craftsmanship* is intended as a practical guide for potential candidates. The book manages to touch on radio, television, print and media advertising, as well as the use of telephones in a political campaign. Schwartzman also touches on more complex and expensive technological advances available to campaigns.

Thompson (1986) in "Computerized Video Wizardry" discusses the emergence of computer-generated graphics and how they have given media consultants the technology to expand their creative horizons.

In "On-line Opposition Research," Anders and Marlowe (1987) detail how on-line legislative databases which sort through bills and votes enable challengers to know every facet of incumbents' records and then design strategies that emphasize the weaknesses of opponents. They also compare major commercial databases. A complete survey of the new communication technologies that have come into use, such as videotext, teletext and on-line databases can be found in Aumente's (1987) *New Electronic Pathways*. In "Campaign Software Reviews" (1987), a panel of campaign and computer experts examine the features of seven software packages, comment on their relative strengths and weaknesses and then suggest the particular campaign each is best suited to serve.

Muncey (1987) in "More Power To Ya" tells how a new generation of microcomputers promises to bring changes to campaign management by offering individual campaign organizations the chance to gain much of the power previously reserved for large organizations. He examines these increased capabilities and the resulting benefits for campaigns and asserts these systems will play a greater role in future campaign management.

The availability of inexpensive microcomputers for campaigns is treated by Haber (1988) in "Computers for Microcampaigns." He concludes that a more computer-literate population will help smaller campaigns computerize themselves.

### Finance and Fundraising

A standard work on direct mail advertising is the Direct Mail Marketing Association's *Direct Marketing Handbook* which contains chapters on production, testing, fulfillment, creative approaches, and many other aspects of direct mail.

Kobs' *Profitable Direct Marketing* and Stone's *Successful Direct Marketing Methods* contain case studies and helpful approaches concerning direct mail techniques.

In "The Telephone as a Political Tool," Roman (1980) notes that the telephone will generate more contributions than any other existing media—if the operation is subject to a strict set of professional guidelines and businesslike controls. He also presents a guide to using the telephone productively for political purposes.

According to Craver (1985) in "Direct Mail and the Political Process" direct mail fundraising has enhanced participation in the political process by making it easier for people to participate. He is troubled, however, by the argument that direct mail only benefits certain groups. He claims it is neutral and merely allows ideas to compete.

An argument advanced by Jacobson (1980) in *Money in Congressional Elections* is that whether or not congressional campaigns are seriously contested depends on the resources mobilized by challengers. Jacobson also traces the politics of campaign finance legislation and the potential consequences of further changes in campaign finance policy.

Sabato (1981) in *The Rise of Political Consultants* devotes a chapter to the world of political direct mail. His "Direct Mail: The Poisoned Pen of Politics" is a thorough examination of how direct mail operates.

Heller (1987) uses "Mail, Money and Machiavelli" to spotlight California's unique reliance on highly sophisticated, targeted direct mail due to large jurisdictions, a diverse population and expensive media markets. He discusses how geographic targeting and its uses for voter contact are emphasized in that state, and the chances of such techniques becoming more widespread.

Several useful newsletters and periodicals that deal with direct mail and fundraising applications for political campaigns are available. These include *Fundraising Management Magazine, Advertising Age, Direct Mail News, Congressional Quarterly's Campaign Practices Reports*, the *Fundraising Institute's Newsletter* and the *KRC Letter.*

## Future Developments

The coming years promise to deliver a broad range of innovative communication technologies that will continue to influence and transform politics and the political process. Although scholars disagree on the effects and magnitude of such technological changes, none dispute their inevitability and importance.

In *The Coming Information Age* Dizard (1982) discusses whether full access to information, now drawing closer due to technological advances, is one of our basic rights. He also examines the ability of new technologies to permit manipulation of a wider range of information resources than ever before.

According to Brotman's (1980) "New Campaigning for the New Media," the western world is approaching a new level of democracy—one marked by a preeminently electronic community where opinion can be measured instantly.

Williams (1982) in *The Communications Revolution* sees the advent of "dial-in voting" and "part-time diplomacy," thanks to cable TV services.

In "The Political Impact of Information Technology" Lowi (1983) stresses that information technology will increase the power people have over their environment, but that susceptibility to manipulation will rise. Craver and Hallett (1987) discuss how the emergence of high speed microcomputers and the existence of more than 3,500 electronic databases give users access to vast amounts of information by using the common microcomputer and modem. "The Online Crystal Ball" goes on to discuss how issues can be tracked through various media to see how coverage differs. They conclude with a presentation of issues that emerged in management literature in the mid-1980s and are now receiving attention from politicians.

In "Is TV Losing Its Campaign Clout?" West (1986) discusses whether computers can transform campaigns in the late 1980s and 1990s in the same manner that television began radically altering modern politics three decades ago. He argues that recent advances in technology offer an enormous array of other options—such as cable TV and computer-targeted telephone solicitations. He posits that as a result of these changes standard television will no longer be such a dominant force in politics in future years.

Roan (1987) discusses how artificial intelligence will enable campaigns to rely on knowledge-based software in "Strategic Software for the '90s." He speaks of future computer systems which will allow information about a specific audience to be fed into a computer. The program will then compose audience-sensitive outlines which may be inserted into an integrated software package for final editing.

In "Communication in the Year 2000," a chapter in *Media: The Second God*, Schwartz (1981) sees the rise of new methods of communication technologies that will have profound effects on the political process. He cites the growth of interactive cable television systems, electronic political "town meetings" and voting from home via computer.

*The Electronic Commonwealth* by Abramson, Arterton and Orren (1988) discusses how different conceptions of democracy will be altered by the arrival of new political technologies. The book details the uses of the new electronic media in election campaigning and how organizations and government officials can use these and future innovations in their policy making.

# REFERENCES

Abramson, J.; Arterton, F.C.; and Orren, G. *The Electronic Commonwealth*. New York: Basic Books, 1988.

Anders, C. and Marlowe, H. "On-line Opposition Research." *Campaigns & Elections*, 7(6), (1987), 61-64.

Arterton, F.C. *Teledemocracy*. Newbury Park, CA: Sage Publications, 1987.

Aumente, J. *New Electronic Pathways*. Newbury Park, CA: Sage Publications, 1987.

Blumenthal, S. *The Permanent Campaign*. New York: Simon and Schuster, 1982.

Brotman, S.N. "New Campaigning for the New Media." *Campaigns & Elections*, II(3), (1981), 32-34.

"Campaign Software Reviews." *Campaigns & Elections*, 8(1), (1987), 22-29.

Craver, R.M. "Direct Mail and the Political Process." In *New Communication Technologies in Politics*. Edited by Robert Meadow. Washington, DC: Annenberg School of Communications, 1985.

Craver, R.M. and Hallett, J. "The Online Crystal Ball." *Campaigns & Elections*, 8(4), (1987), 46-49.

Denton, R.E. and Woodward, G.C. *Political Communication in America*. New York: Praeger, 1985.

Diamond, E. and Bates, S. *The Spot: The Rise of Political Advertising on Television*. Cambridge, MA: The MIT Press, 1984.

Dizard, W.P. *The Coming Information Age*. New York: Longman, 1982.

Fishel, M. "Electoral Targeting, Part I; For the Do-It Yourself Campaign." *Campaigns & Elections*, IV(1), (1983), 11-19.

Fishel, M. "Electoral Targeting, Part II: Analyzing the Data." *Campaigns and Elections*, IV(4), (1984), 61-66.

Fishel, M. and Kinsey, D. "Electoral Targeting, Part III: Computerizing the Process." *Campaigns & Elections*, IV(4), (1984), 61-66.

Getter, R.W. and Titus, J.E. "Voter Registration Tapes: Mining for New Votes, New Voters and New Money." *Campaigns & Elections*, IV(4), (1984), 67-74.

Goldberg, B. "Political Campaigns and New Technology: Winning Elections with a Computer." *Legislative Policy*, March/April 1984, 5-11.

Haber, J. "Computers for Microcampaigns." *Campaigns & Elections*, 8(5), (1988), 55-58.

Heller, D.J. "Mail, Money and Machiavelli." *Campaigns & Elections*, 8(4), (1987), 32-45.

Kobs, J. *Profitable Direct Marketing: How to Start, Improve or Expand Any Direct Marketing Operation*. Chicago: Crain Books, 1979.

Kramer, K.L. and Schneider, E.J. "Innovations in Campaign Research: Finding the Voters in the 1980s." In *New Communication Technologies in Politics*. Edited by Robert Meadow. Washington, DC: Annenberg School of Communications, 1985.

Lowi, T.J. "The Political Impact of Information Technology." In *The Microelectronics Revolution: The Complete Guide to the New Technology and Its Impact on Society*. Edited by T. Forester. Cambridge, MA: The MIT Press, 1983.

Mockus, J. "Geodemographics II: Targeting Your Turnout." *Campaigns & Elections*, I(2), (1980), 55-63.

Muncey, C. "More Power To Ya." *Campaigns & Elections*, 8(4), (1987), 61-65.

Napolitan, J. *The Election Game and How to Win It*. Garden City, NY: Doubleday and Co., 1972.

Paley, W.C. and Moffett, S. "The New Electronic Media—Instant Action and Reaction." *Campaigns & Elections*, IV(4), (1984).

Perry, J.M. *The New Politics*. New York: Clarkson N. Potter, Inc., 1968.

Power, J. "Plug In To Cable TV." *Campaigns & Elections*, 8(3), (1987), 54-57.

Reese, M. "From Telephone to Telelobby: Two Decades of Targeted Communications." In *New Communication Technologies in Politics*. Edited by Robert Meadow. Washington, DC: Annenberg School of Communications, 1985.

Reilly, C. "Direct Mail on Target." *Campaigns & Elections*, 7(6), (1987), 36-40.

Roan, R.F. "Strategic Software for the 90s." *Campaigns & Elections*, 8(1), (1987), 69-72.

Robbin, J. "Geodemographics: The New Magic." *Campaigns & Elections*, I(1), (1980), 25-46.

Roman, M. "The Telephone as a Political Tool." *Campaigns & Elections*, I(3), (1980), 53-64.

Sabato, L.J. *The Rise of Political Consultants: New Ways of Winning Elections*. New York: Basic Books, Inc., 1981.

Sabato, L.J. *The Party's Just Begun*. Glenview, IL: Scott, Foresman and Co., 1988.

Schneider, E.J. "Geodemographics Refined: An Alternative to Standardized Clustering." *Campaigns & Elections*, III(4), (1983), 62-73.

Schwartz, T. *Media: The Second God*. New York: Random House, 1981.

Schwartzman, E. *Political Campaign Craftsmanship For Public Office*. 2nd ed. New York: Van Nostrand Reinhold, 1984.

Steinberg A. *Political Campaign Management: A Systems Approach*. Lexington, MA: D.C. Heath and Co., 1976.

Steinberg, A. *The Political Campaign Handbook: Media, Scheduling and Advance*. Lexington, MA: D.C. Heath and Co., 1976

Stone, B. *Successful Direct Marketing Methods*. 3rd ed. Chicago: Crain Books, 1984.

Teixeira, Ruy A. *Why Americans Don't Vote*. New York: Greenwood Press, 1987.

Tkach, J.R. "Micros: How to Buy and Use Them in Campaigns." *Campaigns & Elections*, IV(1), (1983), 68-74.

Tkach, J.R. "Microcomputers: Their Use in Small-scale Political Campaigning." *Campaigns & Elections*, III(3), (1982), 69-72.

Thompson, R. "Computerized Video Wizardry." *Campaigns & Elections*, 7(2), (1986), 31-34.

Tobe, F.L. "New Techniques in Computerized Voter Contact." In *New Communication Technologies in Politics*. Edited by Robert Meadow. Washington, DC: Annenberg School of Communications, 1985.

West, P. "Is TV Losing Its Campaign Clout?" *Washington Journalism Review*. Vol. 8, October 1986, 14-16.

Williams, F. *The Communications Revolution*. Beverly Hills: Sage Publications, 1982.

Wilson, P.O. "Presidential Advertising in 1988." *Election Politics*. 4(4), (1987), 17-21.

*Marcus Matthews* is a 1987 graduate of Dartmouth College and is a member of the initial class of the Graduate School of Political Management, the first school in the nation to offer a professional degree in the field of practical politics. Mr. Matthews' interests lie in the area of research and design of political and corporate strategies. He is employed as a Junior Associate with the political consulting firm of Dresner, Sykes, Jordan and Townsend while he finishes his graduate studies. Mr. Matthews is also completing work on his first novel.

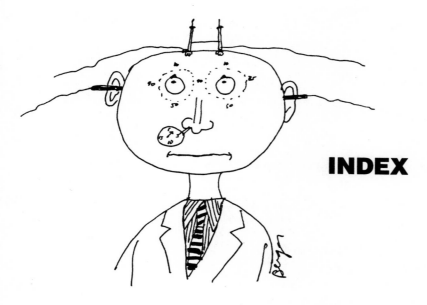

# INDEX